PEARL HARBOR

MARK E. STILLE

PEARL HARBOR

JAPAN'S GREATEST DISASTER

OSPREY PUBLISHING
Bloomsbury Publishing Plc

Kemp House	29 Earlsfort Terrace	1385 Broadway
Chawley Park	Dublin 2	5th Floor
Cumnor Hill	Ireland	New York
Oxford OX2 9PH		NY 10018
UK		USA

E-mail: info@ospreypublishing.com
www.ospreypublishing.com

OSPREY is a trademark of Osprey Publishing Ltd

First published in Great Britain in 2025

© Mark Stille, 2025

Mark Stille has asserted his right under the Copyright, Designs and Patents Act, 1988, to be identified as Author of this work.

All rights reserved. No part of this publication may be reproduced or transmitted in any form or by any means, electronic or mechanical, including photocopying, recording, or any information storage or retrieval system, without prior permission in writing from the publishers.

ISBN: HB: 9781472865311; PB: 9781472865328; EBOOK: 9781472865335;
EPDF: 9781472865281; AUDIO: 9781472865304

25 26 27 28 29 10 9 8 7 6 5 4 3 2 1

Maps by www.bounford.com
Index by Fionbar Lyons

Typeset by Six Red Marbles India
Printed and bound in Great Britain by Clays Ltd, Elcograf S.p.A.

Osprey Publishing supports the Woodland Trust, the UK's leading woodland conservation charity.

To find out more about our authors and books visit www.ospreypublishing.com. Here you will find extracts, author interviews, details of forthcoming events and the option to sign up for our newsletter.

For product safety related questions contact productsafety@bloomsbury.com

Contents

Acknowledgements	6
Introduction	7
List of Illustrations	23
List of Maps	29

1	The Road to Pearl Harbor	31
2	Yamamoto and the Great Debate	56
3	The Japanese Plan	83
4	The Striking Force	119
5	The Pacific Fleet and Pearl Harbor Defenses	145
6	The Striking Force Approaches Pearl Harbor	186
7	The First Attack Wave	195
8	The Second Attack Wave	234
9	The American Reaction and the Myth of the Second Attack	270
10	The Forgotten Offensive: Japanese Submarines off Hawaii	295
11	The Reckoning	317
12	Why Pearl Harbor Matters	328
13	Kimmel and Short: Responsibility Misplaced?	352

Appendices	374
Bibliography	403
Notes	414
Index	441

Acknowledgements

Many people helped in the completion of this book. Those reviewing the text included David Winkler, Evan Mawsley, David Leick, and Hal Stine. In particular, Alan Zimm and Charlie Hart went well beyond the call and provided thoughtful comments saving the author from innumerable errors of fact and judgement. Any errors still remaining are solely the responsibility of the author.

All thanks go to the Osprey crew under Marcus Cowper who took a sprawling manuscript and turned into a finished product, especially Serena Kerrigan-Noble who managed the book through the process, Julie Frederick who copyedited the manuscript and Venetia Bridges who proof read it.

Introduction

Pearl Harbor is recognized as the most important event of the Pacific War (with the possible exception of the atomic bombings of Japan), and one of the two most important events of World War II (the other being the German invasion of the Soviet Union in June 1941). Even so, parts of the Pearl Harbor attack remain poorly understood. These main points of confusion and mythology are the central themes in the book.

Many titles in the continuing flood of Pearl Harbor books focus on the failure to avoid conflict in the months before the attack or on the deeply flawed concept that "Washington" conspired to let the Japanese take the first shots of the war while not informing the commanders at Pearl Harbor what was coming. These accounts largely ignore the military aspects of the attack. When they are mentioned, the Pearl Harbor attack is described as a meticulously planned and brilliantly executed operation. As detailed in this military account of the battle, there is much more to the story than accepting the notion that the Japanese flawlessly conducted the attack and that its result was a brilliant success.

This book focuses on the military aspects of the attack. The first chapter deals with the road to war only to dispel the notion that there was a chance to avoid conflict in the Pacific as long as Japan was run by militarists. A large portion of the book examines the background factors that shaped the attack and determined whether or not it would result in a Japanese defeat or victory. As with any military operation, the most important factor shaping how an operation is conducted and whether it succeeds is the planning by both sides. In the case of the Pearl Harbor attack, the Japanese planning process and the plan that resulted from it is particularly important. Both are examined in great detail.

Other fundamental factors were the tactics, training, ships, aircraft, and men of both sides. Though touted as one of the best defended places on the planet, the fortress of Oahu was not as formidable as it appeared. However, in spite of some deficiencies, the Americans had the capability to mount a robust defense of the Pacific Fleet in harbor and the facilities on the island. That the Americans failed spectacularly in this regard is one of the major themes of the book.

In planning their Pearl Harbor attack, the Japanese were endeavoring to do something never before attempted. Massing the air groups of six fleet carriers into a single formation with over 400 aircraft was a game changer and gave Japanese planners tremendous capabilities. The Japanese faced major technical challenges in creating weapons that were suitable for attacking the United States Pacific Fleet in port. These challenges were overcome through a combination of technology and training, but only at the last second and with some residual problems. Overall, the effectiveness of the forces employed was limited by the rigidity of the planning process and the inability to adjust to emergent conditions.

A major factor often forgotten is how quickly the Japanese put together the capability to conduct large-scale carrier operations. The entity that carried out the Pearl Harbor attack was only created in April 1941, and the last two carriers of the force only joined in August and September. Placing six carriers under a single command was revolutionary; much harder was creating the doctrine for large-scale carrier operations. This was developed quickly and in secrecy and concurrently with planning for the Pearl Harbor operation. Not surprisingly, the Americans were left totally unaware of this new capability. US Navy (USN) intelligence assessed Japanese naval air power as inferior to its own by virtue of poor Japanese aviators and aircraft. The undetected emergence of the Imperial Navy's carrier force was a major reason for the strategic surprise gained at Pearl Harbor.

This book does not rely on a stream of personal accounts that usually serve only as filler and often cloud a deep understanding of the main issues of the event. There is usually little utility in these accounts since they convey universal emotions. For the Japanese aviators assigned the task of striking targets on Oahu, the overwhelming emotion was a steadfast determination to do their duty. They did not concern themselves

INTRODUCTION

with the morality of their actions, but only with the best way to cause destruction to the enemy. By their accounts, few felt hatred for the Americans. The experience of Yoshioka Masamitsu was shared by the aviators ordered to attack Pearl Harbor. He was a 23-year-old flying as a navigator in a torpedo bomber from carrier *Soryu*. Before the attack, he trained hard and was proud to have been selected for an important mission. When he finally learned that the target was Pearl Harbor, he was shocked to learn that Japan intended to attack the United States and was sure he would die in his first wartime mission. Despite all his preparation, Yoshioka and the rest of the crew of his torpedo bomber failed on the morning of December 7 when they expended their torpedo at a demilitarized battleship they had been instructed to ignore. After Japan's defeat, Yoshioka professed sorrow for what he had done. He expressed remorse for the men killed on the ship he torpedoed because they were just young men like himself. His death was announced on August 28, 2024. Passing away at 106, he was the last surviving Japanese aviator of the 770 who took part in the attack.[1]

On the American side, the universal emotion was shock and surprise as the first Japanese aircraft appeared and the first bombs and torpedoes found their targets. Shock turned to anger as men searched for ways to fight back. The outraged Americans fought bravely, determined to avenge their fallen comrades. This attitude was shared by Warren Upton, the oldest survivor of the Japanese attack on Pearl Harbor, who died aged 105 in December 2024. He was also the last survivor from USS *Utah*, Yoshioka's target. He recalls that the ship was hit by two torpedoes, but that he was able to slide down the side of the ship as she was capsizing. He survived, but 58 other men onboard *Utah* that morning did not.[2] Following the attack, American emotions turned into anger and outrage, leading to a determination to take revenge upon the treacherous Japanese.

Another key theme in the book is the use of intelligence. For one of the few times in the Pacific War, the Japanese won the intelligence war in the weeks before the Pearl Harbor attack. Though usually disdainful of intelligence, and usually incapable of producing solid intelligence assessments, Imperial Navy intelligence efforts for the Pearl Harbor operation were successful overall. Targeting intelligence for the operation was an essential ingredient for success. This was performed very well, but only because American authorities on Oahu gave free rein to Japanese operatives working out of the Honolulu consulate. The resulting bonanza of tactical intelligence was critical for whatever degree of success the Japanese enjoyed on December 7. However, on the operational and strategic levels, Japanese intelligence underperformed, as it would for the remainder of the war. Critically, the Imperial Navy never produced any intelligence on the assumptions used in planning the attack. These assumptions provided the rationale for conceiving and approving an operation that everybody knew to be extremely risky. Had they been examined, they would have been found wanting, but that would not have deterred the Japanese from carrying out the operation.

Closely related to the Imperial Navy's intelligence efforts was its deception campaign surrounding its intentions and movements in the opening phase of the war. The location of the Pearl Harbor carrier force was camouflaged in the background noise as the world's third largest navy prepared for war and moved the bulk of its forces into position to execute a major offensive in the Western Pacific. Added to the natural cover of the impending offensive into Southeast Asia, the Imperial Navy instituted a campaign of radio signal deception and call sign changes to hide the movement of its carrier fleet. On this occasion, it was sufficient to fool US Navy intelligence.

On the other side of the equation, USN intelligence totally failed to provide warning of the impending attack on Pearl Harbor. There are many reasons for this, but they boil down to the essential truth that the Americans were not able to ascertain Japanese intentions, as they lacked the ability during this period to read the Imperial Navy's operational codes. Having no real insight into Japanese intentions, the resulting assessment was that the Japanese would not attack the United States, but if an attack were to happen only the Philippines were at immediate risk. Pearl Harbor was thought to be beyond the reach of Japanese attack, except by submarines. Had the Americans examined Japanese capabilities, they would have come to the quick realization that Pearl Harbor was a potential target, as the Imperial Navy had the means to direct a powerful attack against the Pacific Fleet's home base. Though the fact that the Japanese were experimenting with the means to employ massed carrier air power was unknown, the knowledge that the Imperial Navy had more fleet carriers than the USN should have given the Americans reason not to be complacent. The performance of American intelligence in the months before Pearl Harbor provides a textbook study of intelligence failure. Even with the lessons learned

INTRODUCTION

from Pearl Harbor, it has not prevented similar failures since 1941. An obvious analogy is the 9/11 World Trade Center attack in which intelligence analysts were aware of the various components necessary for such an attack, but nobody was able to connect the dots to place them in the context of a new and more powerful capability.

Mythology abounds regarding the planning, execution, and aftermath of the Pearl Harbor operation. Examining these myths is a central theme of the book. The most salient myths are discussed briefly here.

In the months leading to the attack, was there a chance that war between the United States and Japan could be averted?

The war in China was at the heart of the Pearl Harbor attack. Japanese aggression against the Chinese resulted in a brutal conflict. Incidents like the December 1937 Rape of Nanking and the indiscriminate bombing of the Nationalist capital at Chongqing (Chungking) brought the nature of Japanese aggression to the world's attention and turned American public opinion against the Japanese. American support for the Chinese became a major issue between Japan and the United States in the period before Pearl Harbor.

American support for China was an imperative for the Roosevelt administration. It was not for moral or financial reasons, but most importantly for geostrategic reasons. Chinese resistance was responsible for tying down some 800,000 Japanese troops. If China collapsed, Japan would be free to direct its next aggressive move against the Soviet Union or against French, British, and Dutch colonial possession in Southeast Asia. The threat against the Philippines, an American possession, would also be magnified. Roosevelt's first concern was Nazi Germany and its defeat. Anything that detracted from the ability of other nations to resist Germany had to be avoided.

Roosevelt had to handle American public opinion carefully. Even the bombing of an American gunboat in Chinese waters by Japanese aircraft in December 1937 failed to stir the American populace into confronting Japan. World events eventually changed American public opinion from its willful ignorance of the growing threat overseas. The shift was moved by Chinese resistance but most markedly by German ascendancy in Europe.

In an era when the United States was the most important industrial power in the world and a major exporter of resources, it possessed huge potential economic leverage. Much to the shock of the Japanese, the Americans turned this leverage against the Japanese in the form of a total trade embargo in July 1941. Faced with the unpleasant situation of being held to account for their aggression in China and for their occupation of French Indochina in July, the Japanese had essentially two paths. One was to submit to the United States and withdraw from China and French Indochina. The other was to go to war and seize the resources Japan needed to withstand American economic pressure in 1941 or in the future.

Given their unwillingness to withdraw from China, combined with the inability of the government in Tokyo to even seriously consider or enforce such a decision, the choice was never really in doubt. Negotiations with the Americans were pursued from November 1940 until November 1941, but these were a smokescreen as Japan prepared for war. Assumedly, a nation goes to war only if it hopes to win. In the case of Japan in 1941, it was clear to many Japanese leaders that the outcome of a war against the United States was anything but certain. Even this realization did not stop Japan's march to war. The lack of moral courage from Japan's leaders during this period remains breathtaking.

There is no doubt the Americans were content on letting the Japanese fire the first shots of the coming war. This was not some master Roosevelt plan to provoke the Japanese into starting the war but reflected the need for the United States not to be seen as initiating the war for domestic political reasons. Making sure the Japanese were seen as the aggressor was an essential precondition for American entry into the war. This was even more true in the event the Japanese only attacked British and Dutch colonies and left US possessions out of the opening roud of hostilities.

Thus, it should not be surprising that negotiations failed. The diplomatic objectives of Japan and the United States, reflecting their strategic interests, were too far apart to make negotiations ever viable. Unable to face the alternative to war, Japan added the United States and Britain to its list of enemies in a war it was destined to lose.

How did Admiral Yamamoto Isoroku, the man who warned against attacking the United States, come to embrace the attack on Pearl Harbor and then risk everything to get it approved?
Yamamoto is the central figure in the Pearl Harbor saga. It is no exaggeration to state that without his involvement the attack would never

INTRODUCTION

have taken place. Unfortunately, for such an important figure, there is little reliable information available in English. He was a man of paradoxes. He was dedicated to the Emperor and to expanding the Japanese Empire by force if necessary. He warned of a war against the United States because he purportedly saw its outcome. Yet when faced with the question of national survival, he did not object to a war with the United States; in fact, he went out of his way to expand it. If he felt so strongly, then why not threaten to resign – which turned out to be a favorite Yamamoto tactic – to save the nation?

The Japanese planning process for the Pearl Harbor attack, overseen by Yamamoto, was a dangerous exercise in speculation. Yamamoto decided to conduct the operation before it was actually feasible. Despite the many problems existent at the time, Yamamoto declared his ironclad determination to proceed with the attack even though the Japanese lacked a functioning torpedo for the shallow waters of Pearl Harbor or a bomb capable of piercing battleship armor. Even getting a large task force to Hawaii was not possible given Japanese refueling capabilities at the time.

The supposed reason for Yamamoto's Hawaii Operation was to cripple the Pacific Fleet for six months so as to preclude it from interfering with the Japanese Southern Operation to seize the resource areas in Southeast Asia. At least that was the rationale used by Yamamoto to get his risky operation approved by the Naval General Staff. In fact, Yamamoto had much greater ambitions for his Pearl Harbor operation. He wanted nothing less than to shatter American morale by sinking a number of battleships, still seen as the yardsticks of naval power, leading to a negotiated peace favorable to Japan. That Yamamoto believed sinking a handful of battleships would crush America's fighting spirit speaks poorly of his skills as an observer of the United States and his skills as a strategist. The psychological aspects of Yamamoto's plan have been underappreciated since 1941, probably because they turned out to be so wrong.

From April until October 1941, Yamamoto sparred with the Naval General Staff to get his Pearl Harbor operation approved. For its part, the Naval General Staff contended that the plan was too risky, as there was no guarantee that it would achieve the all-important element of surprise. In addition, the carriers necessary to attack Pearl Harbor were needed to support the Southern Operation, which was a higher strategic necessity. Even most of the officers on Yamamoto's Combined Fleet staff and the commander of the force entrusted to carry out the operation were against Yamamoto's vision for the same reasons. For the reasons outlined above, Yamamoto was adamant his plan was necessary for Japan to successfully fight a war against the United States. In mid-October, Yamamoto emerged victorious against the Naval General Staff but only after he threatened to resign.

Why was Yamamoto so powerful? Was it simply due to the threat that in the period immediately before the war he and his entire staff would resign? Why was it so unthinkable for the Japanese not to have Yamamoto at the helm of the Combined Fleet? The answer remains elusive. It is clear that Yamamoto was a man of immense charisma and that his stature was unmatched among the leaders of the Imperial Navy. It was unfortunate for Japan that he was allowed to fulfill his unhealthy obsession to attack Pearl Harbor.

Did the Japanese have military options other than to attack Pearl Harbor?
In the months before Pearl Harbor, there was little debate within the Japanese leadership about the necessity to fight. This course of action offered a way out of the American economic stranglehold since seizure of the lightly defended oil resources in the Dutch East Indies, together with the resources of the British possessions in Asia, could negate the effects of the American embargo. The price of this solution was war with Great Britain and the Netherlands, and much more importantly, probably with the United States as well. In the mind of the Japanese leadership, all three Western powers were linked strategically. Since the Netherlands was already occupied by the Germans and Great Britain was fighting for its very survival, only the United States possessed the military means to threaten Japan's potential march south.

The Japanese assumption that the United States would go to war to defend European colonial possessions in the Western Pacific was flawed. As Roosevelt himself understood, he lacked the support necessary to declare war in such a scenario. Militarily, attacking the British and Dutch while leaving American forces on the Philippines intact was risky, as it left a potentially hostile force on the flanks of the sea lines of communication to Japan's new conquests in Southeast Asia. Nevertheless, it is interesting to imagine what would have happened

INTRODUCTION

had the Japanese done everything possible not to bring the United States into the war in December 1941.

Even if a decision to attack American forces in the Pacific was made, there were other options besides conducting a risky attack against Pearl Harbor. The alternative was neutralizing American forces in the Philippines and remaining on the strategic defensive in the Pacific. This was what the Imperial Navy had been preparing to do for some 20 years – fighting a decisive battle in or near Japanese home waters. This was too passive for Yamamoto, who changed the location of the decisive battle from the waters of the Western Pacific near Japan to the Central Pacific. Now, as war with the United States appeared increasingly certain, Japanese naval strategy was transformed again under Yamamoto. The Imperial Navy would not be content to lie in wait for the United States Navy as it sailed across the Pacific; instead, the Japanese would seek to cripple the United States Pacific Fleet in its main base.

Though the entire strategy of the decisive battle concept was deeply flawed, Yamamoto's Pearl Harbor operation was not only flawed but also dangerous and self-defeating. An attack directly on American sovereign territory in Hawaii was a glaring act of aggression. If accomplished as planned, it would be viewed by the Americans as an unprovoked sneak attack. As such, it would inflame American passions for revenge and provide a divided country with a clear war aim. It undermined the tenuous Japanese plan for victory by making a negotiated peace with the United States more difficult, if not impossible.

The Japanese attack plan at Pearl Harbor has been almost universally viewed as brilliant. But was it?
The notion that the Pearl Harbor plan was brilliant and that it was brilliantly executed persists more than 80 years after the event. Much of this book examines the plan and details its many shortcomings.

Because the Japanese were the instigators of the Pearl Harbor attack, much of this book examines events through their perspective. Instrumental to this approach is the work of Gordon Prange, who remains the premier historian of the Pearl Harbor attack. His efforts after the war to capture the views and actions of the Japanese participants are incredibly valuable. They give us immense insights into Japanese planning as well as the attitudes and actions of key participants. However, it needs to be pointed out that Prange became friends with these people; if Prange can be faulted for anything, it would be his reluctance to criticize the Japanese participants.

The most important of Prange's interviews were with Rear Admiral Kusaka Ryunosuke (chief of staff of the Striking Force – the Japanese carrier force), Commander Genda Minoru (air officer of the Striking Force and chief planner of the operation), and Commander Fuchida Mitsuo (another key planner and leader of the first attack wave). Can their accounts be trusted? Kusaka comes across as trustworthy. Genda largely does as well; given his pivotal role, he had no need to exaggerate it. The problem is with Fuchida, who routinely engaged in untruths and exaggerations. Prange makes this problem even worse since he often states that Genda and Fuchida were responsible for a given action without distinguishing between them.

The actual attack plan was created by Genda. After Yamamoto himself, Genda was the most important figure in bringing the plan to fruition. To be fair to Genda, he was attempting something never done before – a massed carrier air attack on a well-defended base. However, there were errors in the plan, including a failure to take weather into account, faulty target allocation, improper use of fighters, and lack of a coherent backup plan if things did not go as planned. Perhaps the largest error was Yamamoto's decision to use midget submarines in the operation and allow them to proceed up the channel to Pearl Harbor before the execution of the air attack. Such a foolhardy decision had the real potential to sacrifice surprise and thus jeopardize the entire operation.

During the execution of the attack, all these issues were clearly evinced. Massive damage was inflicted on the Americans, but the damage was limited by overconcentration on a few targets, faulty ordnance, and poor target prioritization. The supposedly elite dive-bomber pilots put in a particularly poor performance. All of this has been overlooked for the last 84 years because of a few spectacular successes, such as the destruction of the battleship *Arizona*, and the total lack of preparedness of the Americans which made the Japanese attack as effective as it was.

How ready was the United States Navy's Pacific Fleet, and were defenses on Oahu adequate to defend the fleet?
It is stating the obvious to point out that American defenses were caught by surprise on December 7, 1941. As the Japanese themselves

INTRODUCTION

realized, surprise was the most essential ingredient for success. After the November 27 "War Warning" message from Washington, the overall readiness condition of the forces on Oahu actually decreased by the time of the attack on December 7.

With six operational radars, some 100 fighters, and literally hundreds of Army and Navy antiaircraft guns on Oahu, the Americans had most of the building blocks necessary to mount a solid defense. Crucially, the air warning system was not complete, so even with radar data on the approaching Japanese strike, the fighters remained grounded, and almost all of the antiaircraft guns were initially unmanned.

Even if American defense could have been more effective, it wouldn't have entirely defeated the attack. American losses would still have been considerable, but not at the cataclysmic levels of the actual event. Japanese losses were very light, but had the potential to climb dramatically had the Americans been more prepared. There is ample evidence of this. The last attack group of Japanese torpedo bombers took very heavy losses, and overall losses to the second wave were much heavier than those of the first.

Did the Japanese first attack wave live up to expectations?
Since the Japanese objective was to sink the capital ships of the Pacific Fleet, meaning its battleships and carriers, the first wave was critical to Japanese prospects. With surprise in effect, the torpedo and level bombers could do their work. Only these aircraft had the capabilities to sink battleships. Carriers were an important target, more so than battleships in the mind of Genda, but none were present on the morning of December 7. Of the eight battleships in harbor that morning, five were potentially vulnerable to torpedo attack. Of these, two were the victims of overconcentration by Japanese torpedo-bomber aircrews. Both were hit by multiple torpedoes and sank. Another battleship took two torpedoes and began a slow process of settling to the harbor floor. A fourth battleship took a single torpedo hit but was able to get under way. Of the 40 torpedoes allocated against ships inside Pearl Harbor, only 19 hit a target, well below Japanese expectations of 27 hits. In addition to the battleships, torpedoes accounted for a target ship sunk, and two light cruisers damaged.

The level bombers were equipped with a specially designed heavy bomb capable of defeating battleship armor. Of the 49 bombs dropped, ten hit a target, which was about what the Japanese expected. However, most of the bombs that struck a target failed to function properly. One that did function correctly achieved the best possible result for the Japanese. It set alight the magazine of *Arizona* and killed 1,177 men. This provided the iconic moment of the entire attack and has overshadowed the disappointing performance of the level bombers and their faulty bombs.

While the harbor was under attack, the Japanese were also busy attacking key air facilities on the island. With the benefit of surprise, great damage was done. In fact, throughout the day, more sorties were devoted to attacking airfields than naval targets. Overall, the first wave generally met Japanese expectations. However, more damage could have been achieved if secondary targets had not been attacked by the torpedo bombers, and if the torpedo bombers had not overconcentrated on the two easiest targets immediately in front of them when they conducted their attack runs.

Generally unnoticed in accounts of the attack was the underperformance of the Japanese second attack wave. What happened and why?
The Japanese realized that most damage to naval targets inside the harbor would be caused by the first wave, which would hopefully be attacking with the benefit of surprise. In the second wave, the dive-bombers from four carriers, totaling 78 aircraft, were allocated to attack naval units. Despite the fact that these were elite crews attacking stationary targets, the results were dismal for the Japanese. Only 16 hits were scored, well below Japanese expectations, and most of these were against targets not on the dive-bombers' prioritized target list. Only two destroyers were sunk in this attack, representing a very marginal gain for investment. The primary reason for this unknown debacle was a failure to plan for unfavorable weather and having no solid backup plan in place if things did not go as planned. Also, by this point, the Americans had fully recovered from their initial shock and put up a strong defense.

Did the Japanese consider a second attack?
Probably the most prevalent myth surrounding the Pearl Harbor attack is the question of a second Japanese attack. It is commonly accepted that there was a debate on the bridge of Vice Admiral Nagumo Chuichi's flagship after which Nagumo (foolishly) decided not to mount another attack. This feeds the corollary myth that this lack of a second attack

was a strategic mistake, as it could have easily destroyed the naval base infrastructure. Once destroyed, this would have precluded USN fleet operations out of Pearl Harbor, thus crippling American naval operations for months.

In fact, there was never any prospect of a second attack being approved by Nagumo. He made this very clear during the planning process in the months before the attack. There was never any debate on the bridge of *Akagi* over a possible second attack – this was a fabrication by Fuchida created many years later. Had there been any real prospect of a second attack, Genda would have had a plan ready. The lack of a plan, combined with the remaining time before sunset and many other factors, made any second attack impossible on December 7 even if Nagumo had experienced an epiphany and decided he wanted to mount one. The only window for a possible second attack was December 7 – there was never any chance Nagumo would keep his task force in enemy waters for several days to wait for the next opportunity.

Had a second attack been approved, it is very probable the Japanese would have concentrated on remaining naval targets. In their view, this was the key to sea control, not bombing port facilities and fuel tanks, which were last in priority on the pre-attack target list. However, had the leaders on the scene ignored the precepts embedded in every Imperial Navy officer and decided to concentrate on naval base infrastructure, the Japanese lacked the capability to deliver a knock-out blow against them. Rendering them partially destroyed would have been insufficient to cripple operations at Pearl Harbor and fails to consider the USN's considerable powers of regeneration. The triple-headed myth of the second attack, and the failure to destroy the naval base and the impact of that destruction, is as incorrect as it seems to be enduring.

A huge part of the Japanese plan was a submarine offensive by midget subs inside the harbor and by fleet submarines ringed around Oahu. This was an absolute failure. Why?

It is usually forgotten that the Hawaii Operation was more than just a massive carrier air raid against Pearl Harbor. Yamamoto also employed every modern fleet submarine in the Imperial Navy to complement the air attack. Ringed around Oahu, the Japanese assumed these well-trained units would reap a rich harvest of American naval units fleeing the air attack. In fact, this part of the operation was a total failure. No

American naval units were lost to submarine attack or even exposed to an attack by a Japanese submarine. This was just the start of a long war of futility by the Combined Fleet's submarine force. With the exception of some attacks on USN high-value units in 1942, Japanese submarines were ineffective in attacking its primary target – the Pacific Fleet.

The best-known aspect of Japanese submarine operations in support of the Pearl Harbor attack is the use of midget submarines. Carried to Oahu on the decks of fleet submarines, these top-secret weapons were ordered to transit the channel into Pearl Harbor before the air attack, if conditions were judged to be right. Invariably, these slow submarines, unable to navigate without use of their periscopes, were detected before the air attack. Just as Genda and the other aviators had feared, this jeopardized the element of surprise for the air attack. Given the unsuitability of the primitive midget submarines in this scenario, they were totally ineffective. All five were lost, and only two even had a chance to fire their torpedoes.

Did the Japanese attack on Pearl Harbor cripple the Pacific Fleet?
Most accounts of the battle assert that the attack resulted in the crippling of the Pacific Fleet. This is false, whether it be in the short or long term. Of the 100 ships present in the harbor that morning, 18 were sunk or damaged. If the resulting war after the carrier air raid on Pearl Harbor was going to be a war of battleships, then the attack may well have been crippling, at least in the short run. Of the eight battleships present, four were sunk and the other four damaged to some degree. This sounds like an impressive achievement, but in fact it was irrelevant. In the aftermath of the Pearl Harbor attack, it was obvious that the battleship had been usurped as the standard of naval power by the aircraft carrier. Clear evidence of this was that the new commander of the Pacific Fleet, Admiral Chester Nimitz, could not find a use for his rebuilt battle line in the six months after Pearl Harbor culminating in the Battle of Midway.

Under Nimitz, the "crippled" Pacific Fleet began an aggressive series of raids on Japanese-held areas in the Central and South Pacific. Aided by mismanagement of the Combined Fleet's numerical advantage by Yamamoto, the Pacific Fleet defeated a Japanese thrust into the Coral Sea in May and then inflicted a decisive defeat of the carrier force responsible for the Pearl Harbor attack at Midway Atoll in June.

INTRODUCTION

Almost to the day, within six months of the Pearl Harbor attack, the Pacific Fleet stemmed the tide of Japanese expansion and turned the tide of war in the Pacific.

Of the 18 ships sunk or damaged on December 7, all but two (both old battleships) returned to service. Given the flood of new production naval units, which began to reach the Pacific Fleet in the second half of 1942, the long-term impact of the Pearl Harbor attack was minimal. In fact, it would be no exaggeration to state that even if every ship inside Pearl Harbor had been sunk, the long-term impact on the naval balance in the Pacific would have been minimal.

What was the true strategic impact of the attack?
From Japan's strategic perspective, attacking Pearl Harbor was entirely unnecessary. The main Japanese strategic goal in the opening months of the conflict was to secure the resource areas it needed in Southeast Asia to allow it to build a viable wartime economy. Since these areas were only lightly defended by British, Commonwealth, and Dutch forces, the only potential impediment to their quick seizure was the United States Pacific Fleet. However, this capability was strictly theoretical. The Pacific Fleet was outnumbered by the Imperial Navy at this point and lacked the logistic capabilities to mount an aggressive drive into the Central Pacific in anything like the timeline required to affect events in the Western Pacific.

Japan gained almost nothing of strategic value from its Pearl Harbor operation. The naval balance was not significantly altered in the short term, and in the long term the effect was minuscule. The true strategic effect of the attack was disastrous for Japan since not only was the United States thrust into the war, but it entered as a unified nation determined to gain victory against a treacherous foe. Thus, the attack undermined any prospect of a negotiated peace, which was the only Japanese path to any kind of victory.

Were Kimmel and Short scapegoats?
Admiral Husband E. Kimmel, commander of the Pacific Fleet, and Lieutenant General Walter C. Short, commander of all Army forces in Hawaii, exhibited a lack of mental readiness and intellectual unpreparedness, combined with a lack of imagination, in the months leading up to the attack. Despite warnings from Washington and an obvious

heightening of tensions between Japan and the United States, the actions they undertook, together with the actions they did not take, combined to virtually ensure that the Japanese would gain surprise. The result was a heavy loss of life and an embarrassing defeat.

It would have taken only a single well-placed American search aircraft to spot the approaching Japanese carrier force and change history. Yet there was not a single American aircraft aloft on the morning of December 7 conducting searches for a potential enemy force. The Americans had six functional radars on Oahu; on the morning of the attack, these picked up the approaching raid. Combined with reports of submarine activity in the channel to Pearl Harbor earlier that morning, American commanders on the island had all the information they needed to indicate a combined attack was imminent. Yet no Army anti-aircraft guns were manned, no fighters were airborne, and the ships in the harbor were caught unprepared.

Kimmel and Short's only defense was that they were not given information from Washington about when an attack might develop. While true, it was because Washington did not have any intelligence regarding specific Japanese actions against American forces. Both Washington and Oahu agreed that an attack on Oahu was almost impossible. For commanders of Kimmel's and Short's stature and experience, claiming that Washington was responsible for their forces being surprised is a hollow and self-serving defense that should be beneath senior commanders.

The final chapter of the book deals with this subject. It seems the debate will continue because the heart of the revisionist school on the Pearl Harbor attack is the notion that Kimmel and Short were merely scapegoats. The author's views on this issue are clear, as is the commonsense proposition that the two senior commanders on the island were responsible for the fighting condition and fate of the forces under their charge.

Mark Stille
Annapolis, Maryland
April 2025

List of Illustrations

The driving force behind the Pearl Harbor attack was the commander of the Combined Fleet, Admiral Yamamoto Isoroku. His vision for the attack was to inflict not just a blow on the Pacific Fleet but also to shatter American morale. (Naval History and Heritage Command)

The man charged to execute Yamamoto's risky venture was Vice Admiral Nagumo Chuichi. In April 1941 he assumed command of the world's first massed carrier force and was thrust into planning the Pearl Harbor operation. (Naval History and Heritage Command)

After Yamamoto himself, the man most responsible for seeing the Pearl Harbor attack plan through from planning to execution was Genda Minoru. At the time of the attack he was Nagumo's air officer. (Public Domain)

Admiral Husband E. Kimmel commanded the Pacific Fleet before and during the attack on Pearl Harbor. In this image, taken on February 1, 1941 aboard fleet flagship battleship *Pennsylvania*, Kimmel (in the center of the photo extending his hand) assumes command from Admiral James O. Richardson. (National Park Service)

This view shows the senior Army commander Lieutenant General Walter Short with the senior Navy commander Admiral Husband Kimmel flanking Royal Navy Captain Louis Mountbatten. In the rear is the commander of the Army Air Force on Oahu, Major General Frederick Martin and the principal Navy air commander, Rear Admiral Patrick Bellinger. (National Park Service)

Nagumo's flagship for the Hawaiian Operation was the carrier *Akagi*. She was paired with the converted battleship *Kaga* to form the elite Carrier Division 1, one of three carrier divisions concentrated in the Striking Force. (Naval History and Heritage Command)

Japanese fleet carriers *Soryu* and *Hiryu* formed Carrier Division 2. Both ships were able to carry a large air group at the expense of protection. (Imperial Japanese Navy, now in the Public Domain)

With the addition of Carrier Division 5, the Striking Force had six fleet carriers available for the Hawaii Operation. This is *Zuikaku* pictured before the start of the war; she was identical to sister ship *Shokaku*. (Imperial Japanese Navy, now in the Public Domain)

This panoramic view shows the main facilities located in the Pearl Harbor area. Taken on October 30, 1941, the perspective is from the southwest. Ford Island is in the center of the picture. Across the channel to the left is the Navy Yard; to the left of the Navy Yard is the submarine base. Hickam Field is the large airfield in the upper left of the image. (Naval History and Heritage Command)

This photograph, taken on November 10, 1941, gives a close-up of Ford Island and the mooring points around it. In the upper left is Battleship Row with five battleships. Carriers were usually moored on Ford Island's northwestern side. The Naval Air Station is visible on the upper right and was home to several squadrons of patrol aircraft and hosted carrier aircraft when their parent ship was in port. (Naval History and Heritage Command)

Kaga steams through heavy North Pacific seas en route to Oahu. This image was taken from *Akagi*; *Zuikaku* is at right. (Naval History and Heritage Command)

At 0637, over an hour before the attack opened, destroyer *Ward* spotted a submarine and engaged it with gunfire. This is the crew of Number 3 4-inch gun, which scored a direct hit on the sail of the midget submarine. (Naval History and Heritage Command)

Only one of the five midget submarines succeeded in penetrating inside the harbor. After firing its two torpedoes without success, it was rammed and depth-charged by a destroyer. This is the midget submarine after it was raised off the harbor floor two weeks later. (Naval History and Heritage Command)

In this view, aircraft prepare to take off from *Akagi* at about 0600 on December 7. The lead aircraft is an A6M2 "Zero" fighter flown by

LIST OF ILLUSTRATIONS

Lieutenant Commander Itaya Shigeru, commander of all fighters in the first attack wave. (Imperial Japanese Navy, now in the Public Domain)

This is a group of D3A1 "Val" dive-bombers from *Shokaku*, which were assigned to strike the airfield on Ford Island and nearby Hickam Field. Only 16 of 78 dive-bombers in the second wave scored a hit, and most of these were against secondary targets. (Imperial Japanese Navy, now in the Public Domain)

The second attack wave from *Shokaku* prepares to launch. These aircraft were assigned to attack American airfields. (Naval History and Heritage Command)

The heart of the entire Pearl Harbor operation was the torpedo attack against the battleships moored along Battleship Row. This view shows that attack in progress. In this photograph, taken from a Japanese aircraft, Ford Island is in the center of the scene with Battleship Row on its far (eastern) side. (Naval History and Heritage Command)

This view of Battleship Row was taken by a Japanese aircraft early in the attack. The time is about 0800 as the torpedo planes are in the process of conducting their attack, and the horizontal bombers have not yet made their appearance. (Naval History and Heritage Command)

One of the major tragedies of the attack was the capsizing of battleship *Oklahoma* with the loss of 415 men. This view shows *Oklahoma* after she capsized; moored next to her is battleship *Maryland*, which suffered only light damage during the attack. (Naval History and Heritage Command)

This low-quality photograph taken from a Japanese aircraft of the western side of Ford Island shows the results of the first-wave torpedo attacks. (Naval History and Heritage Command)

This view of Battleship Row shows the early phases of the horizontal bombing attack. A bomb has just hit *Arizona* at the stern, but she has not yet received the bomb that detonated her forward magazines. (Naval History and Heritage Command)

This view of Battleship Row was taken from a Type 97 "Kate" carrier attack plane right after the bomb hit *Arizona*, which resulted in a magazine explosion and the ship's destruction. From left to right are *Nevada*, *Arizona* (burning intensely) with *Vestal* moored outboard, *Tennessee* with *West Virginia* moored outboard, and *Maryland* with the capsized *Oklahoma* alongside. Smoke from the bomb hits on *Vestal* and *West Virginia* is also visible. (Naval History and Heritage Command)

The single most deadly aspect of the entire attack was the destruction of battleship *Arizona*, captured in this iconic image, which shows the moment the ship's forward magazine exploded after being hit by a 1,760-pound armor-piercing bomb. A total of 1,177 men lost their lives in the explosion, constituting almost half of fatal American casualties on December 7. (Naval History and Heritage Command)

The forward magazine explosion sank *Arizona* and caused an intense fire that engulfed the forward part of the ship, as shown here. At left, crewmen on the stern of *Tennessee* are using fire hoses to keep burning oil away from their ship. (Naval History and Heritage Command)

Naval Air Station Kaneohe Bay was a principal target of the Japanese. Undefended by antiaircraft guns, it was strafed relentlessly and suffered bomb attack from Japanese horizontal bombers. (National Park Service)

Most of the 12 B-17 bombers that arrived in the middle of the attack survived the experience. Shown here is a B-17E at Hickam Airfield after landing safely. In the background is a B-17C/D. Smoke from burning ships at Pearl Harbor is visible in the distance. (Naval History and Heritage Command)

As the main fighter base on Oahu, Wheeler Field was a primary target. In this picture, probably taken by a dive-bomber from *Zuikaku*, hangars and fighters lined up on the apron are burning after the first-wave attack. Other undamaged fighters can be seen still lined up on the left part of the apron. (Naval History and Heritage Command)

The burned-out wreckage of a P-40 fighter pictured near Hangar 4 at Wheeler Field. Of the 99 P-40 fighters present on the island before the attack, only 27 were operational at the end of the day. (Naval History and Heritage Command)

Lined up in rows, the fighters at Wheeler Field suffered heavily at the hands of strafing Japanese aircraft, like the P-40s in this view.

LIST OF ILLUSTRATIONS

Only a few were able to get airborne, with most being caught on the ground. (National Park Service)

Results from the second-wave dive-bomber attack were extremely disappointing for the Japanese. This photograph, taken southwesterly from the hills behind the harbor, shows the low-hanging cloud cover and smoke obscuring the target area of the second-wave dive-bomber attack. The large column of smoke in the lower right center is from the burning *Arizona*. The smoke further to the left is from the destroyers *Shaw*, *Cassin*, and *Downes* burning in the drydocks at the Navy Yard. (Naval History and Heritage Command)

The greatest success of the Japanese second-wave dive-bombers was the destruction of destroyers *Downes* and *Cassin* in Drydock Number 1. Ravaged by fire, *Cassin* capsized against *Downes*, as seen in this view. (Naval History and Heritage Command)

Destroyer *Shaw* was undergoing maintenance in Floating Drydock Number 2 when she was attacked by Japanese dive-bombers from the second attack wave. Hit by bombs, the resulting fires reached the forward magazine with the results shown in this dramatic photograph. (Naval History and Heritage Command)

Naval Air Station Pearl Harbor was a key Japanese target. Among the aircraft in this scene are PBY Catalina patrol aircraft and OS2U Kingfisher and SOC Seagull floatplanes normally based on cruisers and battleships. Sailors survey the damage and watch as destroyer *Shaw* explodes in the center background. Battleship *Nevada* is also visible in the middle background. (Naval History and Heritage Command)

Battleship *Nevada* was the only one of the eight battleships present to get under way during the attack. In this view, she is headed toward the channel after being subjected to a heavy attack by Japanese dive-bombers. (Naval History and Heritage Command)

Battleship *Nevada* is aground in the center background of the image. The large column of smoke to the left of her is from destroyer *Shaw* burning in floating drydock. Battleship Row is in the right center, with the heaviest smoke coming from *Arizona*. (Naval History and Heritage Command)

This is a Zero fighter that crashed at Fort Kamehameha near Pearl Harbor during the attack. Markings on the Zero indicate that it is from *Akagi*'s air group. This was the only *Akagi* fighter lost in the attack and one of only nine overall. (Naval History and Heritage Command)

Fifteen of the 29 Japanese aircraft shot down over Oahu were Type 99 "Val" dive-bombers. Here one of *Kaga*'s Vals is being recovered from the harbor after the attack. (Naval History and Heritage Command)

This view shows the submarine base (right center) and part of the fuel farms in October 1941. Among the 26 tanks visible are two, which have been painted to resemble buildings. (Naval History and Heritage Command)

On December 8, 1941, President Franklin Roosevelt delivered an address to a joint session of Congress and requested a declaration of war against Japan. (Naval History and Heritage Command)

Admiral Chester W. Nimitz assumed command of the Pacific Fleet on December 31, 1941. The ceremony took place onboard submarine *Grayling* at Pearl Harbor. (Naval History and Heritage Command)

List of Maps

Map 1: United States Defense Installations on Oahu   87
Map 2: Route of the Striking Force   95
Map 3: Pacific Fleet Ships and Craft located in and near Pearl Harbor on December 7, 1941   156
Map 4: The Japanese Attack Plan   199
Map 5: The Torpedo Bomber Attack   204
Map 6: The Level Bomber Attack against Battleship Row   208

I

The Road to Pearl Harbor

As early as 1914, Japan and the United States began thinking of each other as possible future enemies. This potential came more sharply into focus when Japan openly embarked on a path of aggression. Beginning in 1931, Japanese military actions indicated that their goal was to dominate East Asia. Fulfilling its imperial ambitions in Asia would give Japan the empire that its national pride demanded and the economic capabilities required to become self-sufficient. The initial focus of Japanese aggression was a weakened China. Far from being over in a short period as the Japanese optimistically assessed, the war in China dragged on and became the central issue between Japan and the United States in the period leading up to the start of the Pacific War.

The Japanese Kwantung Army, stationed in Manchuria, had more than its share of firebrands who espoused expansion at the expense of the inferior (as was the universal view at the time) Chinese. These officers acted beyond the control of the Imperial Army's central command or the government in Tokyo. A faction of Kwantung Army officers demonstrated their disdain for central authority in September 1931 when they exploded a small bomb near a rail line of the Japanese South Manchuria Railroad. Falsely accusing Chinese dissidents of the attack, and using this as a pretext, they initiated military operations against Chinese forces and seized control of Jilin province. After the Tokyo government protested ineffectively, it resigned in December 1931. By February 1932, the Kwantung Army was in control of all three Manchurian provinces and declared that these provinces constituted the independent state of Manchukuo. Within months they installed

Puyi, the last Emperor of China who had been forced to abdicate in 1911, as the puppet ruler of Manchukuo.[1]

The actions of the Kwantung Army had huge implications for Japan's fledgling democracy. In May 1932, Prime Minister Inukai Tsuyoshi was assassinated because he did not support the Kwantung Army's unauthorized seizure of Manchuria. After this incident, the Japanese Emperor appointed the prime minister instead of having the post filled by a popularly elected politician. Since the Emperor usually selected an army or navy officer as prime minister, this gave the military tremendous power as it could collapse the government by simply having its prime minister resign. At this point, the military was effectively beyond civilian control.

Japan's invasion of China proper began with the Marco Polo Bridge incident on the night of July 7–8, 1937. In this seemingly insignificant event, a Japanese unit on night maneuvers was fired upon and a soldier was reported lost (he later turned up after missing the initial rollcall). The unit was part of the Japanese garrison stationed in Beijing as an aftermath of the Boxer Rebellion of 1899–1901 to protect foreign legations. The next day the incident escalated when the Japanese responded to more firings with a full-scale attack on Chinese forces in the area.

Using the Marco Polo Bridge incident as an excuse, Japan expanded its operations and realized rapid advances in northern China. In August 1937, the focus of operations turned to Shanghai. The ensuing contest became a huge urban battle in full view of the international community which had a large presence in the city. It took until late October for Chinese resistance to be broken. The next Japanese objective was the Nationalist Chinese capital of Nanjing. After a brief urban fight in December, the conquering Japanese resorted to a frenzy of murder, arson, rape, and looting, all in front of Western witnesses. So horrendous was the violence it has gone down in history as the "Rape of Nanking." Trying to calculate the human terms of this atrocity is difficult, but a death toll of between 100,000 and 200,000 seems likely.[2] The scope of the violence marked the Japanese as brutal aggressors and highlighted the victimhood of the Chinese, at least in the eyes of foreign observers.

In 1938, the Japanese continued their advance as the bitterness of the conflict increased and the Chinese adopted a scorched earth strategy. The important city of Wuhan in central China fell on October 25. Nevertheless, at the close of the year, and despite a number of mistakes, the Chinese position seemed to brighten. The Chinese experienced military success at Taierzhuang and in a stubborn defense of the Yangtze valley. Morale increased, as did Chinese determination to prevail in a protracted war. International opinion shifted solidly in favor of the Chinese.

Despite advances since the opening of the conflict, even the Japanese recognized they were embroiled in a quagmire. They had no political strategy for ending the war after their military superiority produced apparent successes but promised no end of the war. Some 800,000 Japanese troops were bogged down in China in a war that was draining Japan of men and money.

Japan's war of aggression in China, as brutal as it was, did not prompt the Roosevelt administration into action. However, the images coming out of China moved American public opinion vastly in favor of the Chinese by 1940. Though public opinion was moved, it did not translate into pressure for action. The predominant mood of the day was "anti-interventionist" (versus the more commonly used "isolationist"), a term encompassing all factions opposed to American overseas involvement.[3] Reflecting this sentiment was the 1937 Neutrality Act prohibiting the kinds of things that might drag the United States into another conflict. Provisions included a mandatory arms embargo on foreign combatants, no loans or credits to such combatants, and a ban on travel by Americans on ships of belligerents.

Given the mood of the nation, Roosevelt's options were constrained when it came to the war in China. Even outright hostility by the Japanese failed to change the fact that Americans were not ready for war. On December 12, 1937, Imperial Navy dive-bombers attacked and sank the United States Navy gunboat *Panay* in the area of Nanjing.[4] Two Navy crewmen and a civilian were killed, and 43 Navy personnel and five civilians were wounded. As the gunboat was clearly marked as American and the pilots flew close enough to the ship to determine its nationality, there was no doubt that the act was intentional.[5] Japan acted quickly to defuse the incident by paying reparations of over $2.2 million (approximately $50 million in 2025 dollars) and offering a formal apology.

Defeat of the Ludlow Amendment in the aftermath of the *Panay* bombing was an important turning point. It was a measure up for vote in the House of Representatives stating that, in the absence of a direct attack on the nation, a declaration of war by Congress could only be effective after a national referendum. It was voted down in January 1938, marking the first setback for the "anti-interventionists." The national mood was changing and was helped by the growing effectiveness of the Chinese against the Japanese in 1938. At this point, the Americans provided the embattled Nationalist government its first tangible support, arranging a $25 million loan for the Chinese to purchase arms.[6]

As war in China continued, with the Japanese unable to force a military solution, events on the border of Manchuria would have major implications as the Japanese faced the decision of how to open hostilities in 1941. Across the border from Manchuria was the Soviet Far East. Despite a regular number of low-level incidents between the Japanese and Soviets, an uneasy peace held until a large-scale clash in July–August 1938, named the Changkuofeng Incident by the Japanese. A Japanese force seized a hill across the border and managed to hold it in the face of the more numerous and better armed Soviets. The Japanese eventually withdrew following a diplomatic settlement. However, again, the Kwantung Army acted against the wishes of the Imperial Army's commanders in Tokyo and against those of the Emperor himself.

Apparent success at Changkuofeng led the Kwantung Army to another much larger and more impactful incident beginning in May 1939 along the ill-defined border between Soviet-controlled Outer Mongolia and Manchuria. After losing an initial clash in May, the Kwantung Army escalated the incident with a reinforced division, again concealing its intent from Tokyo. A major Japanese attack in July ground to a halt short of its objective, even though the Kwantung Army committed its most modern armor and artillery units. In response, the Soviets massed a force of 57,000 men with 500 tanks under General Georgiy Zhukov to administer a lesson to the Japanese. Beginning on August 20, Zhukov launched a double envelopment attack against the overextended Japanese division, employing a huge advantage in armor, artillery, and aircraft. In only five days, the Japanese were routed, losing almost 18,000 men. The Nomonhan Incident, as it was called by the Japanese, shocked the Imperial Army to its core. Even the arrogant Kwantung Army was forced to recognize its vast inferiority to the better-equipped Soviet Army. The Imperial Army would think twice before challenging the Soviets again unless it assessed the odds were weighted in its favor.[7]

In 1940, the stalemate in China remained unresolved. In an effort to break the logjam, the Japanese resorted to aerial bombing of strategic and political targets in central China. The focus of this effort was Chongqing (formerly romanized as Chungking), the new Nationalist capital. This first-ever strategic bombing campaign, conducted by both the Imperial Army and Navy, was ultimately unsuccessful despite the fact that 182 attacks on the city were conducted in 1940 alone.[8] On top of this military failure, the press coverage of the brutal campaign, directed at helpless civilians, drew international condemnation for the Japanese and increased sympathy for the valiant Chinese.

Events in Europe cast a shadow over Asia in 1940. In June, France surrendered to Germany, the Netherlands were occupied, and in July the British Empire was left to face the German juggernaut on its own. In the eyes of many foreign observers, including the Japanese, British collapse seemed possible. The Japanese were counting on a German victory and signed the Tripartite Pact with Germany and Italy on September 27, 1940. The fall of France and the seemingly perilous state of the British Empire altered the balance of power in the world. In this new environment, European colonial possessions in Asia seemed ripe for the picking.

The new world order placed the United States in a delicate situation. Protected by two oceans, the American public did not see a threat initially, but this changed with Nazi ascendancy in Europe. Roosevelt was faced with a new and much more dangerous global situation while still declaring his intent to avoid bringing the United States into the war. In this new security environment, he was able to convince Congress to pass several important measures.

America's first peacetime military conscription was approved in 1940, but only for a period of one year. It was impossible to expand the military on this basis. In the summer of 1941, Roosevelt sought to extend the length of service to 30 months or the duration of the emergency despite the fact that only 51 percent of Americans were in favor of the measure. When it came up for a vote, the Senate gave it tepid support with only 45 senators voting for it and then for only 18 months. The House passed it on August 12 by a single vote. Although Roosevelt got his way, it was clear that the United States was in no mood to go to war. Also in 1940, the defense budget dramatically increased. To deter the Japanese, Roosevelt ordered the Pacific Fleet be moved from the West Coast to Hawaii.

Roosevelt had other, more potent, options to deter Japan. In July 1940 Congress passed an act giving the administration the power to control critical exports. An export control administrator was appointed, but his power could only be used with the concurrence of the State Department. Roosevelt was reluctant to use this new power aggressively and rejected a total oil embargo on Japan. However, restrictions on high-grade aviation petroleum products were instituted.

On July 17, 1940, a change of government occurred in Japan. The Emperor ordered Prince Konoe Fumimaro to form a government. Known for his indecision, Konoe came into office with an anti-Western bias. Matsuoka Yosuke was named as foreign minister. Fluent in English from his time in the United States from ages 13 to 22, Matsuoka was favored by the Army and given a free reign in foreign relations by Konoe. He had the support of the military for his program of incorporating European colonies in Asia into Japan's economic sphere while avoiding conflict with the United States. As War Minister, Konoe appointed General Tojo Hideki. Tojo had established a solid reputation as an able administrator and thus seemed suited for his new post.

One of Matsuoka's goals was an agreement with Germany. The problem was the Imperial Navy. Navy Minister Admiral Yoshida Zengo, former Navy Minister Yonai Mitsumasa, and the Navy Vice Minister, Yamamoto Isoroku, were against it. All feared that if Japan hitched its star to Germany it would ultimately lead to war with the United States. When Yoshida fell ill, he was replaced by Admiral Oikawa Koshiro on September 5. Against the Navy's wishes, on September 27 Japan signed the Tripartite Pact. The heart of the agreement, aimed at the United States, was a provision that each of the three powers (Germany, Italy, and Japan) would come to the aid of the others if any were attacked by a power not already at war. Though the agreement enhanced his reputation, Matsuoka failed to understand that the Tripartite Pact gained Japan important enemies in the form of the United States and Great Britian. Behind the war in China, Japan's embrace of the Tripartite Pact was the second most divisive issue in its relations with the United States. Matsuoka claimed that he had no choice because it was what the Army wanted.

Matsuoka's decision to join an alliance with Germany was not his only mistake in the summer of 1940. In another stunning display of insubordination, officers in the Army General Staff orchestrated an invasion of northern French Indochina on September 23.

Matsuoka wanted to emphasize diplomacy and had concluded an agreement with the Vichy French that did not include an invasion. Gen Tojo Hideki tried to restore order by dismissing the officers responsible, but the action could not be reversed. Matsuoka made matters worse in a liaison conference[9] on December 12, 1940 when he appeared to bless a move from northern Indochina into southern Indochina, a move not yet decided upon by the Army. Moving into southern Indochina was a red flag with the European powers and the United States as it brought Western colonies in Southeast Asia under direct threat. Japanese bombers flying from airfields in southern Indochina had the range to attack Singapore, Britain's most important outpost in Southeast Asia.

Matsuoka's next move was to secure Japan's northern flank with an agreement with the Soviet Union. Though Matsuoka wanted a full non-aggression pact, he came away in April with a five-year neutrality pact. In addition to both parties agreeing to respect the territorial integrity of the other, the pact called for Japan to stay neutral in the event of a war between Germany and the Soviet Union and for the Soviets to stay out of a war between Japan and the United States. With its northern frontier safe, Japan was free to strike south.

In a bid to bolster the Nationalists, Roosevelt granted a $50 million (worth over $1.1 billion in 2025 money) loan to China on April 25, 1940. He also achieved a major milestone by getting the Lend-Lease Act approved on March 11, 1941 with strong majorities in both houses of Congress.

THE DECLINE OF JAPAN–UNITED STATES RELATIONS

Matsuoka's greatest challenge was guiding Japan's relations with the United States. On November 8, 1940, retired admiral Nomura Kichisaburo was appointed ambassador to the United States. Despite the fact that Matsuoka saw him as just a figurehead to create the impression that friendly relations could be maintained, Nomura became a central figure in Japan–United States relations. Critically, he was given no real instructions by Matsuoka on how to proceed. Matsuoka, in keeping with the rock-star diplomatic persona he was building, had visions that he would personally negotiate an agreement with the Americans.

Nomura was an earnest man who came to the job with a determination to avoid war between the two countries. Unlike some of his other

Imperial Navy counterparts (including Yamamoto), he possessed a completely realistic view of the United States. He clearly understood the disparity in industrial power between the two countries, so was convinced that a war had to be avoided. Nomura also recognized that there was an ideological component to American foreign policy, identifying that Roosevelt and most Americans viewed current events as a struggle between democratic and totalitarian camps.[10] He was personally acquainted with Roosevelt and was seen by the Americans as a man genuinely invested in peace. However, he had difficulties with English. His attitude toward diplomacy and unprofessional methods were a detriment in official communications between the two parties.[11]

In Nomura's mind, the role of the Imperial Navy was critical to avoid war. Its leadership needed to be resolute and emphasize that Japan stood no chance of victory in a war against the United States. Navy Minister Oikawa recruited Nomura for his assignment in Washington with this in mind. Others in the Imperial Navy saw Nomura's job as nearly impossible and Yamamoto saw no prospects for a negotiated settlement. Many lower-ranking officers supported the Tripartite Pact and viewed war with the United States as inevitable. Armed with an assurance from Prime Minister Konoe and Oikawa that the Tripartite Pact did not commit Japan to war with the United States, Nomura went to Washington and presented his credentials to Roosevelt on February 14, 1941.

Negotiations between Washington and Tokyo were always going to be difficult given the issues at stake and the interest groups working behind the scenes on both sides. Further handicapping the prospects for real progress was friction between Matsuoka and Nomura and the diplomatic incompetence displayed by Nomura.

Informal talks between Japan and the United States began around November 1940. On April 16, 1941, Ambassador Nomura and Secretary of State Cordell Hull met to discuss Hull's envisioned basis for negotiations. Hull wanted to shift the discussions to gaining an agreement on "the four principles": 1) respect for the territorial integrity and sovereignty of all nations; 2) noninterference in the internal affairs of all nations; 3) equality of economic opportunity for all nations; 4) no change in the status quo in the Pacific except by peaceful means. The four principles were clearly incompatible with the "Draft Understanding between Japan and the United States," a curious plan for peace in the Pacific drawn up by private citizens from both nations that was favorable to Japan and gave the Japanese a false idea of how far the United States was willing to go to meet Japanese demands. This amateur diplomacy only served to cloud the negotiations since the Japanese failed to understand that the two American clerics primarily responsible for drafting it were acting on their own.[12] Nomura decided not to forward Hull's principles to Tokyo but instead sent the pro-Japanese Draft Understanding and portrayed it as an American proposal. This version was understood and accepted by Tokyo as an official American proposal; in fact, it was not an officially approved document. Matsuoka discovered this, but the misimpression was significant – Tokyo concluded that the Americans were so intent on avoiding war that they might "yield on some important issues."[13]

The next time Nomura and Hull met was between May 7 and 11, 1941. Nomura intentionally failed to give the Americans Matsuoka's statements designed to scuttle the Draft Understanding. He did pass Hull's four principles to Tokyo without making it clear how important they were to the Americans. On May 11, Matsuoka sent a counterproposal that appeared to close the door on future serious negotiations. The Japanese demanded that the United States stop its opposition to Germany and force the Chinese government to accept a one-sided Japanese proposal to end the war in China.

Hull crafted an "unofficial" response to Matsuoka's demands. It rejected all Matsuoka's revisions of the Draft Understanding on the Tripartite Pact, China, and potential Japanese expansion into Southeast Asia. This exchange confirmed the distance between the two sides. It was delivered to the Japanese on May 31. Meanwhile, Nomura met with Hull nine more times between May 12 and June 7. Yet, he failed to report to Tokyo that the Americans were not willing to capitulate to Japanese conditions. Matsuoka only determined American views through Ambassador Joseph Grew in Tokyo. At this point, Matsuoka began to pursue a new course of action – direct talks between him and Roosevelt to arrive at a comprehensive settlement.

On June 21 Hull presented his formal response to Matsuoka's radical revisions of the Draft Understanding. In his verbal comments to Nomura, Hull criticized Japan's leaders (singling out Matsuoka) and declared that it would be "illusory" that an agreement could be reached.

In the midst of these exchanges, a seismic event took place. On June 22, Hitler invaded the Soviet Union. Now Japan was afforded another opportunity, engendering intense debate between the Imperial Army and Navy. The Imperial Army, supported by Matsuoka who wished to assist the Germans, wanted to strike the Soviet Union in its hour of weakness. The Imperial Navy wanted to strike south to take the resources of Southeast Asia, even if it meant war with the United States. The result of these polemics was a decision to wait to see how the situation developed. Preparations would begin for both a northern and a southern advance. No decision was made to go to war with the Soviet Union or any Western power, but the decision to move into southern Indochina was sure to provoke a reaction. If it did, "The Empire shall not flinch from war with Britain and the United States."[14]

These critical decisions, worked out at a series of liaison conferences, were presented to the Emperor at the July 2 imperial conference.[15] Imperial conferences were rare and usually were held to mark a major policy decision. According to Hirohito himself, the Emperor had no power of decision, so imperial approval was just a formality. The Emperor would listen to the proposals being made. If he had questions, they were posed by the President of the Privy Council. Once a proposal was given imperial sanction, the decision acquired a divine and apolitical character.[16]

The July 2 imperial conference was the first of four held in the months before the opening of the Pacific War. Of note, this was the first time that a supreme-level policy contemplated war with the United States and Britain. It is also worth noting that the consideration of war with the Western powers was conducted before the trade embargo was launched by the United States and its allies. At the July 2 conference, Hirohito listened quietly as the Privy Council asked the attendees a series of questions about the bellicose rhetoric directed towards the Western powers. He was assured that the occupation of southern Indochina would be peaceful and that the government considered the chance of the United States going to war over Indochina as low.

On July 10 and 12, liaison conferences considered Hull's June 21 reply. Both services did not want to reject the proposal out of hand as negotiations with the French were ongoing for the occupation of southern Indochina. Days later, at Konoe's behest, the abrasive and ruthless Matsuoka was forced out of the cabinet and replaced with Vice Admiral Toyoda Teijiro. The new foreign minister had no diplomatic experience and seemed more concerned with his position and that of the Imperial Navy rather than that of Japan.[17] As a Navy officer he was well aware of the Imperial Navy's lack of resources compared with the United States Navy but he never tried to make the case to his government counterparts that Japan must avoid a war.

Things came to a head when the Japanese gave the Vichy government an ultimatum on July 12 regarding the occupation of southern Indochina. The French had no choice but to submit, which they did on July 22 by allowing the Japanese access to eight air bases and two naval bases. In response, the Americans warned that such a move might lead to the cessation of talks with Nomura. Roosevelt offered the Japanese a proposal that called for the neutralization of Indochina. It was one of many attempts by the President to decouple Indochina from the larger issue of the war in China. Neither measure dissuaded the Japanese from their next move – on July 28 Japanese troops entered southern Indochina.

Despite Roosevelt's efforts to keep negotiations going, nothing could change the fact that Japanese aggression was expanding. To Roosevelt, with his eye on defeating Germany first, it was essential to keep the Japanese tied down in China, hopefully preventing them from attacking the Soviet Union or weakening Britain by attacking its possessions in Southeast Asia. Toward the goal of strengthening China's capability of resisting, on July 23 Roosevelt authorized an American military mission to China to coordinate Lend-Lease assistance. A more visible sign of American support was the establishment of the American Volunteer Group (aka "The Flying Tigers") in July 1941. Led by Claire Chennault, it initially comprised 99 recently discharged American military pilots to fly 100 P-40 fighters relinquished by the British from Lend-Lease stocks.

Outside support for China was a major irritant for the Japanese. In order to curtail it, they seized major Chinese ports, instituted a blockade of the coast, and occupied northern Indochina. After the German invasion, the Soviets stopped supplying China with arms. The British were able to funnel small amounts of supplies and weapons through Hong Kong. But the major conduit was the Burma Road which snaked from the port of Rangoon in Burma to Kunming in China. A more treacherous route could hardly be imagined, and the physical limitations of this method were increased by graft and corruption. Under Japanese pressure, the British closed it from July to October 1940.

Japan's move into southern Indochina prompted Roosevelt's controversial decision in late July to increase trade restrictions with Japan.

Effective July 26, all Japanese financial assets in the United States were frozen. The Japanese now had to obtain a license to unfreeze funds for each purchase. The biggest blow came on August 1 when the United States government revoked Japanese licenses for outstanding oil shipments. The British and Dutch followed suit. Whether it was Roosevelt's intention to create a flexible tool he could use to deter the Japanese by cutting off oil shipments whenever he wanted, or whether he intended to cut off all oil from reaching the Japanese, the effect was the same. The future of American oil shipments was uncertain as long as the funds were frozen. After returning from a meeting with British Prime Minister Winston Churchill in Placentia Bay, Newfoundland, on August 9–12, Roosevelt took no steps to alter the suspension of Japanese funds. The oil embargo against Japan would continue indefinitely.

As the Japanese imported 90 percent of its oil, of which 75–80 percent came from the United States and the rest from the Dutch East Indies (DEI), the new reality focused the minds of Konoe and others. On August 6, the Japanese finally responded to Roosevelt's neutralization proposal. As viewed by the Americans, it was clearly a step back since it only promised a withdrawal of troops from Indochina after the end of the war in China. The Japanese also asked for American assistance in negotiating a peace in China, but only if Japanese domination was assured. Thus, Japan rejected what Roosevelt thought was a conciliatory proposal and thrust the China issue right back into the center of negotiations. After overcoming his shock that the Americans were using their economic leverage in the form of an oil embargo, Konoe instructed Nomura to seek direct talks between himself and Roosevelt. Nomura delivered this proposal on August 8. The timing of the proposal was inept, coming just two days after the Japanese quashed Roosevelt's neutralization proposal. Nevertheless, Roosevelt was open to the idea, but only if the Japanese made concessions and agreements before the conference. Clearly, the Americans were leery of negotiating with a man who had presided over a parade of Japanese aggression.

As the diplomats struggled for some way forward, the thoughts of the Japanese military were encapsulated in a paper entitled "The Essentials for Carrying Out the Empire's Policies." In it was the intent to conduct operations into Southeast Asia and "if necessary" go to war with the United States, Britain, and the Netherlands. Concurrently, efforts would continue to defuse the crisis diplomatically. The key passage was "In the event that there is no prospect of our demands being met by the first ten days of October ... we will immediately decide to commence hostilities against the United States, Great Britain, and the Netherlands."[18] For diplomatic efforts to be considered successful, Japan's "Minimum Requirements" included: the United States and Great Britain would have to agree not to interfere with Japanese efforts to settle the China Incident, agree to close the Burma Road, and stop all assistance to China. The Western powers would also have to lift the trade embargo. In return, the Japanese agreed "in principle" to withdraw troops from China after a settlement. This was a meaningless concession, as the withdrawal was to take place over 25 years.[19] There was no chance such demands would be seriously entertained by the United States government. With its adoption of "The Essentials for Carrying Out the Empire's Policies," there was no real alternative to war.

On the basis of this paper, Konoe went to get the Emperor's approval on September 5. On this occasion, Hirohito was anything but compliant since to his eye the paper clearly emphasized military preparations over diplomacy. When pressed on the details of the plan, Konoe deferred to the heads of the Army and Navy General Staffs. General Sugiyama Hajime and Admiral Nagano Osami were summoned to the imperial palace. During the ensuing session, in the words of a Japanese historian, the Emperor "displayed the incisiveness he was capable of when utterly compelled – which did not happen often."[20] When asked by Hirohito how long a war with the United States would last, Sugiyama replied, three months. To this, the Emperor pointed out he was told that the war in China would be over in a month and had now going on four years. Sugiyama replied that China's vast depth prevented a quick end to the war. Hirohito blasted him with the retort, "If you say that China has a huge hinterland, the Pacific Ocean is even bigger. On what basis are you now telling me three months?"[21]

Nagano intervened, stating he spoke on behalf of the high command. He provided this analogy to the Emperor:

> If we were to compare today's U.S.–Japanese relations to a sick patient, the patient is in dire need of an operation. If we don't operate, and instead leave him be, the patient will gradually be weaker and weaker. Not that there isn't any hope of recovery. But we must decide while there is still a chance. The high command

desires diplomatic negotiations to reach a successful conclusion.
But in case of its failure, I am afraid that we must pluck up enough
courage and operate.[22]

When the Emperor asked Nagano if he had confidence in victory, he gave a nuanced response: "I cannot say 'definitely' because it depends not just on manpower but on divine power, too… If there is even a remote chance of [war] working out, we must do it." For his final question, Hirohito delivered another admonition: "Then I'll ask you again: Is it correct for me to understand that the high command intends to put more emphasis on diplomacy as of today?" Both men agreed that was the case.[23]

On the following day, an imperial conference was held to review the paper.

After Konoe finished, Nagano gave his view on what must be done:

Accordingly, if our minimum demands, which are necessary for
the self-preservation and self-defense of our Empire, cannot be
attained through diplomacy, and ultimately we cannot avoid war,
we must make all preparations, take advantage of our opportunities,
undertake aggressive military operations with determination and a
dauntless attitude, and find a way out of our difficulties.[24]

By striking now, Japan could seize what it needed to prepare for a prolonged war. Nagano described Japan's long-term military prospects as such:

If this first stage in our operations is carried out successfully, our
Empire will have secured strategic areas in the Southwest Pacific,
established an impregnable position, and laid the basis for a
prolonged war, even if American military preparedness should
proceed as scheduled. What happens thereafter will depend to a
great extent on overall national power – including elements, tangible
and intangible – and on developments in the world situation.[25]

After the parade of ministers finished their rehearsed comments, and Privy Council President Hara Yoshimichi asked a few questions on behalf of the Emperor, the ritual took a turn to the dramatic. Instead of making his exit in silence, the Emperor pulled a paper from his pocket and stunned all those present by reading a poem from his grandfather, Emperor Meiji:

> In as much as all
> The seas in all directions
> Seem twins of one birth
> How often must the winds and
> The waves clash in noisiness?[26]

To this he added: "I always read this composition with humility, endeavoring to be instructed in the late Emperor's peace-loving sprit." After Nagano and Sugiyama again promised to place emphasis on a diplomatic solution, the conference ended "in an atmosphere of unprecedented tenseness."[27] The Emperor's subjects were left to ponder the meaning of his remarks, but his intent seemed clear. Whatever the Emperor's attitude, at the conclusion of the conference, Japan was on a path for war.

In a time when Japan needed moral courage to curb the appetite of the militarists, Hirohito provided none. He clearly had doubts on the plans of Konoe and his military leaders. As Konoe hid in silence, the nation's top military leaders provided the Emperor with the weakest possible rationale for bringing the nation into a war in which the outcome was anything but certain. For his part, all the Emperor could muster was a passive protest in the form of a poem.

While the Emperor's preference was clear, the elements in the "Essentials" paper went unchanged. The imperial conference did nothing to brake preparations for war. In fact, the opposite was true since the timetable for reaching a diplomatic solution was still in motion and time was growing shorter.

By early September, the Japanese government was moving toward war – it was not a question of if war was coming, but when it would begin. To delay war meant Japan grew weaker as its fuel reserves were drained. From a Western perspective, Japan's rush to war was inexplicable, and the failure of the nation's leaders to stop it could be described as moral cowardice since the prospects for victory were at least uncertain, and if examined critically, bleak. This "rational" framework fails to appreciate the views of the military elite and its Bushido-warrior culture. In their narrative, the Japanese were a superior race but lacked the colonies and resources equal to the other major powers. That situation had to be rectified by an advance against inferior races. To retreat at the behest of Japan's inferiors (like withdrawing from China and Indochina), was nothing less than a humiliation. Failure to address Japan's lack of resources and to gain autarky placed Japan in a perpetual position of military and economic inferiority. The current situation presented a window of opportunity – that opportunity had to be seized now.[28]

As the last few weeks of peace dwindled, there were several reasons why an agreement was unlikely. One was the deadlock over China, which even the Japanese had identified as the fundamental issue standing in the way of an agreement with the United States. After the imperial conference, Konoe sent a reply to Roosevelt that included the demand that the United States cease all support for China, a dealbreaker for the Americans. There was no common ground to reach any agreement.

Even as doubts grew regarding the outcome of a war between the United States and Japan, there was a pervasive lack of moral courage among Japan's leaders. The Emperor could muster only a passive protest. Konoe increasingly became an opponent of going to war, but never publicly denounced the plans for war. With the Army advocating war, the Imperial Navy became a key player. Since any war against the United States would be primarily naval, the Imperial Navy's views on its prospects carried real weight. But the Imperial Navy's leaders also failed at this critical juncture.

The Imperial Navy never pressed the Army or the political leaders to stop the rush to war. On September 29, Yamamoto wrote Nagano that "a war with so little chance of success should not be fought." Nagano held the same assessment, yet at the October 4 liaison conference he told the Army: "It is no longer time for discussion. We should [set a timetable for war] right away." At a conference of the Imperial Navy's leaders on October 6, a consensus emerged to avoid war, even if it meant withdrawing from China. Even after learning this, Nagano failed to press the Army with his lack of confidence.[29]

Navy Minister Oikawa was a weak man, who despite his reservations about war, could never bring himself to make a stand against it. He put the onus on Konoe, stating the decision for war was a political one. This was not true since, under the constitution, the prime minister alone did not decide on war and peace – the entire cabinet had to agree. Had Oikawa put the needs of the nation first, instead of his personal reputation or that of the Imperial Navy as an institution, he could have quit his post. By law, the Navy had to appoint an active-duty admiral as Navy Minister. By refusing to do so, the rush to war could have been slowed and possibly the deadline for action averted. Behind the scenes, many military leaders, even Tojo, saw that a humiliating withdrawal from China was better than a war with the United States. Yet, publicly, there was no talk of compromise from any of Japan's leaders.

At least the Imperial Army was consistent in its support for going to war. Tojo, despite his personal qualms, was the public face of the hardliners. The view of the Army was encapsulated in the November 24 entry in the Confidential War Diaries of the Army Staff Office of Imperial General Headquarters: "Nomura and Kurusu [Kurusu Saburo, Japan's ambassador to Germany], who are desirous of a negotiated settlement, and the Army, particularly the General Staff, which is hoping for a breakdown of negotiations, are indeed diametrically opposed to one other."[30] The entry for November 28, after the receipt of the Hull Note, was clear: "This is nothing more than an effort to attain world hegemony by upholding the global status quo. The only path left is war."[31]

At the liaison conference on September 25, Sugiyama and Nagano proposed an October 15 deadline for reaching a diplomatic agreement. Another stunning example of the abdication of responsibility by Japan's leaders was provided during a liaison conference on October 7 when Tojo tried to gauge Oikawa's level of confidence in a Japanese victory. "That, I am afraid, I do not have ... if the war continues for a few years, we do not know what the outcome will be... What I have said should not go beyond this room." This shook Tojo, but the next day he continued his public bellicose statements by telling Konoe, "Occasionally, one must conjure up enough courage, close one's eyes and leap off the veranda of Kiyomizu [a temple near Kyoto]."[32] By using this expression, Tojo meant Japan should take the risk of going to war.

Increasingly uneasy with the march to war and under pressure from Tojo, Konoe resigned on October 16. Lord Keeper of the Privy Seal Kido Koichi recommended that Tojo take his place in the hope that he would be able to control the Army and because he might be able to reverse the decisions of the September imperial conference.[33] Actually expecting to be admonished for his role in bringing down the Konoe cabinet, Tojo was instead asked by the Emperor to form a new government on October 17. The new cabinet included Togo Shigenori as foreign minister and Shimada Shigetaro as Navy Minister. Tojo retained his position as War Minister.

After the fall of Konoe, Emperor Hirohito's principal advisor, Kido, relayed to the new government the Emperor's desire to reexamine the state of relations between the United States and Japan without regard to the September 6 imperial conference. However, in a singular oversight, the suggestion was not couched in terms that it had to done with whatever was needed to avoid war. Even though his awareness of the Navy's lack of confidence meant that Japan was better off if it reversed its trajectory toward war, Tojo lacked the vision to execute the Emperor's desire. This was exemplified during a series of liaison conferences between October 23 and 30.

During this period, a number of issues with direct bearing on Japan's ability to successfully prosecute a war were examined. However, the review was superficial and in some areas simply falsified. Representatives from the military were intent on a decision for war. This mentality was best represented by the Army General Staff's convoluted cart-before-the-horse thinking: "It is first and foremost necessary, at this point, to make up our minds [for war]. Then and only then can we calibrate our national capabilities and direct the nation to prepare for war."[34] The new foreign minister lamented his lack of support from the Navy; in fact, the new Navy Minister Shimada had changed his mind and joined the pro-war camp.[35]

Tojo made sure to cover all his bureaucratic bases during the October 23–30 meetings. Only Foreign Minister Togo and Finance Minister Kaya Okinori remained uncommitted to war. The liaison conference on November 1, lasting a marathon 17 hours, was a critical event. All sides recognized that a decision had to be made. The first matter was a demand from Navy Minister Shimada for a greater steel allocation in exchange for his vote for war. After hours of debate, Shimada got his way. This was yet another example of moral cowardice on the part of the Imperial Navy's leaders. More serious matters followed when the conference turned to the three options open for Japan. The first, giving in to American demands, garnered no support. The second, an immediate decision for war advocated by the Army General Staff, also failed to gain widespread support. Option three, in which a decision for war was made but with war preparations and diplomacy both proceeding apace, was accepted. However, there were issues with the third option – the Imperial Army wanted a deadline of November 13 for determining if diplomacy would work, and the Imperial Navy wanted November 20. After Togo protested, the military backed off and agreed to a deadline of midnight on November 30.[36]

When the issue of negotiations with the United States came up, Togo had two plans for a diplomatic settlement, The first, labeled Proposal A, included four main issues:[37]

1. Japan would withdraw its forces from China within two years of peace being established in China. After that, Japanese troops would remain in areas of North China, Mongolia, and Hainan Island for "as long as necessary." As long as necessary was defined as 25 years.
2. Japan would respect the sovereignty of French Indochina and would withdraw its troops there once peace was established in China or the Pacific.
3. Japan would agree to the principle of nondiscrimination for trade in the entire Pacific region, including China, if that principle was applied throughout the world.
4. In regard to the Tripartite Pact, Japan would "act independently."

Togo was fearful that Proposal A stood no chance with the Americans. He therefore devised Proposal B in the hope of creating some diplomatic maneuvering room. The four points were:[38]

1. Japan and the United States both pledged not to make any advances of forces into Southeast Asia and the South Pacific region, except French Indochina.
2. Japan and the United States would cooperate so that Japan's procurement of necessary materials from the DEI will be assured.
3. Japan and the United States will restore trade relations to levels prior to the American trade embargo. The United States will promise to meet Japan's petroleum needs.
4. The United States will not take actions to hinder peace efforts between China and Japan.

The hardliners objected to Proposal B so had the third point modified and added the fourth point that the United States government would not interfere in peacemaking efforts in China – in other words, the Americans would have to cease providing aid to China.[39] Both these proposals had little chance of being accepted by the United States. As the deadline approached for the end of negotiations, they were in essence an ultimatum.[40]

The longest liaison conference ever conducted ended with both Proposal A and B being adopted. The November 30 deadline for negotiations was also approved.

For the first time, Nagano and Sugiyama presented the detailed war plan to the Emperor on the afternoon of November 2. At this time, he learned about the planned attack on Pearl Harbor scheduled for December 8 (December 7 Hawaii time). On November 4, the Supreme War Council met, again with Hirohito present. All this led to the third imperial conference of the year on November 5. The conference blessed both Proposal A and B as well as the 30 November diplomatic deadline.

TIME GROWS SHORT

In November, Togo sent Kurusu Saburo to Washington as a special envoy to assist Nomura. The reason was to ensure that Nomura adhered to instructions from Tokyo. As the man who signed the Tripartite Pact, his reputation was tainted with the Americans. Proposals A and B reached Nomura on November 4. On November 7, Nomura presented Proposal A to Hull. Three days later, Nomura met Roosevelt. That same day, Togo informed Ambassador Grew in Tokyo that the latest proposal represented as far as Japan was willing to go. Togo also explained to Grew that if the Japanese were forced to abandon their gains in China that "she would inevitably collapse" and that American economic pressure "menac[ed] the national existence to a greater degree than the direct use of force."[41]

Roosevelt and Hull gave no traction to Proposal A. Roosevelt became personally involved in negotiations, probably in response to a plea from Army Chief of Staff General George Marshall and Chief of Naval Operations Admiral Harold Stark to avoid a war in the Pacific. They even advocated sacrificing aid to China since aid to Britain and Russia was more important. Marshall advocated "clever diplomacy" to buy time until defenses in the Philippines could be reinforced.[42] With this in mind, during the November 10 meeting with Nomura and Hull, Roosevelt for the first time raised the possibility of coming to an interim agreement. Roosevelt was thinking in terms of a six-month truce during which the Americans would ease trade restrictions for a Japanese promise not to advance north or south or to meet its obligations under the Tripartite Pact to enter a war between the United States and Germany.

On November 17, Kurusu entered the picture and during a meeting with Nomura, Hull, and Roosevelt pleaded that Tokyo desired peace, but that a withdrawal from China was impossible. Time, he stated, was critical.

Nomura and Kurusu met again with Hull the next day. At this time they presented a modified point from Proposal B – Japan would withdraw troops from southern Indochina if the Americans would unfreeze assets and resume trade relations. This seemed like a promising start to the Americans and might fulfill Roosevelt's desire for a temporary agreement. Any prospect for a temporary agreement was smashed when Foreign Minister Togo learned of what his Washington diplomats had done. He ordered them to retract the offer and submit the original version of Proposal B while emphasizing that the fourth point required America to abandon its support for China. On November 20, Nomura and Kurusu complied. Hull promised only to examine the proposal but voiced his concern over the point that required the United States to stop supporting China.

Both Proposal A and B included the demand for the United States to stop all aid to China. Given this, there was almost no diplomatic room for Nomura and Kurusu and little for the Americans to consider. In response to the latest Japanese proposal, Hull considered both a short-term and a long-term solution. To extend the time for negotiations, he mulled over a three-month moratorium during which the Japanese would pull back from southern Indochina to northern Indochina where the size of their garrison could not exceed 25,000 troops. The Japanese also had to agree to stop further aggressive military moves. In exchange, the United States would partially reopen trade, including lower-grade petroleum for civilian use. The key issue of China was not a central feature of the potential proposal, with the United States only offering to sponsor peace talks between China and Japan in the Philippines. American diplomatic goals were much more explicit in the comprehensive proposal. In order to reach a settlement for peace in the region and to restore trade, the Japanese had to withdraw from China and Indochina and recognize the Nationalist government as the legitimate government in China. Japan was also expected to renounce the Tripartite Pact.

Just how unlikely it was for the Japanese to accept the interim or comprehensive proposals was made clear in the decryption of Japanese diplomatic traffic (the so-called "Magic" intercepts) during the period November 22–24. "Magic," a combined US Army and Navy cryptoanalysis effort, revealed that the Japanese deadline for an agreement was November 28 and "after that things are automatically going to happen." Even more important than the looming deadline was what the Japanese needed for an agreement. The proposal by the United States for a return to the July status quo was insufficient. Only a restoration of oil supplies and a stop of all aid to China would suffice.

Events were already spinning beyond the efforts of the diplomats. American intelligence was tracking clear Japanese preparations for war. From November 20, a huge part of the Imperial Navy was departing home waters and headed south. The size of the force left no doubt as to Japanese intentions – one light aircraft carrier, two battleships, 11 heavy and ten light cruisers, and at least 55 destroyers, 14 submarines, and a commensurate number of auxiliaries.[43] Not just the combat units of the Imperial Fleet were on the move. Over 100 transports were also in motion carrying five divisions. Most of these forces were moving to Hainan Island, which served as the staging area for an attack on Thailand and Malaya. A large convoy was sighted south of Formosa headed south. Other forces were staging at Formosa and the Pescadores in preparation to move against the Philippines. Secretary of War Henry Stimson was aware of these movements on November 25. He called Hull the same day and sent copies of the report to Roosevelt.

The impact of the report detailing the scope of Japanese movements was immediate. Roosevelt was enraged that the Japanese were seemingly not negotiating in good faith. Hull abandoned his work on the interim and comprehensive proposals and on November 26 delivered the so-called "Hull Note" to Nomura and Kurusu. It contained the strongest American conditions, including:

1 A non-aggression pact signed by all major Pacific powers.
2 Japanese withdrawal from China and Indochina.

3 Japanese recognition of the Nationalist government as the legitimate Chinese government.
4 Japan and the United States to cede their extraterritorial rights in China and to work with other governments to give up theirs.
5 A provision for Japan to make the Tripartite Pact essentially void.

These were issues that both sides knew could not be successfully negotiated in the few days remaining before the Japanese deadline. Therefore, Hull knew it would not be accepted. While the note was technically not an ultimatum since it contained calls for additional negotiations and had no deadline, it shocked the Japanese. After seeing the American response, Togo, one of the last leaders unwilling to approve a decision for war, changed his mind.[44] He considered it tantamount to an ultimatum.[45] On the same day that negotiations broke down, the Pearl Harbor strike force departed Japanese waters headed toward Hawaii.

At this point, all negotiations were dead. On November 27, Hull informed Stimson that he had "washed my hands of [the negotiations] and it is now in the hands of you and Secretary of the Navy Frank Knox – the Army and the Navy."[46] In Japan, the militarists in the government saw it in the same light and considered it as "nothing short of a miracle" since it highlighted the fact that diplomacy had failed.[47]

It should not be surprising that negotiations failed. The diplomatic objectives of Japan and the United States, reflecting their strategic interests, were too far apart to ever make negotiations viable. The Americans assessed that when the Japanese had to finally select between peace and going to war with the United States, they would decide to avoid a humiliating defeat. This belief held even as the evidence indicated such a revelation was not forthcoming. The militarists in Japan, who controlled the government and who had been driving the population and military toward war, were not interested in examining the situation rationally. Going to war, even a war that many understood to be unwinnable, was preferable to national humiliation and betraying the souls of the men who had died in China.

China was the most important issue between the two powers. To the United States, the reasons for inserting China into the forefront of negotiations was not financial or moral; it was the much more pressing concern that China was a valuable ally holding down much of Japan's military strength and restricting its freedom of action for additional aggression in Asia. China had demonstrated that it was capable of frustrating Japanese attempts to subject it by force of arms. Now Japan was trying to gain diplomatically what it could not achieve militarily. Both the Americans and Japanese assumed that if the United States and Britain stopped supporting the Nationalist government that a Chinese defeat was inevitable. The Japanese insistence that the Americans abandon China and the American refusal to do so became the most salient stumbling block in the negotiations. In Roosevelt's mind, that of his advisors, and the British, if China collapsed, then the Japanese were free to expand their aggression by attacking the Soviet Union or the colonial possessions of the British or Dutch. Had this happened, it would have meant a reduction in the ability of these nations to withstand Germany. The defeat of Germany was Roosevelt's paramount strategic objective.

With regard to the Japanese, at least Togo, Nomura, and Kurusu were aware of the central role of China in the minds of the Americans. When Togo drafted Proposal B, he was trying to work around the China issue. Nomura and Kurusu also tried to sideline the China issue by offering an interim solution based on Proposal B. On both occasions, the military hardliners in charge of the government frustrated their efforts. Togo's gambit was quashed when the hardliners added a provision to Proposal B that the United States had to abandon China; Togo crushed the attempt of his diplomats in Washington to gain negotiating momentum by ordering them to present the original demands of Proposal B with its requirement that the United States abandon China. Likewise, had Prime Minister Konoe been able to set up a meeting with Roosevelt, any prospect for success was contingent upon the most improbable event that the Japanese militarists would make concessions. With further diplomatic negotiations deemed futile and unwilling to retreat from China, Japan's military was prepared to act swiftly.

The last week of peace in the Pacific passed quickly. Nomura and Kurusu met with Roosevelt and Hull on November 27. The Americans offered no modifications to the Hull Note. On December 1, the final prewar imperial conference was held. Per the deadline set on November 5, the final decision for war was made. At this point, there was no other path possible. The Japanese war machine was in full gear with orders to strike targets throughout the Pacific. Among these planned operations was a bold attack on the principal American base in the Pacific – the home of the United States Navy's Pacific Fleet at Pearl Harbor, Hawaii. The next day, the Commander of the Combined Fleet sent a message to the Pearl Harbor Striking Force: "Climb Mount Niitake 1208."[48] Negotiations had failed – Japan was going to war.

The Pearl Harbor strike was only one of a series of synchronized Japanese attacks across the Pacific. Preceding the coordinated assault was a planned final communication with the United States government breaking off further negotiations. This would be delivered at 1300 hours Washington time on December 7. This was 0730 hours in Honolulu. With the attack scheduled to begin at 0800, it left no room for any delay or problems if the note was to be delivered before hostilities were initiated.

2

Yamamoto and the Great Debate

> A decision has been made that is diametrically opposed to my attitude as an individual. There is no other choice but to pursue this course with determination and energy. This current situation is indeed strange for me. I suppose I should regard it as my destiny.[1]
>
> Yamamoto Isoroku,
> Commander-in-Chief of the Combined Fleet

THE IMPERIAL NAVY AND ITS DECISIVE BATTLE

Imperial Navy planning against the United States Navy (USN) began as a reactive defensive strategy. From the 1920s until the late 1930s, the strategy matured and changed locations, but it remained defensive. In the earliest iteration it was built around a decisive battle fought by the Combined Fleet's surface forces in Japanese home waters; by the late 1930s it was much more complex and featured all elements of the Combined Fleet engaging in a decisive battle in the area of the Bonin and Mariana Islands. This decisive engagement was prompted by an American advance into the Western Pacific – in any conflict with the United States, it was assumed that the Japanese would quickly seize the Philippines and Guam and that the USN would attempt to recapture them.

By 1936, with the end of the Washington Naval Treaty (which prohibited building new fortifications in the Pacific) approaching and with the advent of more capable long-range aircraft, the Japanese considered moving a large portion of their land-based naval air force to the Marshall and Caroline Islands in the Central Pacific to combat the American fleet as it moved westward. Though the Japanese were slow to actually build facilities on these islands, by 1940 they had decided to move the place of the decisive battle from east of the Marianas to northwest of the Marshalls.[2]

Even in this context, Japanese naval strategy against the USN was still reactive. As the USN advanced across the Pacific, it would dictate the time and place of the decisive battle. To many Imperial Navy leaders, this purely defensive strategy was no longer suitable, for several reasons. Foremost, it placed the initiative in the hands of the USN and allowed it to conduct a prolonged war, something that the Imperial Navy feared it would lose. The Imperial Navy understood that it would be mismatched in a war against the USN. Upon the fall of France, Congress passed two legislative acts to create a "Two Ocean Navy." This was a wake-up call for the Imperial Navy since it was the first time it had to deal with the reality of the United States' capability to build a navy that would far outstrip what the Japanese could produce. By Japanese calculations, the Imperial Navy would be 76 percent of the USN at the end of 1941. Once the fruits of the Two Ocean Navy were realized, the ratio of capital ships would drop to 50 percent by 1943 and to about 30 percent by 1944.[3] Time did not work in favor of the Japanese.

THE SOUTHERN OFFENSIVE

Another factor not in Japan's favor was the emerging imperative to seize Southeast Asia to gain the strategic resources required by their war economy. As early as May 1940, the Imperial Navy conducted map exercises to examine naval operations in Southeast Asia within the new context of great power relations in the Pacific.[4] A consensus quickly emerged that a war against only the vulnerable Dutch was not possible – the Americans and British were sure to get involved. There also emerged concerns over the obvious problem of securing the sea lines of communications (SLOCs) between Japan and its conquered resource areas in Southeast Asia. From the beginning, it was assumed that a war of conquest would involve the Americans. The embargo crisis in the summer of 1941 forced the Imperial Navy to begin detailed planning for an offensive into the southern resource areas.

As was the case on most issues, the Imperial Army and Navy had different views on how to conduct the attack into Southeast Asia. The Army wanted to attack British Malaya first, followed by the Dutch East Indies (DEI), and finally the Philippines. The Navy saw matters in a different light, since it assumed that any attack on British or Dutch possessions would bring the Americans into the war. Navy planners did not want to bypass the Philippines, primarily because they sat astride the SLOCs from Japan to Southeast Asia.[5]

Predictably, the Army and Navy settled their differences by agreeing to attack Malaya and the Philippines concurrently, thus leaving both parties content. This was a real risk given the relatively small forces the Japanese committed to these operations. Japanese operations in the opening weeks and months of the war were much more intricate than just attacking Southeast Asia. In the first stage operations, Guam and Wake Atoll, the Gilbert Islands, Thailand, northern Malaya, British Borneo, Hong Kong, and the Philippines were all targeted. Once these were secured, second stage operations would complete the conquest of Malaya and Singapore, and seize southern Burma and key islands in the northern DEI. Finally, in the third stage, the rest of Burma would be captured along with Sumatra and Java in the DEI.[6]

Imperial Navy responsibilities for these operations were extensive. Not only would it have to defend the invasion convoys to this list of far-flung objectives and then support the landings from Allied attack, but the Imperial Japanese Navy Air Force (IJNAF) would have to provide the great majority of air power required to gain air control over a vast theater. Only control of the air would make seizure of the many objectives with relatively small naval and ground forces a possibility. The critical role of air power was at the heart of the Naval General Staff's objections to Yamamoto's Pearl Harbor operation. If all fleet carriers were assigned to attack Hawaii, only a single light carrier was left to support the southward advance.[7] The only recourse was to rely on land-based air power flying out of Formosa to neutralize American air power in the Philippines and from Indochina to attack British air bases in Malaya. The 11th Air Fleet, based on Formosa, was tasked to destroy American air power in the Philippines. As the Americans sent more aircraft to the Philippines, including B-17 heavy bombers, the potential threat was growing. This had to be eliminated at the earliest point possible so that landings on the Philippines could proceed.

Principal American air bases were located in the Manila area, some 500 nautical miles (nm) from Japanese bases on Formosa. That meant that although they were within range of Japanese bombers, Japanese fighters initially lacked the combat radius to accompany them. Even this assumed that the American aircraft were not placed on airfields further away in the Philippines out of the range of bombers based on Formosa. Given this, the need for the carriers of the 1st Air Fleet was manifest.

Two main factors alleviated the Naval General Staff's concerns that the carriers were needed to support the advance into Southeast Asia. With the proper techniques for reducing fuel consumption on long flights, the standard Imperial Navy fighter demonstrated its capability to accompany the bombers. In addition, Imperial Navy officers observed and took heart from the performance of the German Luftwaffe in 1940, especially those operations off Norway, which in many ways resembled potential operations in Southeast Asia.[8]

It took a series of map exercises in September 1941 for the Imperial Navy to feel comfortable with operations supporting the intended southward expansion. Aside from the carrier force, which was (tentatively) allocated to the Hawaii Operation, most of the remainder of the Combined Fleet was devoted to operations in Southeast Asia. After five exercises, the Imperial Navy worked out the details of the major offensive into Southeast Asia, defending the SLOCs between the southern resource areas and Japan, and synchronized those with operations in the Western Pacific.[9]

In its entirety, the advance into Southeast Asia represented an enormous risk. It had to be accomplished on a very strict timetable, lest the Allies move reinforcements into the area or gain the time to destroy the facilities used to extract the very resources for which Japan was so desperate. Another reason for the quick pace of operations was to minimize the amount of time merchant ships were retained to support the military instead of being used for carrying imports to Japan. The Japanese understood that Allied forces in the region were weak. However, Japanese forces were also small. By gaining the initiative and using it to keep the Allies off balance, the Japanese planned to use their forces to execute a series of quick operations, always under air cover. The only issue with the potential to disrupt the Japanese timetable and deny them the much-needed resources of Southeast Asia was a rapid counterattack by the USN's Pacific Fleet across the Pacific.

THE MAN BEHIND THE PEARL HARBOR ATTACK

While many Imperial Navy officers were not content with the reactive defensive strategy against the USN, a single figure was responsible for replacing this strategy with a much more aggressive plan – attack the Pacific Fleet at its home base of Pearl Harbor, Hawaii. This man was Yamamoto Isoroku, commander-in-chief of the Combined Fleet.[10] The story of how the Pearl Harbor attack was approved illustrates Yamamoto's pivotal role.

Yamamoto's unique background and standing made possible his long fight to get his Pearl Harbor plan approved in the face of overwhelming opposition within the Imperial Navy. He was a key member of the group of Imperial Navy officers with moderate views. They saw the Navy as a deterrent force, not as a tool for expansion, and supported the naval arms limitation system.[11] Yamamoto was an iconoclast in several regards. As one of the Imperial Navy's air advocates, he became a staunch critic of the big-gun mentality and of Japan's plans to build superbattleships. He also opposed attempts to draw Japan closer to Nazi Germany. His views angered extremist factions and led to death threats against him. This was part of the reason he was appointed to lead the Combined Fleet in August 1939 – to get him out of Tokyo. His background brought unmatched prestige to his new role. It also afforded Yamamoto the means to seek and attain greater strategic decision-making authority.[12]

It should not be forgotten that Yamamoto was a traditional Japanese Nationalist, dedicated to serving the Emperor, who supported the aggressive war in China and the planned war of aggression in the Pacific. As such, he was not a man of peace as he is most often falsely portrayed. While he was supportive of wars he thought Japan could win, he was not in favor of a war with the United States since he clearly saw such a conflict as unwinnable. In a crucial time in Japan's history, he was in charge of the Japanese fleet, a post of critical importance and influence. Despite his views that Japan could not win a war with the United States, he recognized Japan's unstoppable war-bound trajectory and used his position to plan an expanded war that included a preemptive attack against the United States. He was the only man who could have achieved this dramatic change in Japanese naval strategy. Understanding Yamamoto and his background is essential to explaining how this happened.

YAMAMOTO AND THE GREAT DEBATE

In 1884, Yamamoto was born Takano Isoroku in northern Honshu to a samurai father, 56-year-old Takano Sadayoshi. His father was on the losing side of the 1877 Satsuma Rebellion in which disaffected samurai rebelled against the new imperial government. Consequently, young Isoroku spent his early years in poverty and uncertainty. His way out of poverty was through naval service. In 1901 he gained an appointment to the Imperial Naval Academy at Etajima by scoring the second-highest result of applicants from all of Japan. When he graduated in November 1904, he was the seventh-highest graduate in a class of over 200. He was assigned duty on a cruiser and fought in the Battle of Tsushima in May 1905, the final naval battle of the Russo-Japanese War. Yamamoto was wounded in this action, losing two fingers on his left hand, and was recognized for his bravery.

Clearly an officer with a bright future, he attended the Naval Staff College in 1913. In 1916, Takano Isoroku became Yamamoto Isoroku. Both his father and mother died in 1912, and since Isoroku had several older brothers from his father's first marriage, he had no future in the Takano clan. In a process that was common for samurai families in Japan at the time, he accepted an offer to join the wealthy and influential Yamamoto clan to perpetuate the family name. After marrying in 1918, he was sent on special duty to the United States as a lieutenant commander the following year. He enrolled at Harvard University to study English before withdrawing early in 1920. Yamamoto continued his studies on his own and took it upon himself to learn about oil, the lifeblood of any modern navy. By all accounts, he also took time to play hard, spending time playing bridge and games of chance. Yamamoto returned to Japan in July 1921.

Despite his background as a gunnery officer, Yamamoto was interested in all matters pertaining to aviation. As a captain in 1924, he took up his first aviation command and established himself as an aviation expert. From January 1926 to March 1928, Yamamoto was posted back to the United States as an attaché. His opinion of the United States Navy was formed in this period; it was, he said, "a social organization of golfers and bridge-players."[13] From December 1928 to October 1929, he commanded carrier *Akagi*. Following that tour, he was sent as an assistant to the Japanese delegation to the London Naval Conference of 1930.[14] Two more aviation billets followed – head of the Technical Division of the Aeronautics Department for three years and then commander of Carrier Division 1.

In September 1934, as a vice admiral, he was appointed chief delegate to the preliminary talks of the Second London Naval Conference. Though a member of the treaty faction, the "fleet" faction, with its demand for a 70 percent limit compared to the USN, was in control. Instructed by his government to negotiate terms he knew the Americans and British would never accept, he was forced to witness the collapse of the Washington Naval Treaty and the London Naval Treaty.

After a period of forced idleness that he described as the worst point in his career, he was given the assignment as chief of the Aeronautics Department of the Navy Ministry in December 1935. By this time, Yamamoto was a full-fledged air advocate, but he was never as radical as often portrayed. After only a year, his career took another turn. In December 1936, he assumed the job as Navy Vice Minister serving under Admiral Nagano.

Yamamoto and Nagano (and later Admiral Yonai when he assumed the job as Navy Minister) worked to curb the influence of the Imperial Army and radical factions within the Imperial Navy. This was a losing battle – during this period Japan began a war of aggression in China and moved closer to a military alliance with Nazi Germany. Yamamoto's opposition to the Tripartite Pact with Germany and Italy placed him in personal danger. In the aftermath of the German non-aggression pact with the Soviet Union in August 1939, the cabinet resigned and Yamamoto lost his job. Before this occurred, Yonai secured the commander in chief of the Combined Fleet position for Yamamoto. Though he was respected within the Imperial Navy, Yamamoto was not the obvious choice for his new position. He was viewed as a political admiral, had little command experience, and had spent the previous six years ashore.

On a personal level, Yamamoto had many admirable qualities. He was a man of undoubted intelligence and moral courage. By all accounts, Yamamoto was a man of considerable charisma. His staff adored him. His concern for the men under his charge permeated to the lowest ranks. Perhaps his rarest attribute was his capacity for making bold and imaginative decisions. This was especially rare in the Imperial Navy, but Yamamoto took this attribute to extremes. His stark individuality was so rare that one of his colleagues called it a "product of mutation."

Another of Yamamoto's salient qualities was his reputation as a gambler. This was true in his personal life – he loved games of skill and chance like chess, poker, or bridge. This carried over to his professional life. According to Watanabe Yasuji, Yamamoto's favorite staff officer and his preferred game partner, "In all games Yamamoto loved to take chances just as he did in naval strategy. He had a gambler's heart."[15]

Yamamoto had no faith in Japan's political leaders and was pessimistic that war could be avoided. Though he expected war to break out, he professed a desire to avoid conflict with the United States. There was a simple reason for this – Japan had little hope of victory in a war with the United States. Yamamoto was one of Japan's few senior leaders who saw this clearly. His time in the United States gave him a glimpse of that country's industrial, technological, scientific, and natural resources. In a quote widely attributed to him, Yamamoto painted the Combined Fleet's chances as such in a meeting with Prime Minister Konoe in September 1940: "If I am told to fight regardless of the consequences, I shall run wild for the first six months or a year, but I have utterly no confidence for the second or third year."[16] Of course, this proved prescient.

If Japan was to survive a great power contest with the United States, it had to have access to natural resources. This was only possible by moving into Southeast Asia. Even in this eventuality, Yamamoto saw problems:

> The probability is great that the launching of our operation against the Netherlands Indies will lead to an early commencement of war with America, and since Britain and Holland will side with America, our operations against the Netherlands Indies are almost certain to develop into a war with America, Britain and Holland before the operations are half over.[17]

Later in the same letter, Yamamoto explained his thinking on how a war with the United States should develop: "If … it is felt that war cannot be avoided, it would be best to decide on war with America from the beginning and to begin by taking the Philippines, thereby reducing the line of operations and assuring the sound execution of operations…"[18]

From a strict military perspective, Yamamoto's thinking that an attack on Pearl Harbor was a vital prerequisite for the Southern Operation had merit. His assumption that an attack into the Southeast Asian resource areas had to include an attack on American forces was also the correct Naval Staff College solution. Failure to attack the Americans left the Philippines in the rear of the Japanese southern advance and posed an obvious threat to Japanese SLOCs from Japan to the attacking forces. If the Pacific Fleet was left unmolested, it posed a threat to Japan's eastern flank. The Americans would also be left with the initiative and could begin hostilities when they chose.[19]

A much more subtle view of how to handle the Americans was held by Nagano and the Naval General Staff. Nagano assessed that an attack on Dutch and British possessions in the Far East did not necessarily entail war with the Americans. In this view, Nagano was almost certainly correct. In December 1941, President Roosevelt could not have secured congressional approval to enter the war to defend European colonies. Only Japanese aggression against the Philippines or other American possessions would have moved the Congress to war. Since there were other reasons driving Japan and the United States to war in late 1941, Nagano's assessment that war with the United States could have been avoided was probably only true in the short term.

Nevertheless, Yamamoto's driving requirement to attack the Pacific Fleet to prevent it from interfering with the vital southern advance was entirely unnecessary. For political reasons, the United States lacked the ability to respond immediately to Japanese aggression in Southeast Asia that left the Philippines untouched. More importantly, as will be addressed later, the Pacific Fleet lacked the logistical means to begin an immediate advance into the Western Pacific. Perhaps there was a reason why the Naval General Staff was charged to formulate strategic plans and the Combined Fleet was tasked to refine them. While the Combined Fleet pursued its myopic view of naval strategy, the Naval General Staff had to consider other factors, including economic conditions and the views of the Imperial Army and the Foreign Ministry.

Yamamoto also supported the view that wars could be decided by decisive battles. If the Pacific Fleet could be crippled at the start of the war, American resolve could be undermined and a negotiated peace made more likely. But this is not the way that major industrial powers are defeated – this occurs only after a sustained struggle.[20] Yamamoto did not understand the nature of modern warfare, but, to be fair, he represented the majority opinion within the Imperial Navy.

While Yamamoto was the father of the concept to attack Pearl Harbor with massed carrier air power and the man who pushed the plan forward until it was approved, he was not the primary planner of the attack. This fell upon Genda Minoru, a noted air power advocate and renowned operations planner. It needs to be stressed that the only individuals involved in the plan from the opening phase of planning to its execution were Yamamoto and Genda. Genda was the man with the detailed experience and knowledge to put the plan together, but only Yamamoto had the weight and prestige to have the plan adopted. Simply put, without Yamamoto as its driving force, the Pearl Harbor attack would never have happened.

Captain Kuroshima Kameto was a key staff officer to Yamamoto. He and Commander Watanabe Yasuji best knew the mind of their boss. Yamamoto would often discuss his thinking with them. During 1940, the discussions included what Japan's strategy should be if it came to war with the United States. On this issue, Yamamoto was clear. Because Japan was the weaker nation, it had to strike first.

Kuroshima was Yamamoto's senior staff officer and had been with him since the autumn of 1939. Kuroshima was a Naval Staff College graduate and was in overall charge of planning on the Combined Fleet staff. He was a brilliant planner, but also was extremely eccentric. When he turned his skills to the Pearl Harbor plan, nobody on the staff worked harder on it. As the duel with the Naval General Staff grew more intense, Kuroshima was trusted by Yamamoto to present the plan and advocate for it.

ORIGINS OF THE PEARL HARBOR PLAN

Though Yamamoto has been forever linked with the Pearl Harbor attack, he was not the first naval officer to think of such an operation. Yamamoto began to get serious about the plan in 1940, but it was a matter discussed in literature well before then and was a consistent theme in American naval exercises.

Many American, British, and Japanese writers included a Japanese attack on Hawaii as part of a fictional American–Japanese war in the 1920s and 1930s. The most heralded of these was British journalist Hector Bywater who published a novel in 1925 titled *The Great Pacific War: A History of the American Japanese Campaign of 1931–33*. However, references to any attacks on Hawaii were too generalized and vague to be useful to the Japanese during planning for the attack in 1941. Keep in mind that the Pacific Fleet was not moved to Pearl Harbor until the late spring of 1940, so a direct parallel between these fictional attacks and the real one does not exist.[21]

Attacking Pearl Harbor was a persistent theme of the USN's annual fleet exercise during the 1920s and 1930s. In particular, the 1932 exercise featured a pre-dawn attack by 152 aircraft from two carriers against air bases on Oahu and Pearl Harbor. In 1938, a single carrier repeated a similar attack against Pearl Harbor and Lahaina anchorage. It is doubtful that any useful details of the attacks were available to the Japanese since they were not observers to the actual event and were not privy to the reports afterward.[22]

On the other hand, Yamamoto was almost certainly aware of studies undertaken by Imperial Navy officers on a possible Pearl Harbor attack. In 1927, a tabletop war game was conducted at the Naval Staff College in which two Japanese carriers were used to attack Pearl Harbor. The attack was judged to have been "rash" and therefore unsuccessful. In November of that year, Kusaka Ryunosuke, then a lieutenant commander (but later chief of staff of the force conducting the Pearl Harbor attack), proposed a series of air attacks against Hawaii to make the USN's Battle Fleet depart its home bases on the West Coast to cross the Pacific where it would be annihilated in a set-piece battle.[23]

The most direct prewar exploration with parallels to the actual attack took place in 1936 at the Naval War College. In the study, opening attacks on American forces in the Philippines and against the Pacific Fleet in Pearl Harbor by "sudden and unexpected attacks" from aircraft carriers and flying boats were proposed.[24] So, even before Yamamoto thought about a Pearl Harbor attack and then proposed it, the idea was circulating in Imperial Navy and USN circles.

It was one thing for Yamamoto to have been aware of the concept of attacking Pearl Harbor and quite another to actually propose such a risky operation in contravention of existing Imperial Navy strategy. The impetus pushing Yamamoto to conduct a bold opening attack using carrier air power is not fully appreciated. He realized that the Imperial Navy possessed a new capability but he had not found a way to employ it. Yamamoto's thinking was clearly foreshadowed by the Combined Fleet's training programs in 1939–40 that began to emphasize air training. Part of this were exercises by carrier-launched torpedo aircraft against enemy warships at anchor or in harbor. Torpedo bombers were also noted to be successful against capital ships under way.[25]

Japan's growing naval air power provided Yamamoto with the means to execute the kind of bold opening strike he saw as necessary in a war against the United States. He and key members of his staff were already thinking in terms of a preemptive strike. In Yamamoto's mind, there was a sound rationale for such a bold step. Given the vastly superior industrial might of the United States and the navy that would be created from it, Yamamoto did not want the war to be a battle of attrition. This was what he saw as the likely outcome of the Imperial Navy's existing strategy of waiting for and reacting to an American naval advance across the Central and Western Pacific. It was unlikely that the Combined Fleet could bring the Pacific Fleet to battle under favorable terns, meaning that the decisive battle concept was flawed. The basic outline of the American naval strategy against Japan was known to the Japanese. In it, the Americans were expected to advance into the Marshall Islands and establish forward bases. From there, the advance would continue into the Carolines and Marianas. If the Americans elected for a methodical advance, then the early decisive battle would not unfold, and the war would be prolonged. In this case, the industrial strength of the United States was sure to prevail.[26] The place of a decisive battle would be taken by an attritional struggle, much to the Imperial Fleet's detriment. But how could the Combined Fleet avoid being ground down into defeat? A preemptive strike using air power was the only possible solution. When the Pacific Fleet was moving from its safe bases on the West Coast to Hawaii in May 1940, placing it within range of a carrier strike, Yamamoto was presented with the opportunity he had been waiting for.

Not everybody among the Imperial Navy's upper echelons was happy with the prevailing decisive battle strategy. It stood to reason that the members of the "Battleship Clique" were content with the plan since it preserved the central role of the battleship in the decisive battle. However, air-minded officers, among them Yamamoto, saw the plan as out of touch. Their criticisms were based on three main points. The first was the most cogent, since the existing strategy assumed that the Americans would at some point steam blindly into an elaborate trap. Yamamoto and others assessed that the existing reactive plan left the initiative in the hands of the Americans and it was unlikely they would rush across the Western Pacific only to engage the Combined Fleet on disadvantageous terms. Secondly, the rise of naval aviation made a climactic big-gun clash unlikely. More likely was a series of battles over air bases that the Japanese were belatedly building in the Marshalls and the Carolines.[27] Of course, the view of the air admirals proved to be prescient. Instead of waiting for the enemy to make his move, they believed that the Japanese should use their emerging carrier capabilities to make a preemptive attack.

OBJECTIVES OF YAMAMOTO'S PLAN

Yamamoto's plan was breathtaking in its audacity and had enormous potential to swing the early balance of naval power in the Pacific in Japan's favor. Planning for it began in February–March 1941. Yet at this point it was not certain that the United States and Japan were headed for war. Even more incredible than Yamamoto's conviction (and arrogance) that he should be guiding the Imperial Navy's war planning was the fact that he was aggressively pushing his plan before it was even feasible. Many of the issues surrounding the plan could be solved with more training or focused staff work. However, in March as Genda began to flesh out the concept, several problems had the potential to be showstoppers. Among these were developing the capability of refueling at sea, developing the means to successfully attack battleships with heavy bombs and torpedoes, getting the required intelligence on the Pacific Fleet and its base, and devising the means to achieve surprise without which the attack was impossible. None of these were simple problems – some were not satisfactorily solved until just weeks before the attack.

The attack had military and psychological dimensions to it. On the strategic level, it was necessary to cripple the Pacific Fleet long enough to keep it out of the Western Pacific while the Japanese completed the essential conquests of the resource areas. The time required was at least six months.

Yamamoto also saw the advantage of opening the war with a surprise attack. This was a preferred Japanese tactic in war and was used to begin the war against Russia in 1904. In a discussion with his fellow admiral and friend Vice Admiral Ozawa Jisaburo, he made this point clearly:

> The lesson which impressed me most deeply when I studied the Russo-Japanese War was the fact that our Navy launched a night assault against Port Arthur at the very beginning. I believe this was the most excellent strategic initiative ever envisaged during the war. But it is regrettable that we were not thoroughgoing in carrying out the attack, with the result that we failed to achieve a satisfactory result.[28]

There was also a psychological aspect to the plan. In the words of Onishi, the first planner Yamamoto shared his scheme with, "Yamamoto not only intends to cripple the US Pacific Fleet severely at the beginning of hostilities; he counts heavily on smashing the morale of the American people by sinking as many battleships as possible." The premise here was that since battleships were widely seen as the ultimate arbiter of victory at sea, the destruction of a number of them would have a paralyzing effect on American morale.[29]

THE IDEA IS BORN

According to his chief of staff, Vice Admiral Shigeru Fukudome, Yamamoto first mentioned a plan to attack the Pacific Fleet in Pearl Harbor in March or April 1940. The idea surfaced again during the late fall of 1940 after the completion of the Combined Fleet's annual maneuvers. At this time, Yamamoto told Fukudome of his desire to have Rear Admiral Onishi Takijiro study a Pearl Harbor attack under the utmost secrecy. It is clear that the conceptual framework of an attack on Pearl Harbor launched from carriers was in Yamamoto's mind in 1940. After the attack, he wrote to a fellow admiral and friend that he had decided to launch such an attack in December 1940. This is startling because it is clear Yamamoto had decided on a risky course of action before it was even determined whether such an operation was technically feasible and before the benefits of such an operation had been weighed.

The first time Yamamoto committed his bold gambit to paper was on January 7, 1941, in a memorandum to Navy Minister Oikawa. Aside from clearly laying out his thinking, which bordered on the heretical, the memo was notable for another reason. Yamamoto was attempting to usurp the role of the Naval General Staff, the prime planning body for Japanese naval strategy. Only somebody with Yamamoto's confidence and standing would attempt this.

In the memo, Yamamoto made his case for a carrier air strike by several carrier divisions on the Pacific Fleet in Hawaii. The overarching reason was that as the weaker naval power, Japan had to strike a crippling blow in the opening hours of the war. In his mind, crippling the Pacific Fleet had several benefits. It would break American morale (both civilian and military) and place Japan in the best possible position for a prolonged war. Another benefit was that the USN would lack the strength to interfere with Japan's southward offensive to seize the strategic resources necessary for a prolonged war. Also, the home islands would be secured from attack. The alternative was to let the Pacific Fleet threaten the flank of the southward advance and even attack the Japanese home islands with carriers.[30]

Yamamoto was not blind to the fact that his proposed operation was very risky. He also admitted that the diversion of forces to attack Pearl Harbor might imperil the timelines for the southern advance. To ensure that the Pearl Harbor attack fully met its objectives, he proposed that he be allowed to lead it.[31] Even before serious discussion of his plan began, Yamamoto tasked a growing number of Combined Fleet officers to begin planning it. While this was progressing and these officers began to tackle the many technical and operational issues that needed to be addressed, Yamamoto initiated a complementary effort to get the Naval General Staff to agree to it.

YAMAMOTO VS. THE NAVAL GENERAL STAFF

On April 10, Admiral Nagano took over the Naval General Staff. At this time, he was 62, making him the oldest officer serving in the Imperial Navy. On paper, he had all of the qualifications necessary to assume the role as the Imperial Navy's lead strategist and the man with the final say over operational planning. Nagano had been a full admiral since March 1, 1934. He had held a number of important posts, giving him a wide array of experience. Among these were commander in chief of the Combined Fleet, vice chief of the Naval General Staff, and Navy Minister. To top this off, he spent five years in the United States as naval attaché and studying English at Harvard. In reality, he had lost his youthful vigor and proved no match for the energetic and forceful Yamamoto. According to one of his principal staff officers on the Naval General Staff, "He was not a forceful character or the type to lead his nation to war."[32] In the end, he never really tried to assert control over his impetuous subordinate.

In the Imperial Navy's existing structure, the Naval General Staff was responsible for developing strategy and providing planning guidelines for the Combined Fleet to follow. In times of peace, the Combined Fleet focused on training and the Naval General Staff was responsible for planning. In wartime, the Combined Fleet was tasked to produce operational plans, but only within the framework provided from the Naval General Staff.³³ Mounting a surprise attack against the United States at the start of a war was certainly a strategic decision that the Naval General Staff should have taken the lead on, working with its counterparts on the Army General Staff. Yamamoto failed to see his role was subsidiary to the Naval General Staff. How he took his operational concept and got it incorporated as the centerpiece of Japan's war plan is a remarkable story.

On the same day Nagano took over, Yamamoto's chief of staff, Fukudome, left the staff of the Combined Fleet to assume the job as Chief of the First Bureau on the Naval General Staff. In this capacity, he was responsible for reviewing operational plans. Fukudome's transfer exposed Yamamoto's Pearl Harbor scheme to the Naval General Staff for the first time, since Fukudome was fully aware of Yamamoto's thinking. Shortly after Fukudome assumed his new post, Onishi paid him a visit to give him a copy of his Pearl Harbor draft plan and to discuss it with him. He was instructed to leave the draft plan with Fukudome for safekeeping. Fukudome thought the plan had made progress, but that there were many problems left still unsolved.³⁴

In late April, the first tentative steps of negotiating with the Naval General Staff began. Yamamoto entrusted the eccentric but brilliant Kuroshima with the task of presenting the plan to the skeptical Naval General Staff. Receiving Kuroshima was the Operations Section of Fukudome's First Bureau under the direction of the very competent and well-respected Captain Tomioka Sadatoshi. Under normal conditions, it was Tomioka and his staff that should have been initiating war plans.

Kuroshima explained Yamamoto's plan. From the very beginning, Tomioka was not impressed. According to Tomioka, this was the first time he had heard of it. He immediately came up with a list of objections. They began to talk past one another – Tomioka briefed Kuroshima on the Naval General Staff's overall plans for going to war, and Kuroshima requested that the Pearl Harbor attack be incorporated into the Naval General Staff's planning. Tomioka's lengthy argument boiled down to these points: the Navy's air strength could not be risked in such a manner, as it was needed for other major operations; diversion of so much strength to conduct the Pearl Harbor operation placed the success of the southern offensive in jeopardy; and if the Pacific Fleet was not attacked, it would proceed to attack the Marshall Islands, a contingency the Japanese were prepared to deal with. Tomioka also pointed out the difficulties with refueling. After the meeting was over, he failed to inform Nagano of the Combined Fleet's bold plan.

The campaign to convince the Naval General Staff resumed on August 7 when Kuroshima returned to Tokyo to plead Yamamoto's case. He requested that the annual war game be held in September in order to leave time for the Combined Fleet to absorb any lessons and that the war game include a realistic examination of the Pearl Harbor plan. With the recent American trade embargo and the need for a response in mind, the Naval General Staff agreed to include an examination of Yamamoto's plan. However, when Kuroshima pressed the case to include the Pearl Harbor attack into the war plan, he met more resistance led by Tomioka who pointed out that the plan depended on a combination of gaining surprise, developing refueling techniques, and developing adequate torpedo and level bombing experience to deliver sufficient air power to guarantee results. The First Bureau clung to the belief that a major fleet clash in the area of the Marshall Islands would develop to Japan's favor, making the risky Pearl Harbor attack unnecessary. By the end of the meeting, nothing had been resolved. Both sides agreed to examine the other's plans again. But the real significance of the meeting was that Yamamoto's risky adventure survived contact again with the reluctant Naval General Staff. The officers of the First Bureau did not take the issue to Nagano to gain his veto.[35]

In early September, Rear Admiral Kusaka (1st Air Fleet chief of staff) informed the staff of the 1st Air Fleet about Yamamoto's intention to attack Pearl Harbor. As the staff turned its attention to a number of problems, the fate of the entire Pearl Harbor plan was still in the balance. Amidst this uncertainty, the Imperial Navy's annual war game began on September 11 at the Naval Staff College in Tokyo. The first phase lasted through September 16 and focused on a rehearsal of the Southern Operation.

Using officers to play both Blue (Japanese) and Red (American and British) forces, the teams ran through the Southern Operation in all its phases. Yamamoto left these operations in the hands of his fleet commanders and other subordinates since he was engrossed in the Pearl Harbor attack. One lesson learned from the Southern Operation rehearsal was that land-based air power had problems keeping up with the advance as it went deeper into the DEI. As a result, most of the participants advocated for the carriers being used to support the southern offensive.[36] In addition, operations against the Gilberts, Guam, and Wake were tested.

On September 16, Yamamoto turned his full attention to the Hawaii Operation. He invited some 30 vetted officers, including representatives from his staff, Nagumo and some of his principal commanders and staff, the commander of the Sixth Fleet and two of his staff officers, and several representatives from the Naval General Staff, including Fukudome and Tomioka. Nagano was invited to attend but never did. The examination keyed on two major points: was the operation technically feasible, and what were the prospects for surprise? Beyond that, the exercise was meant to convince the skeptical participants from the Naval General Staff and the Striking Force of the plan's validity.[37]

One of the first issues to be discussed was the best route for carriers to take to Oahu. Vice Admiral Nagumo Chuichi, commander of the Pearl Harbor attack force, preferred the southern route; Genda preferred the northern route with its greater chances of gaining surprise. This was the route supported by most of the other participants, and Nagumo was forced to acquiesce. After deciding whether to fly reconnaissance missions from the carriers during the transit (the decision was not to), the exercise continued to examine a potential operation with a theoretical attack day of November 16.

When the exercise commenced, the first iteration of the attack was judged to be a fiasco for the Japanese. Nagumo's force was discovered by a long-range reconnaissance aircraft before it had a chance to launch its attack. The Americans had time to prepare their defenses – when the Japanese aircraft reached Pearl Harbor, they met a determined American defense and inflicted only minor damage on ships in the harbor and shore facilities. Half of the 171 aircraft were lost. In return, American air raids sank two of Nagumo's four carriers and damaged the other two. It was a dramatic illustration of what might happen if the element of surprise was lost.[38]

The same day, a second exercise was conducted. With the lessons just learned and with the intelligence that American air reconnaissance was inadequate to the north, Nagumo adjusted his approach track further to the north and modified his time of arrival within the potential

American search zone. Using this new approach, Nagumo made a high-speed run south to his pre-dawn launch position. With these important adjustments, surprise was judged to have been gained. Results of the air attack were spectacular, with four battleships, two carriers, and three cruisers sunk, with another battleship, a carrier, and three cruisers damaged. Japanese air losses were assessed to be light. When the Americans located Nagumo's force, counterattacks accounted for one Japanese carrier sunk and another damaged.[39]

The following day, the same participants gathered again to hear the chief umpire explain the results of the attack and to discuss the tactics used by the Japanese team. The exercise fulfilled its purpose of presenting the players with various scenarios to refine their reactions. It was also noteworthy for several other points. There was no discussion of whether the attack should be conducted. Perhaps this was not unexpected given that the participants were screened by Yamamoto with an eye to including those who had a role in the attack or in its approval. Overall, the operation was demonstrated to be feasible, as long as surprise was obtained. Other thorny issues were brought up but not resolved. Whether or not to conduct repeated attacks was not directly discussed during the session, but many of the planners mentioned the need to not lose the carriers. On the issue of how many carriers should be allocated to the attack force, no consensus was reached. The Naval General Staff wanted three and no more than four in order not to remove all carriers from the southern advance. Of course, Genda, an advocate of the attack, wanted every available carrier allocated to the attack. The commander of the Striking Force's escort force, Vice Admiral Mikawa Gunichi, stated that the two battleships assigned to his command were insufficient and stated a desire to get the other two Kongo-class battleships assigned to him. This demand was refused since the Southern Operation also needed the same ships and it was a higher priority. One issue that was settled was whether to include an invasion of Hawaii in the attack. Yamamoto and Kuroshima were not ready to discuss the matter seriously, so it was dropped. The problematic fuel issue was not covered and was pushed over to a future staff study.[40]

One thing that struck many of the participants was the propensity of the judges to underestimate the Americans and give the Japanese forces the benefit of every doubt. For example, one Zero fighter was judged to be worth three American aircraft. In another case, a squall blew up as Nagumo's force was withdrawing, saving it from further air attack and losses. The results of the exercise did nothing to quell the concerns of Nagumo and his staff. Kusaka viewed the game as too theoretical and that "The results depended too much on the various personalities of the umpires."[41] Another member of the staff felt that the plans of the American team were arbitrarily restricted when they threatened the Japanese plan. The same officer was admonished for pointing out some of the self-indulgent aspects of the game.

The exercise also served to intensify the debate between Yamamoto and his supporters and the Naval General Staff. Fukudome reported to Nagano on the results of the exercise and simply stated his opinion of it: "It is an alarming risk."[42] His concern was driven by fears that surprise was anything but guaranteed and that the Southern Operation would be placed in jeopardy if the carriers were lost. He was also aware of the criticality of intelligence. After listening to Fukudome's pessimistic assessment, Nagano weighed in: "In case of war I do not favor launching operations as risky as Yamamoto's proposal. I think it is best for the Navy to limit its plans and concentrate on capturing the southern regions."[43]

Recognizing the wide chasm between the Naval General Staff and the Combined Fleet regarding the Pearl Harbor attack, Fukudome and Yamamoto's new chief of staff, Rear Admiral Ugaki Matome, set up a meeting to thrash things out on September 24 at the Operations Section of the Naval General Staff. Fukudome and some of his staff were present, while Ugaki, Kuroshima, and Commander Sasaki Akira represented Yamamoto's views. Nagumo was allowed to send representatives. He selected Kusaka, Genda, and another staff officer.[44]

Playing the part of a neutral moderator, Fukudome oversaw the proceedings. For his part, Kusaka argued against the plan based on its riskiness, and stated presciently that the attack might offer temporary advantages, but that any strategic advantages were limited. Tomioka and one of his assistant staff officers laid out a cogent argument against the attack. When Genda spoke, it was to outline the potential damage to the Pacific Fleet if the attack was spearheaded by torpedo bombers or high-level bombers. Other staff officers discussed the issue of how best to gain surprise. When it came to setting the actual day of the attack, there were more issues. Fukudome proposed a date around November 20 to begin operations. Kusaka countered with the fact that the 1st Air Fleet would not be ready by that date. This was news to Ugaki who thought the Combined Fleet staff had settled on an attack date of November 21. Based on Yamamoto's desire to have the most ships in Pearl Harbor, a Sunday was needed. This meant either November 16 or 23.[45]

The ever-loyal Kuroshima did not speak until the end of the conference. When he did, he forcefully advocated adoption of Yamamoto's great gambit. Fukudome was unmoved but promised to place all of the problems involved with the Pearl Harbor attack under study by the Naval General Staff. He promised a decision as soon as possible. When Kuroshima reported the results of the conference to Yamamoto, the admiral exploded in anger. Not only did the Naval General Staff doubt that Yamamoto's plan would be successful, but the Combined Fleet was also filled with officers that saw the plan as simply too risky.

In late September, Nagumo, Kusaka, Genda, and other principals from the 1st Air Fleet's staff went to Kanoya Air Base to work out with the principals of the land-based 11th Air Fleet (tasked to support the Southern Operation), including Vice Admiral Tsukahara Nishizo and Onishi (the same Onishi that Yamamoto first turned to for help with planning for the Pearl Harbor attack), the proper allocation of air assets for the upcoming operations. Pressed by Tsukahara for support, Nagumo and Kusaka agreed to send him some of the 1st Air Fleet's air strength. Another result of the conference was an agreement by Kusaka and Onishi to personally present their reservations about the Pearl Harbor attack to Yamamoto.[46]

According to the Japanese official history, the meeting took place on October 3.[47] Speaking in a mild voice, Onishi began with the same objections – the Southern Operation was the primary concern, and the carriers were needed to crush American air power in the Philippines. Plus, he added, gaining surprise was less likely as the diplomatic crisis played out and the Americans were on a higher state of alert.[48]

Kusaka pulled out all the stops in his comments. In a postwar interview he claimed to have pushed the bounds of politeness by attacking Yamamoto's pet project "very severely." He went as far as to tell his boss, "You are an amateur naval strategist, and your ideas are not good for Japan. This operation is a gamble."[49]

Yamamoto agreed that the operation was a gamble, and then called on Kuroshima to address Onishi's and Kusaka's points. Yamamoto remained resolute, declaring, "I understand your viewpoints very well, but this operation has my immovable confidence. Without this operation, I cannot carry out the overall plan of war in the Pacific."[50] The drama was not yet over. As Kusaka was leaving the flagship, Yamamoto gave him this send-off:

> What you recommended is understandable, but as Commander-in-Chief I have resolved to carry out the Pearl harbor attack no matter what the cost. So please do your best to develop the plan from now on. I will place the details of the project in your hands.[51]

Yamamoto told Kusaka to relate these wishes to Nagumo.

Because the results of the September conference were not satisfactory, Yamamoto decided to bring things to a head. He called all his principal commanders to a conference on his flagship battleship *Nagato* to run through the Southern Operation and then the Hawaii Operation. From October 9 to 11, the assembled staffs conducted a tabletop exercise on the Southern Operation. On the morning of October 12, attention turned to the Hawaii Operation. Present for this phase were all the component commanders from the Striking Force and the commander and staff from the Sixth Fleet. Two representatives from the Naval General Staff were also invited.[52]

Compared to the September tabletop exercise, there were several important differences. For the first time, fleet and midget submarines were included in the planning. Their participation caused much concern on the part of the aviators who feared that their premature discovery threatened the security of the entire operation. According to the commander of the Sixth Fleet and other participants, a 600nm circle was drawn around Oahu and designated as a "danger zone." Within this area, all submarines would stay submerged during the day and surface only at night. According to the Japanese official history, Yamamoto also gave his approval for using midget submarines in the operation.[53]

Another major change was that only three carriers were used – *Kaga*, *Zuikaku*, and *Shokaku* – because they had the radius to steam to Pearl Harbor without refueling; *Akagi*, *Soryu*, and *Hiryu* were reserved for the Southern Operation. Even with this smaller force, the attack was judged a success. Nagumo agreed with Kusaka's recommendation to use isolated Hitokappu Bay on Etorofu Island as the rendezvous point. Leaving from there, the Striking Force took the northern route and arrived at its launch point 200nm north of Oahu without being detected. The two attack waves were judged to have inflicted "moderate damage" on the Pacific Fleet, while the Striking Force escaped without serious damage.[54]

Again, the exercise raised many points of discussion and many officers present spoke out against the Hawaii Operation. There was the prickly problem of how to synchronize the Southern Operation with the Pearl Harbor attack. What if the large troop convoys steaming through the South China Sea were detected before the Pearl Harbor attack. Should the British aircraft be shot down? The commander of the invasion forces, Vice Admiral Kondo Nobutake, wanted to dispatch enemy aircraft before they could report his position. Nagumo objected and was supported by Yamamoto, who instructed Kondo not to begin hostilities until the Pearl Harbor attack had been launched. Kondo went on to criticize the entire Pearl Harbor operation. Mikawa again brought up his desire for all four of his Kongo-class battleships to be allocated to the Striking Force.

On October 13, a review of the exercise was conducted. After a session to examine the tactics used, the main event began at 1600 in a special conference held with top commanders and senior staff officers. Yamamoto indicated that all comments made in this session were off the record. When invited by Ugaki to comment, Mikawa, Onishi, Kondo, Nagumo, and Kusaka all railed against the Pearl Harbor attack. Genda recalled that the consensus was that the deterioration of relations between Japan and the United States made surprise very unlikely. The only admiral present to support the attack was Yamaguchi.[55]

The last to speak was Yamamoto. Clearly he had had enough of the bickering within the ranks of his own command:

> I have been studying the entire strategical situation for some time, and I have noted all the points various officers have made today. These ideas will be considered carefully and any constructive suggestions incorporated into the forthcoming fleet order. I realize that some do not think well of my plan, but the operation against Hawaii is a vital part of Japan's grand strategy. So long as I am Commander-in-Chief of the Combined Fleet, Pearl Harbor will be attacked. I ask you to give me your fullest support. Return to your stations, and work hard for the success of Japan's war plans. Good Luck![56]

This was a turning point in the Pearl Harbor saga, but Yamamoto still had to get the Naval General Staff to acquiesce.

Many of the officers from the 1st Air Fleet were distressed over the use of only three carriers in the October exercise. Though still not full converts, Nagumo and Kusaka wanted the maximum number of carriers at their disposal to inflict as much damage as possible and to deal with any unexpected developments. Of course Genda was always in favor of an all-out attack. With the commissioning of Carrier Division 5, the number of fleet carriers rose to six. To bring the matter to a head with the Naval General Staff, Kusaka got Nagumo's approval to go to Tokyo to get a decision. Before he left, Kusaka asked Genda for his opinion. Being an advocate of the all-out attack, he stated that the operation needed all six carriers to be successful.[57]

Kusaka left *Akagi* on October 17 and headed for Tokyo to make the case as forcefully as possible that all six carriers were needed. Meeting with the Operations Section, led by Tomioka, Kusaka was rebuffed again. Tomioka was insistent that the Southern Operation needed at least two carriers and continued to point out the riskiness of the Pearl Harbor plan. It became apparent to Kusaka that he was not going to change any opinions. But in the aftermath of this latest defeat, he took another approach. Instead of returning to *Akagi* to lament matters with Nagumo, he proceeded to *Nagato* to make Yamamoto fully aware of what had happened.[58]

In explaining what had happened, Kusaka cleverly turned the tables on Yamamoto. He reminded him that when he promised Yamamoto to stop opposing the plan at the end of September, Yamamoto promised him every effort to make the attack successful.[59]

If Yamamoto was looking for the opportunity to bring this matter to a conclusion, now was the time. Time was running short, so he promised Kusaka his immediate support. Accordingly, the next day, October 19, he dispatched Kuroshima to Tokyo to gain a final clarification on the Naval General Staff's view of the operation and to address the carrier allocation issue. Kuroshima was given a powerful weapon to play in the ongoing and seemingly endless debate.

When the conference began, Kuroshima and Tomioka immediately got into it. Time was of the essence, since Yamamoto needed an immediate answer, stated Kuroshima. As he had in July, Tomioka rehashed his reasons for opposing the attack. Kuroshima responded with his best arguments.

Realizing that both sides' entrenched views were not going to change, Kuroshima played the powerful weapon given to him by Yamamoto:

> Admiral Yamamoto insisted that his plan be adopted. I am authorized to state that if it is not, then the Commander-in-Chief of the Combined Fleet can no longer be held responsible for the security of the Empire. In that case, he will have no alternative but to resign, and with him his entire staff.[60]

Just as Yamamoto intended, the mere threat of his resignation changed the entire framework of the debate. The idea of going to war without Yamamoto at the helm of the Combined Fleet was inconceivable. Tomioka's will crumbled but not before he made Kuroshima agree to three conditions: only six carriers were to be involved in the attack; the Combined Fleet had no further demands on Japan's remaining naval air power; the 1st Air Fleet would assist in the Southern Operation as soon as possible. Kuroshima agreed.

Though head of the Operations Section, Tomioka did not speak for Fukudome or Nagano. Accordingly, Tomioka and Kuroshima next went to see Fukudome to gain his approval. The same scene played out, with Kuroshima strongly advocating for the attack and Fukudome giving the same well-rehearsed reasons why it should not be executed. Sensing the futility of continuing the argument, Kuroshima again played his ace card of mass resignation. This sufficed to get Kuroshima ushered in to see Vice Admiral Ito Seiichi, Vice Chief of the Naval General Staff. Such a decision had to be made at the very top. While Kuroshima waited in Ito's office, Ito, Fukudome, and Tomioka went to see Nagano.[61]

According to Fukudome, he spoke first, followed by Ito. The outline of the disagreement was covered, as was the need for an immediate decision on an issue that had been lingering for weeks, and Yamamoto's threat. After listening to the two men, Nagano gave his approval with the comment, "If Yamamoto is that confident, I'll leave it to him."[62] After the war he stated he had done so to prevent Yamamoto from resigning and because Yamamoto had studied the problem more than anybody else so should be allowed to conduct his plan. His only condition was that the Combined Fleet not interfere with the Southern Operation and a promise not to weaken the air strength allocated in support of it.

YAMAMOTO AND THE GREAT DEBATE

After a hard-fought battle, Yamamoto got his operation approved. He did so not on the logic and power of his arguments, but on a raw power play. Nagano had the chance to bring his subordinate to heel, but never really tried to do so. In the end, he agreed because he felt Yamamoto was not bluffing, though it would be difficult to see Yamamoto actually carrying out his threat as the nation was headed to war.

Even after the Naval General Staff folded under Yamamoto's pressure, there was widespread sentiment that the operation should not be attempted. There were still technical and training problems that the 1st Air Fleet had to work hard on to be ready for the opening of hostilities, now scheduled for December 8 (December 7 Hawaii date). That date was chosen for a number of reasons. One of those reasons has already been discussed – the available intelligence indicated that Sunday was the day that most ships of the Pacific Fleet would be in harbor. There were also weather factors. If the Hawaii Operation was delayed until January or February, the seas in the North Pacific would be much rougher. The Imperial Army wanted to start operations in Southeast Asia to avoid the worst of the monsoon season. This time was also preferred since the phase of the moon provided the most moonlight which was important for night operations. In addition, time was not moving in favor of the Japanese. Stocks of oil were being reduced with each passing day. Finally, the Japanese were fearful that the American strength was increasing in the Pacific, particularly in the Philippines.

After the Naval General Staff's capitulation, it worked earnestly to incorporate the Pearl Harbor attack into the overall plan for the opening series of attacks against the Allies. On November 5, the Naval General Staff issued Navy Order No. 1. It was very short and simply confirmed Japan's intention to go to war with the United States, Great Britain, and the Netherlands in the first ten days of December.[63] On the same day, the Naval General Staff issued the implementing orders for the opening of the war under Navy Directive No. 1. Yamamoto wanted his Combined Fleet orders to come out the same day. This document, titled "Preparations for War and Commencement of Hostilities," was an 89-page order that went far beyond what the Naval General Staff expected. Authored primarily by Kuroshima, it was actually a strategic war plan more than an operational order. In it was the genesis for future disagreements between Yamamoto and the Naval General Staff.

If Nagano and his staff thought they could exert their veto power in the future, they were to be proven wrong.

A final synchronization between the Combined Fleet and the Naval General Staff was held on November 7 in Tokyo. The talks between the Operations Section and Yamamoto's staff were over in a day, after which the Combined Fleet's order was published. The path to Pearl Harbor was set.

3

The Japanese Plan

> ...the Japanese attack was brilliantly conceived and flawlessly executed.[1]
>
> The Dorn Report on Kimmel and Short

History has recorded that the Japanese plan used at Pearl Harbor was brilliant and that it led to strategic success. Though some parts of the plan were inspired, the reality was that it had many shortcomings. After all, from the American perspective, only a brilliant plan could have provided the Japanese with the means to accomplish what they accomplished. Such a narrative is much more palatable than to point out that American unpreparedness allowed a flawed plan, executed in a mediocre manner, to inflict heavy losses.

One of the first misconceptions regarding Japanese planning for the attack was that it was based on the Royal Navy's attack on the Italian battle fleet inside Taranto harbor on the night of November 11, 1940. In what was one of the greatest successes achieved by carrier air power early in the war, 20 British Swordfish attack aircraft were launched from carrier *Illustrious* to attack the Italian battle fleet inside the well-defended base at Taranto in southern Italy. Even this meager force was able to torpedo three Italian battleships. One was able to return to service in four months, the second by July 1941, but the third never did. It is natural to assume that the Japanese took careful notes on the operation and that they were able to exchange details with their Italian ally. On the surface, the similarities between the actual British attack and the planned Japanese attack were real and, since it occurred over a year before the Pearl Harbor attack, there was sufficient time to benefit from any insights gained.

The reality was quite different. In general, the Japanese dismissed the attack since the Italian ships were "sitting ducks."[2] In fact, besides both plans being built around a torpedo attack against battleships in a shallow harbor, the two operations were vastly different. In the area of carrier operations, the Japanese had very little to learn from the Royal Navy.[3] Aside from the surface similarities, and the obvious fact that the British had achieved success in a shallow-water torpedo attack inside a defended base, the Japanese do not appear to have studied the British operation in detail and did not receive information from the Italians on how it was conducted.

Part of the uncertainty in determining if the Japanese benefitted from an understanding of the Taranto attack lies in the lack of knowledge as to how and when any details from it were passed to them by the Italians. One possible route might have been from the Japanese assistant naval attaché to Berlin, Lieutenant Commander Naito Takeshi, who travelled to Taranto in December 1940 to discuss the attack with the Italians. No report from Naito after his visit has been found. After he returned to Japan in October 1941, Fuchida met with him and questioned him for a full day on October 24 without revealing why he was so interested.[4] It is important to note the meeting took place very late in the planning process for the Pearl Harbor operation. Though he was greatly encouraged after the meeting with Naito, Fuchida never mentioned any specific information he received from Naito. Another chance for the Japanese to learn details of the Taranto attack and feed it into their Pearl Harbor planning came when a Japanese military mission visited Italy and Germany. From May 18 until June 8, 1941, the mission was in Italy and visited Taranto. Again, no germane reports prepared after this Taranto visit have been found. Aside from the general encouragement that a torpedo attack in shallow water was possible, it is unlikely that any hard information was provided to the Japanese that was useful during the Pearl Harbor planning process.[5]

JAPANESE INTELLIGENCE

In general, Imperial Navy intelligence efforts were marked by indifference and a lack of resources. Intelligence was not a field valued by

THE JAPANESE PLAN

aspiring Imperial Navy officers. In almost all cases, the Imperial Navy exhibited a disdain for intelligence and treated it as an annoyance. Operations shaped intelligence assessments, instead of the other way around. The bottom line was that the Imperial Navy usually went into battle with a weak or even nonexistent understanding of the enemy's intentions, capabilities, or even its location. The exception was Pearl Harbor.

Overall, Japanese intelligence supporting the attack was of mixed value. At the strategic level in the months leading up to the attack, Imperial Navy intelligence supporting Pearl Harbor attack planning was poor. There was no examination of the potential political or naval impacts of an attack on Pearl Harbor. Yamamoto's assertion that the loss of a few battleships would shock the Americans into a new framework for war termination was taken at face value, despite it being simply his opinion. Japanese intelligence was also poor at the operational level. The composition of the entire Pacific Fleet was not clearly known. The recent transfer of several key units to the Atlantic was not fully understood, though agents in Hawaii reported the absence of the three New Mexico-class battleships, carrier *Yorktown*, and four light cruisers. At the time of the attack, Japanese intelligence indicated that three carriers were based at Pearl Harbor.[6] In fact, only two carriers had been active out of Pearl Harbor since October, a fact clearly reported by the Japanese consulate on Oahu.

At the tactical level, the state of Japanese intelligence was entirely different. Given the fact that the Japanese consulate in Hawaii was open for business and allowed freedom of movement around Oahu, the Japanese took the opportunity to assemble an excellent tactical baseline for targeting. The primary agent of this intelligence picture was Yoshikawa Takeo, a former Imperial Navy officer who had been discharged from active duty for medical reasons. His new way to serve the Emperor was an assignment to the Japanese consulate on Oahu as a spy with diplomatic cover.

Yoshikawa spent little time even pretending to be a diplomat. Instead, he focused on fulfilling essential elements of information regarding American naval units inside the harbor. Good targeting required precise knowledge of anchorages and moorings used by American naval units along with a record over time of their arrivals and departures. This information was sent by diplomatic channels to the Naval General Staff.

In addition to his reporting on naval units, Yoshikawa had the chance to visit most of the bases on the island.

Regular arrivals of Japanese commercial passenger ships in Oahu gave ample opportunity for the consulate to receive instructions from the Naval General Staff and to send intelligence cables back to Japan. *Tatuta Maru* arrived at Honolulu on October 23 with three Navy officers to confirm the information being provided from the consulate. They also carried a high-priority request for essential elements of information on USN units in Pearl Harbor and detailed maps of every military installation on Oahu.[7]

The decision on how best the Striking Force might achieve surprise was also supported by excellent intelligence efforts. Passenger liner *Taiyo Maru* departed Japan on October 22 and took the same route that the Striking Force was planning to use a few weeks later. No ships were encountered during the voyage and the first American patrol aircraft was not encountered until the ship reached a point some 200nm north of Oahu. Taking weather and sea condition observations along the route was also helpful. Among the passengers on *Taiyo Maru* were planners from the Naval General Staff. Upon arriving at Honolulu, they conferred with the Consul General on three occasions and passed detailed questions to Yoshikawa. Working nonstop, Yoshikawa provided a wealth of updated information by the time *Taiyo Maru* departed on November 5. All this was accomplished under the noses of American counterintelligence agents who inspected personnel boarding the ship. By the time *Taiyo Maru* departed, she did so with a treasure trove of raw intelligence. Among the assessments made by Yoshikawa and the eagle-eyed Navy officers who remained aboard the liner was the probability that surprise could be gained.[8]

Overall, the level of targeting information gained by the Japanese on Pearl Harbor and its defenses before the attack was highly detailed and extremely useful. It was also very timely, though it was not provided in real time. The latest report was provided to the Striking Force the night before the attack was launched. Without this level of insight, Genda's planning would have been much less effective.

Gathering information on American facilities was easy if agents were allowed to move around Oahu unchecked, but accurate analysis and dissemination of the information was more difficult. In this area the Japanese fell short. On November 22, Lieutenant Commander Suzuki

THE JAPANESE PLAN

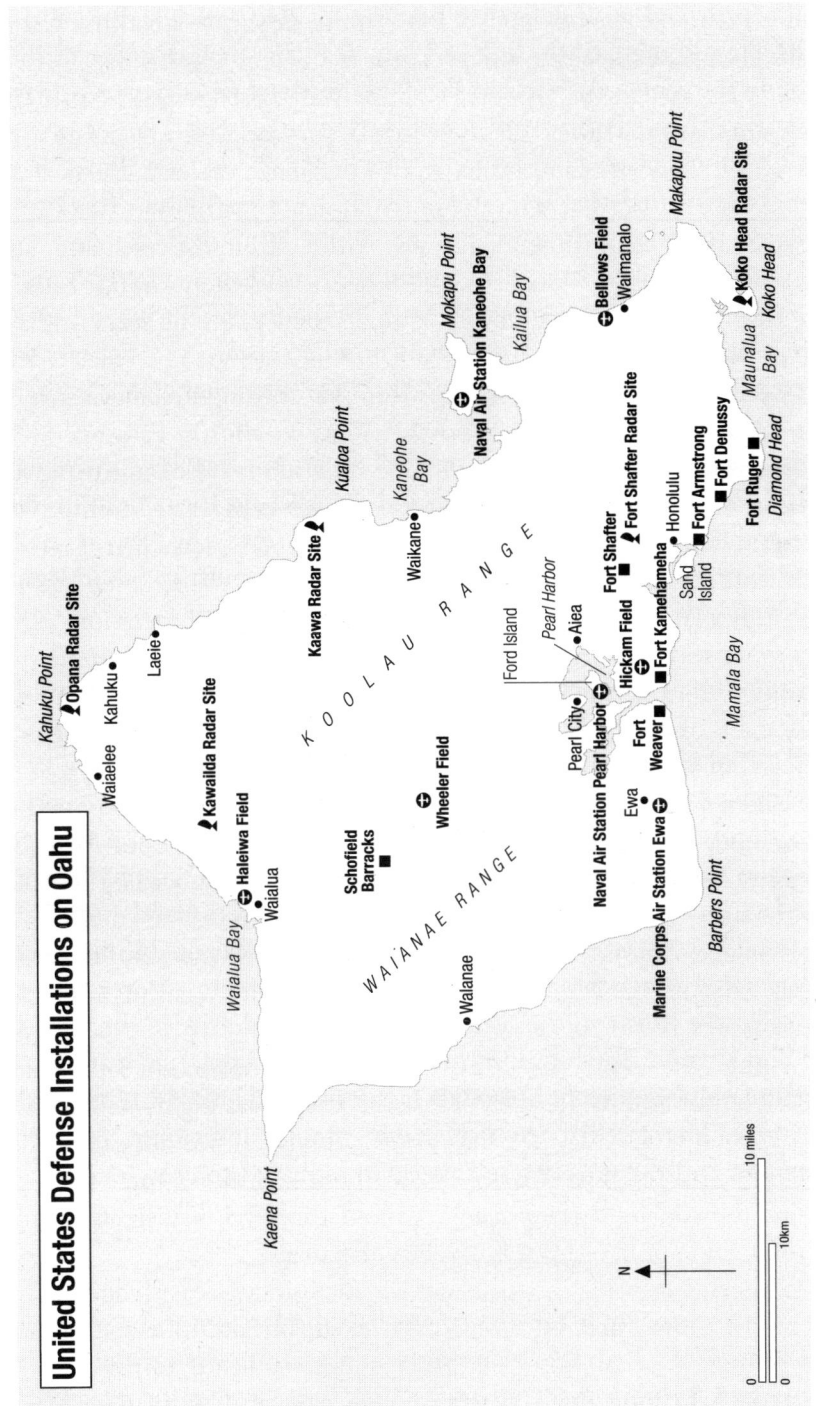

Eijiro provided an intelligence briefing on *Akagi* to Nagumo and his staff. He summarized the assessed American air strength at the facilities around the island. At Hickam Field, 40 four-engine and approximately 100 twin-engine bombers were believed to be present. Fighter strength on Oahu was assessed to be some 200 P-40s, P-38s, and P-36s. In all, Suzuki estimated that 455 Army planes were on Oahu. This greatly inflated American strength and no doubt reinforced the determination of the strike planners to annihilate American air strength on the ground. In fact, the number of Army bombers present was 12 B-17s, and a mix of 50 medium and light bombers. Only 152 fighters were present (99 P-40s, 39 P-36s, 14 P-26s). The true total of Army aircraft was 227 aircraft, including 13 observation aircraft.[9]

In the area of American air operation patterns, Japanese intelligence was more accurate. The Americans did not use large formations in training, and flight operations did not take place at night. The Navy's Catalina patrol aircraft focused their searches on the areas south and southwest of the island, while the northern sector was not adequately covered.[10]

Information on USN ship movements was less useful. In particular, the movement of American carriers was uncertain. Suzuki indicated that three carriers were based at Pearl Harbor and that they regularly came in and out of port. In fact, there were only two, as reported by Yoshikawa. The prospect of operating in the same waters as three American carriers was deeply unsettling to Nagumo and Genda. Kusaka also admitted that the brief was sobering to him as well.[11] It must be emphasized that the last intelligence summary provided to the command staff of the Striking Force seemed to indicate that surprise was possible but greatly exaggerated American air power. The number of aircraft on Oahu was an offensive threat to the Striking Force and a defensive threat to the raiding aircraft. The locations or intentions of three American carriers was the most significant unknown factor of all. There is little doubt that the prevailing intelligence assessment, though inaccurate, reinforced Nagumo and Kusaka's determination to retreat after a single strike.

PLANNING THE ATTACK

At the same time that Yamamoto was fighting for permission to execute his Pearl Harbor attack, planning was already under way on it. It is important to note that Yamamoto was not involved in the detailed planning for his grand operation.[12] He provided his vision to others who then did the necessary work. Though not involved in the details of the operation, Yamamoto fully understood the difficulties of his scheme, describing it as "so difficult and so dangerous that we must be prepared to risk annihilation."[13]

The first officer Yamamoto asked to start looking at the Pearl Harbor operation was Rear Admiral Onishi Takijiro. He was an air power advocate who was instrumental in creating the Imperial Navy's air arm. Like his fellow air power zealot, Yamamoto, Onishi was outspoken and loved to gamble. In another parallel, he was known to frequent geisha houses as a young officer.[14] Yamamoto had full trust and confidence in Onishi, a man respected as an excellent tactical planner and as somebody who would focus on a problem and accomplish it.[15]

Yamamoto reached out to Onishi in January 1941 in the form of a three-page letter. He tasked Onishi to study the concept and present his views as soon as possible. On either January 26 or 27, Yamamoto summoned Onishi to his cabin on his flagship *Nagato* and discussed the concept in person. Immediately after conferring with Yamamoto, Onishi returned to his headquarters at the 11th Air Fleet to begin work. He called upon his senior staff officer, Commander Maeda Kosei, for help. Maeda was an expert on employing torpedoes from aircraft so was the perfect person to work with Onishi at this early point. When presented the theoretical question if air-launched torpedoes could be used in the waters of Pearl Harbor, Maeda replied that the shallow depths in the harbor made such an attack virtually impossible. However, Maeda believed high-altitude bombing might be profitable. For his part, Onishi was convinced of the value of dive-bombing since it was more accurate.[16]

Onishi continued work but realized he needed more insight into the complexities of such an attack. He also needed a man who could think out of the box and solve "impossible" problems. Onishi had the perfect person in mind, an officer that he shared personal and professional bonds with – Commander Genda Minoru. In early February, Onishi summoned Genda from his job as air officer on *Kaga* to help him in the planning effort. Onishi chose well – Genda immediately became the principal planner for the attack and the man most responsible for its execution after Yamamoto himself. Known for his honesty and creativity, Genda's opinion on the concept mattered greatly.

Onishi outlined Yamamoto's plan and showed him the original letter. The importance of the attack was outlined in this passage:

> If we go to war with the USA and fail to destroy the US fleet in Hawaii, there is no chance that we will win. And even if we do destroy it, there is still no certainty that we will win. This operation is in any case essential. The attack is to be carried out by the First and Second Carrier Divisions.[17]

After carefully reading the entire letter, Genda thoughtfully answered, "The plan is difficult but not impossible."[18]

From the start, Genda put his stamp on the plan. He took Yamamoto's somewhat naïve framework and developed it into a workable plan. For example, according to Onishi, Yamamoto's original vision was built on a torpedo-bomber strike launched from carriers some 500–600 miles from Oahu. The aircraft would conduct a one-way attack; instead of returning to their carriers, the aviators would be recovered by submarines and destroyers. The only advantage of this plan was that the carriers could retreat more quickly from a possible counterattack. To Genda, sacrificing the aircraft and probably many highly trained aviators was a non-starter. His view was that the carrier force needed to approach the target as near as possible and that multiple strikes be launched to accomplish the mission. In addition, he wanted to expand the attack to include more than just torpedo bombing.[19]

Following the meeting, Onishi tasked Genda to prepare a draft plan and report back in seven to ten days. After returning to *Kaga*, he produced a preliminary draft in about two weeks. In late February, Genda returned for a second meeting with Onishi. Genda had taken a vision and turned it into something resembling a plan. So insightful was Genda's thinking that each of the basic elements of the plan survived largely intact in the final version. These elements were:[20]

1. The total requirement for surprise. Without surprise, Genda believed the entire attack should be called off. The reason was obvious – without surprise, there was the likelihood of heavy Japanese losses with no corresponding chance of inflicting losses on the Americans.

2. The need to sink carriers as the primary objective. As an air power zealot, Genda's view that sinking carriers and not battleships, as Yamamoto wanted, should be the primary objective of the operation should not be surprising. This is not to say that Genda did not want to sink battleships, but it does highlight the somewhat different target prioritization from that held by his superior.
3. The requirement to destroy American air power on Oahu. Again, as an air power advocate, Genda believed that land-based American air power must be destroyed to preclude a counterattack against the Japanese carriers.
4. The need to employ all carriers in the operation. Yamamoto's original vision had only one or two carrier divisions participating in the attack. Genda wanted all available carriers to take part (including the new Carrier Division 5 when it became available in August) to deliver the most powerful blow possible and to be able to contend with the American response.
5. The need to use all types of attacks. Genda was fearful that torpedo attacks would not be possible and warned Onishi as to the shallow water issue and American anti-torpedo measures. He still viewed torpedo bombing as the preferred method of attack, but as a backup wanted dive-bombing used as well. Genda also considered high-level bombing.
6. The need to include fighters in the attack. This was no surprise given Genda's background, but he foresaw the obvious need for fighters to take part in the attack to gain air control over the targets. Those fighters not allocated to offensive missions would be used to protect the fleet.
7. The need for a morning attack. Genda proposed that the strike occur at dawn, necessitating that the aircraft take off before sunrise to arrive at Pearl Harbor at dawn. This turned out to be impossible since the new aviators of Carrier Division 5 lacked the training to fly at night. The plan was eventually modified so that the first strike took off at dawn and attacked at 0800.
8. The requirement to refuel at sea. This seems obvious from the perspective of the current day where this technique is commonplace. However, at the time the Imperial Navy

was not well practiced in this. Because not all the ships in the attack force had the range to reach Hawaii and return, refueling was a major issue.
9 A requirement for the utmost secrecy. To gain the all-important benefit of surprise, tight security around every aspect of the plan was a necessity.

In addition to advocating the all-out strike outlined above, Genda recommended an invasion of Hawaii in the immediate aftermath of the attack. Such an operation would give the Japanese control of the Central Pacific while denying the Americans a base for launching future operations. Onishi pointed out to Genda that Japan lacked the resources to take the offensive in both the Western and Central Pacific. After Genda presented his draft, he and Onishi discussed the operation again for about two hours.

Onishi used Genda's draft for his more detailed report to Yamamoto. According to Genda, the final report was ten pages and contained most of Genda's points, but with additions and modifications. Some of the known modifications were adding cruisers as the number two target priority behind carriers (Onishi was dismissive of the value of battleships). Onishi placed horizontal bombing as the most effective form of attack. He believed torpedo bombing could be ineffective and that if it was attempted would result in excessive losses in aircraft and men. Because dive-bombing would also be expensive in terms of casualties and lacked the ability to penetrate the deck armor of capital ships, Onishi also downplayed its importance.[21]

Another of Onishi's ideas was to deploy two merchant ships in advance of the attack force to act as scouts. If discovered, they would not receive the same level of scrutiny as a submarine or destroyer and might help maintain surprise.[22]

With his expanded draft in hand, Onishi went to see Yamamoto on about March 10. It needs to be noted that the final version of the plan was very close to Genda's original draft. All of Onishi's substantial modifications were dropped as the plan neared fruition. Notably, Onishi later distanced himself from the plan altogether, which he considered too risky.

According to the Japanese official history, Yamamoto tasked his staff to study the Pearl Harbor attack no later than January. In mid-January,

Captain Kuroshima directed Commander Sasaki Akira, the staff air officer, to look at three potential scenarios. Each assumed that the Americans were on alert and that surprise was not possible. The first assumed that the Japanese carriers would approach to within 350nm of Pearl Harbor to launch a strike focused on American carriers. The second was more traditional – the Japanese carriers would come to within 200nm of the target and launch a full strike. The last scenario was a one-way attack with only bombers, with submarines rescuing the aircrews.[23]

Kuroshima, Sasaki, and Commander Watanabe Yasuji (who was a personal favorite of Yamamoto) were made privy to the draft plan created by Onishi and Genda in late March. At that time, Yamamoto was reported to have stated: "Since we cannot use a torpedo attack because of the shallowness of the water, we cannot expect to obtain the results we desire. Therefore, we probably have no choice but to give up the air attack operation."[24] Whatever doubts Yamamoto had about his pet project at the time, in early April he again approached Kuroshima and Watanabe about the attack.

Shortly after the April meeting, Kuroshima divided the staff into four groups. These were focused on Operations and Supply; Communications and Information, Navigation and Meteorological Conditions; and Air and Submarine Attack. Not only did this greatly expand the number of people aware of Yamamoto's great secret, but it was an unusual step. Creating an operational plan in peacetime was not the prerogative of the Combined Fleet's staff. But Yamamoto was a man in a hurry. His plan had to be developed quickly enough so that it was incorporated into the opening strike at the start of the war. It was only during this period that the all-important element of surprise would exist.[25]

At the end of April, Kusaka was brought into the planning. In a meeting with Fukudome, he was allowed to look at the Onishi–Genda draft. From the start, he thought the proposed operation would be very challenging. When he returned to *Akagi*, he briefed Nagumo on the plan. Nagumo was unimpressed and thought it would be impossible to pull off. As he pointed out the problems with the plan, Kusaka also began to have doubts. He preferred that the Imperial Navy not overextend itself and wanted to stick to the long-planned decisive battle strategy to let the Americans overextend their fleet. Thus, a strange dynamic began in which the two most senior officers of the force slated to conduct an audacious and risky plan were firmly against it.

Kusaka brought in Commander Oishi Tamotsu, Nagumo's senior staff officer, and Genda to work on developing an operational plan. Of course, Genda was already aware of the plan and was hard at work on it.[26]

Planning continued through the summer as the debate raged between Yamamoto and the Naval General Staff. The need for secrecy limited the number of people involved in planning, but according to the Japanese official history, Nagumo's staff completed its draft of the plan on August 28.[27] This conflicts with the recollections of both Kusaka and Genda, who stated that there was a meeting on *Akagi* in early September during which Kusaka revealed the plan for the first time to the collective staff. By doing so, he brought the entire staff into the planning process to examine the discrete parts that needed more work. Genda was named head of the study group and was charged to coordinate the efforts of the other officers who tackled problems within their own areas of expertise. This was the point that Yamamoto's vision began to take on the characteristics of an operational plan.

Even at this date, several important issues remained unresolved. The most important was how to get the Striking Group to Hawaii without being detected. The matter was so important that Nagumo, Kusaka, and Genda had all begun to work on it months before. As usual, Genda's thoughts were the most mature and he developed a range of possibilities for presentation to Kusaka and Nagumo. In his study, he worked on a southern, central, and northern route. Each of the routes had advantages and disadvantages.

Genda had two variants for his southern route. In the first, the Striking Force departed from either Kyushu or the Inland Sea and headed in sections to Wotje Atoll in the Marshall Islands. Wotje was big enough to accommodate the entire fleet and close enough to Japan that no refueling was required to get there. From Wotje, Genda looked at two alternatives. In the first, the Striking Force would move around Johnston Island and steam to a launch point 200–250nm south of Pearl Harbor. While this route did not have onerous fuel requirements and was through an area of calm seas, it offered little in the way of concealment. In the second route from Wotje, the Striking Force would steam farther south until it reached Christmas Island, from which it would head north until it reached its launch point 200nm southeast of Pearl Harbor. This route was not favored for the same reasons as the previous route, and it carried with it extensive fuel requirements.[28]

THE JAPANESE PLAN

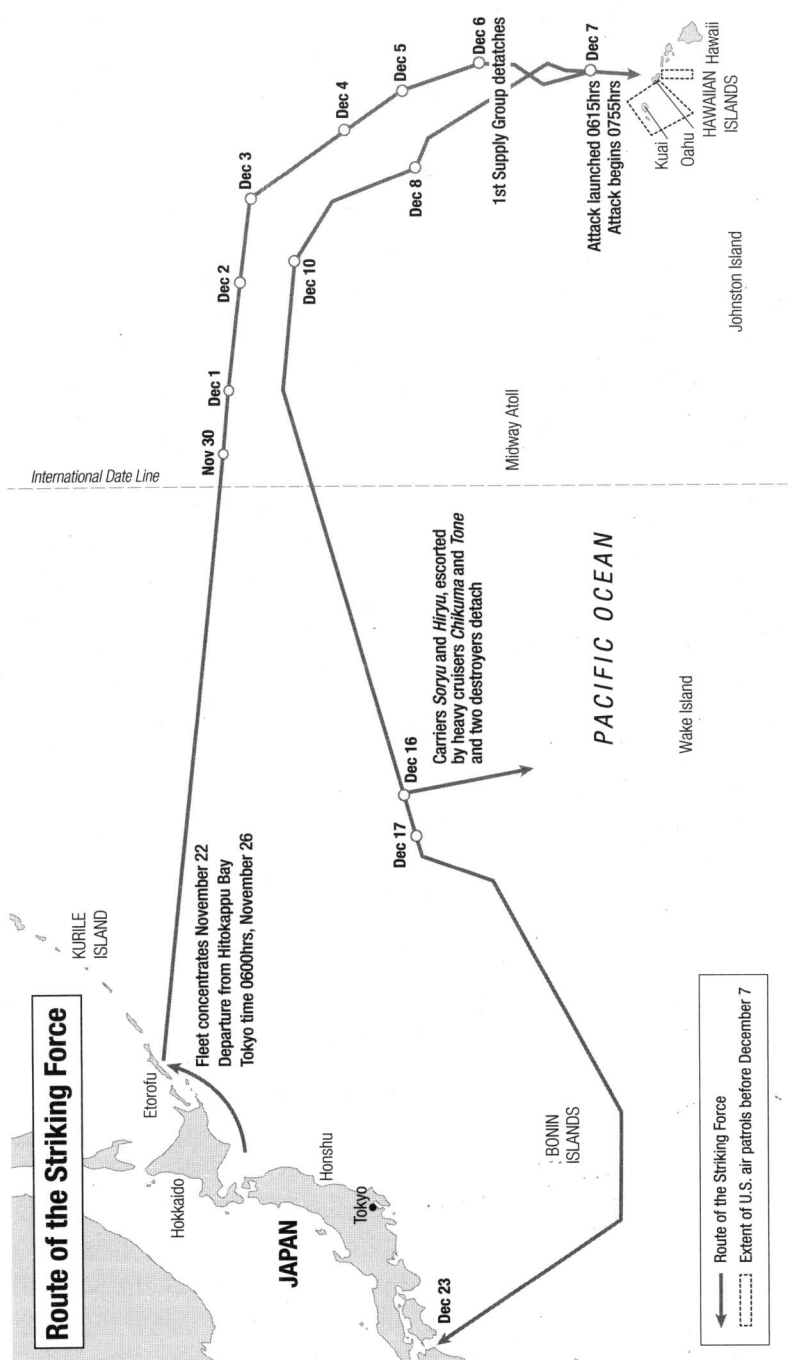

For the central route, Genda had the Striking Fleet departing from two points on Honshu and then heading to desolate Chichi-Jima, some 700nm southeast of Tokyo. From there, the fleet would head to a point 500nm north of Midway Atoll before heading to a point 750nm north of Oahu. Only then would the carriers head south to be within range of Oahu. Genda did not favor this option for several reasons. The rendezvous point at Chichi-Jima was too small for the entire fleet, and, most importantly, the fleet was exposed to possible detection by air patrols from Midway.[29]

From the start, Genda thought the northern route was the most promising. Leaving from the Inland Sea, the fleet would take a route through the North Pacific that balanced late autumn weather conditions with the possibility of concealment. Two routes were proposed, with both having the attribute that they were south of the merchant routes from North America to Japan or the Soviet Union. In addition, approaching Oahu from the north meant that there was a much reduced possibility of detection since intelligence indicated that American air searches were inadequate in this direction. Just as there were positives about the route, there were also negatives. There was no obvious answer to where the fleet could rendezvous. Taking this route meant that several refuelings were necessary. This would be difficult because of the heavy seas in the area during December. Finally, there was the possibility of discovery from merchant ships and aircraft moving between the US mainland and Hawaii.[30]

When Kusaka was presented with these options, he saw the advantages of the northern route. The enhanced possibility of surprise was the primary determinant. However, Nagumo was never in favor of the northern route because of the challenges that heavy seas presented to refueling. According to Genda, this stalemate was only resolved after a concerted campaign highlighting the criticality of surprise. Nagumo's reluctance to use the more challenging northern route stemmed from his assumption that surprise was impossible since the Striking Force was sure to be spotted by American search aircraft. Therefore, he wanted his force to be in the best condition possible to fight its way to Pearl Harbor. Calm seas and support from Japanese bases in the Marshalls seemed to offer that eventuality.[31] Only before the September 11 wargame did Nagumo make up his mind. Under a constant barrage from Genda and Commander of Carrier Division 2, Rear Admiral

THE JAPANESE PLAN

Yamaguchi Tamon, on the security advantages of the northern route, Nagumo finally relented.

Another issue with security implications was whether or not to fly air patrols from the carriers. Genda, who valued surprise above all else, advocated against any patrols for fear that an accident might reveal the presence of the fleet or that the Americans might spot one of the patrolling aircraft. Yamaguchi was strongly in favor of flying patrols in order to not be surprised by ships and aircraft in the area of the Striking Fleet. In the end, Genda convinced Yamaguchi of the wisdom of his views without having to force Nagumo to decide.[32] Though no flight operations were conducted during the transit, each carrier kept six fighters and three dive-bombers on alert.

THE FUEL QUANDARY

One of the most vexing problems for the Japanese was how to get the Striking Force across the Pacific to Hawaii. Using the northern route, only seven ships in the fleet had the range to steam the entire way without refueling. Among these were the carriers *Kaga*, *Shokaku*, and *Zuikaku*; battleships *Hiei* and *Kirishima*; and cruisers *Chikuma* and *Tone*. Given its plans to fight close to Japan, the Imperial Navy had not fully developed the techniques required for underway replenishment. By mid-1941, the Japanese were proficient using the trailing astern method, in which the tanker trailed a fuel hose to a ship astern. Both ships were able to keep moving, making them less vulnerable to attack. This technique was easy with smaller ships (like the destroyers of the Striking Force) because they could easily maneuver out of danger if required.[33]

With his background in the surface navy, Kusaka took on this problem personally. He took a two-prong approach to the issue. By convincing the appropriate people in the Navy bureaucracy, he received permission to lift the restriction on carrying fuel in vacant spaces. By doing so, much extra fuel could be carried in drums and in the trim tanks of the three carriers and the two battleships that lacked the necessary range. Even this was not sufficient for a round trip, so a new method of underway refueling had to be devised. Kusaka simply reversed the position of the heavy ships with the oilers so that the big ships were in front and thus had more maneuver room. The method was tested in October and was found to work. The light cruiser *Abukuma* and the nine destroyers lacked the strength and space to carry extra fuel internally, so had to refuel several times during the transit. The destroyer and tanker crews practiced refueling three at a time with one destroyer astern and the other two on each side of the oiler. Due to intensive practice, the problem was considered solved by the time the Striking Force departed in late November.[34]

ATTACK PRIORITIES

Yamamoto's entire reason for conducting the attack was to sink battleships. This priority did not translate directly down to the Striking Force. The plan put together by Yamamoto's staff – Combined Fleet Operations Order No. 1, Annex 3, issued on November 1 – laid out targets in this order: "Targets for attack are airfields; aircraft carriers; battleships, cruisers, and other warships; merchant shipping; ports, facilities; and land installations."[35] Placing airfields at the top of the list reflected the Naval General Staff's concern that the Striking Force be protected from counterattack. Looking at the war from a broader perspective, the Naval General Staff feared losing a large portion of the Combined Fleet's combat power in the opening hours of the war.

As Yamamoto's top priority was sinking battleships, it is clear that this failed to sink in fully with the staff of the Striking Force actually planning the attack. Genda's priorities were different – being a full-fledged air power advocate, he placed a heavy weight of fire against carriers, believing that they were the most important ships in a modern fleet. However, in the Carrier Striking Task Force Operations Order No. 3, issued on November 23, Genda appeared to support Yamamoto's priorities by stating this attack priority for the first wave: "The targets for the first group will be limited to about four battleships and four aircraft carriers; the order of targets will be battleships and then aircraft carriers."[36] Note that he wanted to ensure the destruction of at least four battleships instead of just damaging many. The inclusion of four carriers as a target would prove troublesome since none would be present on the day of the attack. For the dive-bombers of the second wave: "The targets for the second group will be limited to four or five enemy aircraft carriers. If the number of targets is insufficient, they will select targets in the order of cruisers and battleships."[37] Note

Genda's determination to hit the carriers again with dive-bombing, hoping to make their salvage impossible.

In the final analysis, the competing target priorities were largely meaningless. It was clearly essential to destroy American air power on the ground, and the inexperienced pilots of Carrier Division 5 were only suited for this mission. Given that the first-wave horizontal bombers were carrying weapons suited for attacking battleships, the only issue with regard to asset allocation was the torpedo bombers. With 40 available, both the carriers and battleships vulnerable to torpedo attack could be covered. Even if the Japanese wanted to overconcentrate on one or the other, this was not feasible because of the crowded air space in the harbor area and the fact that the initial targets had to be struck quickly while surprise was in effect.

While the planners could lay out target priorities, the final choice of which target would actually be struck was up to the men in the cockpits. All pilots were given targets, but in the heat and confusion of battle, with other attacking aircraft jockeying for favorable positions, preplanned targets were mere guidelines. When confusion and chaos replaced planning, the danger was that pilots would select unimportant targets for attack or overconcentrate on the few really important targets. For the torpedo bombers from *Soryu* and *Hiryu*, if their primary targets were not there or were already destroyed, they were ordered to find alternative targets in the form of battleships and then cruisers. For the torpedo bombers from *Akagi* and *Kaga*, their alternative targets were other battleships.[38] This was very generic guidance where more precise planning should have been in place. Keep in mind that the attacking aircraft had no radio communications with each other and had little means to coordinate their actions.

As for the timing of the attack, Sunday was selected because the data from the Japanese spies on Oahu indicated that this was the day when the most ships would be in port. The actual time of day for the attack was altered late in the planning process. To accommodate the relatively unskilled airmen of Carrier Division 5, who could not conduct night flying, the time of the attack was moved from dawn to 0800. This required a launch at 0600 just as dawn was breaking (sunrise was at 0606) and still put the raiders over the target in daylight and early enough to gain surprise.[39]

In retrospect, with the result of the attack on the Pacific Fleet in harbor well known, it is easy to overlook the uncertainty of the Japanese in determining the actual location of the fleet in the hours directly before the attack. Although the stream of intelligence from the consulate in Honolulu provided an excellent overview of American naval units, the Japanese considered it essential that a last-minute check be made to confirm the location of the Pacific Fleet. If it was not in Pearl Harbor, the entire operation would have to be reshaped and the strike aircraft organized and armed accordingly.

A day prior to the attack, a submarine was directed to reconnoiter the Lahaina Roads anchorage off Maui and transmit a report. Pre-attack scouting was key in the mind of Genda. It was vital to get last-second information on the location of the American fleet so that Fuchida could deploy his forces accordingly. In the original plan, the reconnaissance aircraft from *Tone* and *Chikuma* were scheduled to take off one hour before the first attack group to scout Pearl Harbor and Lahaina. When the aviators learned of this during a briefing held on November 23, objections were raised that an hour was too much time as it gave the Americans a chance to prepare for the attack. Not surprisingly, the first to raise this objection was Lieutenant Commander Murata Shigeharu, leader of the vulnerable torpedo bombers. His objection spawned a prolonged discussion, with the majority of the aviators siding with Murata. Eventually, Genda changed his mind and cut the time to 30 minutes. After some discussion with Nagumo, he agreed.[40]

At 0600 hours, the launch of the first attack wave would begin. Just as the first wave was departing at 0630, the battleships and heavy cruisers were scheduled to launch the bulk of their floatplanes to search the waters around the Striking Force. About one hour after the first wave had departed, at 0730, the launch of the second wave would commence.

When the first strike wave was approaching Oahu, Fuchida had to make the decision about how to deploy his aircraft. If he believed that surprise had been achieved, Fuchida would indicate this by launching a single signal flare from his aircraft. With that, the torpedo bombers would start their attack first to gain the full benefits of surprise. They would be followed by the fighters to gain air control and then the dive-bombers and horizontal bombers. In the event that surprise had not been achieved, Fuchida would fire two flares. In this scenario, the dive-bombers would attack, followed by the level bombers.

THE JAPANESE PLAN

Amidst the resulting confusion, the torpedo bombers would attack last. The Japanese hoped they could sneak into attack positions while the Americans were focused on the other attacking aircraft.

THE FIRST-WAVE ATTACK PLAN

With the air groups of six fleet carriers, Genda had a wealth of resources at his disposal. But there were constraints as well since the air groups of *Shokaku* and *Zuikaku* were very inexperienced and could not be trusted to successfully handle difficult tasks. Therefore, they were assigned to target easy-to-hit airfields, instead of ships in harbor. Each of the six carriers would only launch a single strike squadron in the first wave; the other strike squadron had to wait until the second wave. Finally, the torpedo bombers were by far the most vulnerable of the strike aircraft. They had to be employed while the effects of surprise were still in play. Between attack waves, the flight decks of the six carriers had to be re-spotted with aircraft and then their engines warmed up. It took 45–60 minutes to accomplish this.

The first wave was planned to commence launching at 0600 while 230nm north of Oahu. If all went according to plan, the attack would begin at 0800 hours Hawaii time, catching the Americans at their most vulnerable. The first wave included 189 aircraft. In it, and key to the entire operation, were the 40 torpedo bombers under the command of Murata and the 50 level bombers under Fuchida. By Japanese calculations, the 40 torpedo bombers were expected to make 27 hits. The same calculations indicated that this would be sufficient to sink six battleships. The 50 level bombers with the heavy armor-piercing bombs were expected to deliver eight hits. This was expected to cripple one or two battleships. Fifty-four dive-bombers under Lieutenant Commander Takahashi Takashi were ordered to attack air installations at Ford Island, Wheeler, and Hickam Fields to cripple any American air response. First-wave fighters were charged with first gaining air control and then attacking the various air installations.

According to Fuchida's testimony after the war, he instructed each of the level bomber groups to carefully assess their situation before releasing their bombs. The level bombers would approach against the wind to improve accuracy. Each group of five was ordered to make as many passes as necessary to ensure an accurate drop. The pilots were ordered to mass their fire against a few targets in order to ensure their destruction. Fuchida also told the level bombers to attack the ships berthed in pairs, not those moored singly, in order to increase the chances for a hit. In Fuchida's mind, minor damage against a number of targets was considered a failure. According to Fuchida, he also emphasized to his aviators the benefit of sinking a fleeing ship in or near the channel.[41] However, given his later record of half-truths and outright lies, Fuchida's account of his prestrike instructions cannot be taken at face value. For example, his orders for the level bombers to concentrate on a few targets rather than many seem to have been ignored. On the other hand, the instructions to concentrate on ships in the channel may have been carried out, based on the target selection of the second-wave dive-bombers. Alternatively, his postwar statements may have been an effort to give cover to those pilots after the fact.

Murata's 40 torpedo planes were to attack in two groups, ideally at the same instant. The Nakajima B5N2 "Kates" would come down to low altitude and split into two groups to approach from two directions. Murata himself would lead the main section of 24 aircraft which were to fly to a point south of the harbor entrance, then swing north over Hickam Field and attack Battleship Row. Twelve aircraft from *Akagi* would be followed by 12 more from *Kaga*. Sixteen more Kates with torpedoes from *Soryu* and *Hiryu* were targeted against the carriers that typically moored on the west and northwest sides of Ford Island. All 16 would approach Pearl Harbor from the west.

Pre-attack planning suggested that at least two carriers were operating out of Pearl Harbor. With 16 torpedo-carrying Kates allocated against them, this meant a potential of eight torpedoes against each target. These were expected to easily deliver the three or four hits that the Japanese thought necessary to destroy a carrier. The second-wave dive-bombers were under orders to bomb the sunken carriers in order to make any salvage impossible.

Only a proportion of the battleships present in the harbor would be vulnerable to torpedo attack. If they were moored singly, this number could be as high as six. If they were moored in pairs, as the Japanese expected, the number could be as low as four. With 24 torpedo-carrying Kates allocated against them, approximately six torpedoes were dedicated against each battleship. Four to five torpedo hits were thought necessary to sink a battleship.[42] The goal was to spread the torpedo onslaught against all the vulnerable battleships, leaving none free from significant attack. One of the battleships was known to berth along the 1010 Dock. This required a different attack route than the ones used to attack battleships on Battleship Row, which was adjacent to Ford Island. On the day of the attack, this battleship was missing, as *Pennsylvania* was secured safely in a nearby drydock.

The torpedo bombers were ordered to conduct their attack in a long string formation. Fuchida claims he made this decision because "the long thin line [was] especially well suited to Pearl Harbor with its narrow channel and many obstacles."[43] In order to cover all the potential attack angles, Murata developed 18 different attack routes: Six against Battleship Row, two against battleships moored on the 1010 Dock, five against the carrier moorings located northwest of Ford Island, and five against other cruiser locations. Of course, when the attackers arrived at Pearl Harbor they would have no precise information on the location of specific units. Because of this, aircraft were not assigned pre-designated attack routes. Each section or aircraft commander would make the decision what to attack upon arrival.

Given his emphasis on sinking carriers, Genda's plan included an overconcentration against them. Even after learning the day before the attack that the carriers were out, he kept the attack plan in place. When another staff officer pointed out that the carriers might return before the attack, Genda revealed his true opinion of the attack, stating, "If that happens, I don't care if all eight battleships are away."[44]

One of the more bizarre aspects of the plan was the provision for dealing with torpedo nets. Despite consistent reporting from the agents based at the Japanese consulate that no nets were present, the Japanese gave much thought to the matter since it had the potential to derail the entire attack. September tests conducted at Yokosuka on ways to cut the nets were not promising, so Fuchida and Genda came up with a new solution. In typical Japanese fashion, the answer involved self-sacrifice. In order to create a hole big enough for other aircraft to exploit, it was decided that one or several of the torpedo aircraft would dive into the net. It was a harebrained idea with little hope of success, and it was not disclosed to the pilots before the Striking Force left Japan.[45] It was also an example of not thinking in terms of combined arms since using a dive-bomber to blow a hole in the nets had a greater chance of success.

The first-wave dive-bombers were focused on American airfields. Twenty-seven Aichi D3A1 "Vals" from *Zuikaku*, escorted by six Mitsubishi A6M2 "Zeros," would break into two groups to attack Wheeler Field from the east and west. Wheeler was the principal fighter field on Oahu. *Shokaku*'s dive-bombers were slated to attack Naval Air Station (NAS) Pearl Harbor on Ford Island and Hickam Field. Ford Island was the primary USN air base on Oahu, and Hickam was a particularly important target since it was the primary bomber field on the island.

Per the Striking Force Operations Order 3, "The targets of the Fighter Combat Units will be enemy aircraft in the air and on the ground." Later, the order stated, "In the event that no enemy aircraft are encountered in the air, the units will immediately shift to the strafing of parked aircraft."[46] This reflected Imperial Navy doctrine, in which fighters were expected to seek combat with enemy fighters at the expense of providing escort to friendly bombers. This worked well if the enemy was surprised and friendly bombers faced no fighter opposition. However, if the enemy had time to scramble fighters, this had the potential to place Japanese strike aircraft at risk.

Nine Zeros were assigned to accompany the torpedo aircraft until they were some 10nm from Pearl Harbor, at which point they would divide from the bombers to attack the Marine Corps Air Station at Ewa Field. Another 12 Zeros were assigned to attack NAS Kaneohe Bay; this facility was the home base for 36 USN PBY Catalina flying boats. Other fighters were ordered to attack Ford Island, Hickam, and Wheeler.

In total, 189 aircraft were allocated to the first wave (in the actual event, only 183 actually attacked, with six aircraft aborting after launch). Of these, 90 were assigned to hit the Pacific Fleet, while 99 were assigned to attack airfields (in what would now be called offensive counterair missions – the Japanese did not use this term). The success of the entire operation rested on the outcome of the torpedo bomber attacks in the first wave. If their attacks were successful, Yamamoto's vision of a shocking blow to the essence of American naval power could be realized.

Organization of Pearl Harbor Attack Force

First Attack Force (First Wave)

Commander: Commander Fuchida Mitsuo

Carrier Aircraft Type/Number Target

First Flight – Horizontal Bombing Force (Commander: Fuchida)

1st Attack Unit	*Akagi*	Kate	15	Battleship Row
2nd Attack Unit	*Kaga*	Kate	15 (1 abort)	Battleship Row
3rd Attack Group	*Soryu*	Kate	10	Battleship Row
4th Attack Group	*Hiryu*	Kate	10	Battleship Row
		Total:	50 (49 actually attacked)	

All aircraft armed with a single Type 5 1,764-pound bomb

First Flight Special Group – Torpedo Force (Commander: Murata)

1st Torpedo Attack Unit	*Akagi*	Kate	12	Battleship Row
2nd Torpedo Attack Unit	*Kaga*	Kate	12	Battleship Row
3rd Torpedo Attack Unit	*Soryu*	Kate	8	Carriers, Battleships
4th Torpedo Attack Unit	*Hiryu*	Kate	8	Carriers, Battleships
		Total:	40	

All aircraft armed with a single Type 91 air-launched torpedo

Second Flight – Dive-Bomber Force (Commander: Lt Commander Takahashi Kakuichi)

15th Attack Unit	*Shokaku*	Val	27 (1 abort)	17 against Ford Island
				9 against Hickam Fld
16th Attack Unit	*Zuikaku*	Val	27 (2 abort)	Wheeler Fld
		Total:	54 (51 actually attacked)	

All aircraft armed with a single 551-pound general purpose bomb

Third Flight – Air Control Force (Commander: Lt Commander Itaya Shigeru)

1st Fighter Combat Unit	*Akagi*	Zero	9	Ford Island/Hickam Fld
2nd Fighter Combat Unit	*Kaga*	Zero	9	Ford Island/Hickam Fld
3rd Fighter Combat Unit	*Soryu*	Zero	9 (1 abort)	Wheeler Fld/Ewa
4th Fighter Combat Unit	*Hiryu*	Zero	6	Wheeler Fld/Ewa
5th Fighter Combat Unit	*Shokaku*	Zero	6 (1 abort)	Kaneohe
6th Fighter Combat Unit	*Zuikaku*	Zero	6	Kaneohe
		Total:	45 (43 actually attacked)	

All aircraft armed with two 20mm cannon and two 7.7mm machine guns

Total aircraft in first wave: 189 (183 actually attacked)

Second Attack Force (Second Wave)

Commander: Lt Commander Shimazaki Shigekazu

First Flight – Horizontal Bombing Force (Commander: Shimazaki)

5th Attack Unit	*Shokaku*	Kate	27	18 against Ford Island
				9 against Kaneohe
6th Attack Unit	*Zuikaku*	Kate	27	Hickam Field
		Total:	54	

One-half of the aircraft armed with two 551-pound bombs; half armed with one 551-pound bomb and six 132-pound bombs

Second Flight – Dive-Bomber Force (Commander: Lt Commander Egusa Takashige)

11th Attack Unit	*Akagi*	Val	18	Various naval targets
12th Attack Unit	*Kaga*	Val	27 (1 abort)	Various naval targets
13th Attack Unit	*Soryu*	Val	18 (1 abort)	Various naval targets
14th Attack Unit	*Hiryu*	Val	18 (1 abort)	Various naval targets
		Total:	81 (78 actually attacked)	

All aircraft armed with a single 551-pound bomb

THE JAPANESE PLAN

Third Flight – Air Control Force (Commander: Lt Shindo Saburo)

1st Fighter Combat Unit	*Akagi*	Zero	9	Ford Island/Hickam Fld
2nd Fighter Combat Unit	*Kaga*	Zero	9	Ford Island/Hickam Fld
3rd Fighter Combat Unit	*Soryu*	Zero	9	Kaneohe
4th Fighter Combat Unit	*Hiryu*	Zero	9 (1 abort)	Kaneohe/Bellows Fld
		Total:	36 (35 actually attacked)	

All aircraft armed with two 20mm cannon and two 7.7mm machine guns

Total aircraft in second wave: 171 (167 actually attacked)
Total attacking aircraft: 360 (350 actually attacked)

THE SECOND-WAVE ATTACK PLAN

Commanded by Lieutenant Commander Shimazaki Shigekazu, the second wave would arrive shortly after the first, allowing the defenders little time to recover. The second wave was very different than the first. No torpedo planes were included because with the element of surprise lost, the low and slow attack profiles of the torpedo bombers would have resulted in heavy losses. All of the Kates present in the second wave were level bombers under Shimazaki's personal command. These were targeted on Hickam, Kaneohe, and Ford Island to complete the destruction of American air power. Each Kate carried two 551-pound ordinary bombs or one 551-pound bomb and six 132-pound bombs. The real punch of the second wave was the 81 dive-bombers under Egusa. Each carried a 551-pound ordinary bomb. All 81 aircraft were slated to attack naval targets. The dive-bombers were ordered to make the carriers their priority target. Of particular emphasis were any carriers damaged from the first wave. The dive-bombers would attack them again, even if they were already capsized or sunk, and complete their destruction in hopes of making any salvage impossible.

Second-wave Zeros were under orders to strafe Ford Island and Kaneohe Bay, and Bellows and Hickam Fields, unless they were occupied with attacking any American fighters that managed to take off. In all, 171 aircraft were allocated to the second wave. The majority of these, 90, were assigned targets to reduce American air power. The other 81 were allocated against naval targets in the harbor.

Combining the assets of both waves, it is significant to note that two-thirds (to include the fighters) were assigned to strike airfields. The aircraft assigned to strike naval targets were split roughly evenly between Kates (conducting torpedo and horizontal bombing attacks) and the dive-bombing Vals. Because the weight of the weapons devoted to attacking ships was so much greater, 71 percent of the total payload was dedicated to attacking naval targets. Kates were responsible for carrying 65 percent of the total payload for the attack.[47]

The large number of aircraft allocated against airfields was necessary since destroying large numbers of aircraft on the ground was difficult if the aircraft were dispersed. This passive step was even more effective if aircraft were in revetments, which made every revetment its own target. One well-placed bomb could destroy only a single aircraft inside a revetment. Given the nature of the targets and the types of aircraft the Japanese had at their disposal, Kates were best suited for attacking large targets such as aircraft hangars, fuel tanks, and maintenance areas. In order to attack small targets, like revetments, much more accurate dive-bombers would have to be used. In this regard, the math did not work in the favor of the Japanese. There were many more small targets than dive-bombers available to attack them. For example, Wheeler Field had 85 revetments for the 109 aircraft at the field, but Genda could only allocate 27 dive-bombers and some fighters to attack this facility.[48] If the Americans had placed their aircraft inside revetments and dispersed the rest, the Japanese would have found it difficult to achieve significant results against aircraft on Oahu.

Japanese fighter allocation was an even bigger potential issue. Again, it needs to be pointed out that Genda did not consider fighters to be simply escorts for the attack aircraft. Fighters were attack elements in their own right and were assigned important targets. The more fighters assigned to attack airfields, the more American aircraft could be destroyed on the ground. Nagumo was accepting a high degree of risk since both the Japanese and Americans assumed that land-based aircraft would have success against a carrier task force, even one defended by fighters on combat air patrol (CAP).[49] The reality was much different, but this was unknown to both contestants in December 1941.[50] Knocking out American air power was another important reason surprise was essential.

THE JAPANESE PLAN

According to the official Japanese history, only 46 fighters remained to maintain the CAP – 12 each from *Shokaku* and *Zuikaku*, six each from *Soryu* and *Hiryu*, and five each from *Akagi* and *Kaga*.[51] About one-third of the fighters were airborne, conducting CAP, with the rest on deck ready to respond. The first CAP group was ordered to take off right after the launch of the second attack wave and was to stay aloft for two hours. Half of these were ordered to patrol at just over 13,000 feet and the others at about 6,500 feet. After two hours, a second group took over, with the patrols being maintained until sunset.[52]

THE IMPORTANCE OF SURPRISE

With surprise an utter necessity, radio silence was essential. Ships of the Striking Force could receive messages but send none. Accordingly, radio transmission keys were sealed and in some cases the fuses in the transmitters were removed. Information between ships was sent by signals flags during the day and narrow-beamed blinkers at night.[53]

Radio silence extended to the aircraft of the first attack wave. Until Fuchida gave the final attack order, no aircraft was allowed to use its radio. After the signal was given to attack, only flight leaders were allowed to use their radios. In the actual event, radio communications were kept to a minimum, much to the detriment of attack coordination. The key objective of near radio silence was to protect the location of the Striking Force.[54]

An assumption of surprise was woven throughout the Japanese plan. This was a hallmark of Japanese operational planning and was similar to other Japanese plans for major operations early in the war. It speaks to the intrinsic arrogance of the Japanese who never failed to underestimate their enemies in operational planning. In the case of Genda's plan surprise was utterly essential. It was necessary to capture the fleet inside the harbor and make it easy to locate and attack; it was necessary in order for the Japanese to destroy American air power on the ground and thus eliminate the chance of an American counterattack or to mount a successful defense of the fleet; most importantly, it was necessary to allow the vulnerable torpedo and horizontal bombers to deliver hammer blows against the American battle fleet.

Japanese planners gave some thought to what should be done if the Striking Force was detected before it had a chance to launch its strike.

In the event surprise was lost in the 24 hours before the strike was due to launch, the Japanese planned to still mount an attack on Pearl Harbor. In this worst-case scenario, Genda planned to conduct a fighter sweep over Oahu with all the fighters. Once "command of the air" was achieved, the strike aircraft would follow.[55]

This truly was a worst-case scenario. The Americans would have time to alert their defenses. Part or most of the Pacific Fleet would have sortied, forcing the Japanese to locate it and plan how to divide their strike assets to hit the portion of the fleet still inside the harbor and that portion now maneuvering outside the harbor. There would have been little prospect of catching American air power on the ground, making an aerial counterattack on the Striking Force all but certain. When the strike aircraft made their appearance, they would have faced a withering antiaircraft barrage. In short, it would have been near total chaos, and nothing that the Japanese could plan for effectively. Based on their reaction to other unforeseen events later in the war, their response to uncontrolled chaos on December 7, 1941 would not have been good.

THE QUESTION OF A SECOND ATTACK

On the key point of whether additional attacks were planned beyond the first two waves on the morning of December 7, the record is confusing. In Task Force Order No. 1, issued on November 23, it appeared to be clear: "When the attacks have been completed the force will quickly withdraw. Upon returning to Japan the force will be re-equipped and supplied and then assigned a task in the Second Phase Operations."[56] According to Kusaka, he and Nagumo expected the first two attack waves to deliver an "all-out fatal blow," thus removing the need for a second attack. That same day, Nagumo issued Operation Order No. 3, which contained contradictory orders with regard to a possible second strike. In this order, once the aircraft returned:

> ...preparations will be made immediately for the next attack. Carrier attack planes will be armed with torpedoes. If the land based air power has been completely knocked out, repeated attacks will be made immediately in order to achieve maximum results. However, if a powerful enemy force is in route to attack, subsequent attacks will be directed against it.[57]

The second order almost certainly reflects the influence of Genda and Fuchida. Both were more aggressive than Nagumo and more confident in the capabilities of the Striking Force. It is clear that two views prevailed within the command staff of the Striking Force. Nagumo and Kusaka had made up their minds before leaving Japan that the operation was a hit-and-run raid. Genda wanted to look for opportunities to cause additional damage.

What would happen if the United States and Japan reached a political agreement before the attack? If that were to happen, then the fleet would be recalled. But if the Striking Force was discovered prematurely, different rules of engagement would apply. If the fleet was discovered before X-1 day (December 6), the only option was to turn back since all surprise was lost. An exception was provided for: if Nagumo assessed that only a portion of the fleet had been discovered, then the Striking Force would react accordingly and proceed on its mission. If the fleet was discovered on December 7 or was fired upon before that date, the Striking Force would return fire and stay on mission.[58]

The final plan was not completed until the end of October and some parts were still being worked out after the Striking Force departed Japan. On 2 November, the outline of the plan and the role for each participating unit was revealed in a mass briefing aboard flagship *Akagi*. Following two more weeks of exercise, the fleet re-supplied and departed their homeports in ones or twos to rendezvous in Hitokappu Bay in the Kuriles on 22 November. Two final briefings were held aboard *Akagi* on 23 November during which every unit in the fleet was informed of the objective and the aviators fully briefed.

AN EVALUATION OF THE PLAN – STRATEGIC CONSIDERATIONS

Yamamoto's vision, as planned by Genda, was a curious mix of imagination, boldness, and futility. At the macro level, the Japanese need to be given full credit for something never attempted or even seriously contemplated before. They combined this imagination with a concept of operations that was so bold that the Americans never saw it as plausible. But given the inferiority of the Pacific Fleet compared to the Combined Fleet in December 1941, why did Yamamoto press so ardently for his high-risk plan to attack Pearl Harbor?

Yamamoto's extreme efforts at securing his plan seem misplaced both at the time and after the event. His aggressive strategy replaced the reactive decisive battle strategy. It was not really an improvement, but better suited Yamamoto who was a gambler. As he admitted, his Pearl Harbor attack was a calculated risk. It was possible that the Imperial Navy could have lost the war on the first day had disaster befallen the Striking Force. Most significantly, the plan was never going to inflict the level of disruption on American morale as Yamamoto hoped. Instead, the attack guaranteed a tidal wave of American public anger, undermined the prospect for a negotiated peace, and increased the probability that the United States would conduct a protracted war to grind Japan into defeat.

Japan's top priority at the start of the war was to quickly seize the southern resource areas. In this context, it made strategic sense to neutralize the Pacific Fleet to cover the eastern flank of the southern offensive. Whether the Pacific Fleet was inferior or not, Yamamoto's plan had bigger goals. The blow against the Pacific Fleet in its home base not only served the purpose of covering the essential drive into resource-rich Southeast Asia but was meant to shatter American morale and lay the groundwork for war termination.

However, in retrospect, the attack was utterly unnecessary. Even if the Pacific Fleet had not been attacked, it was in no position to interfere with Japanese operations in Southeast Asia. Logistics was the key here, not the number of battleships in the fleet. Even if the Americans had attempted a premature operations to attack the Marshalls, the results would have been uncertain for the Pacific Fleet. In the words of Samuel E. Morison, the Pacific Fleet would have suffered disaster under Japanese air attack.[59]

As bold as Yamamoto's plan was, it never had the potential to be successful in the way Yamamoto intended. From this perspective, it was not well considered since it was based on Yamamoto's dubious premise that sinking a few battleships would crack American morale. It satisfied Yamamoto's desire to go on the offensive instead of letting the Americans come to him, but it never had the potential to shift war termination to a different framework. Why would Yamamoto, with his supposed knowledge of the United States, believe in such a superficial assumption?

In another cognitive disconnect, Yamamoto was convinced to use the revolutionary capabilities of massed carrier air power to strike the old mainstay of naval power, the battle line. If the attack was successful, it would provide only dramatic proof that the era of the battleship as the arbiter of naval power was over, yet the attack was built largely on the notion that sinking battleships was potentially decisive. The Japanese estimated that a third of the Striking Force could be lost in the operation; thus, Yamamoto was ready to lose two carriers to achieve his goal of sinking four battleships.

In fact, the Japanese never did a cost-benefit analysis of the strategic value of the Pearl Harbor operation. The benefit of the plan was to potentially cripple the Pacific Fleet. However, even if all the battleships (and carriers) present had been sunk, it would have provided only a fleeting benefit given the American naval expansion program already under way. For this temporary advantage, the cost was bringing the United States into the war under the most disadvantageous conditions possible for Japan. While the USN was unable to interfere with Japan's southern thrust, something that would have been true even if no Pearl Harbor attack had been conducted, the United States that entered the war did so as a united nation determined to exact revenge. In fact, in terms of US public opinion, the attack had exactly the opposite effect desired by Yamamoto.

AN EVALUATION OF THE PLAN – OPERATIONAL AND TACTICAL CONSIDERATIONS

At the operational and tactical levels, Genda's plan was bold. It had the potential to achieve Yamamoto's goal of devastating the Pacific Fleet's battle line and of realizing Genda's goal of crippling the Pacific Fleet's carrier force. It maximized the potential for surprise. It was a gamble to be sure, but a gamble based on the realistic assumption that surprise was possible. It must be remembered that nothing like it had ever been attempted before – Genda had no template to work from.

Nevertheless, the nuts and bolts of the plan were far from perfect. In his draft plan, which essentially became the attack plan, Genda did not place any emphasis on the installations of the naval base. He was focused on attacking the Pacific Fleet and American land-based air power. This reflected existing Japanese perceptions of sea power. After the attack, Nagumo was criticized for ignoring the naval base – this began with Genda's original draft. The author believes that Genda and later Nagumo made the right choice. As will be detailed later, the Japanese lacked the capability to destroy such a huge target. Any attempt to do so would have meant fewer bombs directed at ships and aircraft on the ground, and reducing the ordnance directed at these targets was never a possibility.

Another related but equally controversial part of the plan was to withdraw as soon as the strike aircraft were recovered. Genda wanted to linger after the strikes with the proviso that American land-based air power had been neutralized. Assuming this had been achieved, operating in the area and mounting robust search operations might have developed other targets. With the knowledge that no carriers were caught in port, lingering in the area presented the potential to find them. Doing so would have required healthy doses of fuel and imagination, something which Nagumo and Kusaka did not possess. In the final analysis, with so many unknowns and with such a critical component of the Imperial Navy in his hands, Nagumo was right not to linger in the area without a clear purpose.

Pre-flight reconnaissance was poorly handled. The use of floatplanes from cruisers *Tone* and *Chikuma* to scout Pearl Harbor and the fleet anchorage at Lahaina was unnecessary and carried with it the potential for loss of surprise. The day before the attack, a submarine reconnaissance of the anchorage confirmed it was empty. Even cutting the launch time to 30 minutes before the launch of the attack wave carried with it the potential for loss of surprise. Even if new information was received regarding American fleet dispositions, Fuchida did not have the means to fully act on it.

The torpedo bombers were the most important element in the entire operation. They were expected to account for 27 hits, accounting for the most significant damage to the Pacific Fleet. The problem was that they were only lightly protected by the Zeros. Worse still was that after the Zeros assigned to accompany the torpedo Kates broke away to attack Ewa, the torpedo bombers would be totally unprotected for the last and most vulnerable part of their attack run.

Yet as the torpedo bombers were left unprotected, 12 Zeros were assigned to attack NAS Kaneohe Bay, which based only reconnaissance aircraft. These Zeros should have been protecting the ingress of the torpedo bombers by being available to attack any American fighters present or to suppress antiaircraft positions. If attacking Kaneohe was so important, the Zeros could still do that after making sure the torpedo Kates made their attacks.

Another problem with the torpedo bomber plan was unclear target prioritization. At Genda's level, the plan was fine since it serviced all the high-priority targets (carriers and battleships). The problem came when one of these targets was missing. Assuming that the pilots could make good decisions within literally seconds as they made their attack runs was unrealistic. With little situational awareness on what targets had been hit and whether they were heavily damaged or not, combined with no ability to communicate between aircraft, the invariable consequence was one of several bad results: choosing an unimportant target for attack; overconcentration on a single important target; or under concentration on an important target. All of these were evinced in the actual event.

The attack formation for the torpedo attack was poorly selected. Genda, almost certainly in consultation with Murata, decided that the torpedo bombers would attack in a long string with some 1,600 feet between aircraft. Fuchida stated this was necessary because of the obstructions in the harbor area. It was a poor choice because it strung out the attack and made the final aircraft attack when surprise was likely to have been lost. If it was, then the defenders could concentrate their fire on a single known point that each aircraft had to fly through. The potential result could be heavy losses for the last aircraft to attack. In addition, placing the squadron leaders at the front of the string formation meant they had no ability to guide follow-on aircraft to the best targets.[60]

Of the 18 pre-planned torpedo attack routes, the majority crossed one another. The only deconfliction done by Genda was to send the torpedo bombers into the attack one at a time separated by only seven seconds. The potential for interference and confusion was accordingly great. The string formation used by the torpedo bombers increased the propensity to concentrate on a few targets as each aircraft followed the preceding one. In the case of the actual attack, it meant that targets in the southern portion of Battleship Row would receive more than their share of punishment. In the November rehearsal, the exact same issue emerged. Yet Genda and Murata did nothing to correct it.

A better solution would have been to attack in the usual line abreast formation used to attack ships at sea. In this case, a number of echelons would have been required. By doing so, the defenders could not have concentrated their fire on a single incoming aircraft and torpedo distribution would have been better since the next echelon could have observed which targets were being attacked and shift their fire to other ones.

As with most Imperial Navy plans, there was little thought given to contingencies. What would happen if the first plan failed to unfold as assumed? Even in the opening hours of the war, inflexibility in Japanese planning was a factor. The best example of this was when the Japanese learned the night before the attack that the carriers were not in port. Despite this knowledge, Genda left the plan intact in the simple hope that a miracle would place the carriers in port before the attack started. No alternate plan was provided to the pilots affected.

In the end, the Japanese plan was executed boldly while the American defense plan was caught in complete disarray. Within this basic framework, the Japanese were certain to enjoy a large measure of success. That Genda's plan failed to create all the damage that it might have misses the central point that significant losses were inflicted on the Americans.

The submarine part of the plan was also a failure and was extremely foolish as it contained the potential to negate any possibility of surprise. Chapter 10 covers this in full detail.

PEARL HARBOR AND YAMAMOTO'S REPUTATION

Yamamoto was a unique figure within the Imperial Navy. Despite being the man behind the Pearl Harbor attack, his reputation as a man who never wanted to attack the United States, and who warned of the consequences if Japan did so, remains unchallenged. In correspondence with friends before the war, Yamamoto identified this as a personal dilemma. As a man of duty, he was compelled to lead the Combined Fleet into a war he knew would result in the fleet's and subsequently Japan's destruction. This was surely an act of moral cowardice, and one Yamamoto is not called to task for. He never exerted his considerable influence to stop or slow Japan's race to war. Had he acted on his moral qualms over an unwinnable war with the United States and taken the extreme act of resigning, it almost certainly would have made no difference. Such an act, though, would have solidified Yamamoto's reputation as an independent thinker and marked him as a man with a

THE JAPANESE PLAN

clear moral compass unpossessed by any of Japan's other senior leaders. Expecting an Imperial Navy officer to take such an action is unrealistic, with Yamamoto being perhaps the sole exception. That leaves him in the ironic situation of being a man who warned of war with the United States and then did everything he could to expand the war.

Yamamoto has gained the reputation of a gifted strategist and able war leader. This is entirely undeserved since this reputation rests almost exclusively on his Pearl Harbor attack. Yamamoto was guilty of confused thinking leading up to the attack for both military and political reasons. His goal to sink battleships at Pearl Harbor was anachronistic, and more than a little ironic as he positioned himself as an air power advocate. More than his miscalculation about the impact of sinking ships inside Pearl Harbor, Yamamoto, despite his supposed wealth of experience in the United States and the insights this should have brought, badly miscalculated the American national character. The course he selected to open the war was the most likely to undermine his goal of a negotiated peace with the United States favorable to Japan. There is no escaping the conclusion that Pearl Harbor was Yamamoto's unhealthy obsession.

After Pearl Harbor, his leadership was increasingly erratic and autocratic. Yamamoto oversaw the advance into Southeast Asia. This offensive was conducted in a bold and ultimately successful manner. It was also marked by reckless advances by dispersed forces. Lacking the means to exploit this, the Allies were never able to deal the Japanese even a temporary setback or to disrupt the Japanese advance. In the Second Operational Phase, Yamamoto acted with confusion and overconfidence. The Midway campaign, including the battle for Coral Sea, ended the period of Japanese expansion in the Pacific. During the period from May to June 1942, Yamamoto squandered his numerical advantage and ended up losing the initiative. Yamamoto tried to fight a decisive battle by setting up a clash with the Pacific Fleet at Midway Atoll in the Central Pacific even though the plan faced considerable opposition from the Naval General Staff. Resorting to his Pearl Harbor playbook, Yamamoto did not get the plan approved on its merits, but through another threat to resign. His gamble at Midway ended in utter failure. Yamamoto the gambler, when combined with the lack of sound operational planning, was a recipe for disaster.

The result of the failed Central Pacific offensive was that the Americans were able to launch their first counteroffensive of the war and land in the southern Solomon Islands in August 1942. Thus, only eight months after Pearl Harbor, the Imperial Navy lost the initiative and was fully on the defensive. After a six-month grueling battle of attrition centered on Guadalcanal, the Imperial Navy suffered a defeat much more crippling than Midway. At Guadalcanal, Yamamoto accepted the type of attritional battle he feared, and the Imperial Navy incurred heavy and unreplaceable losses. Throughout the campaign, the Combined Fleet proved unable to synchronize its operations and employ what was still a numerical advantage in most ship categories. Every battle or campaign Yamamoto planned or oversaw, except for the offensive into Southeast Asia against weak opposition, ended in defeat. Despite this, his "success" at Pearl Harbor has elevated Yamamoto's reputation to the rank of one of the top admirals in naval history.

4

The Striking Force

In every naval battle, three of the greatest shaping factors are the men, equipment, and ships of each side. This chapter examines the Japanese force involved in the Pearl Harbor attack and details its strengths and weaknesses. It is worth remembering that the power of the Striking Force was greater than the sum of its parts. The Japanese were still exploring how to use this assemblage of naval power; the Americans were unaware that it even existed.

After much debate, Yamamoto got his way with regard to which carriers would be committed to the Hawaii Operation. It was agreed that all six of the Imperial Navy's fleet carriers would participate in the attack. Together, these made up the most powerful striking force in the world. Without this massed air power, the Pearl Harbor attack would not have been as successful as it was.

Air power advocates within the Imperial Navy had foreseen the advantages of massing carriers. Doing so alleviated coordination issues between dispersed carrier divisions and presented opportunities for superior offensive and defensive firepower. Genda claimed that he had the inspiration for massing carriers into a single formation by watching a newsreel of American carriers steaming together in a box formation while he was in London in 1940 as assistant naval attaché.[1] The problem with concentrating carriers was that they were all susceptible to being detected by a single enemy search aircraft. Once detected, all the carriers were in danger. The Japanese assessed that if a carrier was attacked there was a high likelihood it would be placed out of action or destroyed. Accordingly, in 1940 the Imperial Navy hedged between concentration and dispersal.

Early in 1941, Yamamoto allowed the Combined Fleet to undertake the first steps to exploring the possibilities of permanently concentrating its carriers. Before this point, the carriers were formed into carrier divisions with two or three ships and placed under the command of the First or Second Fleets. No attempt was made to train the different carrier divisions together. As this arrangement preserved the status quo that the carrier was a supporting element to the battleships, most of the fleet's leaders were content with it.[2]

However, air power advocates were not satisfied with carriers as a mere supporting arm of the battle fleet. The commander and staff of Carrier Division 1 became a hotbed for forming the carriers into a single force. By doing so, Carrier Divisions 1 and 2 could train together and develop the necessary doctrine and techniques to normalize multi-carrier operations. The commander of Carrier Division 1 was Vice Admiral Ozawa Jisaburo, a non-aviator but an astute observer of the potential of carrier air power. With his flagship on *Akagi*, he was exposed to the thoughts of his air group commander, Lieutenant Commander Fuchida Mitsuo. Ozawa twice recommended to Yamamoto that he authorize the formation of an "air fleet." Not wanting to provoke a battle with the traditionalists within the Imperial Navy, Yamamoto turned him down twice. In June 1940, Ozawa brought the issue to a head by taking his proposal directly to the Navy Minister. Though irked by Ozawa's abuse of the chain of command, this move began the argument Yamamoto had been avoiding. By December 1940, Yamamoto was convinced and the other principal officers were ready to back this significant change.[3]

On April 10, 1941, the 1st Air Fleet was formed. It is hard to overstate the importance of this development. In today's terms the creation of the 1st Air Fleet represented what would be called a revolution in military affairs. At one stroke, Yamamoto created a force of unmatched power. As first formed, the 1st Air Fleet included Carrier Division 1 (with fleet carriers *Akagi* and *Kaga*), Carrier Division 2 (with fleet carriers *Soryu* and *Hiryu*), Carrier Division 3 (with light carriers *Hosho* and *Ryujo*), two divisions of seaplane carriers, and ten destroyers. The ships of Carrier Division 3 were too small to be included in the Pearl Harbor operation so were never included in planning for it. In September, the two small carriers were transferred back to the other fleets. That same month, the 1st Air Fleet received a massive reinforcement with the creation of Carrier Division 5, comprised of the two new Shokaku-class carriers, *Shokaku* and *Zuikaku*. The concentration of six fleet carriers gave the first commander of the fleet, Vice Admiral Nagumo, a force with 400 aircraft. The *Kido Butai* (literally "Mobile Force" but better rendered as "Striking Force") was the operational component of the 1st Air Fleet.

Even the creation of the Striking Force did not represent the demise of the battleship as the Combined Fleet's centerpiece. The Striking Force was seen as one of several components of the Combined Fleet, though perhaps its most important one. Not until after the Battle of Midway in June 1942 was the carrier recognized as the principal striking force of the fleet, and it took until March 1944 for all other fleet elements to be used in support of the carriers.

As created, the Striking Force was a raiding force unable to undertake prolonged operations on its own. Because of its mobility, it had an increased chance of achieving surprise. This was a critical consideration, since although it possessed considerable offensive power, the Japanese considered it vulnerable to counterattack. In this role, doctrine dictated that when the Striking Force entered the area covered by enemy air patrols it would do so at 25 knots to launch its initial strike at dawn some 200–250nm from the target. After launching the strike, it was usually prudent to retreat at high speed. Only if there was judged to be no danger of an enemy counterattack could a second strike be conducted. This early assessment of the Striking Force's capabilities proved eerily correct during the first seven months of the war.[4]

COMMAND PERSONALITIES

The first commander of the Striking Force was the 54-year-old Vice Admiral Nagumo Chuichi. He seemed an unlikely choice for this new role since his background was in torpedo tactics and he had no experience in aviation. Nagumo was assigned command of the 1st Air Fleet in April 1941 simply because the new command called for a vice admiral and Nagumo was the senior vice admiral available at the time. However, it was normal for a non-aviator to command an aviation formation in the Imperial Navy. Nagumo had built a career around extensive sea time and by avoiding staff assignments. He was generally respected within the Imperial Navy. Though Nagumo was an intelligent and conscientious officer, he was conservative. All factors considered, he was not the right man to command Yamamoto's revolutionary formation.

Nagumo was thrust into an uncomfortable situation when he took over the 1st Air Fleet. Planning for the Pearl Harbor operation was already under way, though this was mainly the purview of Genda. Nagumo and his chief of staff, Rear Admiral Kusaka Ryunosuke, were both against the plan, creating an atmosphere of uncertainty in the staff of the 1st Air Fleet. With Yamamoto pushing the plan forward, Nagumo had to be supportive, at least publicly. Yamamoto never fully trusted Nagumo and Kusaka, stating once to Watanabe, "Perhaps it would be better to rely on young men who can be trusted." Yamamoto kept the heat on Nagumo by visiting the aviators as they trained at Kagoshima, Kasanohara, and Ariake Bay. Yamamoto often summoned the senior officers of the 1st Air Fleet to meet with him on his flagship. They made such a poor impression on Yamamoto and Ugaki that they worried about the morale of the aviators.[5]

One of Nagumo's staff officers perhaps summed up Nagumo's awkward situation best when he stated after the war that his "position in the 1st Air Fleet was something of an adopted son … He was lost in the atmosphere of aircraft, felt insecure, and had to ease his way around."[6]

Rear Admiral Kusaka was Nagumo's chief of staff. Unlike his boss, he had at least some experience in naval aviation since he was the commander of a land-based air flotilla before being appointed as Nagumo's chief of staff. Though Kusaka did not possess a deep knowledge of naval air warfare or operations, he was a very competent staff officer who oversaw the planning for the Pearl Harbor attack and who personally solved one of the critical issues facing the Striking Force in the months before the attack. Like Nagumo, Kusaka was known as a cautious officer.[7]

The staff of the 1st Air Fleet played an important part in the planning process for and during the conduct of operations. By the norms of Japanese culture, command was exercised through consensus, elevating the role of the commander's staff. The paramount role of the 1st Air Fleet's staff was reinforced by Yamamoto's implicit trust in its dynamic duo of Genda Minoru and Fuchida Mitsuo, combined with Nagumo's general ignorance in the specifics of air operations. Kusaka respected Genda and Fuchida, and he determined "to have both Genda and Fuchida freely display their ability as they wished."[8] At the same time, Kusaka viewed Genda as arrogant.[9] Like Nagumo, Kusaka lacked the technical knowledge to evaluate his staff's ideas, so he accepted their recommendations to the maximum extent possible while keeping an eye on their activities.[10]

Without doubt, the most important member of the staff was the aforementioned Commander Genda Minoru, air officer of the 1st Air Fleet. A legend in his own time, he achieved recognition as a daring fighter pilot and then as a planner of complex operations. Yamamoto respected Genda for his "unique and remarkable ideas."[11] This respect approached affection, as Yamamoto probably saw himself in the aggressive Genda. Because he had no choice, Nagumo also trusted him completely. Genda was given complete freedom in planning and his plans were endorsed by Nagumo without comment. Nobody on the staff had the standing or knowledge of air operations to act as a check on Genda.

Commander Fuchida Mitsuo was respected by Yamamoto as an aviator and as a leader. In 1939, he was posted to *Akagi* as air group commander. From there, he was assigned to the staff of Carrier Division 3. In September 1941, he was transferred back to *Akagi* and learned he was to be the commander of all air groups of the 1st Air Fleet. In a late September meeting between Genda and Fuchida, Genda let Fuchida know why he was training so hard – Yamamoto intended to open the war with an attack on Pearl Harbor. Genda also informed Fuchida that he had been selected to lead the attack.

In follow-up discussions with Nagumo's staff on *Akagi*, Fuchida expressed his reservations about the attack. After looking at a chart of the depths of the harbor, he voiced the obvious concern that it was too shallow for a torpedo attack. It was decided that while work continued on a torpedo suitable for a shallow-water attack, Fuchida would continue to train his aviators on the required attack profiles. When the matter of horizontal bombing came up for discussion, Fuchida realized that it was an essential part of the plan since it provided the means to strike the inboard-moored battleships. Knowing the difficulty in gaining the required accuracy, Fuchida proposed bringing the horizontal bombers down to 10,000 feet, stating, "The risk is worth running to ensure maximum destruction."[12]

After his arrival, Fuchida had the task of getting his men ready for the attack by training them relentlessly without telling them the purpose of the arduous training program. Genda admonished him in the same meeting: "Let me repeat – this is the most secret thing of all secrets. I want to take every possible step to keep it even from your flying crews when they train for this mission."[13]

The duo of Genda and Fuchida were the driving force behind the detailed planning and training for the Pearl Harbor attack. Genda was the idea man, relying on Fuchida to shape his visions into reality. Nagumo and his staff were writing the book on large-scale carrier operations as they went along. No other command staff in the world had been challenged in this manner. In addition to tackling how to operate a large carrier formation and handle six carrier air groups, they were trying to figure out how to execute a surprise attack against one of the most heavily defended naval bases in the world.

There were other carrier admirals in the Striking Force aside from Nagumo. The most significant was 49-year-old Rear Admiral Yamaguchi Tamon, commander of Carrier Division 2. Though not a significant factor in shaping the Pearl Harbor attack plans, his views on Nagumo are worth noting. Yamaguchi was held in high regard inside the Imperial Navy, even to the point of being seen as a possible successor to Yamamoto. His career largely mirrored Yamamoto's. He was a member of the Japanese delegation to the London Naval Conference, was a naval attaché in Washington from June 1934 to August 1936, and had become a naval air power advocate without being an aviator. Yamaguchi assumed command of Carrier Division 2 in November 1940. His assessment of Nagumo was that he failed to appreciate the superiority of carriers and did not know how to properly use them.[14] Yamaguchi assessed that Nagumo and his staff lacked boldness and were unable to deal with dynamic situations. He also condemned Nagumo's apparent willingness to let his staff run operations.[15]

Carrier Division 5 was under the command of Rear Admiral Hara Chuichi. His background was as a surface warfare officer before getting command of the Imperial Navy's newest and most powerful carriers in September 1941. Hara had the reputation as an aggressive officer and was given the nickname "King Kong."

THE SHIPS

The Striking Force was comprised of three carrier divisions, each with two fleet carriers. Unlike in the American Navy, Japanese carrier divisions were more than administrative entities. The carriers in each division trained and operated together, and their air groups conducted joint missions.

The cream of the Striking Force was Carrier Division 1, composed of carriers *Akagi* and *Kaga*, the first fleet carriers commissioned into the Imperial Navy. *Akagi*, Nagumo's flagship, was held in particularly high esteem. Given her genesis as a battlecruiser, she could steam at a top speed of over 31 knots and was well protected. By the start of the war she could carry 63 operational aircraft. Rounding out Carrier Division 1 was *Kaga*. Laid down as a battleship, she was selected to be scrapped as part of the Washington Naval Treaty of 1922. She received a new lease on life when *Akagi*'s sistership *Amagi* was badly damaged in the 1923 Tokyo earthquake, leaving *Kaga* as the best remaining choice for conversion into a carrier. She was the slowest carrier in the Striking Force at just over 28 knots as well as the least nimble. However, her size gave her the space to carry up to 75 operational aircraft, the most of any of the Pearl Harbor carriers.

Both *Akagi* and *Kaga* were carrier conversions. The first Japanese fleet carriers designed as such were the two Soryu-class ships. Both were assigned to Carrier Division 2. Lead ship *Soryu* was considered a very successful design and was used as the template for most future fleet carrier designs. Built on a lightly protected but fast hull, she embarked a large air group for her size of 54 aircraft. A high top speed of 34.5 knots was made possible by placing powerful machinery on a cruiser hull. *Soryu* epitomized the offensive mindset of the Imperial Navy when it came to carrier design. However, *Soryu* lacked an adequate level of protection against either bomb or torpedo attack. Near-sister *Hiryu* was completed more than two years later to a modified design. She carried the same number of aircraft, and her additional 1,400 tons of displacement gave the opportunity to add additional protection, though this was still unable to fully protect against bombs and torpedoes.

The two ships of the Shokaku class were commissioned in the months before the Pearl Harbor attack – *Shokaku* in August and *Zuikaku* in September. When complete, both were assigned to Carrier Division 5.

Designed without reference to treaty restrictions, they were the best carriers in the world when they entered service. The ships presented a fine balance of striking power (each could carry 72 aircraft), speed (34.5 knots), a heavy antiaircraft battery, and good protection.

In addition to its six fleet carriers, the Striking Force also included a powerful group of surface ships. Of the Imperial Navy's ten battleships available at the start of the war, two were committed to the Hawaii Operation. These were Kongo-class battleships *Hiei* and *Kirishima*. Both mounted eight 14-inch guns, the same size main battery carried by most of the American battleships in Pearl Harbor. Placed in commission originally during World War I as battlecruisers, both were extensively modernized between the wars and emerged as fast battleships. This extensive modernization included improvements in their protection, but by the standards of 1941 their protection against heavy naval guns and air attack was inadequate. However, with their speed of just over 30 knots, Kongo-class units were the only Japanese battleships to possess the speed necessary to operate with the fleet carriers. In any surface engagement against the Pacific Fleet's battle line, the Kongo class would have been outmatched. However, in any unfavorable tactical situation, *Hiei* and *Kirishima* had a considerable speed advantage over the Pacific Fleet's battlewagons (top speed 20–21 knots), so they could have disengaged at will.

Tone and *Chikuma* were Japan's most modern heavy cruisers and the only heavy cruisers from among the 18 in the Imperial Navy's order of battle to be assigned to escort the Striking Force. Commissioned between 1938 and 1939, both ships were designed to operate with the carrier force. All eight of their 8-inch guns were placed forward, leaving the entire aft portion of the ships available for aviation facilities; each ship could carry five floatplanes. Both cruisers also carried 12 torpedo tubes with 12 reloads. Considering that most Japanese heavy cruisers were well over the 10,000-ton treaty limit, they were superior fighting platforms in a surface engagement compared with their American counterparts.

Escorting the heavy ships of the Striking Force was Destroyer Squadron 1. Given its responsibility for protecting the Imperial Navy's most important ships, the Combined Fleet assigned its most modern destroyers to this formation. For the Hawaii Operation, Destroyer Squadron 1 had ten assigned units. These included the first of the

Yugumo-class, six Kagero-class, and two Asashio-class destroyers. All were modern units commissioned since 1939 and displaced over 2,000 tons at full-load displacement. Designed as torpedo platforms, these ships were powerful surface warfare platforms with eight torpedo tubes and eight reloads. Each destroyer also carried six 5-inch guns. Though excellent surface attack platforms, they were deficient in antiaircraft capabilities and were only mediocre antisubmarine platforms. Acting as the flagship of the squadron was light cruiser *Abukuma*.

Though Nagumo had no intention of being pulled into a surface engagement with American forces, at the start of the war, warships of the Imperial Navy were better prepared for surface actions than their USN counterparts. Japanese ships were generally better armed with longer-ranged weapons and their crews were better trained. In night combat, the Japanese advantage was even more pronounced. Night combat had acquired mythic importance for the Imperial Navy, which trained extremely hard for it and placed it at the center of its doctrine. In addition to superior training, tactics, and techniques, the Imperial Navy developed special optics and other equipment for night battle. Most importantly, Japanese destroyers, and light and heavy cruisers, mounted the Type 93 oxygen-propelled torpedo introduced in 1936. Far superior to any American torpedo, it possessed a warhead of 1,082 pounds, a top speed of up to 48 knots, and a maximum range of 43,746 yards.

JAPANESE CARRIER AIR GROUPS

Japanese fleet carrier air groups were comprised of three squadrons. One was equipped with carrier attack aircraft which could perform torpedo or horizontal bombing missions. A second squadron was equipped for dive-bombing and flew what the Japanese called carrier bombers. The final squadron was composed of fighters. At this point in the war, the Japanese gave priority to offensive capabilities, as evinced by the fact that the great majority of aircraft on each carrier were bombers as opposed to fighters. Even fighters could be used as attack aircraft, as was the case in the Pearl Harbor operation.

Each carrier attack aircraft and carrier bomber squadron was broken down into nine-aircraft *chutai* at the start of the war. The larger carriers carried three *chutai*, while the smaller carriers of Carrier Division 2 embarked only two. Fighter squadrons were broken down into

Striking Force Aircraft Strength, December 1941[16]

	Carrier attack aircraft	Carrier bombers (dive-bombers)	Fighters	Total
Akagi	27	18	18 (3)	63 (3)
Kaga	27	27	18 (3)	72 (3)
Soryu	18 (3)	18 (3)	18 (3)	54 (9)
Hiryu	18 (3)	18 (3)	18 (3)	54 (9)
Shokaku	27	27	18	72
Zuikaku	27	27	18	72
Total	144 (6)	135 (6)	108 (12)	387 (24)

The numbers in parentheses indicate reserve aircraft.

three-aircraft sections (called a *shotai*) built around the section lead and his two wingmen.

Japanese carriers embarked fewer aircraft than their American counterparts, primarily because of the American practice of keeping a portion of each carrier's air group on the flight deck (called a deck park) and not only on the hangar deck. Japanese carriers had two hangar decks, compared with the single hangar deck on American carriers. Since the Japanese kept all their aircraft on the hangar decks, eschewing the deck park technique, they could not embark as many aircraft as the Americans. However, the lack of a deck park provided more flexibility during flight operations. Extensive practice by Japanese deck crews made the carriers of the Striking Force highly proficient in handing aircraft.

The Striking Force was particularly impressive in the conduct of large-scale air operations. Because of the proficiency of deck crews, Japanese doctrine was built around quick launches of large strikes. For a large strike, each carrier brought aircraft from the hangar bays to the flight deck. Those aircraft spotted on the flight deck comprised a single deck load. The strike aircraft and their fighter escort were launched without the need to bring additional aircraft up to the flight deck for a second launch. This greatly reduced launch times and minimized coordination issues. To build a large strike, each carrier usually contributed two or three *shotai* of fighters. The two ships of each carrier division contributed either their carrier attack squadrons or their dive-bomber squadrons. The mix of which strike aircraft were launched in a strike was dependent on the target and other tactical considerations.

The carriers' other strike squadron was used for a second strike or held in reserve.

AIRCRAFT, TACTICS, AND TRAINING

The Striking Force's power rested on its ability to mass air power at key points and moments. Both the aircraft and aircrews aboard the carriers were excellent. The Imperial Navy was obsessed with producing a limited number of outstanding pilots instead of a large number of simply above-average aviators. Such a strategy was only viable in a short war. At the time of the Pearl Harbor attack, the state of training of the aviators on the carriers of Carrier Divisions 1 and 2 was very high; the training level of the new Carrier Division 5 was much less mature. Of the total pool of about 3,500 aviators, some 900 of the most outstanding were assigned to the carriers.[17] The best aviators were fighter pilots. Of these, the best, with an average of 800 flight hours, were assigned to fly carrier fighters.[18]

About 90 percent of the aviators were enlisted. In the Imperial Navy, future command prospects for aviators were limited, so there was little motivation for junior officers to apply for flight training. This meant that senior aviator command positions, like the commanding officers of carriers or their air groups, were not held by aviators. Only three of the six carrier captains at Pearl Harbor had received flight training. The lack of aviators at higher command levels meant they had much less influence over operations.[19]

Under Fuchida's oversight, intensive training began in late September for the Pearl Harbor attack. Fuchida concentrated on the horizontal bombers assigned to attack the ships moored in the harbor, and Lieutenant Commander Murata Shigeharu led the training for the torpedo bombers assigned to attack ships. Lieutenant Commander Shimazaki Shigekazu led the training for the horizontal bombers assigned to attack airfields. Lieutenant Commander Takahashi Kakuichi supervised training for the dive-bombers assigned to attack airfields, while Lieutenant Commander Egusa Takashige drilled the dive-bombers assigned to attack naval targets. Lieutenant Commander Itaya Shigeru was responsible for overseeing fighter training. For six weeks, training was intense. Several sorties per day were not unusual. Night training was attempted until it was realized that the new pilots in Carrier Division 5 would never master this skill in time, forcing the entire idea to be dropped.[20]

Initial training focused on discrete skills required by the different types of aircraft. No attempt was made to conduct combined training. In mid-October, Fuchida decided it was time for group training. Two sections were formed, one of all the fighters and the other with all the strike aircraft. Each engaged in exercise air combat with the other on four occasions. At the same time, the torpedo bombers practiced their attacks by attacking the fleet ten times over a two-week period.[21]

Given the complexity of the attack, a full-scale rehearsal was essential. The more rigorous the rehearsal, the better acquainted the participants were with their part in the operation and the greater the prospects for learning lessons and adjusting the plan where necessary. On November 4, the first rehearsal was conducted. The carriers launched the strike from about 200nm from the target – the first wave took off at 0700 and the second followed at 0830. Arriving in the target area, the first wave of torpedo and dive-bombers struck ships of the Combined Fleet at anchor. The second wave included dive-bombers and horizontal bombers.

The following day, another rehearsal attack took place with the same characteristics of the first. However this time, a defending force of fighters was deployed, prompting a mock air battle at 0900. This variation tested the reaction of the attack force if surprise was not achieved. Overall, the rehearsals were not a rigorous test. The air groups of Carrier Division 5 did not even take part, and the target area was not a close match to Pearl Harbor. Several issues were identified by Genda and Fuchida, covering most aspects of the attack. Among the most important were continuing problems with the torpedoes running too deep, accuracy problems with the horizontal bombers, and overconcentration on certain targets. The identification of the continuing torpedo problem alone made the rehearsal valuable, but based on the results of the actual attack, many of the other problems identified were not properly addressed or corrected.[22]

THE CHALLENGE OF HORIZONTAL BOMBING

Mastering the difficult skill of horizontal bombing was mandatory if the Pearl Harbor attack was to be successful. Horizontal bombing was conducted by the most important aircraft for the Pearl Harbor attack, the Nakajima B5N2 Navy Type 97 Carrier Attack Aircraft. Since Japanese aircraft designations were complex, early in the war the Allied came up with a standardized reporting system. The B5N2 Type 97 was given the reporting name of "Kate." Though neither the Japanese nor Americans referred to this aircraft as the Kate at the time of the attack, for simplicity's sake it will be referred to as such in this book. Introduced into fleet service in 1937, the Kate was approaching obsolescence in late 1941. Its ability to carry a heavy payload, either the Type 91 torpedo or the Type 99 bomb, made it integral to the success of the attack. It possessed decent speed, being capable of 235mph at about 12,000 feet. Even with a full payload, the Kate had a range of 528nm; with no payload this was extended to 1,075nm, making it a good reconnaissance aircraft.[23] The Kate's primary weakness was its inability to absorb punishment. No protection was provided for its three-man crew, and the aircraft lacked self-sealing fuel tanks. Defensive firepower was limited to a single 7.7mm rear-firing machine gun.

To tackle the issue of effectively attacking battleships with their heavy horizontal armor, the Japanese had to develop a new bomb suitable for use by the horizontal bombers. Tests indicated that the minimum weight for such a bomb had to be 1,760 pounds, assuming that it was dropped from 10,000 to 12,000 feet. To create such a weapon, the Japanese decided to modify a 16-inch shell into a bomb. Designated the Type 99 No. 80-3, it weighed 1,753 pounds with a bursting charge of 50 pounds. The 16-inch armor-piercing shell had its nose reshaped for better armor penetration, and the aft part of the shell was tapered for better aerodynamics. The fuse was also modified so that the bomb would explode upon penetration, not impact. Japanese engineers calculated that it could penetrate almost 6 inches of armor, more than adequate to deal with the American battleships at Pearl Harbor.[24]

The Japanese devoted much energy to solving the dilemma of how to hit ships with horizontal bombers flying at medium altitude. It was paramount that such a skill be mastered since only aircraft carrying heavy bombs had the kinetic energy to defeat the heavy armor found on battleships. For any attack on Pearl Harbor to succeed, accurate horizontal bombing was critical given the way that the Americans moored their battleships. Usually, they were moored in pairs around Ford Island, thus making the inner ship impervious to torpedo attack. The problem would be even worse if the Americans deployed torpedo nets around the ships, making any torpedo attack useless. Horizontal bombers carrying heavy bombs were necessary – dive-bombers with their relatively small bombs would make no impression on battleship armor. The problem was that each horizontal bomber carried only a single bomb, and their accuracy was poor.

Led by the carrier attack squadron on board *Akagi* under the dynamic leadership of Lieutenant Furukawa Izumi, the Japanese began to make progress on their horizontal bombing problem. Furukawa arrived on *Akagi* on April 10 and by the end of the month demonstrated that horizontal bombing was a viable tactic. Using a nine-aircraft formation, and attacking from 10,000 feet, he consistently recorded three to five hits on each bombing run. When asked by Genda what was responsible for the improvement, Furukawa's explanation was getting the pilot to work closer with the bombardier. The Japanese institutionalized this by pairing the pilot and the bombardier into a permanent team. The 1st Air Fleet placed one of these highly trained teams at the head of each bombing group as the lead plane. Once the lead pilot dropped his weapon, the rest of the group followed, thus raining nine bombs on the target.[25] The improvement from the previous 10 percent accuracy rate to a consistent 33 percent was a dramatic difference and gave the Japanese hope that the attack would be successful.

At the end of September, tests were conducted with the new bombs against an armor plate target set up to represent battleship *West Virginia*. After ten days, none of the aviators from the Yokosuka Naval Air Corps were able to hit the target. Nagumo agreed to send Fuchida and five hand-picked crews to conduct the test. On the third day of the new round of tests, one of the crews scored a direct hit. The bomb smashed through the armor plate, sending Fuchida to give Nagumo the good news.[26]

Proof that battleship armor could be penetrated by bombs dropped from 10,000 feet was an important discovery. Previously, 13,123 feet (4,000 meters) had been considered the minimum height to generate enough kinetic energy to punch through heavy armor; 18,404 feet (5,000 meters) was the best altitude to escape antiaircraft fire. With the latest test in mind, Fuchida convinced Nagumo, who was worried about the effects of enemy antiaircraft fire, to agree to the lower altitude. At the same time, Genda and Fuchida secured Nagumo's approval to change the standard nine-aircraft formation to a five-plane formation.

By so doing, more attack groups were created and more targets could be struck.[27]

Shaping the former 16-inch shell and adding more space in the internal cavity was a difficult process and was hard on the heavy machinery employed in the task. Only 150 bombs were produced before the machinery broke down.[28] Evidently, the workmanship was not of the highest order, since during the attack an inordinate numbers of bombs failed to detonate or resulted in a low-order detonation. The Japanese performed only a single successful test with the converted bomb yet still chose to rush it into production.

THE PROBLEM OF SHALLOW-WATER TORPEDO BOMBING

The tactic most preferred by the Japanese for attacking ships was using torpedoes. Torpedoes were seen as the most potent threat to enemy warships and could sink any type of ship, even battleships. In 1931, the Type 91 aerial torpedo was developed. It was capable of 42 knots but had a relatively short range of 2,200 yards. The short range was acceptable since the Japanese preferred the higher hit probability provided by launching from shorter ranges. Most of all, the Type 91 was a reliable weapon. Testimony to its excellent design was that it remained in service throughout the Pacific War.

Its capabilities allowed the Japanese to use attack profiles that increased the attacking aircraft's survivability. By 1937, carrier-based torpedo bombers were able to release their weapons up to an altitude of 660 feet at speeds up to 120 knots. In 1941, the attack profile was modified so that the attacking aircraft came in lower (at an altitude of 160–330 feet) and at a slightly higher speed (140–162 knots).[29] This was still a very vulnerable attack profile, and the Japanese expected that their torpedo aircraft would suffer heavy losses.

To use torpedoes in the attack, the Japanese overcame a number of technical and training issues. While the Imperial Navy extensively practiced attacking ships at sea with aerial torpedoes and had developed a mature set of tactics to do so, the attack on Pearl Harbor required a whole new set of skills. A successful attack against the Pacific Fleet while it was moored inside Pearl Harbor required shallow-water attack tactics and weapons. The waters of Pearl Harbor were some 40 feet deep; usually, when an aircraft dropped a heavy torpedo, it would dive to a much deeper depth before adjusting to its pre-set running depth. Not wanting to have their torpedoes settle into the mud of Pearl Harbor, the Japanese endeavored to ensure that their torpedoes did not dive below 33 feet. That such a capability might be required was acknowledged by the Japanese in 1939, well before Yamamoto started to dream about attacking Pearl Harbor. During the Combined Fleet's annual exercise in 1939, it attempted to attack enemy warships in a bay off Kyushu, but the attempt was thwarted by shallow waters. This prompted an examination of the problem. Though not quickly solved, it became apparent that the Type 91 would have to be modified so that it did not go to a depth greater than 39 feet after launch. In addition, an entire new set of tactics was required.[30]

Solving the technical aspects of this challenge was accomplished first. Mindful that the torpedo's technical characteristics had to perform both in flight and in the water, the Japanese came up with a solution that would work in both environments. Wooden extensions were added to the metal horizontal and vertical fins at the torpedo's tail. These slowed the descent of the weapon and made it enter the water at a more shallow angle, which resulted in the torpedo not diving so deeply. The wooden fins broke away when the torpedo hit the water, placing it in a form conducive for hydrodynamic performance. To address the roll problem once the torpedo was in the water, anti-roll stabilizers were placed at the rear of the torpedo.[31] Adding the wooden extensions cut the torpedo's dive to 60 feet or less by February 1940. When dropped from a height of less than 100 feet at speeds below 150 knots, 70 percent of the torpedoes dove to about 40 feet.[32]

If the modified Type 91s were to be successfully employed, a new flight profile had to be developed and the aviators trained to use it. As early as June, Genda began an intensive program of torpedo practice since he believed that this was the hardest technique to perfect. A part of Kagoshima Bay, east of Kagoshima City, Kyushu was selected for the training because of its similarity to Pearl Harbor. In October, the most experienced Kate pilots were selected to train as torpedo bombers; the others were focused on horizontal bombing training. At the same time, Fuchida decided that the torpedo bombers would attack in a single-file formation to avoid the many obstructions inside Pearl Harbor.

Leading the way to develop viable shallow-water tactics was Lieutenant Commander Murata, considered the Imperial Navy's top specialist in

THE STRIKING FORCE

aerial torpedoes. In the summer of 1941, he assumed command of *Akagi*'s torpedo squadron for the express purpose of developing the techniques required for a Pearl Harbor attack. Over the following months, he flew countless mock attacks in the shallow waters of Kagoshima Bay. Promoted to lieutenant commander on October 15, Murata was having problems getting the torpedoes to work as required. Even after extensive training to fly the correct profile, they were still running 66 feet deep. Genda and Fuchida considered telling the men why Murata was pressing them so hard, thinking that would make it easier for them to endure. But, in the end, the torpedo bomber aircrews weren't informed of the real reason for their intense training.[33]

It would take some very skillful flying to employ torpedoes in the shallow waters of Pearl Harbor. Just getting to their launch positions required pilots to navigate the hills around the harbor and shipyard obstructions within it. On their final attack run, pilots had to attain proper air speed and altitude to ensure that the torpedo entered the water at an angle of 17–20 degrees. If the torpedo was dropped at too high of an altitude, the resulting angle of entry caused the weapon to dive too deep. If it was dropped at too low of an altitude, the Type 91 would strike the water at a shallow angle, forcing it to skip on the water or even break up. Only by intense training could the pilots learn to handle the many factors required for a successful launch. Each had to find the correct altitude, based only on his skill, as the aircraft's altimeter did not work at such a low altitude. At the same time, the pilot had to fly the correct speed, select the correct target, and then ascertain the correct range and approach to the target. In addition, he had to launch the torpedo outside of 650 feet to the target or it would not arm in time.[34] While the pilot was trying to keep the correct air speed and altitude, the observer (who was generally the senior airman), provided guidance on the correct azimuth to the target.

As late as the November rehearsals, the torpedoes continued to dive too deep. Almost in desperation, Genda and Murata devised a new flight profile to solve the problem. This required the pilot to fly level with flaps up at about 60 feet off the water at 140–150 knots. Combined with the torpedo modifications, the Japanese finally had a viable method to use torpedoes inside Pearl Harbor. In a series of tests on November 11–13, aircraft from *Akagi* and *Kaga* were able to achieve a success rate of 83 percent. It took until mid-November to solve the torpedo problem. This achievement was remarkable and was essential to the success of the entire operation.

Modifying the torpedoes took time, forcing the Japanese to overcome one more hurdle. Production of the modified torpedo was expedited to meet the attack timeline. By the end of November, the Nagasaki Navy Arsenal had built a total of 120 torpedoes. The first 50 built were distributed to *Akagi*, *Soryu*, and *Hiryu* in mid-November before they moved up to the Kuriles. Another batch of 50 was loaded on *Kaga* but did not arrive at Hitokappu Bay until November 24, just two days before the Striking Force's departure.

THE IMPERIAL NAVY AND DIVE-BOMBING

As was the case for torpedo bombing, the Imperial Navy needed a suitable aircraft before dive-bombing tactics could be fully developed. The first aircraft designed specifically for dive-bombing was the Aichi D1A1 Type 94 Carrier Bomber, adopted in 1934. Its replacement was the Aichi D3A1 Navy Type 99 Carrier Bomber Model 11. This aircraft was later given the Allied reporting name of "Val" and will be referred to as such in this book. Based loosely on a German design, the D3A1 variant entered service in 1940. Despite its antiquated appearance with its fixed landing gear, the Val was a steady and accurate dive-bomber. Like other Japanese aircraft, it was not fitted with self-sealing fuel tanks, making it vulnerable to enemy fire. Flying at about 10,000 feet, the Val could make its best speed of 240mph.[35]

Equipped with two 7.7mm machine guns in the engine cowling and a single rear-firing 7.7mm machine gun, and possessing good maneuverability, the Val stood a chance against enemy fighters. For all its strengths, the Val had one glaring weakness – its inability to carry a large payload. Its maximum payload was a 551-pound semi-armor-piercing weapon fitted on its centerline and two 132-pound bombs under the wings. American dive-bombers of the time could carry 1,000-pound bombs.

Using the Val, in 1940–41 Japanese dive-bombing tactics were refined, led by Lieutenant Takahashi Sadamu. For striking ships at sea, the standard tactic at the start of the war called for the dive-bombers to approach a target starting at about 10,000 feet. Ships were attacked along their length, not their beam, to increase the chances of a hit. Once the attack had begun, the dive-bombers formed an echelon formation, went to full power, and began a 10-degree dive. When the group was close enough to the target, the lead pilot started a 65-degree dive and aimed for the top of the target ship's foremast. Typical bomb release altitude was about 2,000 feet above the target. Subsequent aircraft in the formation adjusted their aim point based on the results of the leading aircraft. Takahashi's new tactics accounted for an improved accuracy of 55 percent in 1941.[36]

In the months of training before the attack, Lieutenant Commander Egusa Takashige, leader of Carrier Division 2's dive-bombers, advocated for a more aggressive attack profile. Egusa was universally seen as the Imperial Navy's best dive-bomber pilot. He was a gifted leader as well – Genda stated that his ability to lead units in combat was "godlike."[37] Egusa was appointed to direct the training of Carrier Division 1 and 2 bomber squadrons. Instead of the accepted attack profile of diving at 65 degrees and dropping the weapon at 2,000 feet, Egusa waited until 1,500 feet until he released his bomb. In dive-bombing, the lower the drop, the greater the accuracy. The difference in accuracy was great enough that Fuchida and later Nagumo approved the new profile even though there was a greater risk of the pilot not being able to pull out of his dive.[38]

The standard weapon for the Val was one semi-armor-piercing Type 99 No. 25 551-pound ordinary bomb. Adopted in 1939, it was assessed to be capable of penetrating about 2 inches of horizontal armor. Due to its relatively small weight and the fact that it was dropped so close to the target, it lacked the power to penetrate battleship armor. The Japanese were confident though that it could cripple carriers and cruisers.[39] Also available was the Type 98 No. 25 532-pound land-attack bomb with a high-explosive warhead fused for instantaneous detonation.

IMPERIAL NAVY CARRIER FIGHTERS

Fuchida, with his background in horizontal bombing, did not spend much time overseeing fighter training. Genda, with his background as a fighter pilot, took a greater interest. The main contribution both men made in this area was securing the best available fighter pilots to fill out the Striking Force's six squadrons of fighters. Both agreed to add energetic fighter pilots to supplement those with China experience who might not readily adjust to new tactics. On September 24, in a meeting between the Combined Fleet and the Naval General Staff, it was agreed to strip experienced fighter pilots from Carrier Divisions 3 and 4 for Divisions 1 and 2, thus allowing an expansion of the fighter squadrons on the ships allocated to the Pearl Harbor attack. Pilots were also stripped from the Yokosuka Air Group, even if it meant a negative impact on training. By such means the fighter squadrons of the six Pearl Harbor carriers were brought up to full strength by early November.[40]

Without doubt, the most famous Japanese carrier aircraft of the war was the Mitsubishi A6M2 Model 21 Navy Type 0 Carrier Fighter. Given the Allied reporting name of "Zeke" later in the war, it was better known as the "Zero" and will be referred to as such in this book. The Zero had many great qualities. Among these was a long range when using a drop tank, heavy armament of two 7.7mm machine guns in the engine cowling and two 20mm cannons in the wings, and outstanding maneuverability. As a dogfighter, it was unsurpassed at low and medium altitudes. The Zero possessed a superb rate of climb and a respectable 331mph top speed.

In the first few months of the war, the Zero achieved legendary status. It did have weaknesses, though these weren't readily apparent on December 7. The Zero's outstanding performance was directly due to it having been designed with an airframe as light as possible. Therefore, it possessed almost no protection and lacked self-sealing fuel tanks as well.

For fleet air defense, Zero fighters were not ideal aircraft. On the one hand, they exhibited a good rate of climb so could get to altitude quickly after scrambling. Their long endurance permitted lengthy patrols. Shortcomings in this role included poor radios and a small ammunition load. For the wing-mounted 20mm cannons, only 60 rounds per gun were carried. Once the 20mm rounds were spent, the Zero's hitting power rested with its woefully inadequate 7.7mm light machine guns.

The basic tactical formation used by the Zero was the *shotai* composed of the leader and his two wingmen. Japanese fighter pilots were highly proficient in gunnery and constant drills made the *shotai* a coherent formation. The preferred tactic was a hit-and-run attack – dogfighting, at which the highly maneuverable Zero was excellent, was not encouraged.

Communication between fighters and their parent ships or even between fighters was a major issue. At the start of the war, the Japanese relied on the Type 96 radio telephone. Though it entered service in 1936, it was still being installed in aircraft when the war began. Transmission was affected by interference and reception was unclear. Radio transmissions could not be used over long distances. Only by means of a radio telegraph could messages be carried at long distances from the aircraft to their home ship. As a result, fighter pilots had to rely on various signal methods to share information.[41] Because the Pearl Harbor attack would be launched over 200nm from the target, all aircrew taking part in the operation had to learn Morse code, even the fighter pilots already overburdened in their single-man cockpit.[42]

With Lieutenant Commander Itaya from *Akagi* overseeing the training, the fighter squadrons focused on basic skills, formation flying, but apparently no combat training. Not even strafing was practiced. Pilots from *Shokaku* and *Zuikaku* spent the bulk of their training achieving basic carrier qualifications. It is important to note that in the course of this training combined training was not attempted. Doctrinally, Japanese fighters did accompany the bombers to their target, but they did not provide a close escort to the strike aircraft.

STRIKING FORCE SEARCH DOCTRINE

Had the Pacific Fleet not been caught inside Pearl Harbor, the Striking Force would have had to execute air searches to find it. Search operations were an area of weakness for the Japanese. The primary reason was the Imperial Navy's offensive mindset. This focus meant the Japanese sought to keep the maximum number of aircraft available for strikes, not searches. By doctrine, the Japanese planned to devote only 10 percent of aircraft to reconnaissance.[43] Given this mindset, the ideal solution was to use the floatplanes on escorting battleships and cruisers for search missions, thus saving the carrier aircraft for strikes. The problem with this was that few floatplanes were available, and of these even fewer were suitable as search aircraft.

For the Hawaii Operation, the Striking Force carried 15 floatplanes. The best floatplanes were the Aichi E13A1 Navy Type 0 Reconnaissance Seaplane Model 11 (later known as "Jake" under the Allied aircraft reporting system). *Tone* and *Chikuma* each carried two of these aircraft. In the search role, the Jake was an excellent aircraft with a long range of 1,128nm and a three-man crew. Top speed was 234mph at just over 7,000 feet.[44] However, its limited top speed and poor defensive armament made it very vulnerable to enemy fighters if it was intercepted. Complementing the four Jakes were ten Nakajima E8N2 Navy Type 95 Reconnaissance Seaplane Model One aircraft. It dated from 1933 and was in the process of being replaced by the much more capable Jake. The Type 95 later received the reporting Allied name "Dave." Both battleships carried three, and the two heavy cruisers embarked two more each. Since it was designed as a spotter aircraft for naval gunnery, its range of only 485nm made it a poor choice for search missions.[45] It was maneuverable, but its low top speed and poor defensive armament made it vulnerable to interception. The final type of floatplane in the Striking Force was a Kawanishi E7K2 Navy Type 94 Reconnaissance Seaplane Model 12 "Alf" carried aboard *Abukuma*.[46] Thus, unless Nagumo allocated Kates to search missions, the Striking Force possessed a limited number of air reconnaissance assets.

There were other problems with Japanese search operations. As demonstrated in the months following Pearl Harbor, the ship recognition skills of Japanese search aircraft crews were weak and accurate navigation also proved difficult. The reporting aircraft had to know its own position to accurately report the location of the target. Communications were also an issue – use of radio telegraphs required skilled Morse Code or other coded signals operators. Aircrew on search aircraft possessed such skills, but aircrew on attack aircraft assigned to search missions usually did not.[47]

STRIKING FORCE AIR DEFENSE CAPABILITIES

Though not understood in December 1941, the Striking Force's air defense capabilities made it vulnerable to air attack. All of the building blocks of fleet air defense were challenges for the Japanese. Had the Americans been able to mount a counterattack, the Striking Force could have suffered losses, just as many Japanese Navy officers feared.

The greatest air defense weakness of the Striking Force was a lack of early warning. Since no Japanese ships carried radar at this point of the war, detection of approaching enemy aircraft was dependent on the visual acuity of lookouts on ships or from fighters aloft.

Japanese air defense doctrine called for a standing fighter patrol (called combat air patrol or CAP). However, the limited number of fighters allocated to defensive patrols made it impossible to conduct a standing CAP with anything more than a token number of aircraft. By doctrine, half of the 18-aircraft fighter squadron was dedicated for CAP, with the other half devoted to escorting strike missions. From the nine fighters allocated to fleet air defense, each carrier kept one *shotai* aloft on CAP (with a patrol time of about two hours), another ready to launch, and the third in a lesser degree of readiness. The other two *shotai* could be launched once a threat was detected.[48]

Successful air defense required adept control of airborne fighters against approaching threats. Here the Japanese had real problems. Direction of fighters was a learned skill, with control of airborne fighters falling upon the air defense officer. Though this was a specialized task, this duty was assigned on a rotating basis, making it impossible for any one officer to gain deep expertise. Perhaps most importantly, actual control of the fighters on CAP was nearly impossible because of the poor quality of voice radios on the fighters.[49] Adding to the confusion was the fact that all airborne aircraft, not just those on CAP, used a single frequency.[50] All of this meant that the fighter pilots themselves had to perform an instant threat prioritization and allocate fighters against threats accordingly. Sitting in a cockpit, a *shotai* leader had very limited situational awareness. Thus, a multi-axis or multi-altitude threat had the real potential to overwhelm the Striking Force's air defense system. However, if the threat was detected early enough and was presented sequentially, the Japanese air defense system could cope.

After the CAP, the next line of defense was provided by the ships' antiaircraft batteries. In theory, since carriers, battleships, cruisers, and even destroyers of the Striking Force were fitted with both long- and short-range antiaircraft weapons, a layered defense against air attack was possible.

Unfortunately for the Striking Force, neither layer was effective. The outer layer was provided by 4.7-inch and 5-inch guns. Only *Akagi* was fitted with the older 4.7-inch weapon; the mainstay Imperial Navy long-range antiaircraft weapon was the Type 89 5-inch High Angle Gun fitted on the other heavy ships of the Striking Force. This was a reliable weapon and possessed a fairly high elevation speed and a high muzzle velocity. However, it was limited by its fire control system, the Type 94 High Angle Fire Control Installation. Because the system required an extensive number of data inputs to be made manually, the Type 94 had issues dealing with high-speed targets. The analog computer-generated fire control solutions were often inaccurate.[51] As a result, long-range antiaircraft fire was reduced to less effective barrage fire instead of aimed fire at individual targets.

The inner layer of fleet air defense was an even greater problem for the Japanese. That was attributable to the Imperial Navy's poor selection of the Type 96 25mm antiaircraft gun as its mainstay short-range antiaircraft gun. Simply stated, the Type 96 was an inferior weapon – its shortcomings included inadequate training and elevation speeds, a low sustained rate of fire, and excessive vibration and muzzle blast that affected accuracy. Its small 0.6-pound projectile was often ineffective against rugged American aircraft.[52] The Type 96 possessed an approximate 1,500-yard effective range, but this was already at the point where the dive-bomber was well into its dive.[53] Other factors inhibiting the Type 96's effectiveness were the low numbers fitted to ships at this point in the war and its fire control system. The Type 95 Short-range High-Angle Director was not accurate and was unable to handle high-speed targets.[54]

If attacking American aircraft survived the CAP and antiaircraft fire, there was one more asset the Japanese could employ to defeat air attack. This was the overlooked but very effective measure of skillful maneuvering. Imperial Navy doctrine recognized its importance and gave maneuver primacy over firepower.[55] Ships were allowed to maneuver freely rather than maintaining formation to provide supporting fire to protect the carriers. Against horizontal, torpedo, and dive-bomber attack, the best hope of avoiding damage was skillful evasive maneuvering. This was easy to accomplish against horizontal bombing, less so against torpedo attack, and very difficult to achieve against well-trained dive-bomber pilots.

After describing all of the potential issues the Striking Force had with air defense, it is worthwhile to review the maritime strike capabilities of the American air forces on and around Oahu. The Japanese were very concerned with land-based air power's capacity to deliver serious blows to the Striking Force. In retrospect, this was severely overblown. None of the strike aircraft on Oahu were trained for maritime attack, and all depended on horizontal bombing. The main strike aircraft was the Boeing B-17 Flying Fortress high-altitude heavy bomber. Touted by the Army Air Force as capable of conducting precision bombing against ships at sea, the reality was much different. Dropping their bombs from an altitude of 18,000–20,000 feet, ships below had adequate time to maneuver out of danger. As an example, when ships of the Striking Force came under B-17 attack at the Battle of Midway just six months later, none of the avalanche of 291 bombs dropped from B-17s found its target. Though ineffective in the maritime strike role, B-17s flying at altitude were virtually immune from Japanese antiaircraft fire. Interception of the heavily armed bombers was difficult for Zeros.

More numerous than the B-17s on Oahu were Douglas B-18 Bolo medium bombers. Obsolescent by 1941, the B-18 was slow, had an inadequate defensive armament, and carried a small bomb load. Delivering their attacks at lower altitudes than the B-17, they would have been very vulnerable to interception from the Zeros on CAP. Also present on Oahu was a small number of more modern Douglas A-20 Havoc light bombers. Though faster and thus more survivable against fighter attack, they possessed little ability to hit ships. Thus, the Army Air Force possessed very limited maritime strike capabilities.

On the other hand, the aircraft aboard USN carriers posed a potential mortal threat to the Striking Force. Each American carrier embarked an air group with one torpedo squadron, two squadrons of dive-bombers, and a fighter squadron. As events in the following months confirmed, the standard American torpedo bomber, the Douglas TBD-1 Devastator, was a minimal threat to well-defended Japanese shipping because of its slow speed and unreliable torpedo.[56] Conversely, the Douglas SBD Dauntless dive-bomber was a superior aircraft to the Val. Its well-trained aircrews could hit maneuvering targets, and their 1,000-pound bombs had the potential to deal mortal blows to carriers. The Japanese were justifiably concerned about Pacific Fleet carriers launching attacks against the Striking Force.

WAS THE STRIKING FORCE CAPABLE OF CONDUCTING ITS MISSION?

In order to make the Pearl Harbor attack possible, the Japanese solved many technical problems and created new capabilities. Foremost among these was a new doctrine for massing its aircraft carriers. Many technical issues, each having the potential to derail the attack, were also solved. Among these was the development of new weapons, in particular a modified torpedo for shallow-water attacks, and a heavy bomb for attacking battleships. In conjunction with the development of these weapons, new techniques were also developed and aircrews were trained in their use.

In just nine months, from April until December 1941, the Imperial Navy had created an entirely new and powerful capability. During this short span of time, the Japanese created the capability to mass carrier-based air power and employ it at long distances from its bases. This was nothing less than revolutionary. The Americans were unable to track or understand this development. As a result, they were caught by surprise when it was unveiled for the first time.

Underpinning the capabilities of massed Japanese naval air power was a combination of good aircraft flown by excellent aviators. The Zero fighter was superior to anything the Americans had on Oahu. Flown by experienced pilots, the Zero could clear the skies of defending fighters and gain temporary air control over the island. Japanese strike aircraft were more than capable of dealing the Pacific Fleet serious damage. American battleships were vulnerable to torpedo attack, and recent Japanese advances in horizontal bombing increased the probability that the bulk of the American battle line could be crippled. Since they were a top-priority target, the American battle fleet faced an avalanche of torpedoes and heavy bombs dropped by aviators honed to a fine edge. If the Pacific Fleet's carriers had been in port, they would have received special attention in the form of torpedo attack and follow-up dive-bombings. Highly trained dive-bomber crews could wreak havoc against their assigned targets. With accuracy honed against ships at sea, the Japanese expected a rich harvest against ships caught in port. A similar result was probable against American Army and Navy aircraft caught on the ground.

In assessing the prospects for Japanese success, the biggest wildcard was the element of surprise. Were surprise to be achieved, the prospects of inflicting the crippling blow Yamamoto was planning increased dramatically. Without it, Japanese aviators would still press home their attacks and cause a lesser degree of damage, though at a much higher price to themselves. Since the actual attack was mounted with the benefit of surprise, the flaws in Japanese planning and the vulnerabilities of their aircraft and ships were largely camouflaged. Whether it gained surprise or not, the Striking Force was ready to open the war in dramatic fashion.

5

The Pacific Fleet and Pearl Harbor Defenses

THE PACIFIC FLEET

Considered the most powerful component of the American military, and stationed in the fortress of Hawaii, the USN's Pacific Fleet appeared to be in an unassailable position in December 1941. After examining its commanders, ships, and aircraft, it becomes immediately apparent that it was less powerful and certainly less ready for war than it appeared. The strength of the fortress charged with the defense of the fleet was also illusional.

The man overseeing the Pacific Fleet was Husband E. Kimmel. Born in 1882 in a small town in northwestern Kentucky, Kimmel unsuccessfully tried to get into the Military Academy at West Point before gaining admission to Annapolis. Upon graduation, he was 13th out of a class of 62. With his insistence on order and efficiency, combined with an unequivocal work ethic, he climbed the ranks. Kimmel's background was in gunnery, and in particular, battleship gunnery. He commanded battleship *New York* in 1933 before assuming an important staff job as chief of staff of Commander, Battleships, Battle Force. After serving in Washington and achieving flag rank in 1937, he returned to sea as commander of a division of heavy cruisers. In 1939, he was appointed as Commander, Cruisers, Battle Force.

Admiral Kimmel assumed command of the Pacific Fleet on February 1, 1941. In every way, he appeared up for the job. Thirty-seven years of naval service had led him to this point. To assume his new job, Kimmel was promoted over 31 more senior admirals. His actual title was Commander in Chief of the United States Fleet, but this was mainly honorific. Kimmel's real job was focused on his duties as Commander in Chief of the Pacific Fleet. Not being a political admiral, he was selected for his new job by virtue of his abilities. Kimmel was a man of energy, strong will, and professional integrity. His physical demeanor spoke of position and authority. He was able to engender loyalty from his staff and showed it in return. Kimmel was able to calm interservice rivalries on Oahu, but this did not translate into a close working relationship with his Army counterpart on the island.

In a far-sighted move, Kimmel moved his offices from battleship *Pennsylvania* to the fleet headquarters building located at the submarine base. It was much more efficient for the fleet commander to work ashore where he could communicate without restriction and not interfere in the training plan of his former flagship.

However, Kimmel was not without faults. According to his superior officer, Admiral Harold R. Stark, Chief of Naval Operations, Kimmel could be brusque dealing with other officers, but was always open to reason. Though usually pleasant and level-headed, he was known for his temper. He worked to excess and dwelled on details and appearances. Thus, it was not surprising that Kimmel was short on imagination.

On February 15, Kimmel sent a letter to his new command outlining possible scenarios for an attack on the fleet. In it, he made the bizarre assertion that while no responsible foreign power would attempt to attack the fleet, irresponsible foreign nationals could. Thus, from the start, he was confident that Japan would not attack the United States, but that some individuals acting without orders might. The letter postulated that an attack could come from submarines attacking ships in Hawaiian waters or by a surface force including aircraft carriers. The mental gymnastics contained in the letter were noteworthy. Kimmel believed that the Combined Fleet would not attack, but some unpredictable commander would be able to take part of the fleet and steam 3,000nm to attack on his own.[1] This was an unrealistic threat framework to start with for the new commander.

Just days later, on February 15, Stark sent a letter to Kimmel dismissing the possibility of a torpedo bomber attack on the fleet inside Pearl Harbor. It stated the prevalent thinking at the time that the harbor was too shallow since a minimum depth of 75 feet was required to

THE PACIFIC FLEET AND PEARL HARBOR DEFENSES

successfully air launch a torpedo. Thus, as stated in the letter, there was no need to employ anti-torpedo nets.

Rising tensions in the Pacific coincided with Kimmel's tenure as commander of the Pacific Fleet. As a matter of course, he acted on these warnings in a half-hearted manner or not at all. When the government of Prime Minister Konoye fell under pressure from hard-liners on October 16, the mood in Washington was that conflict was getting closer. Stark sent a strong warning to Kimmel that Japan might resort to war against the United States and Britain. In response, Kimmel took some measures to defend Wake, Midway, Johnston, and Palmyra and increased security around Pearl Harbor. Aware that the Pacific Fleet was inferior to the Combined Fleet after a series of transfers to the Atlantic Fleet in April, Kimmel requested reinforcements, including the new battleships *North Carolina* and *Washington*, submarines, and cruisers. Stark's reply on November 7 turned down this request. Furthermore, he added a cautionary note that the crisis in the Pacific was coming to a head and that anything could happen in the next month.

On November 27, Kimmel received another warning message from the Navy Department. It needs to be quoted in full:

> This dispatch is to be considered a war warning. Negotiations with Japan looking toward stabilization of conditions in the Pacific have ceased and an aggressive move by Japan is expected within the next few days. The number and equipment of Japanese troops and the organization of the naval task forces indicates an amphibious expedition against either the Philippines Thai or Kra Peninsula or possibly Borneo. Execute an appropriate defensive deployment preparatory to carrying out the tasks assigned in WPL 46. Inform district and army authorities. A similar warning is being sent by War Department...[2]

Immediately upon its receipt, Kimmel's staff began to dissect the message. The key first sentence, meant to be strong and leave no room for misinterpretation, failed to have its desired impact on Oahu. Though not mentioned specifically as a Japanese target, Washington expected forces in Hawaii to make "appropriate defensive deployment." In the mind of the Navy Department, this included a high degree of readiness by all forces and enhanced reconnaissance.

Kimmel saw it differently. He noted that the message appeared to pertain to other locations but not Hawaii. The most likely form of attack against the Pacific Fleet was by enemy submarines, so for the first time he ordered that any submarine contacts around Oahu be attacked by depth charges. That was the extent of new security measures. Kimmel decided against increasing the readiness conditions of ships inside Pearl Harbor. Even more critically, he failed to order additional reconnaissance around Oahu. This measure was specially prescribed in the War Department's message to his Army counterpart, General Walter Short, but as Kimmel was well aware, this mission was solely the responsibility of the Navy. In fact, the matter was not even discussed with the commander of the long-range PBY flying boats based on Oahu. That commander was entirely unaware of the continued warning messages from the Navy and War Departments delivered over the past two months so was not sufficiently informed to recommend increased reconnaissance patrols.

Given Kimmel's mindset that an attack on Pearl Harbor was unlikely and that readiness of the fleet was paramount so that it could undertake offensive operations as quickly as possible, none of Washington's urgings to take more defensive measures registered with him. His thinking is reflected in one sentence: "It was absolutely essential that we maintain training in the Pacific Fleet up to the last minute."[3]

Kimmel never had a clear conception of Japanese capabilities. At times he recognized that the Japanese had the capability to attack Pearl Harbor, but most of his comments to his staff dismissed discrete portions of Japanese capabilities until there was nothing left to worry about. Kimmel downplayed the ability of the Japanese to conduct a carrier air attack given the short range of Japanese carriers. There was something to this, but the Japanese had overcome this limitation. Kimmel gave the Japanese no ability to overcome obstacles. While he understood that the Japanese could send submarines to the Hawaiian Islands, he entirely dismissed any Japanese ability to send submarines into the harbor itself. As a result, the net at the entrance of the harbor was not an antisubmarine net; it was an anti-torpedo net designed to prevent Japanese submarines from sitting outside the harbor and sending torpedoes up the channel.[4]

Foremost among the reasons why no precautionary action was necessary in Kimmel's mind was that the fleet had "to be ready for offensive action."[5] Excessive operations not related to training were

THE PACIFIC FLEET AND PEARL HARBOR DEFENSES

undesirable since they reduced readiness. Another reason was a fuel problem that curtailed the number of ships that could be kept at sea at a given time without depleting the fuel supply for the fleet. In addition, it took time to refuel ships. Only one-eighth of the fleet could be refueled in a 12-hour period.[6] After the "war warning" messages of November 27, another factor entered his calculation. The Army's version of the "war warning" message directed Short not to alarm the civilian population with any measures he took. Kimmel was aware of this stipulation and also took care to comply. This was part of the reason he decided to keep the bulk of the fleet in Pearl Harbor between the November 27 alert and the actual attack – sudden departure of the fleet could have created alarm.

PACIFIC FLEET ORGANIZATION

The previous Pacific Fleet commander, Admiral James O. Richardson, routinely had half the fleet out of harbor at any one time.[7] Kimmel changed this operating posture about one month into his tenure. He divided the fleet into three task forces and kept one or two at sea. Each ship typically spent 40 percent of its time at sea.[8] Each task force nominally included a carrier component and three battleships, but its actual composition was dependent on what ships were operational and what the mission of the task force was at a given time.

Task Force 1 was under the command of Vice Admiral William S. Pye. Pye was the senior officer in the fleet after Kimmel and carried the title Commander, Battle Force (the fleet's battleships). As the next most senior officer, he was the de facto deputy commander of the fleet. Pye had a great reputation as a strategist. He was familiar with the Pacific Fleet's war plans since he had drafted them in his previous tour in the War Plan Division of the Navy Department.

Task Force 2 was commanded by Vice Admiral William F. Halsey, in his role as Commander, Aircraft, Battle Force (the fleet's aircraft carriers). Halsey was the exact opposite of Kimmel: gruff, outspoken, and extremely aggressive. Having earned his aviator wings at the age of 51, he was the Navy's senior aviator and its most experienced carrier commander. Kimmel and Halsey got along well.

Vice Admiral Wilson Brown was in charge of Task Force 3 and also wore the hat of Commander, Scouting Force (the fleet's heavy cruisers).

Brown was new to the Pacific Fleet, having arrived in February, and had a background in submarines and gunnery. When asked about the possibility of a Japanese air attack on Pearl Harbor, his response was typical for American naval leaders of the period: "Japanese fliers were not capable of executing such a mission successfully, and if they did, we should certainly be able to follow their planes back to their carriers and destroy the carriers so that it would be a very expensive experiment."[9]

Task Force 4 was under the command of Rear Admiral Claude C. Bloch, who also wore the hat of Commandant, 14th Naval District. As Task Force 4 commander, he was responsible for the local defense of Pearl Harbor and the other Hawaiian islands, as well as Wake, Midway, Johnston, and Palmyra. In this capacity, Bloch submitted a memo on December 30, 1940, on "Situation Concerning the Security of the Fleet and the Present Ability of the Local Defense Forces to Meet Surprise Attacks." In it, he outlined the threat from a carrier-launched air attack and the inability of air defense forces under Army command to deal with such an attack. The memo went on to state that his local defense forces were similarly unable to cope with enemy submarine attack.[10]

Rear Admiral Patrick Bellinger, a naval aviator, was an important figure in the defense of Pearl Harbor as Commander Task Force 9. In this capacity, he controlled all the long-range patrol aircraft based on Oahu and other outlying locations. Finally, Task Force 7, Commander Submarines Scouting Force, was under the command of Rear Admiral Thomas Withers, Jr., a former submarine and battleship skipper.

SHIPS OF THE PACIFIC FLEET

On paper, the heart of the fleet's fighting power was its contingent of battleships. Of the 15 older battleships in the USN, nine were assigned to the Pacific Fleet in December 1941. This was considered a superior fighting force to the ten Japanese battleships in service at the time since four of the Japanese ships were former battlecruisers with a lighter scale of protection. In general, American battleships were more heavily protected than their Japanese counterparts and possessed at least a comparable level of firepower. However, the weakness of the older American battleships was their low top speed; they were unable to operate with the carriers because of this disparity. Being much slower than their Japanese counterparts would have allowed the Japanese to select the time and place of a major fleet engagement. All older American battleships were heavily modernized between the wars and received upgrades in protection and firepower. Even so, their underwater protection remained suspect. At the start of the war, antiaircraft protection aboard these ships was also deficient.[11]

Both Nevada-class ships (*Nevada* and *Oklahoma*) were assigned to the Pacific Fleet. These second-generation American dreadnought designs were powerfully armed with a main battery of ten 14-inch guns but possessed a maximum speed of less than 20 knots. The succeeding Pennsylvania class (*Pennsylvania* and *Arizona*) had broadly the same capabilities but carried a heavier main battery of 12 14-inch guns. By the time the Tennessee class was commissioned in 1920–21, protection (and underwater protection in particular) had been enhanced. The two ships of this class, *Tennessee* and *California*, were both assigned to the Pacific Fleet. They carried a main battery of 12 14-inch guns. The last American battleships built before the Washington Naval Treaty of 1922 curtailed future battleship construction were the three ships of the Colorado class (*Colorado*, *Maryland*, *West Virginia*). These were effectively Tennessee-class ships with an upgraded main battery of 16-inch guns. With three 16-inch gun ships compared with the Imperial Fleet's two, the USN had a firepower advantage in any potential battle line clash.

While the battleship was still viewed by most Navy officers as the arbiter of naval power, aircraft carriers were a very important component of the Pacific Fleet. In the minds of the USN's air power advocates, the carrier was already the fleet's principal striking component. In December 1941, the USN possessed seven fleet carriers, but at the time of the attack only three were deployed in the Pacific. This included both Lexington-class ships (*Lexington* and *Saratoga*) and the Yorktown-class carrier *Enterprise*. The first two were the largest aircraft carriers in the world, having been converted from battlecruisers and commissioned in 1927. Commissioned in 1938, *Enterprise* was built to an extremely successful design and could carry up to 90 aircraft. American carriers embarked more aircraft than their Japanese counterparts and were better protected, with the exception of the Shokaku class.

In terms of heavy cruisers, the Imperial Navy and the USN were numerically equal, with 18 each. However, the Pacific Fleet only had

12 in December 1941. Washington Naval Treaty restrictions kept these ships to 10,000 tons, but since the Japanese systematically surpassed this limit, while the Americans actually built under the limit, American treaty cruisers were generally inferior in firepower and protection. Even so, American heavy cruisers were very useful ships with a main battery of nine or ten 8-inch guns, a decent antiaircraft suite, and the speed necessary to operate within a carrier task force. The first three classes of American treaty cruisers were underprotected; it was not until the advent of the New Orleans class in 1934 that the USN received a well-balanced heavy cruiser.

Whereas Japanese light cruisers were built to lead destroyer squadrons, American light cruisers were larger and more powerfully armed. The first post-World War I USN light cruisers of the Omaha class were built as scouts. These ships were considered failures, being very lightly protected and possessing an archaic main battery layout. By the start of the Pacific War, they were considered secondary units. The same cannot be said of the Brooklyn class that began to enter service in 1936. The nine ships in the class were powerful and balanced designs with a main battery of 15 6-inch guns and with a better level of protection than the Treaty heavy cruisers. Four of these ships were assigned to the Pacific Fleet and all were in Pearl Harbor on December 7.

American destroyer designs exhibited a different philosophy than their Japanese counterparts. Because of their many roles, American destroyers were built as multi-mission ships. Being charged to conduct attacks on Japanese formations, they had to possess a heavy torpedo battery. They also had to defend the battle line against Japanese torpedo attack, so also required a strong gun armament. The main battery had to be dual purpose since defense against Japanese air attack as the Pacific Fleet advanced across the Pacific was also envisioned. High endurance to operate in the expanses of the Pacific was also a priority.

After a ten-year hiatus, the USN commenced building modern destroyers in 1932. Ships of the first four classes of 1,500-ton designs were all assigned to the Pacific Fleet. The 18 ships of the Mahan class were considered the best ships of this type. They carried advanced machinery for enhanced range and a top speed of 36.5 knots. The ships were also heavily armed, embarking five 5-inch/38 dual-purpose guns and 12 torpedo tubes.

THE PACIFIC FLEET AND PEARL HARBOR DEFENSES

The second type of destroyer active in the Pacific Fleet were flush-deck destroyers built during or after World War I. A massive force of 273 ships was constructed in three classes. Heavily armed for the period, they carried 12 torpedo tubes and four 4-inch guns. By 1941, they were clearly second-line units, but some still remained in service in their original destroyer role. Many others were converted to other roles, including minelayers, minesweepers, and seaplane tenders.

Since many of the ships of the Pacific Fleet were caught in Pearl Harbor and subjected to the heaviest air attack against naval units in history up to that point, it is necessary to examine their antiaircraft capabilities. As was the case for all navies in this period of the war, USN ships possessed inadequate antiaircraft capabilities. Long-range protection was provided by two types of 5-inch guns. The older 5-inch/25 gun, introduced in 1921, was a decent weapon and was fitted on heavy cruisers, battleships, and Lexington-class carriers. It was replaced by the excellent 5-inch/38 dual-purpose gun fitted on modern destroyers and Yorktown-class carriers. Both possessed complex fire control systems, with the Mark 37 fire control director servicing the 5-inch/38 gun. Later in the war, the USN deployed large numbers of the 40mm Bofors and 20mm Oerlikon guns. Neither was available in 1941. For medium- and short-range protection, USN ships relied on a mix of the 3-inch/50 single mounts, a limited number of the unsatisfactory 1.1-inch quad mounts, and the ineffective .50-caliber machine gun. In general, American warships of the period were vulnerable to air attack but did have the capability of exacting attrition from aerial attackers. Ships in Pearl Harbor on the day of the attack mounted 135 3-inch, 232 5-inch, 64 1.1-inch mounts, and 397 .50-caliber machine guns.[12] Once the effects of surprise wore off, these guns produced a heavy volume of fire.

DISPOSITION OF THE FLEET

In the spring of 1941, the German U-boat threat in the Atlantic grew. In accordance with joint war planning conducted with the British, both parties agreed that the Atlantic was the decisive theater and that Germany was the greater threat. Accordingly, President Roosevelt directed that the Atlantic Fleet be reinforced – such a reinforcement could only be accomplished by moving ships from the Pacific. During the summer of 1941, Kimmel lost a significant part of his fleet. In total, the battleships *Idaho*, *New Mexico*, and *Mississippi* were transferred to the Atlantic. These ships were recognized as the best USN battleships modernized in the period between the wars. *Yorktown* was also transferred, taking one of Kimmel's four carriers. In addition, four light cruisers, 17 destroyers, three oilers, three transports, and ten other auxiliaries departed the Pacific Fleet. Transferring one-fourth of the Pacific Fleet made it clearly inferior to the Combined Fleet. The number of ships transferred exceeded the number of ships sunk or damaged in the Japanese attack. In such a condition, the Pacific Fleet was in no position to threaten Japan's drive into Southeast Asia.

On December 7, 1941, the naval balance between the USN and the Combined Fleet was as outlined in the table below. The USN was divided into two even parts, with one in each ocean. The small Asiatic Fleet was responsible for the defense of the Philippines.[13]

When the attack came on December 7, 21 percent of the Pacific Fleet was dispersed in many locations besides Pearl Harbor. However, the bulk of the fleet, 100 warships, coastal craft, and auxiliaries, was berthed at Pearl Harbor.

IJN-USN Naval Balance, December 1941

	Pacific Fleet	Asiatic Fleet	Atlantic Fleet	USN Total Strength	IJN Total Strength
Fleet carriers	3	0	4	7	6
Light carriers	0	0	0	0	3
Escort carriers	0	0	1	1	1
New battleships	0	0	2	2	0
Old battleships	9	0	6	15	10
Heavy cruisers	12	1	5	18	18
Light cruisers	9	2	8	19	17
Modern destroyers	45	0	52	97	69
Old destroyers	21	13	36	70	33
Total destroyers	66	13	88	167	102
Modern submarines	21	23	5	49	32
Old submarines	6	6	43	55	31
Total submarines	27	29	48	104	63

THE PACIFIC FLEET AND PEARL HARBOR DEFENSES

Ships at Pearl Harbor, December 7, 1941 (not including yard craft or ships moored in Honolulu)[14]

Battleships	*Nevada, Oklahoma, Arizona, Pennsylvania, Maryland, West Virginia, California, Tennessee*
Heavy cruisers	*New Orleans, San Francisco*
Light cruisers	*Helena, Honolulu, Phoenix, St Louis, Detroit, Raleigh*
Modern destroyers	26
Old destroyers	4
Gunboat	1
Submarines	4
Minelayers	9
Minesweepers	14
Auxiliaries	26

Many Pacific Fleet ships were not present in Pearl Harbor on the day of the attack. Most importantly, these included two carriers. Halsey departed on the morning of November 28 with orders to deliver a Marine fighter squadron to Wake. After leaving harbor, he headed west with *Enterprise*, heavy cruisers *Chester, Northampton,* and *Salt Lake City,* and nine destroyers under the designation Task Force 8. The remainder of the force, with the original Task Force 2 designation, was built around three battleships. After brief exercises, these ships returned to Pearl Harbor.

Once beyond sight of Oahu, Halsey placed Task Force 8 on full war alert. Weapons were loaded with live ammunition and orders were given to engage hostile (Japanese) submarines and aircraft. Reconnaissance aircraft covered 200nm around the task force. Halsey was taking no chances since he expected the Japanese to strike without declaring war first. He expected a submarine attack, however, not an air attack on Pearl Harbor.[15]

The other carrier based at Pearl Harbor, *Lexington*, cleared the Pearl Harbor channel on the morning of December 5 along with heavy cruisers *Chicago, Portland,* and *Astoria,* and five destroyers. This force had the mission of delivering a Marine dive-bomber squadron to Midway.

Other elements of the fleet were also absent. Admiral Brown and Task Force 5 departed Pearl Harbor on December 5 with heavy cruiser *Indianapolis* and five old destroyers converted into minesweepers. This force headed to Johnston Atoll to conduct amphibious exercises.

PEARL HARBOR

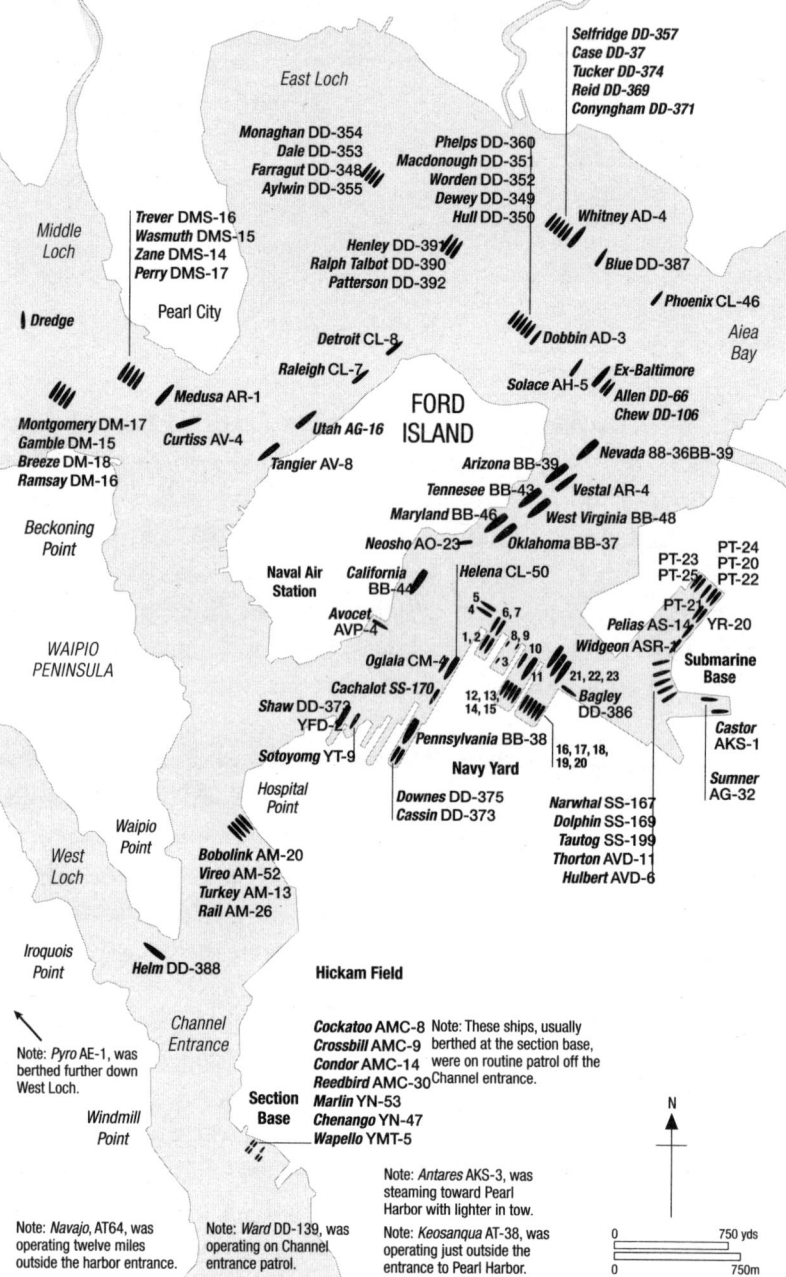

THE PACIFIC FLEET AND PEARL HARBOR DEFENSES

U.S. Navy ship designations	Navy Yard
Auxiliaries	1. *Jarvis*, DD-393
Ae ammunition ship	2. *Mugford*, DD-389
Ad destroyer tender	3. *Swan*, AVP-7 (on marine railway)
Ag miscellaneous	4. *Tern*, AM-31
Ah hospital ship	5. YO-30
Ak cargo ship	6. *Argonne*, AG-31
Aks general stores ship	7. *Sacramento*, PG-19
Ao oiler	8. *Sunnadin*, AT-28 and various Yard craft including: YG-15, YTT-3, YT-119, VT-129, YT-130, YT-142, YT-146, YT-152
Ar repair ship	
As sumbamrine tender	
Asr submarine rescue vessel	
At ocean tug	9. YG-21
Avp small seaplane tender	10. *Ramapo*, AO-12 (with PT-29, PT-30, and PT-42 aboard)
Avd seaplane tender (former destroyer)	
Combatants	11. *New Orleans*, CA-32
Bb battleship	12. *Rigel*, AR-11
Ca heavy cruiser	13. *Cummings*, DD-365
Cl light cruiser	14. *Preble*, DM-20
Dd destroyer	15. *Tracy*, DM-19
Ss submarine	16. *Pruitt*, DM-22
Minecraft	17. *Sicard*, DM-21
Am minesweeper	18. *Ontario*, AT-13
Amc coastal minesweeper	19. *Schley*, DD-103
Cm minelayer	20. *Grebe*, AM-43
Dm destroyer (light) minelayer	21. *San Francisco*, CA-38
Dms destroyer (high speed) minesweeper	22. *St Louis*, CL-49
	23. *Honolulu*, CL-48
Patrol craft	
Pg gunboat	
Pt motor torpedo boat	
Yard craft	
Yfd floating drydock	
Yg garbage lighter	
Ymt motor tug	
Yn boom (net) tender	
Yo fuel oil barge	
Yr floating workshop	
Yt yard (harbor) tug	
Ytt torpedo testing barge	

The same day, another force, led by heavy cruiser *Minneapolis* with four more destroyer minesweepers, left port for gunnery exercises south of Oahu. Heavy cruisers *Pensacola* and *Louisville* were escorting convoys to and from the Philippines. Nine submarines were also absent from port, with two each stationed off Midway and Wake. One of the submarines was operating south of Oahu with a destroyer. A major portion of the Pacific Fleet was on the West Coast, safely beyond Japanese attack. Carrier *Saratoga* was undergoing repairs, and battleship *Colorado* was in Bremerton undergoing overhaul. Also present on the West Coast was light cruiser *Concord*, nine destroyers, ten submarines, and many various auxiliaries.[16] Light cruiser *Trenton* was assigned to defend the Panama Canal.

Given the disposition of the Pacific Fleet on December 7, it is fair to say that fortune was with the Americans. As later events would clearly demonstrate, the most valuable ships of the fleet were its carriers and heavy cruisers. None of the fleet's carriers were in harbor on the day of the attack; of the fleet's 12 heavy cruisers, only two were present and these were in the repair yard where torpedoes could not reach them. Along with the heavy cruisers, the four Brooklyn-class light cruisers were valuable ships, but only two were in exposed positions when the attack began. In the strategic sense, even if the Japanese had sunk every ship present in Pearl Harbor on December 7, that would not have constituted a crippling blow to American naval power.

LOGISTICS

Usually overlooked in an examination of the Pacific Fleet was its logistics capabilities. The Base Force was charged with supplying the fleet with all its needs. Of the four squadrons, Squadron 8 was the most important. Established in July 1941, by August it comprised 18 ships – two store ships, one ammunition ship, four provisions ships, and 11 oilers.[17] The mobility of the Pacific Fleet was not assisted when in April 1941 three oilers were sent to the Atlantic.

Oil was the lifeblood of any fleet, and this reality weighed on Kimmel's mind. All fuel oil used by the Pacific Fleet had to be brought from the US West Coast, some 2,000nm distant. After arriving at Oahu, it was stored in dozens of tanks near the harbor. All were above ground and thus vulnerable to attack. The Pacific Fleet's Achilles' heel was its lack of tankers. Kimmel only had eight available, and of these, only four could perform replenishment of ships at sea. Fuel and the availability of tankers dictated how the fleet operated. After the attack, Vice Admiral Pye, who very briefly served as acting commander of the Pacific Fleet after Kimmel was relieved, suggested that it did not matter how severe losses were because "the fleet could not have operated more than 2,500 miles from Honolulu no matter what its strength."[18]

AMERICAN NAVAL AIRCRAFT

The Pacific Fleet's three carriers embarked air groups larger than those on Japanese fleet carriers. By 1938, USN carrier air group structure was standardized into four squadrons with a nominal strength of 18 aircraft each. The excellent Douglas SBD Dauntless dive-bomber equipped two squadrons. Because of its ability to absorb damage and carry a 1,000-pound bomb load, it was a superior dive-bomber to the Val. On the other hand, the torpedo bomber squadron was still operating the Douglas TBD Devastator that entered service in 1937. By 1941, it was obsolescent and carried unreliable torpedoes, giving it marginal capabilities. The Kate was a superior aircraft with a much better torpedo. Fighters made up the final squadron of an American carrier air group. *Enterprise*'s air group used the Grumman F4F Wildcat. Though it lacked the performance characteristics of the Zero, it was much more able to sustain damage. Used with appropriate tactics, it could match the Zero in certain scenarios. Onboard *Lexington* was a fighter squadron with the much inferior Brewster F2A Buffalo, which was totally outclassed by the Zero.

SHORE-BASED AIRCRAFT

Between the Navy and the Marine Corps, 301 aircraft were on Oahu on December 7. This total is misleading since only 202 were operational on the day of the attack. By far the most important of these were the patrol aircraft assigned to Bellinger's Task Force 9. These were the excellent Consolidated PBY Catalina patrol aircraft, destined to remain in service for the entire war. With an effective radius of 700nm, they were well suited for long-range patrol missions. Both the PBY-5 variant and the less modern PBY-3 were represented.

In total, 67 PBYs were on Oahu assigned to seven patrol squadrons. Three squadrons were stationed at NAS Kaneohe Bay with 36 aircraft (three were airborne on the morning of the attack), with the remaining aircraft and squadrons located at NAS Pearl Harbor on Ford Island (four were airborne). One squadron had 11 of its 12 PBY-3 aircraft deployed to Midway. Of the 67 aircraft, only seven were not operational, an impressive total considering that about half of the aircraft had arrived since October and spare parts were still in short supply.[19]

The PBYs were an important asset in the defense of Pearl Harbor. Without exquisite intelligence that the Japanese were on their way, the only realistic means to detect an approaching Japanese task force was by a PBY on patrol. This was acknowledged by Kimmel who after a meeting on March 1 sent Bellinger to work with the commander of the Army Air Force (USAAF) on Oahu to create a joint plan in case of a Japanese attack. By March 31, the two staffs produced what became known as the Martin-Bellinger Report.

This was a serious and professional estimate of how the Japanese might conduct an attack. It was very close to what the Japanese were thinking at the exact same time. Among its conclusions were:

- A Japanese attack might develop without any intelligence warning.
- Such an attack might precede a declaration of war.
- Forces committed to the attack would be considerable: "Orange might send into this area one or more submarines and/or one or more fast raiding forces composed of carriers supported by fast cruisers."[20]
- The heart of the assessment was this passage: "It appears that the most likely and dangerous form of attack on Oahu would be an air attack. It is believed that at present such an attack would most likely be launched from one or more carriers which would probably approach inside of three hundred miles."[21]
- The report also contained this startling assessment: "In a dawn air attack there is a high probability that it could be delivered as a complete surprise in spite of any patrols we might be using and that it might find us in a condition of readiness under which pursuit would be slow to start."[22]
- On the critical matter of how to prevent a surprise attack, the report offered a simple two-sentence answer: "Run daily patrols as far as possible to seaward through 360 degrees to reduce the probabilities of surface or air surprise. This would be desirable but can only be effectively maintained with present personnel and material for a very short period and as a practicable measure cannot, therefore, be undertaken unless other intelligence indicates that a surface raid is probable within rather narrow time limits."[23]

The report was masterful and was praised by the Navy Department in Washington. One outcome of the report was to transfer responsibility for long-range reconnaissance from the Army to the Navy. It was not ideal to break up the Army's duties with regard to defending the fleet, but it was dictated by reality. The Army possessed only a handful of long-range aircraft (the B-17s), nowhere near enough for an effective search. The Navy was better equipped in this regard. The agreement contained the provision that if the Navy determined it had inadequate resources, the Hawaiian Air Force could make aircraft available "under the tactical control of the Naval commander directing search operations."[24]

From the start, the Navy thought that its PBY resources were inadequate for sustained search operations. Patrol Wing Two had 67 aircraft but lacked relief pilots and crew. The real issue was how these aircraft were being used. They were not devoted to search operations at all. Instead, "The task assigned the Commander-in-Chief ... was to prepare his Fleet for war... The Fleet planes were being constantly employed in patrolling the operating area in which the Fleet's preparations for war were being carried on."[25] In other words, they were supporting fleet training for expected wartime operations at the expense of search operations to provide warning of a potential attack.

It is hard to accept the contention by Kimmel and Bellinger that they lacked the capabilities to perform meaningful search operations around Oahu. This was certainly true had continuous 360-degree coverage been desired, but such extravagant coverage was not required. Only the high-threat areas needed to be covered. East of Oahu did not require coverage, and coverage to the south also could have been reduced. The identified high-threat area was to the north – the exact approach the Japanese planned to use. Other search assets were also available in the form of a variable number of B-17s capable of long-range searches. The other AAF bombers on Oahu were capable of medium-range searches.

It is not accurate to state that Kimmel did nothing with regard to air reconnaissance after the November 27 war warning message, but what was done was too little and misdirected. The PBY squadron on Midway was ordered to fly to Wake on December 1 and scout the area on the way. On November 30, another PBY squadron was ordered to fly to Midway via Johnston Atoll, again scouting the waters on the way. Once at Midway, it conducted searches from December 2 to 6. During this period, *Enterprise* and *Lexington* were active in the same area.[26] This was an adequate search operation to the west, but left the northern sector uncovered. Yet, the northern threat was considered the most vital during the frequent drills against air raids.[27] Upon examining Kimmel's war plan for the Pacific Fleet, it is obvious that this activity was training for the planned offensive and not an effort to guard Oahu from attack.

Since Kimmel and Bellinger agreed that maintaining a 360-degree watch of the waters around Oahu was impossible on any sustained basis, Kimmel decided to prioritize training and force readiness over taxing the PBY force with additional scouting requirements. Without this mindset, there were not enough aircraft to cover the critical northern sector. In the final analysis, any search would have been better than no search. No search rendered the possibility of discovering an approaching threat at exactly zero percent. When his superior officer sent him a message with the first line "This message is intended as a war warning," that was probably the time for Kimmel to initiate intensive search operations along the enemy's most likely approach. That would also have been the proper time to ask the Army for help, which Kimmel never did. In light of subsequent operations during the war, even had Kimmel ordered search operations to the north of Oahu, there was no guarantee that Nagumo's carriers would have been discovered on their approach. However, in the final analysis, conducting no search operations was a serious misjudgment that left Pearl Harbor wide open to attack, and ensured the Japanese strike force had the element of surprise they deemed critical to the success of their plan.

In addition to the critical PBY force, Marine Air Group 21 was based at Ewa Field. Half of a squadron of Grumman F4F-3 Wildcat fighters was present (the rest of the squadron was on Wake Island). Most of one Marine scout bomber squadron was on *Lexington* on its way to Midway; only five Vought SB2U-3 Vindicators remained on Oahu, and the Vindicator was totally worthless as a combat aircraft. A second Marine scout bomber squadron possessed 22 Douglas SBD-1/2 Dauntless dive-bombers (the same aircraft operated by the Navy from carriers). Despite its training shortfalls, this squadron represented the greatest potential threat to the Striking Force from Oahu. Finally, the Navy maintained a large force of non-combat aircraft, floatplanes for cruisers and battleships and a variety of utility aircraft, most at Ford Island.[28]

KIMMEL'S WAR PLANS

To understand the reasons why the Pacific Fleet was caught flat-footed on December 7, it is critical to understand Kimmel's plan for the

THE PACIFIC FLEET AND PEARL HARBOR DEFENSES

fleet when hostilities developed. Kimmel did not see the Pacific Fleet as a means to defend Hawaii. In his mind, the fleet was an offensive weapon. Anything getting in the way of maintaining the fleet's readiness to attack was to be avoided.

Kimmel clearly saw the nature of the offensive he wanted to execute:

> In the Pacific, our potential enemy is far away and hard to get at … and has a system of defense … that requires landing operations, supported by sea forces, against organized land positions supported by land-based air. This is the hardest kind of opposition to overcome… It also requires a preponderance of light force and carrier strength, in which we are woefully deficient in the Pacific. Our present strength is in battleships – which come into play after we have reduced the intervening organized positions…[29]

In his view, the recent transfer of a quarter of his strength was a game changer. He went on to state that the Pacific Fleet was "so reduced in light forces and carrier strength that its capabilities for offensive operations of a decisive nature are severely crippled."[30] This affected Kimmel's strategic calculus since "The Japanese are not going to expose their main fleet until they are either forced to do so by our obtaining a position close enough to threaten their vital interests or it is advantageous for them to do so."[31]

Yamamoto was not the only admiral in the Pacific with big plans. As was the case with all American naval officers, Kimmel was trained to be aggressive. Just like Yamamoto's aggressive plan to attack Pearl Harbor, Kimmel's plans did not exactly comport with the overall plans of his superiors. Like Yamamoto, Kimmel was fixated on his offensive war plan, and this fixation was part of the reason he was caught off guard by the Japanese.[32]

Plan O-1 began to take shape immediately after Kimmel assumed command on February 1, 1941. It was also known as Pacific Fleet Plan WPPac-46 and was part of the overall plan called Rainbow-5. This latest plan was the successor to War Plan Orange (Orange being the color for Japan), first introduced in 1906. It was built around the premise that the fleet would conduct an aggressive thrust to relieve the Philippines where the American garrison was sure to be under attack by the Japanese. This was a rash plan, and was exactly what the Japanese were hoping for, but it took until 1934 for the USN to bow to reality.

Instead of a quick thrust, the Americans now planned a methodical advance, exactly as the Japanese feared. The target of the advance was the Japanese-held islands of the Central Pacific – the Marshalls, Carolines, and the Marianas. By 1940, the plan called for the first amphibious landing somewhere in the Marshalls by the sixth month of the war, with Truk – the main Japanese naval base in the Central Pacific – captured after a year. As events during the war demonstrated, this was an impossibly optimistic schedule.

Events in 1940 forced the Navy to reexamine its plan for a large-scale offensive in the Pacific. The fall of France in June 1940 left Great Britain in jeopardy. Admiral Stark feared that the British might also succumb. He wanted to replace War Plan Orange with a new plan that focused on fighting Germany first. This was the basis for Rainbow-5, a blueprint for a coalition war planned and fought with the British.

Resisting pressure from the British to come to the aid of their base at Singapore, the Americans did agree to assist the defense of Singapore, the Malay Peninsula, and the DEI (the so-called Malay Barrier) indirectly. To accomplish this, the Pacific Fleet was tasked to conduct raids against Japanese positions in the Marshalls. Some in Washington believed that the Combined Fleet would fight for the Marshalls, setting up a potential big fleet engagement. The challenge for Kimmel and his war plans officer, Captain Charles "Soc" McMorris, was devising a plan with enough gravity that it would accomplish its objective of drawing Japanese forces from Southeast Asia to the Central Pacific. Simply attacking Japanese outposts in the Marshalls would not achieve this objective.

Kimmel and McMorris came up with a solution to get at the Combined Fleet. It revolved around the base at Wake Island, which was being built up with a permanent Marine garrison and squadron of fighters. Though Wake was important, it was not reason enough for the Japanese to risk a major fleet engagement. Compelling Yamamoto to react to Kimmel's moves would entail using some portion of the Pacific Fleet as a lure. To do this, Halsey and his three carriers would conduct a scouting mission into the Marshalls, withdraw, and then return a week later to strike worthy targets. Such a risky maneuver was clearly meant to get Yamamoto's attention and draw his forces into the Central Pacific.

Following the carriers, Kimmel's battleships would depart from Pearl Harbor in two waves. After rendezvousing with the carriers on day

12 after the war began, they would head north as the carriers struck targets in the Marshalls. Once reunited with the carriers, and covered by PBYs from Wake and Midway, a massive clash was expected at a point between Midway and Wake on day 16 of the war.

Plan O-1 provides insight into Kimmel's thinking before the attack on Pearl Harbor. The Pacific Fleet was an offensive weapon and had to be in readiness to execute offensive operations on short notice; otherwise it could not support the Allied defense of the Malay Barrier. The entire fleet had a role to play in this offensive. Air power was an important aspect of the plan, especially the PBY force that was necessary to support the final decisive clash.

Examining Kimmel's plan, it becomes apparent how it would have brought the Pacific Fleet into a dangerous trap and into probable disaster. The salient weakness of the plan was the paucity of air power, principally carrier air power. Three carriers were insufficient for the kind of battle Kimmel had in mind, and his plan proposed to expose them to attrition before the main battle. Kimmel treated the carriers as support ships to the battleships. On the positive side, Kimmel understood the important role that long-range air reconnaissance would play and had a large force to execute it.

Had the war begun without the attack on Pearl Harbor, the Japanese would have been in a good position to give battle in the Central Pacific as Kimmel hoped. Forces not engaged in the Southern Operation included the entire 1st Air Fleet and the modern submarines of the Sixth Fleet. The First Fleet was in home waters waiting for such a decisive battle to develop with two battleship divisions with six battleships,[33] Cruiser Division 6 with four heavy cruisers, Cruiser Division 9 with two torpedo cruisers each carrying 40 torpedoes, and two destroyer squadrons. Light carriers *Hosho* and *Zuiho* had been detached from the 1st Air Fleet and sent to the First Fleet.

Other available forces included the Fourth Fleet based in the islands of the South Seas Mandates. It was composed of older units, none being larger than a light cruiser, but had under its command a land-based air flotilla. The remainder of the 11th Air Fleet, the IJN's land-based air force, was committed to the Southern Operation. The Fifth Fleet, based on northern Japan, was also a force with little combat power. Its most capable unit was the 21st Cruiser Squadron with two dated light cruisers and a seaplane carrier.

Kimmel's fleet in December 1941 was no match even for the portion of the Combined Fleet available for operations in the Central Pacific. With only two carriers (the third was under repair), Halsey would have faced certain defeat at the hands of Nagumo's six carriers. Had the Striking Force been able to attack Kimmel's battle force, a disaster greater than the historical attack on Pearl Harbor would probably have ensued. With little or no air cover, the American battleships were vulnerable to air attack and Nagumo's torpedo bombers could have had a field day. Any battleships lost in the Central Pacific would have included a great loss of life and no possibility of salvage. Had the battle occurred, the Japanese would have enjoyed success at least as great as they enjoyed at Pearl Harbor.

Despite Kimmel's aggressive instincts, there is little chance such a massive battle would have actually occurred. The first obstacle was the lack of an adequate fleet train to support the entire fleet. The Pacific Fleet possessed only eight tankers, with only four capable of underway replenishment. Kimmel conceded during the post-attack investigations that to keep the fleet at sea for prolonged periods required 75 tankers, with one-third of the tankers being capable of underway replenishment.[34] Had American intelligence detected the presence of Nagumo's six carriers, it is hard to imagine even the aggressive Halsey would have elected to give battle with only two of his own.

Examining Plan O-1 and its timetable, it is hard not to conclude that Kimmel was being overly ambitious. In the words of one of the post-war investigators, Kimmel was consumed with the notion of becoming "the American Nelson."[35] Under the basic USN war plan, Rainbow-5 (WPL 46), Kimmel was to follow a defensive strategy at least for the first six months of the war. He was to protect Hawaii, but also other American possessions in the Pacific including Midway, Wake, the Aleutians, Johnston, and Samoa. This defensive stance reflected the Germany first policy. Lack of auxiliaries made a major offensive movement impossible anyway. Kimmel's mindset was offensive, but it is unlikely that his superiors would have permitted the outnumbered Pacific Fleet to execute its own grandiose war plan. The transfer of a large portion of the Pacific Fleet indicated that the USN's main effort had temporarily shifted to the Atlantic (especially in terms of light forces) and that the focus of initial operations in the Pacific was defensive.

THE PACIFIC FLEET AND PEARL HARBOR DEFENSES

Even with the apparent contradictions present in Plan O-1 and what the Navy Department envisioned once war began, Kimmel's plan was drafted in March, refined after Rainbow-5, with the final version being submitted to Admiral Stark on July 25, 1941. It was approved on September 9 by Stark. McMorris made the last changes to the plan on December 6. Had the war opened in Southeast Asia, Kimmel was determined to carry it out.

An important aspect of the plan was getting information on Japanese forces as quickly as possible. Though submarines and cruisers were part of this effort, the best method was by long-range PBY aircraft. Five of the Pacific Fleet's nine PBY squadrons were committed in the plan to deploy to advance bases on Wake, Midway, and Johnston. Kimmel needed the PBY force for his offensive, not for what he believed would be fruitless searches around Oahu.

Even if Kimmel had been allowed to fight his fleet action, it is unlikely that the Japanese would have acted according to his script. The Imperial Navy did not plan to fight a decisive battle between Midway and Wake. More likely was a Japanese effort to employ attrition tactics against the Pacific Fleet. However, with Yamamoto in charge, a much more aggressive response was possible.

THE UNITED STATES ARMY

It is not well understood that defense of the Pacific Fleet while in port was the responsibility of the United States Army. The mission of the Hawaiian Department was, in the succinct words of Marshall, "the fullest protection for the Fleet."[36] With 43,177 men on December 7, it was the largest Army command beyond the continental United States.[37] The largest unit in the Hawaiian Department was the Hawaiian Division, a large infantry division with four regiments. In 1941, it was broken up to form the cadre of the 24th and 25th Infantry Divisions. The other large command on the islands was the Coast Artillery Command.

The Army was highly confident in its ability to defend Hawaii. The islands were a modern fortress and could be held, even without the assistance of the Pacific Fleet. This is reflected in a memo prepared by Army Chief of Staff George Marshall's staff and signed by him in April 1941. Since it so clearly reflects the thinking at the time, it is quoted in detail:

The Island of Oahu, due to its fortification, its garrison, and its physical characteristics, is believed to be the strongest fortress in the world. To reduce Oahu, the enemy must transport overseas an expeditionary force capable of executing a forced landing against a garrison of approximately 35,000 men, manning 127 fixed coast defense guns, 211 automatic weapons, and more than 3,000 artillery pieces and automatic weapons available for beach defense. Without air superiority this is an impossible task.

Air Defense. With adequate air defense, enemy carriers, naval escorts and transports will begin to come under air attack at a distance of approximately 750 miles. This attack will increase in intensity until within 200 miles of the objective, the enemy forces will be subject to attack by all types of bombardment closely supported by our most modern pursuit.

Hawaiian Air Defense. Including the movement of aviation now in progress Hawaii will be defended by 35 of our most modern flying fortresses, 35 medium range bombers, 13 light bombers, 150 pursuit of which 105 are of our most modern type. In addition Hawaii is capable of reinforcement by heavy bombers from the mainland by air. With this force available a major attack against Oahu is considered impractical.[38]

This was a very optimistic assessment of the state of defense for Hawaii. While the garrison was capable of repelling an invasion, its capabilities against air attack were more limited and highly dependent on receiving adequate warning. Against naval forces, the Hawaiian Air Force had marginal capabilities.

Walter C. Short, commander of the Hawaiian Department, was born in Illinois in 1880. In 1902 he entered the Army as a direct commission officer and was assigned to the infantry. For the next almost 40 years, Short made his way up the ranks of the Army. During World War I, he skyrocketed up to colonel, but reverted to his permanent rank of major after the war. In the small Army between the wars he worked his way up to brigadier general in 1937. Short was sent to Hawaii with the temporary rank of lieutenant general just days after Kimmel's arrival.

THE PACIFIC FLEET AND PEARL HARBOR DEFENSES

Much of Short's career was spent as an instructor in training assignments. From the standpoint that he was faced with training his growing force on Hawaii, he was a good match. Short was undoubtedly a capable and conscientious officer. However, he lacked imagination and was not aggressive. In most situations, he could be expected to play "by the book." In the eyes of many observers, Short was a micromanager who dwelled in the details.

Ordered by Marshall to be as cordial as possible to the Navy, Short reported back that he found Kimmel and Bloch to be "most approachable and cooperative in every way; and that "our relations should be extremely cordial."[39] Short made cooperation with the Navy his top objective and was fully aware of the importance of his responsibility to protect the fleet. He also made efforts to bridge the gap between the Army and civilian authorities on the islands.

THE HAWAIIAN AIR FORCE

Major General Frederick L. Martin (co-author of the Martin-Bellinger Report) was appointed commander of the Hawaiian Air Force when it was established on November 1, 1940. At the time of this appointment, Martin was the Army Air Corps' (changed to the Army Air Forces in June 1941) senior pilot and had over 2,000 hours of flight time in his logbook. The 58-year-old Martin was not a well man, with a severe and chronic ulcer. Though promoted to major general to deal with Short from a position of near equality, he stepped into an awkward position when he reached Hawaii. He was under the direct command of Short, who was an infantryman in every sense of the term. At the same time, he had direct access to the commander of the Army Air Forces, Major General H. H. "Hap" Arnold. Martin was under instructions from Arnold to improve relations between the Hawaiian Air Force and the regular Army and Navy. In this regard, he was successful as relations improved in 1941. The price was that Martin had to concede on points and acquired a reputation for being too eager to please.[40]

Under Martin were two flying commands: the 18th Bombardment Wing controlling the bombers on Oahu, and the 14th Pursuit Wing controlling all fighters. There was also a separate command for each major airfield on Oahu – Hickam, Wheeler, and Bellows Fields. One of Martin's objectives after taking over was to create a dispersal field for each of the combat squadrons. He often pleaded with Arnold for more modern aircraft.

In addition to a personnel strength of 754 officers and 6,706 enlisted men, the Hawaiian Air Force possessed a seemingly impressive total of 234 aircraft on December 7.[41] Of these, 152 were fighters. This was also a misleading figure since only 99 were modern P-40-B (87) and P-40-C (12) aircraft. If flown with the proper tactics, the Curtiss P-40 Warhawk had the potential to counter the aircraft flown off the decks of the Striking Force. Compared to the Zero, the P-40 was much more able to take battle damage, was better armed, with two .50-caliber and four .30-caliber machine guns, and was faster in a dive. However, it was clearly unable to match the Zero's maneuverability. Trying to dogfight with a Zero was asking for trouble, but if the American pilots used the P-40's higher dive speed for slashing attacks, they could create problems for the Japanese. On the morning of December 7, 64 P-40s were operational, though they were unarmed.

The Curtiss P-36 Hawk, which first flew in 1935, was considered obsolete by the AAF in December 1941. Thirty-nine were present on Oahu on the day of the Japanese attack; 20 were operational. Finally, 14 Boeing P-26 Peashooters were on Oahu of which ten were operational. This open-cockpit fighter was the Army Air Corps' standard fighter until 1938, but by 1941 was a museum piece.

Wheeler Field was the primary fighter base. Its commander had built over 100 dirt revetments, each about 10 feet high, to protect his fighters. Wheeler was not fenced, so it was difficult to defend the aircraft against potential sabotage if dispersed around the perimeter of the base.[42] Accordingly, on the day of the attack, the fighters were lined up on the concrete tarmac in front of the hangars. Here, under Short's orders, they were under armed guard. All fighters had their ammunition removed at night and secured in hangars.

About one-third of the fighter pilots at Wheeler were just out of flight school with only 200–300 flight hours. This was adequate for a basic level of training but was devoid of gunnery training. Some of the newly arrived pilots had never fired an aircraft weapon. There were also some very experienced pilots on Oahu, though they did not possess combat experience. Squadron commanders and flight leaders typically had about 1,000 flight hours.[43]

While the Hawaiian Air Force was fairly well off in terms of fighters, the same cannot be said for its bomber force. Defense of Hawaii centered on the long-range B-17 heavy bomber, but only limited numbers were available in late 1941. Since the Philippines were expected to be the first Japanese objective, most of those that were available were sent there (35 at the start of the war). Only a token number was left for Hawaii. On December 7, only 12 B-17Ds were on Oahu, of which only six were operational.

The AAF considered the B-17 to be a wonder weapon. It possessed a long range (some 750nm), was well armed for self-defense with seven machine guns, and carried an impressive bomb load of 4,800 pounds. It would have been possible to use the B-17 as a long-range reconnaissance aircraft, but the AAF did not want to misuse them on reconnaissance. If used for reconnaissance, several problems would have been exposed including a lack of training for long-range overwater missions and ship recognition. The AAF much preferred to use the B-17s as a striking force. Though held up by the AAF as a maritime strike weapon of unsurpassed power and range, it was virtually worthless in the role for the simple reason that bombing from high altitude against a maneuvering naval target offered only a remote prospect of gaining a hit.

Aside from the B-17 force, there were an equally small number of other modern bombers. One B-24A heavy bomber was present, as were 12 A-20A light bombers. In addition, 38 obsolete bombers were still kept in the force, including 33 Douglas B-18 Bolos (introduced in 1937), three Martin B-12s, and two Curtiss A-12s. The B-18s possessed marginal capabilities with a top speed of only 217mph, only three machine guns for self-defense, a short radius, and a modest bomb load. Rounding out the Hawaiian Air Force's order of battle were another 24 various trainers, transports, and tactical observation aircraft.

Training of AAF personnel was a matter of contention between Short and Martin. In this matter, Short showed his true colors as an infantryman. In July 1941, he instituted a six- to eight-week training program to indoctrinate Hawaiian Air Force enlisted personnel as infantrymen. His reasoning was that with 7,229 men on hand, exactly 3,344 were surplus to requirements given the number of available aircraft. Rather than allow them to continue their AAF training, Short felt it was more valuable to provide them with brief training as infantrymen.[44]

THE AIR WARNING SYSTEM

In the month after he took over, Short was ordered by General George Marshall to provide an assessment of the capabilities of the Hawaiian Department to defend against air attack. Short's answer indicated some clear thinking on the subject and keyed on the importance of establishing a reliable early warning system.[45] Though Short did not possess the aircraft to mount a proper long-range reconnaissance, he did possess a surveillance and warning system in the form of radar. What could have been a real advantage was mismanaged into irrelevance. After the last three radars were set up on November 26, there were six mobile SCR-270B air-search radar systems on Oahu with a theoretical detection range of between 75 and 125nm.[46] However, these were only operated daily for short periods. Having radar was fine, but it had to be integrated into an air warning system to be fully effective. Only rudimentary steps were taken to organize an operational air warning system in which all aircraft operating over and around Oahu were accounted for. Such a system was required before effective fighter control could be exercised.

On December 7, all that existed was the so-called Information Center located at Fort Shafter. When it was operating during duty hours, it consisted of a group of plotters working around a large table with a map of Oahu and the surrounding waters. The plotters marked the location of contacts reported by the radar stations. There was no way to distinguish between friendly and hostile contacts.

In addition to the radar and the misnamed Information Center, the Army had set up 100 lookout stations on high ground around Oahu. They were in place to report on the movement of aircraft and ships. This would have been a useful augment to the radar since observers could presumably provide the identity of contacts. As useful as they might have been, none of the stations were manned on December 7 because there was no alert for an air attack or for a possible landing. So, in the words of Pearl Harbor historian Gordon Prange, "the stations supposed to warn of approaching ships or planes were not on duty because nobody expected the attack of which they were supposed to warn!"[47] The Army also had sound detectors on the island to augment the radar, but again since no alert was in place, they were not used.[48]

THE PACIFIC FLEET AND PEARL HARBOR DEFENSES

ANTIAIRCRAFT GUNS

A major part of any air defense system was antiaircraft guns. The Army had big plans for augmenting the antiaircraft defense on Oahu. One hundred 3-inch guns were planned, but only 86 were present on the day of the attack. Available numbers of medium and light weapons were much lower – of 144 37mm guns, only 20 were present; 516 .50-caliber machine guns were planned, with only 109 present. Ammunition for these weapons was limited.[49]

On the day of the attack, the fixed batteries of 3-inch guns had some ammunition nearby, but it was boxed up. The mobile batteries had none since their ammunition had been moved to Aliamanu Crater several miles away. Additionally, the mobile batteries were not in firing positions.[50] On the day of the attack, these factors, plus the reduced personnel readiness on a Sunday, meant the antiaircraft guns of the garrison provided no meaningful protection to the fleet. Even though some guns were firing by the end of the first attack wave, Army antiaircraft artillery was too few in number and was poorly located to make any difference.[51]

READINESS

With the forces on hand, Generals Short and Martin had the means to mount a credible defense. However, that assumes a reasonable condition of readiness. Between April and November 1941, 13 exercises were conducted to test the air defenses of Oahu. All involved some level of participation by Army and Navy aircraft and Army antiaircraft units. These exercises were meant to showcase the readiness of air defense forces to defend the islands. In reality, they were highly scripted and bore no resemblance to reality. The exercise directors knew the direction of the attacking aircraft and received artificial assistance in identifying them. In May, the Army and Navy cooperated on a large-scale exercise to repel an invasion. As Short described it later to Marshall, the exercise was a resounding success and was comprised of three phases. In the first, his aircraft located and bombed an enemy carrier 250nm out to sea. According to the press, the bombers struck just as the carrier was in the process of launching aircraft. Coordination with the Navy was described as very good.[52] The only realistic aspect to the exercise was the dispatch of 21 B-17s from the West Coast to reinforce the Hawaiian Air Force.[53] In the second phase, the garrison prepared for an invasion; in the final phase, the garrison maneuvered to repel the invasion and dealt with sabotage by the local population.[54]

Though Short was happy with the exercise and thought it advanced Army–Navy cooperation, it demonstrated that Short did not understand his primary mission, which was to defend the fleet. Most exercise scenarios are artificial in some facets in order to allow all aspects of the force to participate, but the May 1941 exercise failed to include any phase in which the fleet was being defended. In fact, the scenario assumed that the Pacific Fleet was somewhere at sea or was so inferior to the Japanese that it failed to intervene. The focus on an invasion also suggests Short's true emphasis – repelling an invasion of Hawaii. Worst of all, the exercise failed to foresee the most likely Japanese operation against Oahu – an air raid aimed at the Pacific Fleet without an accompanying invasion.

After the emplacement of the first two radars on September 27, Martin mounted the first dress rehearsal of the air warning system and its centerpiece, the Information Center. On November 12, the Navy kicked off the exercise by launching a simulated strike from *Enterprise* 80nm from Oahu. The approaching formation was detected by radar, and the Information Center quickly gave the assessment that the approaching formation was hostile. Within six minutes, fighters were launched and intercepted the enemy formation about 30nm from Pearl Harbor.[55] Though far from a realistic exercise, it did demonstrate what could be done if operational radars and fighters at a high state of readiness were combined with a fully staffed Information Center. On December 7, none of these conditions existed.

Short had three alert postures. The first was focused on anti-sabotage measures. The Army, beginning with Marshall, was convinced that widespread sabotage, coordinated by Tokyo, was a certainty. Since about one-third of the population of Oahu was of Japanese descent, Short needed little convincing that sabotage was his primary concern. The November 27 war warning message from the War Department did not mention sabotage directly, but the next day both Short and Martin received direct warnings as to the sabotage threat. Short's reply that he had taken appropriate precautions against sabotage, but nothing to

THE PACIFIC FLEET AND PEARL HARBOR DEFENSES

counter an external threat, was reviewed by the War Plan Division at the War Department without comment.

The second included all anti-sabotage measures and defense against air, submarine, and surface attack. The last was directed against an all-out attack, including an invasion.[56] In the aftermath of the November 27 message from Marshall (the War Department's version of the War Warning message sent to Kimmel by the Navy Department on the same day), Short concluded that the last two measures were unnecessary as a Japanese attack was unlikely. A full-out alert also had the undesired consequences of alarming the local population and disrupting ongoing and essential training programs. Because he had always considered sabotage as the primary danger, he opted for the first alert stage (Alert No. 1). After conferring with Martin, it was decided to do nothing that would interfere with training or ferrying B-17s to the Philippines.

The one concession Short did make to the possibility of an air attack was to order the six mobile radar stations to extend their hours to include from 0400 to 0700. This was in addition to the regular hours from 0700 to 1100 for training (except for Sunday) and from 1200 to 1600 for training and maintenance (except for Saturday and Sunday). This measure was undertaken even though Short had no faith in the new radar systems.[57]

Though ordered to conduct reconnaissance in the November 27 message, Short declined to do so since the Navy had already agreed to take over that responsibility. He did not offer to augment Navy patrols with his B-17s, but with the small numbers available this would have constituted a token effort.

Short's Alert No. 1 included provisions for disarming aircraft and massing them together so they could be more easily protected against sabotage. He believed that the aircraft could be dispersed with 30–35 minutes' warning, but that getting them airborne would take longer.[58] According to the Air Force official history, the aircraft were on four hours' notice to be ready to fly.[59] Antiaircraft ammunition was also kept stored. Perversely, the alert instituted by Short made his air units more vulnerable to air attack than they were before the alert.

Short showed a gross misconception of his responsibilities. He gathered his aircraft into easy-to-hit targets and made it impossible for them to launch immediately. His antiaircraft ammunition was secured and not readily available for the guns. The only means he had of detecting an incoming threat was by radar. This was not manned around the clock and on the weekend was only operating for a few hours. He failed to conduct reconnaissance as ordered, and failed to ascertain if the Navy was conducting a robust scouting program as had been agreed.

When it came to ensuring readiness, the actions of the commanders in Washington were not above reproach. They provided the best warning possible given the information available, but the warning went out in two versions, one from the Navy Department and another from the War Department. This caused unnecessary confusion. Furthermore, the messages were ambiguous with regard to the exact measures that Washington wanted carried out. The War Department asked for a report of what measures were taken, but when it received Short's response it failed to indicate that the steps taken were inadequate. On balance, the response taken to the November 27 War Warning messages virtually guaranteed that the Japanese would achieve surprise.

AMERICAN INTELLIGENCE

Underwriting the lack of readiness on Oahu on December 7 was weak intelligence in the weeks and months preceding the attack. The reasons for this total failure to provide indications and warning to the commanders on Oahu remain hard to understand over 80 years later.

Beginning in the middle of 1940, the United States was able to read Japanese diplomatic messages. This was very useful since virtually all traffic between the Foreign Office in Tokyo and various embassies and consulates around the world could be decrypted. This top secret program was named Magic. Lower grade diplomatic codes (using the so-called J-code system) used between the Japanese Foreign Office and consulates had also been broken. This meant the messages between Tokyo and the Honolulu Consulate were being read by the Americans.

Magic cryptography was an undeniable success, but mundane factors prevented this information from getting to Oahu on a timely basis. By 1939, with German assistance, the Japanese were using a code (given the codename Purple by the Americans) that used modified Enigma machines. Although Magic could decrypt Purple, there were insufficient Purple decoding machines (used to decipher Japanese diplomatic traffic) in 1941 to position one in Hawaii. There was also an insufficient number of Japanese translators.[60] Further, not all raw intercepted messages could be delivered to Washington where they were deciphered in a timely basis. When the number of radio circuits was inadequate, messages were sent by airmail. If this was made impossible by the weather, then they were sent to Washington by ship and train.[61]

Official distribution of Magic decrypts was very selective. The distribution list did not include anybody on Oahu. In April 1941, Kimmel's senior intelligence officer attempted to gain access to Magic diplomatic intelligence but was rebuffed. This included the low-grade J-code intercepts.

Among the potentially useful warnings from diplomatic traffic that the Americans were able to decipher was a September 24, 1941 message from Tokyo to the Honolulu consulate. It provided Yoshikawa (the lead Japanese spy on the island) with a reporting grid covering Pearl Harbor and ordered him to use it to report the precise locations of ships in the harbor. While it was normal that the consulate would be reporting on USN ship movements, as was occurring at other Japanese consulates throughout the Pacific, this was the only occasion where this level of detail was being requested. As such, it could be seen as a potential precursor to attack. None of the Navy officers in Washington who reviewed the message saw its significance. Kimmel and Short were not informed of its existence.

Intercepted and deciphered diplomatic traffic lacked any reference to Japanese intentions to attack Pearl Harbor. It might have provided more data points as to Japanese intentions, but nobody was able to fully connect the dots. Select analysts in Washington with access to Magic were unable to piece together Japanese intentions. Diplomatic traffic by itself was insufficient to provide indications and warning of a specific Japanese move at a specific time and place.

NAVAL INTELLIGENCE

The focused efforts of American naval intelligence also proved unable to provide indications and warning of the attack. This reality has been clouded by the performance of American naval intelligence after the attack. Just a few months later, the same analysts were able to penetrate Japanese naval codes enough to provide the new Pacific Fleet commander with such a level of insight that he felt comfortable enough to commit all his remaining strength based on intelligence provided by the same people who had failed Kimmel just weeks before.

Producing intelligence assessments for Kimmel's consumption was performed at two levels. At the national level, the Navy Department had an Intelligence Division which relied on the Office of Naval Intelligence (ONI) for intelligence assessments. In 1941, this situation was in flux due to an old-fashioned turf battle between the Intelligence Division and the War Plans Division in the Navy Department. The head of the War Plans section, Captain Richmond Kelly Turner, wanted more control over the important function of producing assessments on Japanese intentions. In early 1941, he went to Captain Theodore S. Wilkinson, head of the Intelligence Division, to tell him that he should make no assessments of Japanese intentions but rather give the raw intelligence to the War Plans Division, which would produce the required estimates. Wilkinson stood his ground, as producing assessments of enemy intentions was clearly an ONI responsibility. After being rebuffed the first time, Turner tried again when Captain Alan C. Kirk took over the Intelligence Division. Kirk tried to stand his ground, but Turner was adamant that ONI was merely a collection and distribution agency and took the matter to Admiral Stark. This time, the abrasive Turner prevailed.[62]

The net effect was just as Turner desired – ONI was reduced to impotence. Critically, assessments of Japanese intentions were no longer in the hands of those with the most in-depth knowledge of Japan or its armed forces. Instead, officers with no intelligence training or insights were producing these assessments. Not surprisingly, these generally reflected the views and requirements of the planners.

The second source of assessments reaching Kimmel was from the intelligence personnel on his own staff. The Pacific Fleet intelligence officer was Lieutenant Commander Edward T. Layton. As the fleet intelligence officer, he was charged with making all-source intelligence assessments. Layton assumed his job one year before the Pearl Harbor attack. He knew Yamamoto personally and related to Kimmel his intelligence and skills at games of chance. When it came to what Yamamoto might do with his carriers when war began, Layton was of the opinion that he would not "gamble too much wherein Japan might lose the war in the first battle when she had larger stakes, more vital stakes at hand."[63] Layton had regular access to Kimmel, briefing him daily at 0815. He was able to gain Kimmel's confidence.

THE PACIFIC FLEET AND PEARL HARBOR DEFENSES

As part of Kimmel's inner circle, Layton was in constant contact with all the important members of the staff. What comes across in the recorded discussions inside the staff was a clear case of groupthink. Nobody thought the Japanese would attack the United States. This included Kimmel, and the highly regarded strategic minds of his deputy, Admiral Pye, and chief planner, Captain McMorris. At the same time these men believed that war was coming, but only allowed for the possibility that American forces in the Philippines were threatened.

Intelligence and cryptographic assessments were different disciplines and were under different masters. Intelligence made up its own department both at the Navy Department and Pacific Fleet levels. Cryptographic activities were under the Communication Division. There were several cryptographic stations in late 1941 working Imperial Navy targets, including those supporting the Navy Department in Washington, Station Cast on Corregidor in the Philippines, and Station Hypo on Oahu. Station Hypo, also known as the Combat Intelligence Unit, was under the command of Commander Joseph J. Rochefort.[64]

NAVAL INTELLIGENCE SOURCES AND METHODOLOGY

There were few sources available to American naval intelligence analysts before the start of the war. Human intelligence was not available since the Americans had no sources within the Imperial Navy and there were no Japanese prisoners to interrogate. Observations by friendly forces were also not available since the forces were not in contact. This left the various disciplines of communications intelligence – cryptanalysis, direction finding, and traffic analysis.

Potentially the most fruitful source was cryptanalysis of enemy radio messages. If these messages could be intercepted and deciphered, even in part, enemy intentions could be laid bare. By the fall of 1941, USN cryptanalysts were still unable to read the Imperial Navy's main operational code (JN-25(b)) or its Flag Officer's Code. The cryptographers at the main Navy station in Washington were assigned to attack the operational code but lacked the resources necessary to crack it. Early in 1941, Station Cast was also directed to attack JN-25(b). Meanwhile, Station Hypo on Oahu was fruitlessly trying to decipher the Flag Officer's Code.

Intercept of an enemy signal yielded very important information even if the signal itself could not be deciphered. When an enemy unit communicates, these messages can be intercepted. The location of the transmitting unit can be ascertained by direction-finding. Once the identity of the transmitter is determined through identification of its call sign, its location can be determined if multiple lines of bearings are gained.

Another method to exploit enemy radio traffic is through traffic analysis. Once enough enemy signals are intercepted, patterns can be deduced, such as command relationships. The frequency and urgency of the messages are useful for assessing the timing of enemy operations and the units likely to conduct them. Traffic analysis is an art form since the analysts are relying on the externals of the message instead of a deciphered version of its internals. For example, through traffic analysis, ONI had a very good idea of the organization and order of battle of the Imperial Navy in 1941. However, when it came to the 1st Air Fleet, established in April 1941, ONI was unclear. In mid-1941, it was assessed that all ten Japanese carriers were assigned to a single entity. Previously, the carrier divisions were assigned to different fleets. However, the new entity, called by USN analysts the Carrier Fleet, was believed to be an administrative unit, not an operational one.[65]

Of course, all types of communications intelligence can be thwarted by the simple measure of instituting radio silence. If enemy units do not transmit, their location cannot be determined, nor can the external or internal content of the messages be used to assess intent. Radio silence is possible if the enemy unit can still communicate with its higher echelon commanders by use of landlines or communicate with other units in a naval force by signal lamp or flags. Though a powerful deception tool, radio silence cannot be used for extended periods. It is an abnormal state and is often an indicator of high-interest operations by the unit or units exercising such a condition.

Part of the staff-planning process was to assess enemy courses of action (COA). Both the most likely and most dangerous enemy COAs are useful for planning purposes. There are two basic ways of discerning the enemy's COAs. One is by assessing his intentions, the other by assessing his capabilities. In the frequent absence of the former, the latter is often used.

Discerning enemy intentions is difficult since it requires deep penetration of the target. In the case of the months before Pearl Harbor,

American communications intelligence had the potential of providing such a high level of insight had the Americans successfully penetrated JN-25(b). Without real insight, ONI, Layton, and Rochefort were left to make their assessments with little data, but plenty of bias and ill-founded impressions. The Japanese were sure to avoid war with the United States since it was simply too strong to attack. American analysts attributed a high degree of rationality to Japanese decision makers, failing to realize that in the minds of the Japanese they were facing a question of national survival. In the final analysis, the Americans had no firm basis for assessing the entirety of Japanese intentions.

In the absence of a well-founded assessment of Japanese intentions, the Americans failed to consider Japanese capabilities. Here again, mirror imaging was at work. The main potential threat to Hawaii was from Japanese carriers, but the magnitude of the threat was downplayed. The USN operated carriers singly, so they presumed that was surely how the Japanese would operate theirs. The Americans failed to understand that the formation of the 1st Air Fleet gave the Japanese revolutionary new capabilities. To be fair, this is unsurprising since the formation had only existed since April, and the last two fleet carriers to join it did so in August and September.

The same lack of imagination was at work in the months and weeks before Pearl Harbor as the Americans attempted to understand how the Japanese would open a war in the Pacific. The Japanese focus on Southeast Asia was obvious and logical since it was the only way Japan could gain the resources necessary to avoid economic strangulation. It was also a convenient and convincing smokescreen for other Japanese naval operations, like an attack against Pearl Harbor. In an analysis of the most dangerous Japanese COAs, it should have been clear that to the Japanese the only force capable of thwarting their move south was the Pacific Fleet. But could the Japanese effectively attack it? Again, the answer was obvious. As had been done many times in exercises before the war, the Pacific Fleet in Pearl Harbor was vulnerable to attack. With six fleet carriers, the Japanese had the means to launch a powerful attack on the fleet. With the Japanese predilection for surprise attacks, such a move became more than simply theoretical. It was a total lack of imagination that prevented Navy intelligence officers in Hawaii or Washington from seeing the potential threat to the Pacific Fleet.

In his book published well after the war, Layton failed to take responsibility for his lack of imagination. He should have raised his voice to Kimmel along these lines: "Yes, the prevailing assessment is that the Japanese won't attack Pearl Harbor, but you need to be fully aware that they have the capability to do so and in the absence of proof of their actual intentions, you need to be prepared for this worst case eventuality." Just like Kimmel did after the war, Layton tried to shift the blame to Washington. The basis for this argument was Washington's failure to share the fruits of Magic with the Pacific Fleet. This led to Kimmel being unaware of the imminence of war as portrayed in Japanese diplomatic codes and the information being passed from Yoshikawa on the location of ships in Pearl Harbor. While true, this does not excuse the lack of imagination on Oahu and does not guarantee that Layton and others would have made the mental leap that the first move in Japan's new war would be an attack on Pearl Harbor.

A perfect example of the collective lack of imagination on Oahu was provided on December 3, when the Navy Department sent a message to Kimmel and Bloch that Tokyo had ordered its diplomatic facilities in several key Pacific countries to destroy most of their codes and ciphers. A second message indicated that the same facilities had been ordered to destroy most of their Purple cipher machines, leaving only one functioning. This was an indication of impending hostilities, a view shared by Rochefort and Washington. However, Layton failed to make this point clearly to Kimmel. Kimmel also missed the importance of this development, stating in 1946, "I didn't consider that of any vital importance when I received it."[66]

WHAT THE AMERICANS KNEW

On April 1, only a day after the prescient Martin-Bellinger report was issued, Naval Intelligence in Washington sent this message to all naval districts, including the 14th Naval District on Oahu:

> Personnel of your Naval Intelligence Service should be advised that because of the fact that past experience shows the Axis Powers often begin activities in a particular field on Saturdays or Sundays or in national holidays of the country concerned they should take steps on such days to see that proper watches and precautions are in effect.[67]

THE PACIFIC FLEET AND PEARL HARBOR DEFENSES

Unable to read the Imperial Navy's two most important codes, Rochefort's Station Hypo was forced to rely on traffic analysis.[68] Using this method, Rochefort produced an assessment on September 28: "The general impression grows that preparations are increasing for either maneuvers on a large scale or possibly a hostile operation of some kind."[69] Station Hypo produced a daily summary which Kimmel read through on December 6.

Rochefort was able to track a growing level of Japanese activity in September and October, mostly in the South China Sea. On November 1, the IJN instituted a fleet-wide call sign change for all its units, something done about every six months. In the aftermath of recovering each unit's new call sign, Station Hypo discovered a new unit – the 1st Air Fleet. This was a new organization and was reported to Kimmel on November 3. It was unclear what this development meant.[70]

The Japanese were using every trick possible to hide the movement of their ships. Dummy radio messages and irregular communication addresses were common. Beginning on November 23, the 1st Air Fleet's communications unit was ordered to transmit false radio messages to give the impression that the main units of the fleet were in the western part of the Inland Sea. As the ships of the Striking Force were steaming for the Kurile Islands, radio traffic suggested that normal training operations were ongoing in the Inland Sea. Though Rochefort's analysts were able to identify much of the Japanese deception efforts as a smokescreen, by the time the ships of the Striking Force moved to the Kuriles under strict radio silence, the Americans had lost them. Through November 18, the carriers were believed to be in the Inland Sea. Washington also missed the movement of Nagumo's carriers, assessing that the ships of the Striking Force were in or near their home ports, with the exception of *Shokaku*, which was placed in Formosa in a low-confidence assessment. On November 30, the Imperial Navy changed its call signs for the second time in 30 days. It was an unprecedented move and should have alerted Navy intelligence officers both in Hawaii and Washington.

At the same time that the Striking Force was lost, Rochefort was able to track the large-scale movement of Japanese forces to the south. Nobody on Oahu saw any danger to Oahu at the time, As Rochefort put it, "No one thought in terms of Pearl Harbor at the time."[71]

After Kimmel received the war warning message on November 27, there was a greater urgency in determining Japanese naval intentions.

On the afternoon of November 27, Kimmel and Bloch made their way into the basement where Rochefort's Combat Intelligence Unit worked. In a 90-minute meeting, Rochefort went over his assessments. He reiterated that the Japanese were on the move, but that was in the South China Sea. On the crucial question of the locations of the Japanese carriers, he stated that they remained in home waters. One of two (probably light) carriers may have deployed to the Marshalls, along with a large number of submarines.

On December 2, in response to an order from Kimmel to provide everything he knew about the location of Japanese warships, Layton briefed his latest assessments. Most of the Imperial Fleet was assessed to be headed south, including Carrier Divisions 3 and 4. When asked where Carrier Divisions 1 and 2 were, Layton responded that he did not know but guessed they were in home waters. Both Layton and Rochefort were becoming uneasy about the lack of definitive locating data on the carriers, but this was not alarming since they often went unlocated for sustained periods. On December 6, Rochefort's daily summary on Japanese naval activity focused on the activity in Southeast Asia. There was no update on the carriers or the submarine force, still believed to be in the Mandates.[72] At this point, the carriers were closing in on Oahu and the Sixth Fleet's submarines were taking up positions around the Hawaiian Islands. The Japanese had won the intelligence war.

CONCLUSION

In the final analysis, though American and Allied codebreakers were making slow progress into JN-25(b) before Pearl Harbor, by December 1941 the breakthroughs were unable to reveal any usable intelligence. The Japanese deception plan to prevent the Americans from tracking the Striking Force was successful for many reasons. It was a multi-level scheme relying heavily on the misconceptions of its soon-to-be enemies. The first layer was the detailed plan to deceive Allied intelligence efforts by denying them insights into Combined Fleet movements. This included the change of call signs twice within a month and then new procedures after the second call sign change to make recoveries difficult. Radio silence of the Striking Force was combined with false indications of ongoing training inside the Inland Sea by carriers and their air groups.

THE PACIFIC FLEET AND PEARL HARBOR DEFENSES

Though not part of the deception plan, the massing of the Combined Fleet for the Southern Operation was the perfect cover for the rest of the fleet. Assumedly, if key fleet units were not identified as part of the southern offensive, they were being retained in home waters for possible use against any attempt by the USN to intervene.

While the Japanese deception plan was excellent, it paled in comparison to the self-deception exhibited by the Americans. False logic dictated that a Japanese attack against the United States was an act of suicide, and thus unlikely to occur. If the Japanese wanted to risk self-immolation, the only possible targets were American forces in the Philippines. Pearl Harbor was not under threat because the Japanese possessed little capability to attack it.

American intelligence was totally unaware of the Imperial Navy's new doctrine of massing carriers, and the development of new Japanese weapons which allowed the Pacific Fleet to be attacked in port. For these reasons, combined with the supposed strong defenses guarding Oahu, an attack on Pearl Harbor was simply inconceivable.

Failure of Washington to provide accurate warning of any Japanese attack against Oahu does not excuse Kimmel's and Short's lack of decisive action to defend against a potential attack. By its nature, any Japanese attack on Pearl Harbor would be a surprise operation, and warning could never be guaranteed. Clearly, by late 1941, Japan intended to strike somewhere in the Pacific. Just as clearly, the Japanese possessed the capability to attack Pearl Harbor though the Americans had no idea how strong this capability was. The first responsibility of a commander was force protection. Admiral Kimmel failed to verify that his fleet was actually safe inside Pearl Harbor. Though not directly responsible for the protection of the fleet, he failed to take measures to ensure that a Japanese fleet couldn't approach Oahu undetected despite many warnings that an attack was more than a remote possibility.

General Short bears direct responsibility for failing to organize a coherent defense against potential attack. It is difficult to understand how, after receiving a warning that hostilities were likely, the readiness condition of his forces on Oahu actually decreased. With multiple radars and 100 operational fighters, mounting a credible defense of the fleet was well within his means.

6

The Striking Force Approaches Pearl Harbor

With the final approval of Yamamoto's Hawaii Operation, the pace of preparations increased. On November 3, Nagumo held a briefing for key commanders and staff personnel of the Striking Force. At last, the principal officers of the fleet were told why they had been training so hard over the past months. The next day a full rehearsal for the attack was conducted. On November 5, a second rehearsal was conducted. After the rehearsals, the carriers returned to their home ports for final repairs, maintenance, loading supplies, and taking on fuel. *Akagi*, *Kaga*, and *Hiryu* went to Sasebo; *Soryu* and the two Shokaku-class carriers to Kure. Everything aboard the ships excess to requirements or for safety was removed. Oil drums were loaded in every vacant space. The crews were then given liberty for a brief four-day period.

The first units participating in the Hawaii Operation to depart were those assigned to Submarine Squadron 3. On November 11, its nine boats departed Saeki Bay for a refueling stop in the Marshalls before heading to Hawaii. On November 13, *Akagi* departed from Sasebo and steamed to nearby Kagoshima where her air group flew aboard. The next day, *Akagi* entered Saeki Bay where Nagumo and his staff embarked. The other carriers departed from their home ports on November 16 and 17 and embarked their respective air groups.

On the afternoon of November 17, Yamamoto's flagship, battleship *Nagato*, anchored in Saeki Bay where *Akagi* was already waiting. At 1500, Yamamoto, Ugaki, and other staff officers went over to *Akagi* for the last prewar conference with Nagumo and his staff. According to the postwar recollections of the surviving participants, the purpose of Yamamoto's visit was not to give Nagumo and his staff a pep talk, but to remind them of the capabilities of their soon-to-be enemy. He warned that surprise may not be gained and that the Striking Force might have to fight its way to the target. In the ensuing farewell party, Yamamoto closed by indicating his faith in the men of the task force and his expectation of success.[1]

That afternoon, elements of the Striking Force began to filter out of Saeki Bay. The first to depart and head to Hitokappu Bay in the Kuriles were *Soryu* and *Hiryu* with four escorting destroyers. One by one, the other ships followed. *Akagi* departed after dark. Some ships moved along the coast; others proceeded north only when they were well out to sea. *Kaga*'s departure was delayed a full day. The extra time at Sasebo allowed the final batch of the modified Type 91 torpedoes to be loaded aboard.

The spot selected for the rendezvous of the Striking Force was a point off Etorofu Island. Hitokappu Bay was large enough to accommodate the entire task force and was remote enough to provide concealment. For several days, ships entered the bay by ones and twos. The last to make her appearance was *Kaga*, arriving on November 22.

On November 22, Suzuki gave an intelligence brief to Nagumo and his staff. He had returned from Honolulu aboard *Taiyo Maru* on November 17 with the latest information on conditions along the planned route of the Striking Force and of American dispositions and defenses on Oahu. The following day, *Akagi* was the scene of another important brief. Command personnel from every ship in the task force were summoned to the flagship to hear Nagumo announce, "Our mission is to attack Pearl Harbor."[2]

At 0600 on November 26, the Striking Force departed its anchorage at Hitokappu Bay. From there, its transit to the planned attack launch point north of Oahu required 12 days. The transit was dominated by the need to refuel the destroyers every other day. The Striking Force maintained a cruising speed of 12–14 knots, except when refueling took place and speed was reduced to 9 knots.

The final units with a role in the Hawaii Operation departed Japan on November 28. This was the Midway Bombardment Force. With only three ships, Fubuki-class destroyers *Sazanami* and *Ushio*, and tanker *Shiriya*, this small force was tasked to bombard the airfield on Midway Atoll on the night of December 7 to aid the withdrawal of the Striking Force. Since the accompanying oiler had a top speed of only 8 knots, the force departed from Tateyama in the southern part of Tokyo Bay on November 28 to make its way slowly to Midway. After completing its mission, the small force was ordered to return to the Inland Sea. Of note, *Ushio* was the only ship associated directly with the Pearl Harbor attack to survive the war.[3]

During the first part of the Striking Force's transit, a quarter of the crews on the ships were at their battle stations. In the second part of the transit, half of the crews were at battle stations. A sharp eye was kept for American submarines. No aircraft were flown from the six carriers, but each kept six Zeros on full alert.[4]

According to Genda, work on the attack plan continued throughout the transit. He stated that not a day went by without some change or minor adjustment to the plan. Some of these resulted from the ideas or opinions of Nagumo. The most significant modification was prompted by Yamamoto's pre-departure warning that surprise may not be possible. Genda, Fuchida, and Murata thought about what to do if the Americans were on the alert. Under the assumption that surprise was assured, it was planned for the vulnerable torpedo bombers to open the attack; now Genda and Fuchida came up with a new plan if surprise was not in effect. In this case, the other bombers would do their work first with the hopes of disrupting and distracting the defense. Only then would the torpedo bombers attack. To indicate which attack plan was in effect, the three men devised a signal system using flares. The fact that the Japanese first examined the real possibility that surprise was not a given only during the transit demonstrates a serious flaw in their planning process. Once an assumption had been set, planning proceeded with the absolute belief that it would be fulfilled. This serious process error was exhibited throughout the war.

Not only Genda was busy making last-minute preparations. Aircrews constantly worked on their recognition skills of American ships, and those on *Akagi* had the opportunity to review the scale models of Oahu and Pearl Harbor. By all accounts, morale among the aviators was extremely high; senior officers rarely left the bridges of their commands and when they slept they did so in uniform.[5]

For the entire transit, radio silence and a strict blackout were in effect. This made moving a large group of warships across a great distance very challenging. During the day it was fairly easy to keep the force together.

THE STRIKING FORCE APPROACHES PEARL HARBOR

At night or when fog descended, the only thing to guide the formation was the wake of the ship in front of them or an occasional blink from a signal light. One factor working in Nagumo's favor was that the seas in the northern Pacific were unusually calm for late November and early December. This made refueling much easier and alleviated one of Nagumo's greatest fears. The only weather complication was occasional unseasonably heavy fog.[6]

During this period of the transit, Nagumo used a formation designed to protect the carriers. Four destroyers were deployed in the vanguard about 6nm apart. Then came the six carriers in two parallel columns. Behind the carriers were the seven tankers, The two battleships brought up the rear. The remaining destroyers were deployed on the flanks of the formation. Though he originally planned to use the three submarines as a warning force well out in front of the task force, Nagumo decided that the low visibility from the submarines made it likely they might get lost in bad weather. With radio silence in effect, this could become a real problem. Instead, Nagumo placed the submarines less than a nautical mile to starboard of *Akagi* where they remained for the entire transit. At night and during heavy fog, Nagumo brought the entire formation closer together to make communication by signal light easier. Though on occasion a ship did stray from the formation, overall the transit was conducted without major difficulty.[7]

Even the good weather and lack of any sign of American ships or aircraft failed to encourage Nagumo. He worried that his ships might miss the signal from headquarters whether to proceed with the attack or not. With every ship in the Striking Force ordered to tune into a special frequency, this was unlikely to happen. Still he worried about being detected, refueling, keeping formation, and the many other things that might go wrong. When Kusaka tried to calm his nerves, Nagumo simply replied, "You are too optimistic."[8]

Nagumo also had to endure Genda's persistent pleading to keep his mind open to the possibility of a second attack. Nagumo would have nothing to do with such an eventuality; his response was always, "One attack only! One attack only!" Nevertheless, Genda came up with four different scenarios for Nagumo to consider after the last of the aircraft from the Striking Force's two-wave assault returned. In the first plan, the Striking Force would linger for several days at a point some 200nm north of Oahu. From here, it could launch searches to find American warships not in Pearl Harbor or launch additional strikes against ships and facilities inside the harbor. In the second plan, the Striking Force would position itself as above, but then return to Japan on a different path than that selected by Nagumo. The third variant was the same as the first two, but with a withdrawal route along the Hawaiian Islands passing close to Midway. The intent was to be ready to attack any American ships in the area. The last plan was Genda's preferred course of action. It called for the Striking Force to steam southward, passing Oahu to the west before returning to the Marshalls. Steaming in the area of Oahu offered the possibility of launching repeated strikes over the next three days to complete the destruction of the Pacific Fleet.[9]

Support from the Naval General Staff was provided in the form of daily weather updates. A special communications system was set up to ensure that the Striking Force did not miss any messages. Messages were repeated several times; on every odd-numbered hour, day and night, a message was sent to Nagumo. Every ship was responsible for receiving messages, but battleship *Hiei* had the best communications system so had primary responsibility.[10]

The placid advance of the Striking Force hit a bump on December 4 when the seas turned rough. With the destroyers taking 45-degree rolls, refueling scheduled for the day was canceled. Also on this day, Nagumo clarified his position if the Striking Force ran into an enemy or neutral merchant or warship. In this instance, he instructed the ships of the task force to destroy the ship's communications equipment. If need be, the ship was to be sunk. This determination by Nagumo meant he intended to press on even if he was spotted.

At 1130 on December 5, the Second Supply Group departed the formation. After refueling the entire Striking Force, tankers *Toho Maru*, *Toei Maru*, and *Nihon Maru* headed to the northwest with their escort destroyer *Arare*. If all went according to plan, the tankers would meet the Striking Force on its withdrawal route to Japan.

By the morning of December 6, the Striking Force reached a point about 600nm north of Oahu. Starting at about 0630, Nagumo's ships engaged in their last refueling. The sea was fairly calm, so refueling proceeded uneventfully. The weather continued to be good overall, with cloudy skies and a wind of about 20 knots. This was a critical period of vulnerability for Nagumo, as he refueled within range of B-17 bombers from Oahu. He was unaware that he had no reason to worry since

THE STRIKING FORCE APPROACHES PEARL HARBOR

there were no American search missions looking at the waters north of Oahu. After completing the refueling, the First Supply Group broke away and headed north at about 0830. *Kenyo Maru, Kyokuto Maru, Shinkoku Maru,* and *Kokuyo Maru* with destroyer *Kasumi* would meet the Striking Force again as it departed Hawaiian waters.

With every ship in the force topped off with fuel, at 1130 on December 6 speed was increased to 20 knots and course changed to the south – straight for Oahu. Just ten minutes later, the famous Z flag was raised on *Akagi*. This was significant to every ship in the fleet as it was the same flag hoisted by Admiral Togo before the famous Japanese victory over the Russians at the 1905 Battle of Tsushima. Nagumo passed the message sent from Yamamoto to the entire fleet: "The rise and fall of the Empire depends on this battle. Every man will do his duty."

With the Striking Force on its way to Pearl Harbor, the Japanese heightened their intelligence-collection efforts. Getting the most up-to-date and accurate information on the movements and location of Pacific Fleet units was critical to the success of the attack. As Nagumo endlessly fretted, Kusaka's primary concern was getting the latest intelligence updates from the Naval General Staff. On November 28, the Foreign Ministry issued instructions to the Honolulu consulate to report on the arrival and departure of all capital ships.[11] The following day, the Consulate General received instructions to report not just ship movements but also the lack of movements. When carrier *Lexington* departed with three heavy cruisers, joined by the departure of two other heavy cruisers on December 5, this was reported to Tokyo at 1904 that night.

On December 6, after a prompt from Tokyo, Yoshikawa provided an update on the state of defenses at Pearl Harbor. In his update he indicated that there were still no barrage ballons present and that in his opinion there were no torpedo nets around the battleships. Strangely, the message also included a sentence mentioning that there was a "considerable opportunity left to take advantage for a surprise attack." Previous intelligence updates from the consulate never included reference to a surprise attack. Though sent in a code broken by the Americans, the message was not decoded and translated until December 8.

I-72 checked in from her reconnaissance of Lahaina anchorage the day before the attack. The report was brief: "The enemy is not in Lahaina anchorage."[12] This was a blow because Genda hoped to catch the fleet in the deep waters of the anchorage. If sunk there, no salvage was possible. The message was received by the Striking Force at 1903. Despite the confirmation that the anchorage was clear, Genda left in place the seaplane check of the anchorage the following morning.

More critical intelligence followed. At 0150 hours on December 7 the following message was received:

> In the evening of the 5th (local time), *Utah* and a seaplane tender entered the harbor. Ships in port on the 6th are: nine battleships, three light cruisers, three seaplane carriers and seventeen destroyers, in addition to four light cruisers and two destroyers in the docks… All heavy cruisers and carriers were out of the harbor… No unusual condition was observed concerning the fleet…[13]

At 0200, *Akagi* received the last intelligence update that indicated that no barrage balloons or torpedo nets were in evidence. Last-minute intelligence generated by the Japanese consulate in Honolulu and received aboard *Akagi* suggested that conditions for the attack were favorable. The report concerning the types of ships in harbor was not entirely accurate, but the bulk of the Pacific Fleet appeared to be present. Though Genda later stated he was constantly adjusting the attack plan during the transit, the arrival of this high-quality intelligence did not prompt him to make additional modifications. The presence of the carriers was a huge planning assumption. Instead of modifying the orders of the 16 torpedo bombers assigned to attack them, Genda hoped for the carriers to miraculously appear by Sunday morning. When none did, the result was an unnecessary last-minute scramble on the part of the Kate pilots assigned to attack them.

THE FINAL APPROACH

The seas were heavy on the night of December 6 – even the carriers were being tossed around. On the six carrier flight decks, the aircraft of the first attack wave were spotted and readied for launch. Below, on the hangar decks, the second wave was readied. Each aircraft had been meticulously maintained during the transit and was as ready as it could be.

On the run toward Oahu, the formation's speed increased to 24 knots. In battle formation, the Striking Force was an imposing sight.

THE STRIKING FORCE APPROACHES PEARL HARBOR

In the vanguard was light cruiser *Abukuma* and four destroyers. About 3nm astern of the cruiser were the two battleships in column. Heavy cruisers *Tone* and *Chikuma* were deployed some 4nm off the flanks of the battleships. Behind the heavy combatants were the six carriers arranged in two parallel columns. Leading the starboard column was *Akagi*. Behind the flagship were the Striking Force's two newest carriers *Shokaku* and *Zuikaku*. *Kaga* was the lead ship of the port column, followed by the two smallest carriers, *Soryu* and *Hiryu*. The remaining destroyers were deployed on the flanks and stern of the carriers. Finally, the three submarines brought up the rear of the formation. This was the most powerful naval force on the planet, though its power had yet to be demonstrated. In just minutes, it would begin the launch of one of the most shocking and impactful surprise attacks in world history. This was the Imperial Navy at the height of its power. Never again would all six of these carriers operate together.

Events began to unfold according to plan. At 0530, *Tone* and *Chikuma* each launched a single Jake reconnaissance seaplane to perform a final check of Pearl Harbor and Lahaina anchorage. By 0550, the Striking Force was 220nm north of Oahu. The carriers changed course to the east to steam directly into the wind. Speed was increased again to 24 knots. Conditions were very difficult for launching aircraft. Long heavy swells sent spray over the flight decks. Even the carriers were rolling 11–15 degrees. The weather was so rough the start of the launch was delayed by 20 minutes.

When the launch finally began, the lightweight Zero fighters, arranged at the front of each deck load of aircraft, took off first. Following the fighters, the strike aircraft on each of the carriers were sent aloft. Four carriers of Carrier Divisions 1 and 2 had Kates arrayed on their flight decks. Each of these Kates were comprised of horizontal bombers and torpedo bombers. The horizontal bombers took off first, followed by the torpedo bombers. On *Shokaku* and *Zuikaku*, the decks were crowded with Val dive-bombers. These also took to the sky and began to assemble in formation.

From start to finish, the launch of the first wave took only 15 minutes – the fastest launch yet recorded by the Japanese for such a large group. By any measure, it was an impressive achievement. Of the 189 aircraft planned for the first wave, 183 were now in the air circling the carriers as newly launched aircraft joined the formation. In total, 43 fighters, 49 horizontal bombers, 40 torpedo bombers, and 51 dive-bombers had taken off. The launch was marred by several mishaps. One Zero each was forced to abort its launch from *Shokaku* and *Soryu*; one Val from *Shokaku* and two from *Zuikaku* suffered the same fate; one Kate armed as a horizontal bomber from *Kaga* also failed to launch. Each carrier had a destroyer astern to act as a plane guard during launch in case an aircraft crashed into the water upon takeoff. After assembling this huge formation, Fuchida in his Kate horizontal bomber gave the signal to depart. At about 0620, the formation headed south toward Oahu.

When the launch was complete, Nagumo ordered the Striking Force to the south to close the distance to the target. Aircraft from the second attack wave were moved to the flight deck by the three aircraft elevators on each carrier. Once on the flight deck, the engines were warmed up. By 0705, the second attack was ready to go. Nagumo ordered the fleet to turn east again into the wind. Ten minutes later, the launch began, with the Zeros again being the first to launch.

In this instance, of the 36 Zeros from the six carriers, only 35 took off. One Zero from *Hiryu* aborted. *Shokaku* and *Zuikaku* contributed 54 horizontal bombers – all of these launched successfully. The most important part of the second wave was the huge force of 81 dive-bombers with their elite crews from the carriers of Carrier Divisions 1 and 2. One dive-bomber each from *Kaga*, *Soryu*, and *Hiryu* encountered engine problems and was scratched, leaving 78. In all, the second wave was comprised 167 aircraft: 35 Zeros, 54 Kates, and 78 Vals. Counting the aircraft from both waves, a total of 350 aircraft were winging their way toward the utterly unsuspecting Americans on Oahu.

By the time the launch of the second wave was complete, the Striking Force was about 180nm from the northern tip of Oahu. Not all the flight activity that morning was related to the launch of the two attack waves. After the launch of the first attack wave, the Zeros allocated to CAP were sent aloft. At 0630, search aircraft from *Hiei, Kirishima, Tone* and *Chikuma* were launched to scout the waters south of the Striking Force.

Up to this point, the Japanese plan had gone exactly as intended. Competent planning and a heavy dose of American overconfidence translated Yamamoto's vision and Genda's plan into the surprise attack both contemplated. How successful 350 aircraft could be against an enemy caught off guard was about to be revealed.

7

The First Attack Wave

> If war eventuates with Japan, it is believed easily possible that hostilities would be initiated by a surprise attack upon the Fleet or the Naval Base at Pearl Harbor.
>
> Rear Admiral Richmond Kelly Turner to Admiral Stark, January 24, 1941[1]

The launch of the first wave had gone as well as the Japanese could have hoped. With the exception of the six aircraft that were forced to abort, the entire first attack force was in the air in 15 minutes. After taking off and circling near their carriers, the attack group assembled into a single loose formation. At Fuchida's direction, at 0620 hours it headed south while gradually assuming cruising altitude. The formation of 183 aircraft was led by the 89 carrier attack aircraft from *Akagi*, *Kaga*, *Soryu*, and *Hiryu* flying at between 9,200 and 9,800 feet. Arrayed to their right were the 51 dive-bombers from *Shokaku* and *Zuikaku* flying at 14,100 feet. Fighter cover was provided by the Zeros from all six carriers.

THE LAST WARNINGS

Before the attack, Admiral Kimmel and General Short failed to act on a series of warnings provided by Washington. A Japanese attack on Oahu was simply not believed to be possible. Now, on the morning of December 7, there were multiple indications of potentially hostile activity, but still the Americans failed to react.

The first indication was the most dramatic. It occurred hours before the start of the air attack. It is the most difficult to understand as to how it failed to rouse the Americans from their overwhelming sense of complacency.

Just as the Japanese aviators feared, the discovery of one or more of the midget submarines making their way into Pearl Harbor before the arrival of the air attack had the potential to sacrifice surprise. The midget submarine operation is detailed in Chapter 10, but for the purposes of outlining how their operations jeopardized the security of the Japanese air attack, it is sufficient to state that one of the midgets was spotted at 0342 in the restricted area a mile south of the channel into Pearl Harbor. Duty destroyer *Ward* was called to the scene but found nothing after searching for an hour. Later, at 0630, another ship spotted a possible small submarine. *Ward* was summoned again, and this time her crew clearly identified the object as a conning tower with a periscope. The ship's captain headed for the contact and opened fire at 0645. The second round hit the base of the submarine's sail and the target was observed to sink. After dropping a series of depth charges, *Ward* sent a signal at 0651 reporting what had occurred. A second, more direct, message was sent, stating: "We have attacked, fired upon, and dropped depth charges upon submarine operating in defense sea area." Received at the fleet radio station at 0653, even this development failed to jolt the Americans out of their lethargy. Kimmel had predicted that the Japanese might use submarines to attack his fleet. When it occurred, his command and control system was unable to process developments and respond in a timely manner.

The next warning was the most subtle of the three events. Per Short's instructions, the radar sites on Oahu were operating this Sunday morning from 0400 to 0700. The first unknown contact gained by these radars that morning was recorded at 0613 when the Koko Head and Fort Shafter radars picked up and tracked single contacts south of Oahu. These were the Japanese cruiser floatplanes making their pre-strike reconnaissance flights. Since the Information Center was not fully manned, it was impossible to identify the contacts. As it was, the appearance of two single contacts was not enough to raise an alarm.

The final warning should have been undeniable evidence of an impending attack. At 0645, the radars at Kaawa, Opana, and Kawailoa detected a group of aircraft north of Oahu. All except the Opana

THE FIRST ATTACK WAVE

radar shut down as scheduled at 0700 hours. Just as the Opana radar was due to be shut down, the two-man crew picked up a large flight of aircraft 132 miles north of Oahu at 0702. The crew reported this to the Information Center at Fort Shafter at 0715. By then, the large group of aircraft was only 88 miles away. Only two people were present at the Information Center. The lieutenant in charge was standing his second watch. After recalling that a flight of B-17s was due from the West Coast at this time and that its track was roughly the same as the reported air contact, he instructed the radar team that the contact was of no concern. The time was 0720. The Opana radar continued to track the inbound flight until 0739 when it was only 20 miles from Oahu.

Failure to fully staff the Information Center was a serious error. Even so, had the duty lieutenant explained to the radar crew that he was expecting a flight of only 12 B-17s, he might have learned that the radar operators were tracking a much larger formation. Raising the alarm at this point would have probably been fruitless. None of the fighters were in a combat-ready condition, antiaircraft guns were also unready, and the chains of commands of the Army and Navy were too cumbersome to respond quickly. In a best-case scenario, the radar warning of almost an hour was sufficient to have allowed the defenders some time to prepare for an attack. This would have almost certainly been insufficient to launch interceptors, but some aircraft dispersal might have been possible. Had word been passed to the fleet, sounding General Quarters would have secured all hatches and doors to improve the ships' watertight condition, antiaircraft batteries could have been manned, and preparations could have begun to sortie from the harbor.[2]

FUCHIDA MAKES A MESS

At 0735, the airborne strike received word from *Chikuma*'s search plane that nine battleships, one heavy, and six light cruisers were present in harbor. A subsequent report indicated that weather conditions were perfect. Earlier, *Tone*'s scout plane reported that Lahaina anchorage was clear.

As the formation approached Oahu, Fuchida had to decide which plan to use from between the two he and Genda devised during the transit. If Fuchida felt that surprise was achieved, the torpedo bombers would lead the attack. If he assessed that surprise had been lost, then the dive-bombers would lead with the torpedo bombers holding back.[3]

The importance of which plan to be used was linked to the attack of the torpedo bombers. This was the most critical aspect of the entire attack and had to be successful if its goals were to be achieved. Under ideal circumstances, the torpedo bombers would attack first, coming from two directions, with total surprise. Fuchida, Genda, and Murata knew how difficult the attack profile was for the torpedo bombers. They wanted no interference in the form of exploding bombs from the dive-bombers attacking Ford Island or from dive-bombers recovering from their dives at low altitude. The best that Fuchida, Genda, and Murata could come up with for the no-surprise attack variant was that the dive-bombers attacking Ford Island would occupy American antiaircraft gunners and any fighters, if they were present, to allow the vulnerable torpedo bombers to proceed unmolested. This was not a realistic plan, but fortunately for the Japanese it was not tested.

At 0740, just as the aircraft formation was approaching land off Kahuku Point, Fuchida fired one flare – the signal for a surprise attack. It is not clear how Fuchida made the assessment that the attack had gained surprise other than perhaps no American fighters were in sight. This was another flaw in the plan: by the time Fuchida could make an actual determination regarding surprise, the attackers would be too close to their targets to adjust.

According to Fuchida, after the first flare, Murata was observed to take his torpedo bombers and began to reduce altitude and head toward the target. However, the fighter group leader maintained his position. Fuchida stated he quickly fired another flare to get his attention. With two flares having been fired, Lieutenant Commander Takahashi, the lead dive-bomber pilot, thought that the signal for a no-surprise attack was in effect, so he raced ahead to attack first. In post-war interviews, Fuchida declared his frustration with the way the attack developed, but that there was nothing he could do about it.[4]

As a result of Fuchida's signals, the formation began to execute a no-surprise attack.[5] According to Japanese charts of the attack routes produced after the battle, Murata's torpedo bombers flew further to the west for several more minutes instead of proceeding directly toward the harbor. So, instead of the torpedo bombers entering the target area at the same time under pristine conditions, they arrived minutes after the

THE FIRST ATTACK WAVE

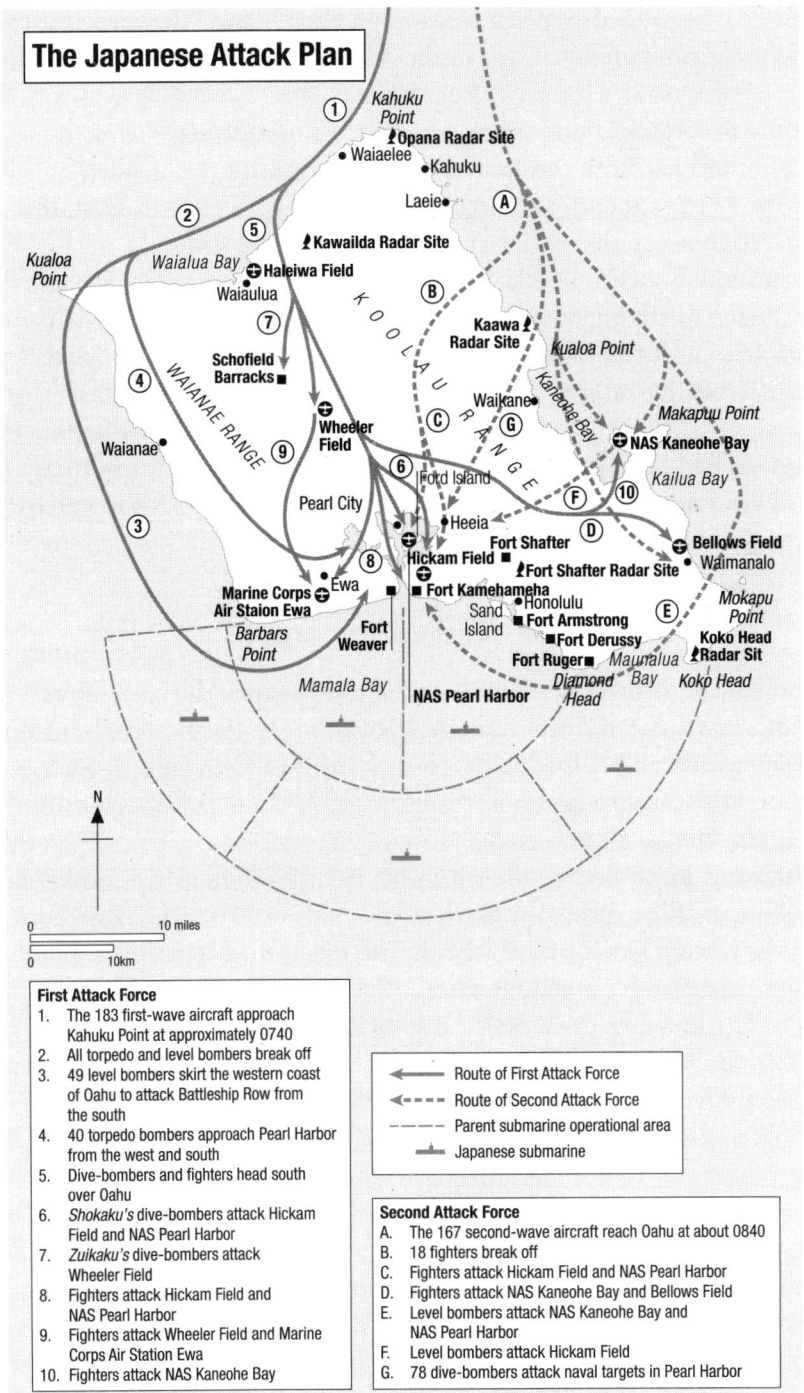

first dive-bomber dropped a weapon on Ford Island. The torpedo attack was not simultaneous – the Kates attacking the mooring points along the northwest side of Ford Island began their attacks several minutes before the attacks along Battleship Row. Consequently, the main targets on Battleships Row received precious extra minutes of warning. This allowed extra time for antiaircraft guns to get into action and additional time to improve the watertight conditions of the ships.

At 0749 hours, Fuchida issued the attack signal "*To, To, To,*" the first character in the Japanese word for "charge." By this time, the formation had already divided into separate groups which were headed for their respective targets. At 0753 hours, Fuchida's aircraft sent the signal "*Tora, Tora, Tora*" ("Tiger! Tiger! Tiger!"), the codeword indicating that surprise had been gained. These signals were not only picked up by the Striking Force, but also aboard Yamamoto's flagship *Nagato* located in the Inland Sea.

THE TORPEDO BOMBERS

Murata's 40 torpedo bombers were targeted against the battleships – the traditional heart of American naval power in the Pacific. At 0751 hours, Murata ordered his formation to split up into four groups, each built around the torpedo bombers from one of the four carriers contributing aircraft. The 24 aircraft under Murata's direct command, 12 each from *Akagi* and *Kaga*, flew to the southeast in order to loop around Hickam Field to enable a direct approach to the ships on Battleship Row located on the eastern side of Ford Island. The remaining 16 torpedo bombers (eight each from *Soryu* and *Hiryu*) flew to the east so as to attack the ships anchored on the western side of Ford Island.

Murata's pilots faced the greatest challenge of any of the Japanese raiders. Flying the planned attack profile and scoring a hit on one of the selected targets, even if it was stationary, demanded great skill. Flying the correct air speed and altitude was critical if the Type 91 torpedoes were to hit the water at the proper entry angle. As the pilots approached the harbor area, each had just seconds to make several critical decisions. First, the correct target had to be identified. Then, the correct range calculation was required since the torpedo needed at least 650 feet to arm itself. Most importantly during this process, the correct speed and altitude at which the torpedo was dropped had to be achieved.

THE FIRST ATTACK WAVE

Because of the intensive training of the aircrews to master all these elements, Japanese planners expected that of 40 torpedoes dropped, 27 would hit their targets.

Since the main torpedo attack group under Murata had swung to the west, the aircraft from *Soryu* and *Hiryu* were closer to their targets, so they opened the torpedo attack on Pearl Harbor. The leader of the 16 torpedo Kates from *Soryu* and *Hiryu* was Lieutenant Matsumura Hirata from *Hiryu*. As his aircraft approached Ford Island from the west, they headed directly into the sun. This made identification of ship types more challenging. On their way along the Wai'enae mountains, Matsumura was bypassed by Lieutenant Nagai Tsuyoshi and the eight aircraft from *Soryu*. Nagai assumed an attack altitude of 150 feet and headed to the target. Nagai was adept enough at ship recognition to understand that there were no carriers in their normal moorings on this side of the island. Genda, Fuchida, and Murata knew from pre-attack reports that the carriers were not present on December 6 but did not change the attack plan in the hopes that one would return by dawn the following day. Actual events proved the old adage that "hope is not a plan"; when Matsumura's 16 torpedo aircraft faced the reality that their primary targets were not present, there was no firm backup plan. Now Matsumara's 16 Kates faced a dilemma that they did not handle well.

The only ships moored on the northwest side of Ford Island were the training ship *Utah*, the light cruisers *Raleigh* and *Detroit*, and the seaplane tender *Tangier*. None of them were suitable targets for a precious Type 91 torpedo, and none were on the target priorities briefed to the pilots. *Utah* was a former battleship, but she had been demilitarized for use as a target ship. She had lost all her main battery turrets and had boxlike structures placed over her empty barbettes so still vaguely resembled a battleship. The pilots had been briefed not to attack her, but with the sun in their eyes and with no real backup plan, many of the pilots could not make this important distinction.

Nagai recognized *Utah* for what she was and quickly decided not to attack. Looking for a suitable target, he spotted a ship to the southeast moored along the 1010 Dock which he identified as a battleship. He and the Kate directly behind him headed for this new target. Unable to communicate with his other pilots, the rest of his group – six aircraft led by Lieutenant Junior Grade Nakajima Tatsumi – headed toward

Utah to make their attacks. Nakajima launched his torpedo and missed so badly that it hit light cruiser *Raleigh* moored in front of *Utah*. The three other aircraft in Nakajima's section also targeted *Utah*. One hit the ex-battleship, but the other two missed. One hit the shore near light cruiser *Detroit* and the other has never been located in the mud of Pearl Harbor. Next to attack were the last two aircraft from Nagai's section. The first of these missed its target and struck Ford Island aft of *Raleigh* (where it was later recovered); the second hit forward on *Utah*.[6]

Utah stood no chance against the impact of two torpedoes. Launched as a battleship in 1910, she was converted into a target ship before the war. In the process, she was demilitarized and lost her belt armor. Her antiquated side protection system was entirely unable to deal with modern weapons.

As the attack started, her crew was caught completely by surprise. Because all the ship's weapons were stored below decks or were under steel houses (used when *Utah* performed her duties as a target ship), she was unable to return fire during the attack. As indicated in her Action Report, which described her attackers as "They appeared to [be] Henkle [sic] 113, or similar type, with very silent engines," her crew never knew what hit them. Both torpedo hits occurred in the same location in quick succession. By 0805, the former battleship developed a list of 40 degrees, and this increased to 80 degrees five minutes later. Abandon ship was ordered just before the ship began to capsize at 0812. Her Action Report mentioned constant strafing by Japanese aircraft during this time, but no Japanese aircraft engaged in this activity against *Utah*'s crew. Sixty-four of the ship's crew were killed and the wreck of the ship still remains where it sank.[7]

Action Reports from the ships under attack seldom agree on the times of events. *Raleigh*'s commanding officer stated that he felt the dull explosion of a torpedo at 0755 as he was taking coffee. The Type 91 struck the Number 2 Fireroom, and soon the Number 1 Fireroom and the forward engine room flooded. Counterflooding was ordered, and all topside equipment that could be removed was jettisoned. The ship's two floatplanes were lowered into the water and taxied to Ford Island. The ship never lost power; this combined with the quick response of the crew kept the ship from capsizing. According to her commanding officer, the ship's antiaircraft crews were firing back within five minutes of the commencement of the attack. In all, 266 3-inch/50 rounds,

THE FIRST ATTACK WAVE

3,270 1.1-inch, and 9,900 .50-caliber rounds were expended. Hits were claimed on five attacking aircraft.[8]

As *Utah* started to capsize and *Raleigh* began her fight for survival, Nagai flew south along Ford Island to head toward a new target along the 1010 Dock with his wingman right behind. According to his wingmen, Nagai's aircraft made a perfect approach and scored a direct hit on the target. It was not a battleship as Nagai had thought, but two ships moored together. The Type 91 ran under the minelayer *Oglala* and hit the modern light cruiser *Helena*. When he got within about 650 yards of *Oglala* and *Helena*, Nagai's wingman recognized that Nagai had wasted his torpedo on a cruiser. He banked away and headed to a new target – the battleship moored at the southern end of Battleship Row.[9]

While *Soryu*'s eight torpedo bombers were trying to figure out a new targeting plan on the fly, Matsumura's eight *Hiryu* aircraft were struggling with the same problem. Confusion reigned from the start as *Hiryu*'s aircraft approached the target area. Since Matsumura identified *Utah* correctly, he led his wingman to the south so they could line up on Battleship Row. However, the last two pilots in Matsumura's section missed their turn. They fell in behind Lieutenant Kadono Hiroharu, who led the second four Kates of Matsumura's attack group, as he temporarily circled near Ewa Field. Kadono saw Nagai's torpedo hit *Helena* and headed for the 1010 Dock to repeat the attack. When Nagai's wingman broke off his attack on *Helena*, Kadono realized that this target was in fact a cruiser. He and a single Kate from Matsumura's section broke off their attack.[10]

The remaining four aircraft from *Hiryu* continued toward *Helena* to launch their attack. By now the Americans were able to direct anti-aircraft fire at the wandering *Hiryu* aircraft. Probably because of this fire, the first aircraft failed to launch its torpedo at the proper altitude and speed, so the weapon plunged into the harbor floor. The next aircraft came under fire from *Helena* and *Oglala*, was heavily damaged (29 holes were later counted in the aircraft), and was forced to launch the torpedo from over 600 feet, much too high for a successful drop. The last two Kates both missed with their Type 91s, with one hitting the shore under the 1010 Dock and the other getting stuck in Pearl Harbor's muddy bottom.[11]

Aboard *Helena*, crewmen spotted the first attacking torpedo bomber at 0757. Ninety seconds later, the torpedo hit the ship as the crew was

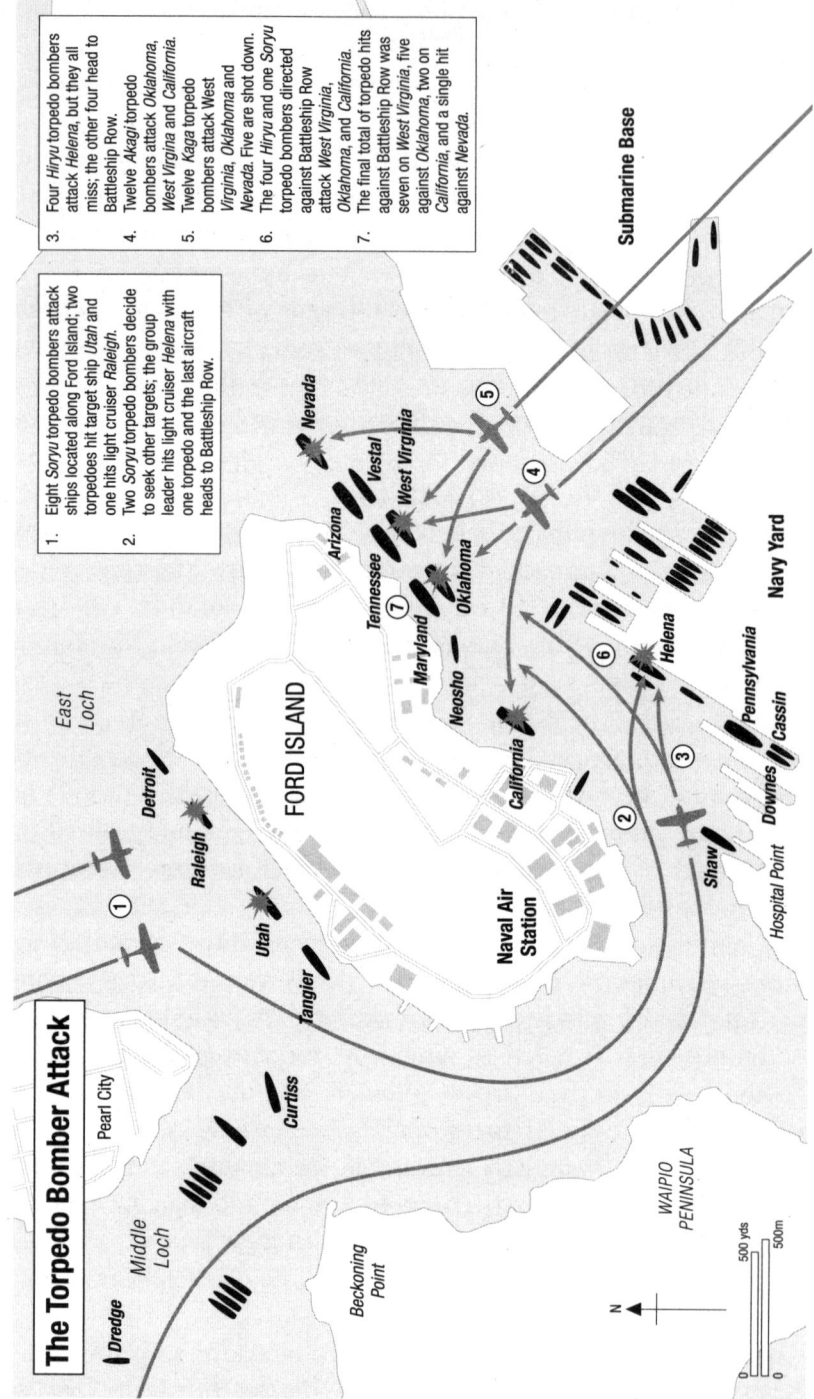

running to their General Quarters stations. The torpedo hit amidships on the starboard side 18 feet below the waterline. Damage was extensive, with three boiler rooms flooded, but the ship was in no danger of sinking. Personnel casualties were heavy – 26 men died outright and 71 were wounded. Five of the wounded later died in hospital. Though *Helena* was unable to bring gunfire against the Kate that torpedoed her, the crew responded quickly against subsequent attacks. A total of 375 5-inch/38 rounds were expended, as well as 3,000 rounds of 1.1/75 rounds and 5,000 .50-caliber machine gun rounds.[12]

Unfortunately for the ancient *Oglala*, she was moored outboard of *Helena* on the morning of December 7. Launched as a cargo ship in 1907, she was purchased by the USN ten years later and converted to a minelayer. *Oglala* possessed no armor or underwater protection, and no internal subdivision. General Quarters was sounded at 0755 with the explosion of the torpedo that ran underneath *Oglala* and hit *Helena* being recorded a couple of minutes later. The force of the explosion ruptured *Oglala*'s hull on the port side. Extensive flooding resulted and a 5-degree list quickly developed. With no power, there was no hope of keeping the ship afloat so two tugs were summoned to move the ship clear of *Helena* and secure her to the pier. Though this was successful, by 0930 the list increased to 20 degrees, forcing the abandon ship order to be given. *Oglala* capsized on her port side 30 minutes later. Three of her crew suffered minor wounds.[13] Few ships can claim to have sunk without having been directly hit, but that was *Oglala*'s fate.

At the conclusion of this fiasco, four *Hiryu* Kates and one *Soryu* Kate were maneuvering to attack Battleship Row. The other 11 Kates from Matsumura's attack group had achieved little. This was the inevitable outcome of forcing each section leader or pilot to individually decide on a new target. In the resulting confusion, made worse by antiaircraft fire and the reflection and glare from the sun, which was directly ahead, most pilots misidentified their targets. Of the targets they struck, only *Helena* was worth a torpedo. The crews of five aircraft who had the patience and skill to avoid this temptation proceeded to Battleship Row where important targets could be found in abundance. Their confusion was not at an end though; they now joined the line of *Akagi* torpedo bombers in the process of conducting their attacks.

BATTLESHIP ROW UNDER TORPEDO ATTACK

Genda's biggest blows were reserved for the American battlewagons moored along Battleship Row. The first round consisted of the 24 torpedo bombers under Murata. Battleship Row was full on the morning of December 7. *Nevada* was moored in the northernmost position. Forward of her was *Arizona* with repair ship *Vestal* moored alongside. Forward of *Arizona* were the first of two battleships moored in pairs. The first pair was *Tennessee* (in the inboard position) and *West Virginia* (outboard). The second pair included *Maryland* (inboard) and *Oklahoma* (outboard). Moored alongside the Ford Island fueling pier forward of the second pair of battleships was fleet oiler *Neosho*. The last major ship moored on the eastern side of Ford Island and the battleship located closest to the harbor channel was *California*.

Against this lineup were Murata's 24 aircraft, now joined by the five Kates from *Soryu* and *Hiryu* that had declined to waste their torpedoes on the ships moored off the northwestern portion of Ford Island. Leading the attack were the 12 torpedo bombers from *Akagi* under the direct command of Murata.

Murata led his formation over Ewa Field at just over 1,600 feet altitude until he turned left to fly over Hickam Field from the southwest. On passing Hickam Field, the formation turned left again to fly over the shipyard and the Southeast Loch toward Battleship Row. The first six of Murata's aircraft were in two parallel lines, one led by Murata and the other by Lieutenant Junior Grade Goto Jinichi. The two wingmen trailed their leaders by about 1,600 feet. The second group of six aircraft was deployed in a long trail formation with the same 1,600 feet between aircraft, but this extended to as much as 6,000 feet separation in the last half of the formation.[14] It is important to note that as Murata's squadron maneuvered into attack formation they were entirely unescorted.

Once on the final run over the Southeast Loch, the pilots had to rely on their training to get into the proper envelope to release their torpedoes. Altitude was reduced to 65 feet, judged by sight, and speed was reduced. Within seconds their targets on Battleship Row came into view. Goto observed that he and Murata came under machine-gun fire even before they launched their torpedoes. Directly in front of them were the two outboard battleships *Oklahoma* and *West Virginia*.

THE FIRST ATTACK WAVE

At 0757, Murata launched his Type 91 torpedo at *West Virginia*; Goto selected *Oklahoma* as his target. Goto observed that both torpedoes hit their targets. Despite the machine-gun fire, Goto's Kate was undamaged, and Murata's was hit by only a single bullet. The quick American response impressed Goto.[15]

The next two torpedo bombers to drop their weapons were the aircraft following behind Murata and Goto. Murata's wingman aimed for *West Virginia*, while Goto's aimed for *Oklahoma*. The last two Kates in the first group to attack both headed for *Oklahoma*. The one in Goto's flight took 21 bullet hits and then had a near collision with Murata's second wingman as both were going for the same target. One of the aircraft, probably Goto's wingman, was forced to jettison its torpedo. The first six *Akagi* torpedo planes scored several hits against *West Virginia* and *Oklahoma* in quick succession and all survived the experience.[16]

Next up was the final group of six torpedo bombers under Lieutenant Negishi Asao. His aircraft approached the target area in a long trail formation. Observing the concentration on only two battleships by the first six *Akagi* aircraft, Negishi led his two wingmen to attack *California*. Both Negishi and his first wingman dropped their weapons against *California*; one was a hit. The second wingman had the same intent but under heavy fire was forced to veer back to *Oklahoma* which was a closer target. One of the crewmen on this aircraft was wounded and died after returning to *Akagi*.[17]

At this point, confusion returned when the final *Soryu* torpedo bomber interrupted the dispersed *Akagi* stream. The pilot was unable to make the tight turn required to line up for a drop against *California*, so was forced to abort the run and go around for another try. Three *Akagi* aircraft had yet to attack. The section leader directed them to the nearest and easiest target, *Oklahoma*. The section leader was able to aim his torpedo at *Oklahoma*, but before his two wingmen were able to attack, the first two remaining aircraft from *Hiryu* inserted themselves into the equation. These were Matsumura and his wingman. Attacking through the turbulence of the preceding aircraft, Matsumura was unable to drop his weapon and was forced to go around for another target run. His wingman launched his Type 91 at *West Virginia*. The final two *Akagi* aircraft were able to complete their attack run against *Oklahoma*. Overconcentration on the unfortunate *Oklahoma* continued when the last two *Hiryu* aircraft, led by Lieutenant Kadono, dropped their

PEARL HARBOR

The Level Bomber Attack against Battleship Row

1. 49 level bombers approach Battleship Row from the south.
2. The formation consists of four groups: 15 torpedo bombers from *Akagi*, 14 from *Kaga*, 10 from *Soryu*, and 10 from *Hiryu*. Each air group is arranged in sections of five aircraft.
3. Three of the four groups have to make more than one pass over the target before dropping all their weapons.
4. Level bombers hit four of the six battleships moored along Battleship Row: *Tennessee*, *Maryland*, *West Virginia*, and *Arizona*. *Arizona* suffers a catastrophic magazine explosion, but the other three battleships suffer only minor damage. The repair ship *Vestal*, moored alongside *Arizona*, is also damaged in the attack.

FORD ISLAND

Nevada
Arizona
Vestal
Tennessee
West Virginia
Maryland
Neosho
Oklahoma
California
Naval Air Station
Shaw
Helena
Downes
Pennsylvania
Cassin
Navy Yard
Hospital Point
Channel Entrance
Section Base
Hickam Field

N

0   500 yds
0   500 m

torpedoes against the same target. Finally, Matsumura flew a complete circle and then lined up against *West Virginia*. He claimed a hit.[18]

The Japanese claimed that 11 *Akagi* carrier attack planes dropped their torpedoes (one jettisoned its torpedo as the result of a near air-to-air collision), and that all 11 hit one of the three battleships targeted. Interspersed among the final six *Akagi* torpedo bombers were the four remaining *Hiryu* aircraft. The first two of these launched at *West Virginia* and the final two selected *Oklahoma*.

Trailing the *Akagi* torpedo bomber group by 3 miles were the 12 aircraft from *Kaga* under Lieutenant Kitajima Ichiro. By this point, the weight of American antiaircraft fire was increasing, mainly from .50-caliber machine guns but also from a few 5-inch/25 guns on the battleships which had been able to break out ammunition. Since the remaining torpedo bombers were in a long trail formation, the Americans were able to concentrate their fire on each one in succession. Of the last seven *Kaga* torpedo bombers to attack, five were shot down – four by machine-gun fire and one by a 5-inch gun.

None of the torpedo planes from the other three carriers were shot down, demonstrating how critical the element of surprise was for the vulnerable torpedo aircraft.

Kitajima and his first wingman both selected *West Virginia* for attack. The second wingman observed that the battleship already had a port list from the effect of previous torpedo hits. Kitajima's second wingman was hit four times by antiaircraft fire before launching against *West Virginia*. As the weight of antiaircraft fire increased, the next two Kate pilots selected *Oklahoma* as their target. Both were hit by antiaircraft fire eight times but were able to return to *Kaga*. The sixth Kate to make its attack run was not as fortunate and was hit by antiaircraft fire and burst into flames. The rear gunner declined to burn to death, so jumped out of the aircraft with no parachute. Amazingly, he was pulled out of the water still alive but died of his injuries within minutes. His aircraft continued on past the 1010 Dock, jettisoning its torpedo on the way. The Kate crashed on the grounds of the Naval Hospital, killing both of the other crewmen.[19]

The final six aircraft to attack were all subjected to heavy defensive fire. The first was led by Lieutenant Suzuki Mimori. A one-in-a-million shot hit the warhead of the Type 91 that Suzuki's Kate was carrying. In the resulting explosion, Suzuki and his crew were killed. Suzuki's first wingman was hit twice but he was able to launch his weapon on *West Virginia*.

Interrupting the *Kaga* attack was the final *Soryu* torpedo bomber that had completed a full circle and then selected *California* for attack. One of the crewmen on board this aircraft confirmed that the Type 91 hit its target. In return, the Kate was heavily damaged by antiaircraft fire. The skillful pilot made it back to the Striking Force but was forced to ditch next to a destroyer after his landing gear failed. The next Kaga torpedo bomber to attack was forced to veer to the right and launched its torpedo at *Nevada*. The torpedo hit the battleship forward but the Kate was shot down. One of the members of this crew was spotted coming ashore on Ford Island near *Tennessee* and was shot by a Marine.[20]

The attack of the final three Kaga torpedo bombers was anticlimactic. The first waded through the antiaircraft fire to launch its weapon against *Oklahoma*. The crew claimed a hit and observed that the battleship was already listing and had water on its deck. The following aircraft was shot down before it could launch its weapon. The final Kaga torpedo bomber suffered the same fate – it was hit by antiaircraft fire, had its torpedo ripped away, and crashed.[21] Of the 12 *Kaga* aircraft, eight dropped their torpedoes against three different battleships; the Japanese claimed all eight hit their target.

The torpedo attack lasted just 11 minutes, ending at 0806. In this short time, the Japanese inflicted the most significant damage of the entire attack. At the cost of five aircraft (and a sixth later forced to ditch), torpedoes sank two battleships and inflicted damage leading to the sinking of two others. Additionally, a target ship and a minelayer had sunk and two light cruisers were damaged. Of the 36 torpedoes launched, the best estimate concludes that 19 hit a target.

Japanese Torpedo Hits at Pearl Harbor[22]

Target	Number of hits
Oklahoma	5
West Virginia	7
California	2
Nevada	1
Utah	2
Raleigh	1
Helena/Oglala	1
Total	19

THE FIRST ATTACK WAVE

By all appearances, the Japanese torpedo attack was a great success. Four battleships were hit, with two sinking immediately. In reality, it was not as successful as the Japanese had planned. As has been detailed, the attack was not executed smoothly. Most of the aircraft from *Soryu* and *Hiryu* wasted their weapons. In the main attack on Battleship Row, Genda wanted a distribution of fire, but the pilots got the last vote. Most of the 29 torpedo bombers attacking Battleship Row concentrated on the easiest targets available – *Oklahoma* and *West Virginia*. Only four went after other battleships. Though the Japanese expected 27 torpedo hits, only 19 were actually recorded. Of these, only 15 were against the primary targets. From this standpoint, only 38 percent of the torpedoes employed furthered the goals of the attack. The inability to execute a coordinated surprise attack against the targets located on both sides of Ford Island, combined with the selection of an extended trail formation, resulted in heavy losses for the last group of aircraft to attack.

THE LEVEL BOMBERS

Forty-nine level bombers constituted the second part of the Japanese one-two combo against Battleship Row. The 49 aircraft were organized into ten groups of five aircraft (one *Kaga* Kate aborted, so one of her groups had only four aircraft). Each group was arranged in a "V" formation with the lead aircraft at the center. The Americans noted that the Japanese formations were impeccable. Aboard the lead aircraft was the lead bombardier. When he dropped his bombs, all other aircraft in the group also dropped theirs so that a single target was subjected to a barrage of bombs. Using this technique, the Japanese believed at least one of the bombs would hit the target.

Fuchida planned for his level bombers to approach the target in a single column formation with each group bombing in turn. This may have been the ideal arrangement for bombing accuracy, but it was not ideal if the enemy was shooting back. After the war, Fuchida made this astute observation: "I further saw that it was not wise to have deployed in this long single-column formation. The whole bombing group could be destroyed like ducks in a shooting gallery."[23] Even though the level bombing attack commenced only minutes after the torpedo attack, it was met by antiaircraft fire. Fuchida was impressed with the rapidity of the American response; his aircraft was hit by shrapnel during its first attack run.[24]

Fuchida's group led the long, impressive formation of level bombers. Coming from the southwest, they overflew Battleship Row with a separation of about 220 yards between groups. Their primary targets were the double-moored battleships in which the ships inboard were immune to torpedo attack. Fuchida states in his account of the attack that his group targeted *Nevada* at the northern end of Battleship Row. This target selection was contrary to his own instructions. One of the Kates in his group was forced to drop its bomb early because of battle damage. When it came time to drop, clouds obscured *Nevada*, so Fuchida banked his group away for another try.[25]

When Fuchida's group returned for its second attempted attack run, smoke from *Arizona*, moored forward of *Nevada*, once again obscured the target. Changing the target to *Maryland*, Fuchida's group dropped its four remaining bombs. Fuchida personally witnessed two hits and two near misses.[26] As usual, Fuchida's account was inaccurate. In fact, all four bombs missed the target, with two hitting Ford Island.

However, the experience of Fuchida's group was typical in many regards. Each group approached the target in perfect formation and made its drop when it had a clear view of the target. From the best reconstruction of the sequence, the three groups from *Akagi* opened the attack from 0805 to 0807. As detailed above, Fuchida's lead group did not drop on the first pass. The next two groups selected *Tennessee* and *West Virginia* as their targets and dropped all ten of their bombs. *Kaga*'s three groups, with a total of 14 aircraft, made their first pass from 0807 to 0808. The first and third groups held their bombs, and the second targeted *Arizona* with *Vestal* alongside. When the first and third groups returned, they delivered their attacks against *Tennessee* and *West Virginia*. *Soryu*'s two groups made their passes from 0808 to 0809. The first group targeted *Tennessee* and *West Virginia*, and the second held its bombs. When the second group returned to make its drop, it targeted *Nevada*. From 0809 to 0810, *Hiryu*'s two groups were the last to make their initial target run. The first dropped on *Arizona* and scored a dramatic hit, detonating *Arizona*'s forward magazines. The smoke from the huge explosion made the second group miss when it later dropped against *California*.[27]

As ordered by Fuchida, groups made as many passes as necessary to get a clear view of the target. The last drop occurred at 0840 when

THE FIRST ATTACK WAVE

California reported being missed by four bombs. Six of the ten groups scored a hit, for a total of ten hits on five different targets. The hits were also well spread out. The primary targets were the two inboard battleships; both *Tennessee* and *Maryland* suffered two bomb hits. Two hits were also recorded against *West Virginia*, and two against *Arizona*. Outboard of *Arizona* was *Vestal* – she suffered two hits as a result of bombs missing *Arizona*. Achieving ten hits in 49 drops was a very respectable achievement. The fate of *Arizona*, examined below in more detail, has become the iconic event of the entire attack and has overshadowed the ineffectiveness of the other bomb hits. Of the ten hits, six failed to explode or resulted in only a low-order detonation. If the bomb that went through *Vestal* before exploding is included, then seven of the bombs failed to perform as designed. Two of the bombs that hit the battleships failed to explode at all, even though they had two separate fuses. The other four rendered only low-order detonations that resulted in minor damage. In some cases this was due to the modifications made on the shells when they were converted to bombs. The removal of the excess weight weakened them enough that they shattered on impact.[28]

The fate of *Arizona* was and still remains the subject of much conjecture, but it is clear that her destruction was caused by a level bomber. Even the number of bomb hits was hard to clarify. Her original damage reports include as many as eight hits; the Japanese claimed four. The true total from the ten bombs dropped from groups from *Kaga* and *Hiryu* was two hits and two near misses. The first five bombs from the *Kaga* group resulted in a hit on *Arizona*'s Number 4 14-inch gun turret, a near miss along the battleship's port side, and a hit aft on *Vestal*. The bomb that hit *Arizona* aft caused minor damage as it glanced off the front of the sloping armor on the face of Turret Number 4 and was deflected aft. After penetrating the main deck, it exploded in the flag officer's pantry, causing little damage.[29]

The fatal blow came from the first *Hiryu* group under the command of Lieutenant Commander Kusumi Tadashi. Upon the signal of Lieutenant Kondo Shojiro, the bombardier on Kusumi's lead aircraft, all five aircraft in the group released their weapons from 10,480 feet. Again, the same pattern unfolded. One bomb hit *Arizona* on her starboard side between Turrets 1 and 2, another scored a near miss on the battleship's port side, and another hit *Vestal*. Observers at the time thought that the near misses were torpedo hits, but it is clear no torpedo bombers targeted *Arizona*.[30]

From this altitude, and with a fully functional No. 80 Type 99 bomb, the weapon had no problem penetrating the 5-inch armored deck and the 1-inch protective deck over the forward powder rooms. In the span of seven seconds, the bomb penetrated to one of the three starboard powder rooms and exploded. Expanding gas from the first powder room spread to the two adjacent powder rooms. Contained by the 13-inch-thick armored bulkhead of the armored citadel located forward of Turret Number 1, the gases vented up three decks and created a burst of fire visible on photography of the event on the deck forward of Turret 1. With nowhere else to vent, the superheated gases ignited the three port-side powder rooms. This caused a catastrophic explosion familiar to anyone who has seen film of the event. Altogether, some 582 tons of powder for the 14-inch guns exploded. The entire forward third of the ship was completely devastated.[31]

The destruction of *Arizona* made the level bombing attack a success and corresponded with Japanese expectations. Had the other bombs functioned as intended, *Maryland* and *Tennessee* could have suffered significant damage. Otherwise, the results were disappointing. *California* and *Nevada* were missed altogether and the hits on *West Virginia* were irrelevant since her fate had already been determined by the torpedo attack.

AGONY ON BATTLESHIP ROW

Oklahoma was the most-attacked battleship by virtue of the fact she was directly in line with the approach route down the Southeast Loch. According to her action report, the first indication of the attack was the explosion of bombs on the southwest hangar of Ford Island. The first indication of the attack resulted in orders to man the antiaircraft battery and then go to General Quarters. Only the port ready machine gun opened fire but was silenced by the force of the explosion of the first torpedo hit forward.[32] Within a few minutes, the battleship was hit by two more torpedoes on the port side. *Oklahoma* immediately listed to port after the first hit, and by the third hit the list increased to 45 degrees. Two or three additional torpedo hits were recorded after that. Within eight to ten minutes after being struck, the ship capsized.

THE FIRST ATTACK WAVE

Oklahoma's quick capsizing resulted in heavy casualties. The rescue of men trapped below decks began almost immediately, and eventually 32 were rescued by salvage teams. Calculations from December 15 indicated that of the 1,353 officers and men present on December 7, 899 survived. Twenty-two were known dead and 26 wounded at the time of the report, with 406 still missing.[33]

The barrage of torpedoes directed at *Oklahoma* would have sunk any battleship of the day, but *Oklahoma*'s underwater protective system made her especially vulnerable to torpedo damage. Though modernized between the wars, even this updated system was inadequate against torpedo attack. The modernization added a torpedo bulge and a torpedo bulkhead of 1.5 inches. The bulge was empty. Behind the original hull of the ship was a protective layer of two fuel tanks, both filled with fuel oil to absorb the blast of an explosion. Behind the fuel tanks was an armored bulkhead covering the hull from the third deck to the double bottom. The same protective system was featured on *Arizona* and *Nevada*.[34]

West Virginia, moored aft of *Oklahoma*, was also subjected to repeated torpedo attack. She carried a much more effective underwater protection system than that on *Oklahoma*. The same system was fitted on *West Virginia*'s sister ship *Maryland*, and both Tennessee-class ships, *Tennessee* and *California*. The superior system covered two-thirds of the *West Virginia*'s hull. It contained five compartments with a total depth of 17.5 feet. The outer compartment next to the hull was a void space 4 feet deep. Next were three fuel tanks, each 3 feet deep. The final layer was another void 4.5 feet deep. The inner boundary was a 1-inch-thick armor plate. All the layers were subdivided by transverse bulkheads; the bulkheads between the layers were designed to bend under pressure from an explosion.[35]

The ship's executive officer was the senior surviving officer. In his action report, he stated that he was getting dressed when at 0755 the word was passed "Away Fire and Rescue Party." This was followed about 30 seconds later by "General Quarters." It was also at this time that the first two torpedo hits were felt. By the time he reached the quarterdeck, the ship was already beginning to list rapidly to port. At this time, the executive officer felt another torpedo hit followed by a fourth. This brought the ship's list to an estimated 20–25 degrees. When *Arizona* blew up, burning debris ranging from a fraction of an inch up to 5 inches in diameter rained down on the quarterdeck of *West Virginia*.[36]

Through the efforts of junior officers and senior petty officers, counterflooding of voids on the starboard side was accomplished in time to prevent the ship from capsizing. By the time flooding forced the evacuation of Damage Control Central, the list had been reduced to 21 degrees. The firefighting teams were unable to extinguish the onboard fires, and a wall of flame was advancing toward *West Virginia* from oil on the water from the doomed *Arizona*. Not until the following afternoon did firefighting teams finally extinguish the blaze.[37]

Post-attack analysis indicated that *West Virginia* was struck by seven torpedoes, six hitting the hull on the port side and the seventh against the rudder, which blew it off its mount. The six hull hits did extensive damage to the outermost plates. Though the tanks of the torpedo defense system were compressed and pushed inward, the innermost bulkhead held. Despite the fact that the system worked as designed, the onslaught of torpedoes was overwhelming. The influx of water into the ship caused by the first four hits created a quick list; when the next two torpedoes hit, they did so above the armor belt. These hits were the most significant since they allowed flooding of the second and third decks. Making things worse were the fires that burned on and around the battleship for the remainder of the day and into the next.[38] By 0940 hours, fire engulfed the ship from her bow aft to Turret Number 1. At 1005 hours, the word was given to abandon ship since there was no power to fight the fires that now engulfed the superstructure. The fires were not brought under control until that afternoon when fire parties returned to the ship.

In addition to the torpedo damage, *West Virginia* was hit by two No. 80 bombs. The first hit the foretop and penetrated all the way to the main armor deck where it was stopped without exploding. The second bomb hit the top of Turret Number 3. This bomb was also faulty. It broke up and did not explode. Fragments from this bomb set the two seaplanes on the catapult on top of Turret 3 afire.

Unlike *Oklahoma*, *West Virginia* did not capsize, resulting in a much smaller loss of life. This was attributable to her better torpedo defense system, prompt counterflooding, and that she was wedged against *Tennessee*. Of her December 1 crew of 87 officers and 1,454 men, two officers and 103 enlisted personnel were killed and another 52 wounded. Among the dead was the ship's commanding officer, Captain Mervyn Bennion, who was hit by a splinter from a bomb which exploded on the adjacent *Tennessee*. He continued to fight the ship despite his mortal abdomen wounds and for this he was awarded a posthumous Medal of Honor.

Maryland suffered the least of any of the battleships moored on Battleship Row. Her gunnery crews promptly manned their weapons at the beginning of the attack. A total of 450 5-inch/25, 4,500 1.1-inch, and 2,500 .50-caliber rounds were expended during the attack. Because of her inboard position, *Maryland* was saved from torpedo damage, but she was a target of Fuchida's level bombers. Two Type 80 bombs hit the ship, but both struck areas where damage was not significant. One hit the forecastle below the waterline; another hit the forecastle but caused little damage. Minor flooding resulted; added to the intentional flooding of the forward magazines, paint stowage, and gasoline stowage, there were about 1,000 tons of water in the forward part of the ship. From her crew on December 1 of 108 officers and 1,496 enlisted, three men were killed and ten wounded.[39]

Tennessee, the other battleship moored inboard, also escaped torpedo damage. When the first Japanese aircraft were observed at about 0755 dropping bombs on Ford Island, *Tennessee*'s crew went to General Quarters and the gunners went into action within five minutes. According to her action report, the ship expended 760 rounds of 5-inch/25 shells, 180 rounds of 3-inch/50, and 4,000 .50-caliber machine-gun rounds. For this, the ship claimed four enemy planes.[40]

When *Arizona* blew up, burning powder, oil, and debris was thrown on the quarterdeck of *Tennessee* (*Arizona* was moored about 75 feet astern of *Tennessee*). This started fires on the stern that were more damaging than the bomb hits. The fires were brought under control by about 1030. Almost immediately after, at about 1035, it was decided to try to move the ship forward to escape the fires from the badly burning *Arizona*. Both engines went ahead 5 knots but the ship did not move because *West Virginia* kept her wedged against the mooring quay. *Tennessee* kept her screws turning over from 5 to 10 knots throughout the day and night in order to wash the burning oil away from her stern.[41]

Tennessee took two hits during the level bombing attack. One struck Turret Number 3, wrecking the catapult on the roof before penetrating into the turret. The bomb broke into large pieces but did not explode, but the explosive charge spilled into the turret and burned. Damage to the training gear and rammers was recorded. The range finder was completely wrecked. Several casualties occurred as a result of this hit. The other bomb to strike *Tennessee* hit the top of Turret Number 2. Penetrating into the turret, it rendered the middle gun inoperative. Fragments from this hit caused casualties at the machine-gun stations. Overall casualties were light – four enlisted men killed, two missing, and 19 wounded. One officer and two Marines were wounded.

The fate of *Arizona* has been described. A single explosion killed most of the ship's crew and utterly destroyed the forward part of the ship so that no salvage was possible. Heavy fires resulted and burned for days. The final casualty count was 47 officers and 1,056 enlisted killed and another five officers and 39 enlisted wounded out of her December 1 crew of 100 officers and 1,411 enlisted personnel. Among the dead were the ship's commanding officer, Captain Franklin Van Valkenburgh, and the embarked Commander, Battleship Division 1, Rear Admiral Isaac Kidd; both were awarded the Medal of Honor posthumously.

Vestal took two bomb hits; the first hit forward and penetrated three decks before exploding in a storage compartment; the second sliced through the ship, creating a 3 by 5 foot hole in her side. The bombs left *Vestal* down by the stern with a starboard list. She got under way at 0845 with the assistance of tugs and beached on Aiea Shoal to keep from sinking.

Also moored near Battleship Row was the fleet oiler *Neosho*. Given the scarcity of ships of her type in service with the Pacific Fleet, a case could be made that she was the most valuable ship moored around Ford Island. At the beginning of the attack she was in the process of unloading fuel. Had she been struck in this condition, a major conflagration would have resulted. Wanting to avoid this, her crew got *Neosho* underway at 1042 and moved her out of the line of fire.

Nevada was moored by herself at the end of Battleship Row. Only a single torpedo bomber selected her for attack. At 0803 the crew recorded a hit by a torpedo on her port side between the two forward gun turrets about 14 feet above the keel. The blast of the torpedo created a 16-foot-long and 27-foot-high hole in the torpedo bulge. The inner torpedo bulkhead held with just minor dishing noted. Some flooding did result, but it was not enough to threaten the ship with sinking.[42]

On *Nevada*, the first Japanese air attack was recorded at 0801, which prompted an immediate call to General Quarters. Only a minute later, the ready machine guns opened fire on enemy torpedo planes approaching the port beam. One torpedo bomber was claimed by machine-gun fire and crashed about 100 yards off *Nevada*'s port quarter. Another Kate dropped the torpedo that struck *Nevada* on the port bow. At about 0803, the 5-inch/25 battery opened fire under local control. It was about this time that the 5-inch battery claimed to have scored a hit on another Kate that disintegrated in midair (this was the *Kaga* torpedo bomber flown by Lieutenant Suzuki and his crew). The machine guns and 5-inch battery continued firing until 0908.[43]

After taking the single torpedo hit, *Nevada* accrued no additional damage during the level bombing attack. When burning oil from the shattered *Arizona* threatened to engulf the ship, the order was given to get under way. At 0840, enough steam was available to back down to clear her mooring station before beginning to move down the channel between the Navy Yard and Ford Island. As she headed into the channel, the second attack wave arrived. The sight of a battleship moving down the channel was too tempting for many of the dive-bomber pilots; *Nevada*'s ordeal had just begun.

California's action report is confusing as to the time of various events and the types of damage suffered. By 0803, the ship's two ready machine guns were firing at torpedo bombers with the 400 available ready rounds. By 0810, the two ready 5-inch/25 guns were in action with 50 rounds of shells in the ready boxes. At 0830, the ship claimed one dive-bomber that was observed to crash. According to the action report, two torpedo hits were recorded at 0805 and a third at 0820 (in fact, only two hits occurred). A resulting list of 4 degrees forced counterflooding. At 0840, four bombs detonated close aboard. The list increased as flooding continued. Its cause could not be determined, though missing or loose manhole covers were suspected. At 1002, the captain ordered the crew off the ship due to fire, but his order was canceled at 1015.[44] *California* continued to slowly settle until she rested on the bottom of the harbor on December 10. Six officers and 92 enlisted men were killed; another three officers and 58 enlisted were wounded from her December 1 crew of 120 officers and 1,546 enlisted.

California's sinking was entirely unnecessary. The torpedo defense system for her and sister ship *Tennessee* was the same as the system placed on *West Virginia* and *Maryland*. It should have been able to protect the ship from the effects of two torpedo hits. Both torpedoes struck the ship's port side. The first struck below the main armor belt between

Turret Number 2 and the bridge; the second struck further aft abreast Turret 3. In addition, one Type 80 bomb exploded close enough to the port bow to rupture some of the plating and cause flooding. This flooding was significant enough to bring the ship's head down by 3.5 feet.[45]

Both torpedo hits struck where the full effect of the torpedo defense system with its 17.5-foot-deep protection layers could be utilized. The first torpedo created a huge 24- by 10-foot-large hole, but the protective system performed as designed. The explosion destroyed the outer plating and the Number 1 bulkhead. Deeper in the ship, the Number 2 bulkhead was deformed and holed in several places; the Number 3 and 4 bulkheads were pushed inward but were not penetrated; the Number 5 bulkhead was almost intact with the exception of some minor indentation. The same result was observed for the second torpedo hit. However, this hit proved more dangerous since it revealed the one weakness of the ship's protective system. Though the system had performed as designed, the need for electricity and ventilation created various runs of piping through watertight boundaries. In this case, it was an 8-inch fuel oil line running through the Number 5 bulkhead that ruptured.[46]

Though the level of flooding was not great, it was enough to expose that missing or loose manhole covers at the top of the space in the areas of the explosions allowed water to enter the ship. The number of missing or loose manhole covers was not determined at the time, but salvage operations found six to be missing and another 12 that were loose. The reason for this is also not clear as no inspection of the area was planned and no maintenance was scheduled. Had the issue of flooding on the third deck been addressed quickly, the ship could still have been saved. This effort was severely handicapped when a bomb-hit during the second attack started a serious fire, forcing the crew to evacuate the ship temporarily. By the time the crew was able to return 15 minutes later, the flooding could not be contained and a flooding boundary could not be established. Thus, it is likely that a minor oversight resulted in the ship's sinking.[47]

ATTACKS ON THE AIRFIELDS

A critical component of Genda's plan was to cripple American air power on the ground so it could not launch a counterstroke against the Striking Force. Since the elite strike squadrons of Carrier Divisions 1 and 2 were

THE FIRST ATTACK WAVE

assigned to strike capital ships moored around Ford Island, the responsibility of hitting American air bases was shifted to the dive-bombers from *Shokaku* and *Zuikaku* and the fighters from all six carriers. Genda increased his striking power in the first wave by using the fighters as attack elements instead of acting as direct escorts for the torpedo and dive-bombers. In the absence of American fighters on patrol, this was an inspired plan; if the Americans had used their ample warnings of an impending attack to get fighters in the air, the lack of direct escorts for the strike aircraft could have been disastrous.

The 43 first-wave Zeros were all given assignments to strafe airfields in the opening moments of the attack. Some Zero groups were assigned more than one airfield to hit. At 0740, the Zeros departed Fuchida's massive formation and headed to their targets. The 14 fighters from *Soryu* and *Hiryu* headed toward Wheeler Field. Lieutenant Suganami Masaji commanded *Soryu*'s fighters, and Lieutenant Okajima Kiyoguma commanded *Hiryu*'s fighters. After departing the formation, 11 Zeros from *Shokaku* and *Zuikaku* flew east to attack NAS Kaneohe Bay. Finally, the 18 fighters from *Akagi* and *Kaga* flew toward Ewa Field, referred to as Barbers Point Airdrome by the Japanese. The nine fighters from *Akagi* were under the command of Lieutenant Commander Itaya Shigeru, while *Kaga*'s Zeros were commanded by Lieutenant Shiga Yoshio.

FORD ISLAND ATTACKED

Naval Air Station Pearl Harbor on Ford Island was an important Japanese target. It was the home station of Patrol Wing Two (PATWING 2) and its four squadrons of PBY long-range patrol boats. One of these, Patrol Squadron (VP)-21, was deployed to Midway Atoll. The others, VP-22, VP-23, and VP-24, were at Ford Island on the morning of the attack, with four PBYs from VP-24 airborne to conduct exercises with a submarine off Lahaina, Maui.

Genda tasked a *chutai* of nine *Shokaku* Vals to conduct the primary attack against NAS Pearl Harbor. Lieutenant Commander Takahashi led this formation; the bulk of his squadron was allocated against Hickam Field, the principal Army airfield on Oahu. Following the confusion with Fuchida's flares, Takahashi went to full throttle and headed directly for the airfields.

Takahashi approached Ford Island from the north. The group of nine aircraft was spotted by multiple observers, but only one aboard *Helena* recognized them as Japanese.[48] Achieving total surprise, he began his 55-degree dive at 0755. Each Val carried a Type 98 high-explosive bomb. As the first bombs were dropping, Commander Logan Ramsey, operations officer of PATWING 2, sent out the first report of the raid to the world with its famous text, "Air Raid Pearl Harbor. This is no drill."

Leading the attack, Takahashi dropped his bomb first. It was a miss, hitting at the water's edge of one of the seaplane ramps. His two wingmen dropped their 551-pound bombs among the aircraft of VP-22 parked on the apron. The second section of three aircraft targeted a hangar to the northeast. All missed the hangar directly, but a near miss on the northeast corner of the structure started a fire. The final trio of Vals targeted other hangars further to the northeast. One pilot scored a direct hit, but the bomb failed to explode. The other two recorded a near miss, and a miss. After dropping their bombs, the dive-bombers used their machine guns.[49]

Following the bomb attack, Takahashi led his *chutai* to make strafing runs from the northwest. The targets were the aircraft of Utility Squadrons VJ-1 and VJ-2. Three aircraft were claimed to have been set afire by the Japanese. After returning to his ship, Takahashi claimed great success from his efforts. Two hangars were destroyed, as well as 20 PBYs and other smaller aircraft. In fact, only seven of his nine bombs exploded, and one (Takahashi's) was a complete miss. Still, the carnage they caused was considerable.[50]

After Takahashi's dive-bombers departed the target area, several Zeros under Lieutenant Ibusuki Masanobu from *Akagi* approached Ford Island from the direction of Hickam. Making a single strafing pass on NAS Pearl Harbor, they flew off in the direction of Hickam, their primary target.

The brief appearance of Ibusuki's fighters concluded the first-wave attack against NAS Pearl Harbor. During and after the attack, American sailors fought the fires and tried to save aircraft from being engulfed in flames. These efforts were greatly handicapped when *Arizona* sank on top of the main water line onto the island. Men broke out .30-caliber machine guns and used small arms to fight back against the Japanese. Despite these efforts, none of Takahashi's Vals or Ibusuki's fighters were lost.

THE FIRST ATTACK WAVE

Even the relatively few first-wave aircraft to attack Ford Island had inflicted severe damage. The Japanese reported 100 PBYs as present, exaggerating the number of aircraft and mistaking the utility aircraft of VJ-1 and VJ-2 as PBYs. Twenty-three PBYs were claimed destroyed. The actual results were not as bad but were still enough to render the squadrons based there almost ineffective. Six PBY-3s of VP-22 were destroyed, and the rest were damaged or disabled. Half of the newer PBY-5s of VP-23 were burned. VP-24 suffered the least as four of its aircraft were airborne. The squadron's single ready aircraft was damaged. By 0830, VJ-2 reported it had no flyable aircraft available.[51]

Adding to the confusion, two groups of American aircraft arrived in the middle of the attack. At 0615 carrier *Enterprise*, located about 215 miles due west of Oahu, launched 18 Dauntless dive-bombers to conduct patrols ahead of the ship. The unarmed aircraft were ordered to recover at Ford Island. The lead two aircraft arrived during the raid and though attacked by Japanese fighters and American antiaircraft fire, both landed safely at Ford Island. The other 16 arrived in pairs, and only one was able to land at Ford Island. Three were shot down by Japanese fighters and another two destroyed by friendly antiaircraft fire. Seven finally landed at Ewa Field and another at Hickam. One landed at a grass field on Kauai.

HICKAM FIELD GETS POUNDED

Adjacent to Pearl Harbor was the Hawaiian Air Force's main bomber base, Hickam Field. Striking it was a critical component of the Japanese plan to cripple American air power and prevent retaliatory strikes on the Striking Force. The base had its primary striking power of 29 B-17s and B-18s parked in the flight line in rows just 10 feet apart and between the hangars. A single B-24A was also present in the same area. Further up the flight line were ten A-20s.

Of the 51 dive-bombers from *Shokaku* and *Zuikaku*, Genda allocated 17 Vals from *Shokaku* to hit Hickam in the first wave. One *chutai* of eight aircraft was under the command of Lieutenant Yamaguchi Masao, while Lieutenant Fujita Hisayoshi commanded a second *chutai* of nine aircraft. The entire formation was under Yamaguchi's command.

The 17 Vals circled Hickam in a counterclockwise spiral to line up an attack from the east-northeast parallel with the hangar line and apron.

Yamaguchi noted the rows of neatly arranged bombers and the complete lack of antiaircraft fire. Tactical surprise was total.[52]

First to attack was Fujita's *chutai*. Their target was two large Hawaiian Air Depot hangars that the Japanese thought contained B-17s. At 0755, Fujita's aircraft commenced its usual 55-degree dive. To ensure a hit, the pilots claimed they held their dives until about 450 feet above the ground before dropping their bombs. All nine aircraft scored direct hits on the hangars. They also fired their 7.7mm machine guns on the way down. The hangar, and the three aircraft inside – an A-20A, a B-18, and an O-47B observation plane – were all destroyed.[53]

Next to attack was Yamaguchi's *chutai*. He had been tasked to destroy eight hangars to the northeast of the Air Depot hangars. Yamaguchi dove first with his two wingmen. The first two Vals planted their bombs on Hangars 11 and 13; the third aircraft hit Hangar 15-17 and set the B-24A parked outside on fire. The second section of three Vals also targeted Hangars 11 and 13. One of the final section of three aircraft hit Hangar 7. Three B-18s inside were destroyed, including General Martin's personal aircraft. The last two pilots missed, but one struck Hickam's water main, which made fighting fires for the rest of the day almost impossible.[54]

Since the bombs were targeted at the hangars, the Japanese planned to finish off the aircraft parked on the apron by strafing. After dropping their bombs, the Vals came in from the east to systematically strafe the bombers on the flight line. Fujita's *chutai* attacked first, followed by Yamaguchi's. All 17 aircraft made a single strafing run but their 7.7mm machine guns made little impression, according to photography of the flight line during this stage of the attack.[55]

Much more deadly was Lieutenant Commander Itaya Shigeru and his nine Zeros. Each fighter carried two wing-mounted 20mm cannons, each with 60 rounds. After the dive-bombers cleared the area, the Zeros began their deadly work just after 0800. Lieutenant Ibusuki Masanobu led the second section of three aircraft:

> I then [led] my flight to Hickam Field where we discovered a long line of B-17s on the field apparently unaware of the raid… I led my flight in a low strafing run. I saw my bullets smashing into the big bombers, I pulled up and swung around. The whole field seemed to

The driving force behind the Pearl Harbor attack was the commander of the Combined Fleet, Admiral Yamamoto Isoroku. (Naval History and Heritage Command)

The man charged to execute Yamamoto's risky venture was Vice Admiral Chuichi Nagumo, who assumed command of the world's first massed carrier force in April 1941. (Naval History and Heritage Command)

Genda Minoru was the principal planner of the Pearl Harbor attack, overseeing all aspects of air operations. (Public Domain)

Admiral Husband E. Kimmel (in the center of the photo extending his hand) assumes command of the Pacific Fleet from Admiral James O. Richardson on February 1, 1941. (National Park Service)

Senior American commanders, Lieutenant General Walter Short, Admiral Husband Kimmel, Captain Louis Mountbatten, Major General Frederick Martin and Admiral Patrick Bellinger. (National Park Service)

Nagumo's flagship for the Hawaiian Operation was carrier *Akagi*. She was paired with the converted battleship *Kaga* to form the elite Carrier Division 1. (Naval History and Heritage Command)

Showing the Japanese fleet carrier *Soryu*. (Imperial Japanese Navy, now in the Public Domain)

Carrier *Zuikaku* from Carrier Division 5 is pictured before the start of the war; she was identical to sister ship, *Shokaku*. (Imperial Japanese Navy, now in the Public Domain)

Panoramic view from the southwest, taken on October 30, 1941, showing the main facilities located in the Pearl Harbor area. (Naval History and Heritage Command)

A close-up of Ford Island and the mooring point around it, taken on November 10, 1941. (Naval History and Heritage Command)

Left A photograph taken from *Akagi* shows carrier *Kaga* steaming through heavy North Pacific seas enroute to Oahu. (Naval History and Heritage Command)

Below The crew of Number 3 4-inch gun on destroyer *Ward*, which scored a direct hit on the sail of a midget submarine. (Naval History and Heritage Command)

A midget submarine after it was raised off the harbor floor two weeks after being torpedoed by destroyer *Ward*. (Naval History and Heritage Command)

Aircraft prepare to take off from *Akagi* at about 0600 on December 7. The lead aircraft is an A6M2 "Zero" fighter flown by Lieutenant Commander Itaya Shigeru. (Imperial Japanese Navy, now in the Public Domain)

A group of D3A1 "Val" dive-bombers from *Shokaku*, which were assigned to strike the airfield on Ford Island and nearby Hickam Field. (Imperial Japanese Navy, now in the Public Domain)

The second attack wave from *Shokaku* prepares to launch. These aircraft were assigned to attack American airfields. (Naval History and Heritage Command)

Photograph taken by a Japanese aircraft, showing the torpedo attack against the battleships moored along Battleship Row in progress. (Naval History and Heritage Command)

View of Battleship Row was taken by a Japanese aircraft early in the attack. (Naval History and Heritage Command)

Above Battleship *Oklahoma* after she capsized; moored next to her is battleship *Maryland*, which suffered only light damage during the attack. (Naval History and Heritage Command)

Inset Low-quality photograph taken from a Japanese aircraft of the western side of Ford Island showing the results of the first-wave torpedo attacks. (Naval History and Heritage Command)

View of Battleship Row during the early phase of the horizontal bombing attack on battleships *Nevada, Arizona, Vesta, Tennessee, West Virginia, Maryland* and *Oklahoma* moored outboard. (Naval History and Heritage Command)

View of battleship Row taken from a Type 97 "Kate" carrier attack plane right after the bomb hit *Arizona*, which resulted in a magazine explosion and the ship's destruction. (Naval History and Heritage Command)

Shows the moment the *Arizona*'s forward magazine exploded after being hit by a 1,760-pound armor-piercing bomb. (Naval History and Heritage Command)

The forward magazine explosion sank *Arizona* and caused an intense fire that engulfed the forward part of the ship, as shown here. (Naval History and Heritage Command)

Undefended by antiaircraft guns, Naval Air Station Kaneohe Bay was a principal target of the Japanese. (National Park Service)

Shown here is a B-17E at Hickam Airfield after landing safely. In the background is a B-17C/D. Smoke from burning ships at Pearl Harbor is visible in the distance. (Naval History and Heritage Command)

As the main fighter base on Oahu, Wheeler Field was a primary target.
(Naval History and Heritage Command)

The burned-out wreckage of a P-40 fighter pictured near Hangar 4 at Wheeler Field.
(Naval History and Heritage Command)

Lined up in rows, the fighters at Wheeler Field suffered heavily at the hands of strafing Japanese aircraft, like the P-40s in this view. (National Park Service)

View from the hills behind the harbor showing the low-hanging cloud cover, heavy smoke from burning ships, and American antiaircraft fire. (Naval History and Heritage Command)

Ravaged by fire, the destroyer *Cassin* capsized against *Downes* as seen in this view. (Naval History and Heritage Command)

Hit by bombs, the resulting fires from destroyer *Shaw* reached the forward magazine with the results shown in this dramatic photograph. (Naval History and Heritage Command)

Naval Air Station Pearl Harbor was a key Japanese target. Sailors survey the damage and watch as destroyer *Shaw* explodes in the center background. (Naval History and Heritage Command)

Showing battleship *Nevada* headed toward the channel after being subjected to a heavy attack by Japanese dive-bombers. (Naval History and Heritage Command)

Showing the destruction to battleships *Nevada*, *Shaw*, and *Arizona* in the wake of the attack, with the heaviest smoke coming from *Arizona*. (Naval History and Heritage Command)

A Zero fighter from the *Akagi* air group that crashed at Fort Kamehameha near Pearl Harbor during the attack. (Naval History and Heritage Command)

Here one of *Kaga's* "Val" dive-bombers is being recovered from the harbor after the attack. (Naval History and Heritage Command)

View of the submarine base (right center) and part of the fuel farms in October 1941. (Naval History and Heritage Command)

On December 8, 1941, President Franklin Roosevelt delivered an address to a joint session of Congress and requested a declaration of war against Japan.
(Naval History and Heritage Command)

Admiral Chester W. Nimitz assumed command of the Pacific Fleet on December 31, 1941.
(Naval History and Heritage Command)

THE FIRST ATTACK WAVE

be aflame. I turned and led another attack to make sure all enemy planes were destroyed.[56]

In total, Ibusuki made six attack runs. Though he noted that the American defensive fire was increasing, none of his aircraft were hit. However, another of Itaya's fighters hit its propellors on the asphalt of the parking apron after it was unable to pull up from a strafing run. It crashed into a building at Fort Kamehameha, killing four airmen on the ground and wounding another nine. *Kaga*'s fighter unit under Lieutenant Shiga Yoshio arrived over Hickam at 0805 in the midst of Itaya's assault.

Ground personnel struggled to return fire using small arms and .30-caliber machine guns. Some men manned intact aircraft to use their machine guns to engage the low-flying Japanese. Airmen tried to disperse the surviving aircraft, sometimes taxiing the aircraft under strafing attack. By 0900, there were few intact aircraft remaining. Hickam was left with virtually no ability to strike back. The few aircraft in condition to fly needed fuel, ordnance, crews, and orders.

In the middle of the strafing attacks, an unarmed flight of 12 B-17s (six each from the 38th and 88th Reconnaissance Squadrons (Heavy)) arrived over Hickam after a scheduled flight from the continental United States. Despite the attention immediately devoted to the newcomers by Japanese fighters and even some Vals, few were lost. Finding Hickam under attack, most of the aircraft attempted to divert to other fields on Oahu, but finding those also under attack several landed at Hickam anyway. One B-17C from the 38th was strafed while landing at Hickam and burned; another B-17C from the same unit crash-landed at Bellows Field and was salvaged for parts. The other four bombers from the 38th recovered at Hickam. Of the six B-17Es from the 88th, three landed at Hickam, two at Haleiwa, with the final bomber landing at Kahuku Golf Course on the northern part of the island. Two more B-17Es aborted before or after takeoff from California and never made the transit to Hawaii.

WHEELER FIELD

Dating from 1922, Wheeler Field was in the midst of an expansion begun in 1939. By December 1941, it was highly developed with four large hangars adjacent to the flight line. Wheeler was the home of the 14th Pursuit Wing under Brigadier General Howard C. Davidson and its subordinate 15th and 18th Pursuit Groups. Nine pursuit (fighter) squadrons were available with 150 fighter aircraft (12 P-40C, 87 P-40B/C, 39 P-36A, and 12 P-26A/B) of which 84 were operational on the morning of the attack.[57]

When Short ordered Alert Number 1, the aircraft were dispersed to their revetments on December 2. This was done even though aircraft dispersal was not required under Alert Number 1. The alert ended on December 5, and the aircraft were moved from revetments to the aprons in front of the hangar line. All the fighters were still fueled but had their machine guns removed for cleaning and maintenance. Movement of the aircraft to the apron was not completed until the early hours of December 7. When completed, the aircraft were parked in two rows per squadron in front of the hangars, wingtip to wingtip.[58]

Located in the center of Oahu, it was the nearest major base to the Japanese first attack wave as it made its way down the island on the morning of December 7. *Zuikaku*'s dive-bomber unit with 25 Vals under the command of Lieutenant Sakamoto Akira was assigned responsibility for neutralizing the Hawaiian Air Force's primary fighter base. When Sakamoto was released by the overall dive-bomber leader, he conducted a pass south of Wheeler to survey the target. It became immediately apparent that the Americans were not ready – the fighters sat in rows.

Sakamoto led the first *chutai*; behind him was Lieutenant Ema Tamotsu and his second *chutai*. Trailing behind was Lieutenant Hayashi Chikahiro's third *chutai*. Each Val carried a No. 25 Type 98 land bomb intended for the hangars. Any aircraft in the open could be taken care of by strafing. Ironically, the first attack on Wheeler was made at 0745 by rear gunners of the *Soryu* torpedo bomber unit as it was making its way to Pearl Harbor. No damage was done and it was unlikely the Americans even knew it had occurred. Once the torpedo bombers were clear, Sakamoto was clear to make his attack.

Sakamoto elected to make his approach from the north-northeast and to conduct a complex attack, contrary to the usual Japanese dive-bomber tactics. He ordered an attack from several directions almost at once, presumably to reduce the period his squadron was potentially exposed to fire over the target. He shouldn't have worried since there was no antiaircraft protection at the base. The first *chutai* was ordered to attack from the northeast along the hangar line; the second *chutai* would approach from the south, and the third *chutai* from the north. The bombers in each *chutai* used "stepladder" tactics in which each section of three aircraft chose a target upwind to minimize smoke interference to subsequent sections.[59]

At 0745, Sakamoto took his *chutai* into its attack dive. He dropped the first bomb – since this was the first bomb to fall on Oahu, it was also the first bomb of the Pacific War. Incomplete records preclude a complete understanding of Sakamoto's attack, but it appears his section missed the hangar they were aiming at and instead hit a warehouse and a machine shop. The rest of his *chutai* also missed, making the attack ineffective.[60]

After delivering their bombs, Sakamoto's eight Vals began the first of many strafing runs. Some pilots reported making four or five runs, all at a very low level. After the other two *chutai* made their bombing attack, they also began to strafe. Adding to the chaos was the appearance of eight Zeros under Lieutenant Suganami Masaji from *Soryu*. Beginning at 0755, the Zeros entered the strafing derby over Wheeler. Meanwhile, six more Zeros, these from *Hiryu* under Lieutenant Okajima Kiyoguma, waited overhead. Okajima ordered his fighters to enter the fray, but quickly changed his mind when he saw that the airspace over Wheeler was already packed with Japanese aircraft. He headed south to Ewa Mooring Mast Field, his secondary target.[61]

The intense strafing resulted in many casualties. Personnel of the 72nd Pursuit Squadron were caught in their tents – 11 were killed and 19 wounded, making it the highest losses for any unit at Wheeler. Even under unrelenting strafing, men flocked to the flight line to find means to fight back. Some set up a .50-caliber machine-gun post on the roof of the headquarters building.

Ema's second *chutai* with nine dive-bombers was the next to make an appearance. He and his wingmen selected Hangar 1 as their target. Pressing their dive to just under 400 feet before releasing their bombs, all three scored hits. The building suffered heavy damage and all four aircraft inside were destroyed. Heavy smoke forced the rest of the *chutai* to hit large buildings behind the flight line. All told, it appears only four bombers hit their primary target (a hangar), two hit the aprons nearby, two hit barracks, and one was dropped well to the west, probably due to a hung bomb on the aircraft.[62]

Hayashi's third *chutai* with eight Vals had a similar mixed bag of success. Attacking right on the heels of the second *chutai*, they targeted Hangars 3 and 4. However, by this time, smoke from the burning aircraft on the aprons determined which targets could be struck and with what accuracy. Two pilots managed to hit Hangar 3, but four bombs landed on the parking apron adjacent to the hangar, making the smoke issue even worse. Two bombs were aimed at the large 600-man barracks, but both missed.[63]

Thousands of machine-gun rounds stored inside Hangar 3 began to cook off, increasing the danger to the men attempting to fight fires in the area. Other men began to taxi intact P-36 and P-40 fighters to revetments and then move machine guns and ammunition to the fighters to ready them for combat. Still others carried machine guns to the tops of buildings to mount a defense against the seemingly endless rounds of strafing. Colonel William J. Flood, the base commander, and General Davidson, commander of the Hawaiian Interceptor Command, helped move aircraft from the flight line.[64]

At 0815, after some 30 minutes of bombing and strafing, Sakamoto ordered his men to rendezvous on him and head back to *Zuikaku*. None of the Japanese aircraft were lost in the attack. Two had flown so low while strafing that they had telephone wires wrapped around their fixed landing gear.[65]

The Japanese assault left the aircraft at Wheeler Field in a shambles. Sakamoto's *chutai* claimed 19 aircraft destroyed on the ground and Suganami's *chutai* another 17. Sakamoto also claimed that his attacks had left six hangars on fire, accounting for another 60 aircraft inside them. While his accounting was faulty, the bottom line was probably close to the actual losses. However, lack of discipline on the part of the dive-bomber pilots and heavy smoke reduced the level of damage that might have been inflicted. Only two of the four hangars were hit. Striking the aircraft on the aprons with bombs was an error since it created huge amounts of smoke which affected the attack options and accuracy of subsequent bombing or strafing.[66]

DISASTER AT KANEOHE BAY

Naval Air Station Kaneohe Bay was the newest air facility on Oahu. It was commissioned in February 1941 and was still a work in progress

THE FIRST ATTACK WAVE

by December. Located on the island's windward side, it is 15 miles from Pearl Harbor. The base was built to accommodate the Pacific Fleet's growing force of patrol aircraft. On December 7, it was the home of Patrol Wing One (PATWING 1). Its three squadrons (VP-11, 12, 14) had a total of 37 PBY-5s. Of these, 33 were present; four were moored in the bay, and five were located in the two completed hangars. The rest were parked on the apron. PATWING 1 was at high state of readiness – 21 of its aircraft were on a four-hour availability and nine were ready within 30 minutes. However, the base was not ready for an attack. There was no antiaircraft protection on or near the base.[67]

Though an important target, Genda did not allocate any bombers from the first wave to hit Kaneohe Bay. Instead, the fighter units from Carrier Division 5 were given the mission. Lieutenant Kaneko Tadashi from *Shokaku* led five Zeros; another six Zeros from *Zuikaku* were under the command of Lieutenant Sato Masao. Under Kaneko's overall control, the fighters were ordered to break off from the main formation and proceed to eastern Oahu with Kaneohe Bay as their main target. If there were not enough targets there, then Bellows Field, just 10 miles south, was designated as their secondary target.[68]

As Kaneko led his charges over central Oahu, his group sighted a civilian plane on an instructional flight. Several Zeros dove to attack and fired bursts at the biplane, but it escaped. These were the first shots of the attack. Upon sighting the air facility at Kaneohe Bay, it was obvious to Kaneko that the Americans were totally unprepared. Many PBYs lined the apron and several were moored in the bay. Kaneko flew over the base to maneuver his formation to make their attack runs from the upwind side, which was from the east. At 0752, the strafing began.

Sato's fighters hit the four moored PBYs and then turned their attention to the aircraft parked on the apron. Among the first aircraft hit on the ground were two utility aircraft (an OS2U-1 Kingfisher and a J2F-1 Duck) located near the incomplete runway. At very low altitude – some observers stated the Japanese came down to 75 feet – the Zeros methodically shot up the helpless PBYs parked in the open. At about 0830, the Zeros departed, having claimed 56 aircraft destroyed on the ground and another five moored in the bay. The Americans fought back with rifles and pistols before breaking out .30 and .50-caliber machine guns from the ready aircraft. This was ineffective; only four of the Zeros, one from *Shokaku* and three from *Zuikaku*, suffered any damage and all returned safely.

By the end of the first attack, about half of PATWING 1's aircraft were destroyed or disabled. VP-14 suffered the least since three of its aircraft were airborne and one other in a hangar was undamaged. Half of its aircraft parked on the apron were destroyed, as well as the two moored in the bay. VP-11 was the hardest hit. Two PBYs inside a hangar were undamaged, but five of the six aircraft parked adjacent to the hangar were destroyed with the last aircraft heavily damaged. VP-12 lost about half its aircraft including its two moored aircraft.[69]

MARINES UNDER ATTACK

Ewa Mooring Mast Field was the home of Marine Air Group 21 with three subordinate squadrons and 47 assigned aircraft, 33 of which were operational. The primary target was the SBD-1/2 Dauntless dive-bombers of Marine Scout Bomber Squadron 232 (VMSB-232). However, there were also seven SB2U-3 Vindicators left behind from VMSB-231 when the squadron embarked on *Lexington* two days earlier, and the remaining F4F-3 Wildcats of Marine Fighter Squadron 211 (VMF-211) after the rest of the squadron deployed to Wake Atoll.

Though personnel at Ewa saw the Japanese aircraft approaching at around 0755, there was no possibility of mounting a defense when Lieutenant Commander Itaya's nine Zeros opened the attack. Descending for their strafing runs, the Japanese focused on the aircraft lined up on Ewa's northwest apron. Itaya's Zeros made only a single pass before heading east to hit Hickam.[70]

Immediately behind Itaya came Shiga and his *Kaga* fighters. Using short bursts from their 20mm and 7.7mm guns, the second wave of Zeros added to the carnage along the neat rows of aircraft on the northwest apron. After their initial strafing run, Shiga's Zeros reversed course and conducted another attack run. In addition to aircraft at Ewa, cars on the road into Ewa were strafed. Among the vehicles targeted was the commander of MAG-21, but he was not wounded.[71]

Though the Americans were unable to respond to Itaya's opening attack, by the time Shiga began his attack he was met by rifle and pistol fire. Shiga himself remembered one Marine who stood without

THE FIRST ATTACK WAVE

fear, ignoring machine-gun fire hitting the ground around him as he unloaded rounds from his pistols against Shiga's aircraft. Later waves were subjected to .30-caliber machine-gun fire from weapons the Marines salvaged from destroyed aircraft. Despite these efforts, Japanese fire proved deadly. After setting most of the aircraft alight on the apron, they proceeded to attack aircraft under repair in other parts of the base and the utility aircraft parked in a different section of the runway. Efforts mounted by Marine ground crew and pilots to man their aircraft or at least pull them out of the line of fire were for nought.[72]

Adding to the destruction was a second wave of strafing runs, this time by Zeros from *Soryu* and *Hiryu*. Fresh from their attack on Wheeler Field, the Zeros headed south to expend the rest of their ammunition at Ewa. Okajima led six *Hiryu* fighters on their strafing runs. After his wingmen suffered damage, Okajima decided he had pressed his luck enough and decided to break off the attack. The last to attack were eight *Soryu* Zeros from 0805 to 0820 hours.

At about 0835, the Japanese onslaught resumed. This time the assault was conducted by Takahashi's dive-bombers from *Shokaku*. The primary targets of Takahashi's squadron were NAS Ford Island and Hickam Field. Having used all their 551-pound bombs on these targets, the Vals flew the short distance to the west to expend their remaining machine-gun ammunition against Ewa.

Intent on making strafing attacks, Takahashi's Vals appeared at treetop level. Tasked to complete the destruction of any aircraft present, the Japanese quickly realized that most of the Marine planes had already been destroyed. Accordingly, they shifted their attention to strafing buildings and personnel. Some Vals conducted steep banks to give the rear gunner a chance to use his 7.7mm machine guns against ground targets. Some Marines also reported that the Vals dropped small bombs – the 132-pounb bombs carried on each Val wing. After the attack, five small bomb craters were noted on the field.[73]

Marine Air Group 21 was virtually annihilated by the strafing from Fuchida's first wave. Usually the claims of aviators were exaggerated, especially when smoke obscured the target and multiple aircraft took credit for the same destroyed target. Total Japanese claims were 60 destroyed aircraft, compared with the 47 actually present. *Akagi*'s pilots claimed 11, *Kaga*'s 15, *Soryu*'s 12, and those from *Hiryu* 22.[74]

ATTACKS ON DISPERSAL FIELDS

Haleiwa Field on the western shore of Oahu had no permanent installations in December 1941. On November 3, the Hawaiian Air Force began to rotate fighter squadrons from Wheeler to Haleiwa. On the morning of the attack, the field was hosting the 47th Pursuit Squadron. When it quickly became apparent that an attack was under way on other parts of the island, the squadron duty officer, Second Lieutenant Karl F. Harris, took steps to ready his squadron for action. Guns were remounted on the P-40s, ammunition loaded, fuel tanks topped off, and engines warmed up.

One of the few American success stories of the day was that of the efforts of the men of the 47th Pursuit Squadron. With their squadron deployed to Haleiwa Field, Second Lieutenants George Welch and Kenneth Taylor were at the Wheeler Field Bachelor Office Quarters when they heard the first explosions at the west end of the flight line. The two pilots jumped in Taylor's vehicle and headed north toward Haleiwa. Close behind was another private vehicle with First Lieutenant Robert J. Rogers and Second Lieutenants John L. Davis and Harry W. Browne. Wheeler is only ten miles from Haleiwa, and Taylor made this distance in ten minutes despite the threat of strafing and the winding road. The car behind Taylor's was strafed at 0820 but continued on its way.

Tension at Haleiwa built with the appearance of two B-17s. These were part of the group arriving at Hickam which decided to divert to fields not under attack. One landed at Haleiwa at 0820, followed by a second five minutes later. After the arrival of the second B-17, the two cars filled with pilots tore onto the field. Taylor and Welch found their aircraft almost ready, but no .50-caliber ammunition was available at the field. The fighters would have to rely on their four wing-mounted .30-caliber machine guns.

Bellows Field, located on the eastern side of the island, was used as a dispersal field for Wheeler. In the spring of 1941, the 86th Observation Squadron with its O-47Bs was moved to Bellows. In July, Bellows was established as a separate command, and work on a 5,000-foot runway was begun in October. As events unfolded on December 7, it took until 0827 to place the base on alert. Kaneko, fresh from shooting up Kaneohe with his Zero, headed to Bellows to judge the state of his secondary target. At 0840, he made a single firing pass approaching from the east. He estimated that 35 aircraft were at the field. In reality, there were two rows of aircraft, one with 11 P-40s and another with 7 O-47B/O-49s.[75]

Kaneko's single pass prompted Bellows' ground crews to ready as many aircraft as possible, but a shortage of personnel meant that only three could be readied by the end of the first Japanese attack. As this was playing out, a B-17C made a landing approach between 0845 and 0900 with two of its engines smoking. On the second attempt, it crash-landed and came to rest in an adjacent pineapple field.

8

The Second Attack Wave

As soon as the first wave was aloft, preparations began for launching the second. In a well-rehearsed ballet, the aircraft were quickly spotted on the flight decks and their engines warmed. At 0705 hours, Nagumo ordered his fleet into the wind again. Beginning at 0715, the second-wave aircraft began to leave the flight decks of the six carriers. The launch was quick and efficient. One aircraft, a *Hiryu* dive-bomber, had engine problems and did not launch. After launch, two more dive-bombers and a fighter had to return due to engine problems. A total of 167 aircraft were left to head south to Oahu.

Included in the second wave were 35 fighters, 78 dive-bombers, and 54 horizontal bombers. The dive-bombers were slated to attack naval targets, while the horizontal bombers were tasked to complete the destruction of land-based air power on Oahu. About 15 minutes after the departure of the first attack wave, the second wave under Lieutenant Commander Shimazaki Shigekazu approached Oahu from the north-northeast. While still off the coast, the formation turned left parallel to the northeast coast. At 0843, Shimazaki ordered his squadrons to deploy. The 35 fighters under Lieutenant Shindo Saburo took up positions over Oahu to cover the bombers. The main punch of the second strike, the 78 dive-bombers under the command of Lieutenant Commander Egusa Takashige, arrived over Oahu near Kaneohe Bay then headed west toward Pearl Harbor. Under Shimazaki's direct control were the 27 level bombers from *Zuikaku*. These headed to Hickam Field. The level bombers from *Shokaku* under Lieutenant Ichihara Tatsuo were divided into two groups. Eighteen level bombers

THE SECOND ATTACK WAVE

headed to NAS Kaneohe Bay and one *chutai* of nine level bombers headed to NAS Pearl Harbor.

THE GREAT DIVE-BOMBER DEBACLE

One of the least known aspects of the Pearl Harbor attack was the almost complete failure of the Japanese dive-bombers to inflict meaningful damage on the Pacific Fleet. On the surface, this development was incomprehensible since the elite dive-bomber crews were going after stationary targets and because later in the war these same crews displayed remarkable precision against maneuvering ships.

The best dive-bomber crews were reserved for the massive second-wave strike. *Akagi* contributed 18 Vals (divided into two *chutai* each with a normal strength of nine aircraft), while *Kaga* assigned 27 to the attack (divided into three *chutai*). However, one *Kaga* aircraft was forced to abort due to engine problems, leaving 26 to head toward Oahu. Both *Soryu* and *Hiryu* launched all their dive-bombers, 18 from each ship in two *chutai*, but one from each carrier had to abort because of engine issues. Of note, the missing *Hiryu* aircraft was that of dive-bomber squadron leader Lieutenant Kobayashi Michio.

Much was expected of Egusa and his well-trained dive-bomber crews. Under Egusa's tutelage, the dive-bomber crews of Carrier Divisions 1 and 2 had become expert at hitting moving targets. During the 1941 Combined Fleet exercises against target ship *Settsu* making 14 knots, 66 hits were scored out of 123 bombs dropped for an accuracy rate of almost 54 percent. Wanting to increase accuracy, Egusa insisted that the bomb release altitude be reduced to 1,312 feet (400 meters). Later, in training for the Pearl Harbor attack, the focus shifted to attacking stationary targets at the expense of more work against *Settsu*. Against stationary targets, an improvement in the dive-bombers' already impressive hit rate was all but certain.[1]

If the attack went according to plan, each squadron leader would allocate his *chutai* to strike specific targets. Typically, the entire *chutai* would concentrate on the same target, but the *chutai* leader had the option of dividing his group into three-aircraft sections. The target priority had been drummed into each crew – American carriers were the highest priority, followed by cruisers and then battleships. Because their heavy horizontal protection could not be penetrated by the No.

25 Type 98 551-pound bombs carried by the Vals, attacking battleships was a waste of ordnance. Topside damage might be inflicted, but no critical damage could be gained. On the other hand, the relatively thin horizontal protection of carriers and cruisers could be penetrated by these bombs, thus explaining why these valuable ships were the top-priority targets.

Japanese target priorities were well thought out, but only effective if the aviators adhered to them. This was the first problem with the dive-bomber attack. Genda gave the American carriers top priority, even to the extent that if they were present and already sunk by torpedo attack, their hulks were to be dive-bombed to prevent them from being salvaged. The carriers weren't present on the morning of the attack, throwing the target selection by the dive-bomber crews into disarray. Typical of Japanese staff work, an assumption was made that the carriers would be present, but no real thought had been given to a contingency plan other than creating a prioritized target list and briefing the pilots on it. There were certainly no exercises of what to do if the top-priority targets were missing. This was a massive oversight since the possibility that the carriers would not be present was an obvious potential outcome. Even more unforgivable was the fact that the Japanese received intelligence on the morning of the attack that the carriers were gone, but even at this point development of a contingency plan was not considered.

Another example of the inflexibility of Japanese planning was the assumption that optimal weather would exist over the target on the morning of December 7. This premise guided their training program, during which the dive-bombers flew over an hour from their bases to the range to conduct the traditional dive from about 11,500 feet against targets under optimal weather conditions. In a full dive and using the Val's bomb sight, results were excellent. However, the assumption that excellent weather would exist over Oahu in December was not factually based. While October and January are usually cloudier than December in Hawaii, the chances of overcast or mostly cloudy conditions range from 30 to 40 percent; if scattered cloud conditions are included, then the percentage grows higher. Clear conditions typically exist less than 50 percent of the time in December. Given this, some training should have been devoted to working under less-than-optimal weather conditions. At the very least, Genda, Fuchida, and Egusa should have brainstormed what to do in this eventuality instead of letting each crew

THE SECOND ATTACK WAVE

or section handle it on their own. Photographs taken during the second-wave attack clearly show the presence of low, thick clouds – conditions clearly not optimal for dive-bombing.

In addition to the cloud cover, another factor facing the dive-bomber pilots was the presence of smoke over the harbor from damage inflicted by the first wave. Both the strikes on NAS Pearl Harbor, and to a lesser degree nearby Hickam Field, created huge columns of smoke. These paled in comparison to the smoke from *Arizona*'s funeral pyre. Again, photos depicting this period of the attack clearly show massive amounts of smoke over the harbor. Finally, by the time the second-wave dive-bombers arrived, surprise was lost and the Americans were returning fire. The volume of American antiaircraft fire over the harbor during this period was remarkable and is displayed on many period photographs.

For all the reasons limiting accuracy delineated above, and given the challenges with target selection, the Japanese second-wave dive-bomber attack was bound to underperform. However, the extent to which it did has not been fully explored. Despite the quality of the aircrews involved, from the Japanese perspective, it was the least lethal effort of the entire attack.

ATTACK OF THE DIVE-BOMBERS

When it became clear that the carriers were not present, the dive-bomber crews were given new orders to attack targets of opportunity. This meant hitting any heavy ship that had survived the first wave.[2] It is not known who issued this order or to what degree the crews were given leeway to ignore their pre-attack instructions. It seems unlikely that the pre-attack plans would be voluntarily thrown into disarray in this manner, but that is exactly what happened. Lieutenant Abe Zenji, an *Akagi chutai* leader, confirmed this by stating that after he took off he was instructed to hit the same targets as the first wave.[3] Evidently, Genda's staff work to determine target priorities had little influence on the men actually executing the attack.

As his formation approached Kahuku Point, Shimazaki ordered his squadrons to deploy at 0843. When Shimazaki gave the order to attack at 0855, Egusa and his *Soryu* dive-bombers crossed into Oahu directly over Kaneohe Bay. *Hiryu*'s dive-bomber squadron was to Egusa's right, and *Akagi*'s and *Kaga*'s squadrons were arrayed to his left. After the formation flew over Honolulu, it headed west to Pearl Harbor. Egusa led the formation in a clockwise circle around the harbor at an altitude of just over 13,000 feet. He could see that the harbor was already filled with antiaircraft fire and that thick smoke was obscuring the target area. While over Hickam Field, at 0902, he gave the order to attack. The plan was for *Soryu*'s dive-bombers to attack first, followed by those from *Hiryu*, *Akagi*, and *Kaga* at short intervals.

Soryu's Dive-bombers

As Egusa approached the target area, it immediately became obvious that this would not be an easy operation. He had problems finding a clear target because of all the smoke. He resorted to following a string of tracers to their source where a target must be located. This was surely not the preferred method to select a suitable target, and Egusa aborted his first dive and set up a new attack. This time the target was heavy cruiser *New Orleans* moored inside the Navy Yard area. Egusa's bomb missed, impacting between the cruiser and repair ship *Rigel* moored nearby.[4]

New Orleans' action report largely backs Egusa's account. Of the ten aircraft that targeted the Navy Yard area, where the cruiser was moored without ship's power, three bombs were dropped near the ship. One exploded between *New Orleans* and *Rigel* and unleashed a barrage of fragments. Twenty-seven small holes were counted in *New Orleans* and 150 in *Rigel*. Neither ship recorded any casualties. *New Orleans* also reported that two more small bombs were dropped near *Rigel* but failed to explode. These may have been the wing-mounted 132-pound bombs loaded on Egusa's Val.[5]

Egusa's two wingmen also had problems with their attack. The largest ship in the Navy Yard was battleship *Pennsylvania* sitting in Drydock Number 1. The two crews selected her for attack but were unable to get a good line on the battleship; their bombs missed the primary target and hit the two ships in the drydock forward of the battleship. These were destroyers *Cassin* and *Downes*. After recovering from their dives, the aircraft strafed destroyer *Dale* as she headed down the main channel to exit the harbor. One of these two aircraft was hit by antiaircraft fire and crashed at the entrance of the harbor.[6]

However, this account from Japanese sources does not entirely agree with the action reports of the ships involved. While *Downes*' action report mentioned the approach of three dive-bombers, *Pennsylvania*'s

THE SECOND ATTACK WAVE

report gives a higher number. *Downes* was hit by a single bomb on her bridge, probably at 0850, which created a huge fuel-fed fire. With no means to fight the fire, it rapidly spread out of control. Destroyer *Cassin* was alongside in the same drydock. Later in the attack, *Cassin* was struck by three bombs. These passed through the ship and detonated on the floor of the drydock, resulting in extensive hull damage. The fire raging on *Downes* and in the drydock spread to the adjacent *Cassin*. Again, with no means to fight the fire, the crew was ordered off the ship. At 0915, a terrific explosion rocked *Downes*. At 0920, the order was given to abandon ship. An attempt to put the flames out was made by pumping water into the dry dock but this merely resulted in the flames riding the water. Finally, *Cassin* fell off her keel blocks and rolled over onto *Downes*, resulting in both ships becoming constructive losses.[7]

Dale's action report stated that she was subjected to severe dive-bombing and machine-gun attack as she approached the channel entrance. Her commanding officer surmised that this was done in an effort to block the harbor, though even sinking a destroyer in this position would not have been sufficient to totally obstruct the channel. One dive-bomber was observed to crash during this attack as a result of antiaircraft fire; *Dale* claimed credit.[8]

Lieutenant Yamashita Michiji led the second section of Egusa's *chutai*. He also selected a battleship for attack – *Maryland*. He missed his target, with his bomb splashing near fleet oiler *Neosho* that was getting under way from the Ford Island fueling pier and was backing down very close to *Maryland*. Yamashita's two wingmen looked across the channel for a target and selected light cruiser *Helena* moored alongside the 1010 Pier. Both Vals missed their target. One of these aircraft was destroyed by antiaircraft fire, with the Japanese giving credit to gunners aboard *Helena*.[9]

Helena had a busy morning. According to her action report, she was subjected to dive- and glide-bomber attacks. The recurring reference to glide-bombing attacks in different ships' action reports indicates that the Japanese dive-bombers were not able to conduct their usual, and more accurate, dive-bombing profile with its steep 55-degree dive. Glide-bombing involves a more shallow-angle dive. *Helena* crewmen observed five Vals head toward the cruiser. Four near misses were reported: one on the dock abreast the bridge, two close on her starboard bow, and one close on her starboard quarter. In a second attack, about ten Vals using a glide-bombing profile (30–40 degrees) were active near the ship. Five appeared to head toward *Helena*, but none reached their release point to attack the cruiser. Two were engaged by antiaircraft fire, left smoking, and crashed near or beyond the Naval Hospital; one veered away; the last two broke off to attack other targets. Using her 5-inch/38 mounts and 1.1/75 quad mounts, *Helena*'s antiaircraft fire was effective. Her action report states that on several occasions aircraft headed directly toward *Helena* were turned away by her intense fire and forced to seek other targets or were forced to wildly drop their bombs. In particular, the ship's 1.1-inch/75 battery was noted as effective. Optimistically, she claimed seven aircraft destroyed during the morning.[10]

The third section of Egusa's *chutai* made scattered attacks. The section leader claimed a hit on *California*. Both his wingmen lined up on a target located north of Ford Island. This was destroyer tender *Dobbin* with a collection of five destroyers moored alongside. The two bombs missed, landing off *Dobbin*'s port quarter.[11] *Dobbin*'s action report stated that three bombs were dropped, resulting in near misses on her starboard quarter, astern, and port quarter. The difference was probably attributable to the fact that each aircraft carried one large and two small bombs, and in the heat of action it was not always possible to tell them apart. In the case of *Dobbin*'s action report, the bombs were identified as 300-pound weapons, something not carried by the Japanese. Fragments from the bomb that landed astern struck the stern of the ship, causing personnel casualties from the 3-inch/50 antiaircraft gun crew located on the after end of the boat deck. Three men were killed and two wounded.[12]

California took a single bomb hit during the second wave, probably from one of *Soryu*'s dive-bombers at about 0900. The bomb struck on the starboard side of the upper deck abreast the foremast. It penetrated to the second deck, setting off an antiaircraft ammunition magazine. The resulting explosion killed 53 men. A serious fire started at about 0905; smoke from the fire reached the second and third decks and even the forward engine room through the ship's ventilation system. Damage control parties restored light and power and brought the fires under control by 1000. A second bomb later scored a near miss and ruptured the ship's bow plates.[13]

As the damage control parties were bringing order from chaos, a new crisis emerged. Burning oil from other ships engulfed *California*'s stern. Captain Joel W. Bunkley ordered the ship to be abandoned. Within 15 minutes, wind blew the burning oil pool away from the ship and the captain ordered the men back on board. Not all the men did so or did so in a rapid fashion. A quick-thinking sailor raised the national ensign (the flag had yet to be raised in all the morning's confusion), which encouraged many men to stream back aboard.[14]

Soryu's second *chutai* was under the command of Lieutenant Ikeda Masatake. It was down to eight Vals since one aborted immediately after launch. Ikeda claimed that he attacked *Pennsylvania* and placed a bomb on the battleship's boat deck. The second aircraft in the section selected destroyer *Shaw* as its target as she sat inside Floating Drydock Number 2. The crew claimed a hit on the destroyer. The final aircraft subjected *Helena* to another attack but missed.[15]

The only battleship not located on Battleship Row was fleet flagship *Pennsylvania* located in Drydock Number 1. She was undamaged in the first wave, but now she came under attack from *Soryu* dive-bombers. At 0906 hours, according to her action report, she took a hit from a 551-pound bomb on her boat deck near a 5-inch/25 mount that penetrated to the deck below and exploded in a 5-inch/51 casemate. Twenty-six men and two officers were killed, and another 25 were wounded. This damage did not prevent *Pennsylvania* from mounting a spirited defense. During the two raids, she expended 650 5-inch/25, 350 3-inch/50, and 50,000 .50-caliber rounds.[16]

After the first section claimed success, the rest of the *chutai* experienced none. The second section had only two Vals. Both selected *California* as their target but both missed. No precise information is available on the activities of the last section. According to Japanese sources, the three aircraft in the section attacked widely separated targets but did not score any hits. Based on American action reports, several candidates exist for these attacks. According to her action report, one bomb was dropped off destroyer *Aylwin*'s bow, though none of the other ships in her destroyer nest reported the event. Ammunition ship *Pyro*, moored at the ammunition piers in the West Loch, reported being attacked by a single dive-bomber. The bomb hit the pier.[17]

Hiryu's Dive-bombers

Lieutenant Kobayashi commanded *Hiryu*'s dive-bomber squadron and was slated to personally lead its first *chutai*. When his aircraft was forced to abort, his place was taken by Lieutenant Nakagawa Satoshi, leader of the second *chutai*. Nakagawa selected *St Louis* moored in the Navy Yard as his target. His bomb missed the cruiser. His first wingman attacked an unknown target in the Navy Yard. He also must have missed as no American reports indicate a ship was hit there. Nakagawa's second wingman looked across the channel to find *West Virgina*. The ship had already sunk in an upright position but was selected for attack anyway. This attack was unsuccessful. The lead pilot of the next section and his first wingman also attacked targets in the Navy Yard. Both reported uncertain results. The third aircraft of this section initially targeted a destroyer but then shifted to *California*. This attack was also unsuccessful.[18]

Twenty ships were moored in the Navy Yard. Most valuable among these were heavy cruisers *New Orleans* and *San Francisco* and light cruisers *Honolulu* and *St Louis* Since these types of ships were high on the pre-attack target priority list for the dive-bombers, the Navy Yard should have been the focus of the attack. As the attack developed, this was not the case, but Japanese sources indicate at least nine dive-bombers did select ships moored there for attack. The only hit of consequence on a target in the Navy Yard was a near miss on light cruiser *Honolulu*. The bomb landed close enough to her port side forward to cause considerable internal damage to electric cabling.[19]

St Louis was moored next to *Honolulu* and her action report provides details of the attack on the Navy Yard. At about 0900, a formation of six dive-bombers was observed diving on the two light cruisers from an altitude of about 6,000–7,000 feet using a shallow dive (40–50 degrees, again indicating a glide-bomb profile). Antiaircraft batteries on *St Louis* (the forward .50-caliber and 1.1-inch/75 machine guns) engaged the attackers. Four Vals veered to the left and released their bombs, which landed between the 1010 Pier and Ford Island. The bomb from the fifth Val landed about 200 feet from *St Louis* and exploded; afterward the Val was observed to bank left, catch fire, and crash. The final dive-bomber in the group was the aircraft that probably scored the near miss on *Honolulu*.[20]

All three Vals of the third section selected *Maryland* for attack. Again, all missed their target. One of these was shot down by antiaircraft fire.[21] *Maryland* claimed seven enemy aircraft shot down with the destruction of four being confirmed, according to the ship's action report. During the attack the battleship expended 450 5-inch/25 shells, 4,500 rounds of 1.1-inch/75 rounds, and 2,500 machine-gun rounds.[22]

Next up was Kobayashi's *chutai*, now down to eight aircraft. The new lead section under Lieutenant Junior Grade Shimoda Ichiro and one of his wingmen attacked *Maryland*. The other wingman selected *Helena*, along with two of the aircraft from the third section. The final aircraft from the third section targeted *Pennsylvania* but missed. Finally, the two aircraft from Kobayashi's section selected destroyer *Helm* for attack outside the harbor.[23]

Only the aircraft that attacked *Helm* had any effect. The destroyer had gotten under way before the attack and was patrolling outside the harbor entrance when the second wave attacked. The ship's action report stated that at 0915 enemy aircraft approached from astern in a medium glide and dropped two bombs, which exploded only 50 yards off the port bow and 20 yards off the starboard bow. *Helm* turned sharply to port to avoid the bombs but was shaken violently by the near misses. Damage was minor with the worst being some sprung seams below the waterline on the starboard side.[24]

Akagi's Dive-bombers

Lieutenant Chihaya Takehiko commanded *Akagi*'s dive-bomber squadron and led the first *chutai*. Chihaya and his two wingmen opened his squadron's attack by selecting *Neosho* as a target. The big oiler was still underway and headed for the Southeast Loch. Despite her large size and slow speed, all three Vals missed their target. *Neosho* reported engaging a number of Japanese aircraft during this period, but the only attack mentioned in her action report was that "several" bombs were dropped astern close enough to shake the ship.[25]

Throughout the attack, Japanese pilots had problems with ship identification. For example, an account from Chihaya's pilot (Flight Petty Officer First Class Furata Kiyoto – Chihaya was in the rear seat as an observer) claimed that he dropped his bomb from the prescribed 1,312 feet against a ship he later identified as *Maryland* based on its position in Battleship Row. Furata was "pretty sure we scored a hit on the enemy ship, but I wasn't able to confirm it because we were flying at such a low altitude." Noteworthy was the observation that American antiaircraft fire was intense even before the attack; during the attack Chihaya's Val was hit countless times by machine-gun fire. Even though the fuel tank was leaking, the aircraft made it back to *Akagi*.[26]

The second section tried to attack *Pennsylvania* but was forced to line up on destroyer *Shaw* instead, located inside Floating Drydock Number 2.[27] In the attack on *Shaw* at 0910, the Japanese claimed three hits. This comports well with *Shaw*'s action report. As the destroyer was sitting in the drydock, the ship was hit by three bombs in quick succession. All were dropped from 1,000 feet and all hit the bridge area. The first two penetrated deeply into the ship and created a tremendous fire from the ruptured fuel tanks. Twenty minutes later, the forward magazine blew up, separating the bow from the rest of the ship. Had water been available to fight the fire, the magazine explosion might have been prevented, according to her action report. However, the crew was able to prevent the fire from engulfing the aft portion of the ship. In addition to the three bombs that hit the ship, the Americans indicated that two or more exploded in the dry dock between the ship and the side walls of the dry dock.[28]

In another example of poor target identification, the third section selected seaplane tenders for attacks. These were large and valuable ships but were still auxiliaries and nowhere to be found on the pre-attack target priority list. The lead aircraft selected *Tangier* moored along the northwest side of Ford Island. Only a near miss was claimed. After delivering its bomb, the aircraft was hit by antiaircraft fire from several ships and crashed on seaplane tender *Curtiss* moored northwest of Ford Island. One of the wingmen attacked *Curtiss* and gained a hit. It was shot down by antiaircraft fire. The third aircraft attacked an unknown target and was also shot down.[29]

At 0850, crewmen aboard *Tangier* spotted the second wave coming in. In the next five minutes, *Tangier*'s .50-caliber machine guns and her forward 3-inch/50 guns claimed two aircraft. The first crashed in the Middle Loch aft of *Curtiss* and repair ship *Medusa*, the second on the shore nearby. *Tangier*'s action report does not mention a near miss but does confirm a bomb hit on *Curtiss* at 0855. The next group of Vals attacked at 0910. *Tangier*'s gunners riddled another dive-bomber that deliberately crashed onto *Curtiss*. From 0913 to 0920, five bombs were dropped by five different planes near *Tangier*. The first failed to press its attack and placed its bomb near Ford Island off the ship's port bow. The other four aircraft conducted glide-bombing attacks but could only manage near misses: two forward and two aft, all between 15 and 40 feet. *Tangier* was struck in 42 places by bomb fragments,

THE SECOND ATTACK WAVE

but there was no serious damage. Only three crewmen received superficial wounds.[30]

Not unexpectedly, crewmen on *Curtiss* gave a different account of the same event. It provides one of many examples of eyewitnesses in the same area recording the same event much differently; seldom do observers agree on timing. *Curtiss*' action report states that her antiaircraft fire brought down the dive-bomber that deliberately crashed into the tender at 0905. Already on fire, the Val hit the ship's boat deck on the starboard side. A gasoline-fed fire took hold. Beginning at 0912, a group of dive-bombers attacked *Curtiss*. After four misses, one bomb hit the ship on the starboard side of the boat deck. It passed through several spaces before entering the hangar and detonating on the main deck. Damage was extensive within 30 feet of the blast, and several fires took hold that were not extinguished until 0936.[31]

Lieutenant Abe Zenji led the second *chutai*. After the war Abe stated that he initially decided to attack *Arizona*. This would have been an impossibly difficult target since there was a massive column of smoke issuing from the stricken battleship. Once Abe recognized that the ship had already sunk, he flew across Ford Island and selected *Raleigh* for attack.[32] Shortly after 0900, what was described as a glide-bombing attack began against the cruiser. Abe's bomb hit near a 3-inch mount, went through the carpenter shop and an oil tank, before exiting the ship on the port quarter below the water line. After hitting the bottom of the harbor it detonated about 50 feet from the ship. *Raleigh* was already struggling to survive from her earlier torpedo hit, but the bomb caused little additional damage.[33]

The next six Vals all targeted *Maryland*. Though smoke made it hard to determine what results had been achieved, the Japanese claimed five hits.[34] Despite the fact that at least 11 dive-bombers selected *Maryland* as their target, she was not hit by any bombs dropped during the second wave. All *Akagi*'s returning pilots commented on the heavy antiaircraft fire they encountered over the harbor.

Kaga's Dive-bombers

The largest group of dive-bombers came from *Kaga*. Three *chutai* were involved in the attack; the first was under the control of Lieutenant Makino Saburo (*Kaga*'s dive-bomber commander), the second under Lieutenant Ogawa Shoichi, and the third commanded by Lieutenant

Ibuki Shoichi. Makino was the only dive-bomber squadron commander to exert any control over the targets of his crews.

Nevada had gotten under way at 0840 and was moving toward the channel. Makino's squadron, the last dive-bomber unit to attack, was circling overhead looking for a suitable target. Believing he had a chance to bottle the Pacific Fleet up in Pearl Harbor, he ordered his dive-bombers to focus on the slowly moving battleship.[35]

Beginning at 0850, *Nevada* underwent the heaviest dive-bombing attack suffered by an American battleship during the entire war. According to her action report, the attack was already under way when the ship was backing down and preparing to swing around *Arizona* and *Vestal*, both moored in front of her. As she began to move down Battleship Row toward the channel entrance, she became too tempting of a target for the Japanese to ignore.[36] The majority of *Kaga*'s dive-bombers lined up to attack her. Over the span of the next few minutes, they scored a total of five hits. The other 18 dive-bombers missed, a very weak performance against a slow, non-maneuvering target.

The five bombs that hit did so nearly simultaneously, so the sequence that follows does not represent the order in which the bombs struck the ship. Crew members claimed that some were dropped from as low as 300 feet. The first hit was recorded well forward, just to starboard of the centerline where the bomb made a 12-inch hole. Going through the main deck, it went through the unarmored forward part of the ship and exited above the second deck. It exploded underwater and created extensive damage to the bow area, including significant dishing of the external plates and opening up the forward edge of the anti-torpedo blister.[37]

Another hit was very close to the first. Striking the unarmored forward portion of the ship, the bomb traveled about 60 feet from the point of impact before exploding. When it did explode, it was between two liquid-backed boundaries, thus creating only minor structural damage. One of these boundaries was a fuel tank with 3,800 gallons of high-octane aviation gasoline, but fortunately the volatile fuel did not explode. The third bomb also hit forward but caused more structural damage than the first two. A fire ensued, fed by gasoline vapors, and burned for two days. The bomb failed to penetrate the second deck (the main armored deck), making only a 4.5-inch distortion.[38]

THE SECOND ATTACK WAVE

The forward superstructure was struck by another bomb. Landing on the antiaircraft director platform, it penetrated the navigation bridge, the signal bridge, the captain's office, and the superstructure deck, before exploding on the upper deck. This also created a huge fire, fed in part by the ready-use ammunition in the damaged area. Damage was limited when the bomb fragments failed to penetrate the secondary battery 5-inch/51 casemates on the upper deck.[39]

The final bomb exploded immediately upon impact, unlike the other bombs. It struck the starboard skylight above the crew's galley. Because of the heavy tile and concrete in this area, penetration was limited. Fragmentation damage was extensive, with one 5-inch/25 mount rendered inoperable. The galley was also wrecked, but no fire took hold.[40]

In response to the fires, the forward magazines were flooded, which brought the bow down further. A communications error resulted in the after magazine also being flooded. Under orders from Kimmel, *Nevada* was run aground at Hospital Point at 0910. At 1030, she was dragged across the channel by tugs.

Only three *Kaga* aircraft ignored the lumbering *Nevada*. Led by Lieutenant Ogawa Shoichi, the third section of the second *chutai* went looking for targets along Battleship Row. They reported bombing *Maryland* and *West Virginia*.[41]

ANALYZING THE DIVE-BOMBER ATTACK

Instead of a quick, devastating attack by the four dive-bomber squadrons involved, the Japanese second-wave attack on naval targets in Pearl Harbor was an almost complete debacle. The long, drawn-out attack by groups as small as one or two aircraft demonstrates what a disorganized mess it degenerated into.

Using the action reports from the ships in the harbor to fully recreate the results of the dive-bomber attack is impossible. The reports are contradictory and often incomplete, even in regard to the numbers of aircraft involved. American records also contradict Japanese sources. The author has opted to use Japanese records as the basis for determining the targets of the dive-bombers, though this still provides an incomplete picture. It also provides an inaccurate picture in the sense that

Japanese Second-Wave Dive-bomber Targets, December 7, 1941

Target Type	Number of dive-bombers
Battleships	44
Heavy and light cruisers	11
Destroyers	9
Auxiliaries	9
Navy Yard (no specific target identifiable)	3
Unknown	2
Total	78

the dive-bomber crews probably identified unimportant targets such as destroyers and auxiliaries as larger warships (cruisers or battleships) and because it does not account for instances where the dive-bombers were aiming at larger targets but missed and hit smaller ships.

The focus on battleships is evident, with over half of the dive-bombers reporting attacking these ships. For good reason, Fuchida instructed his crews not to waste their bombs on these ships. However, when the vague pre-attack instructions morphed into "hit the same ships attacked in the first wave," human nature took over. Crews decided to hit battleships, thought to be the centerpiece of American naval power and easily identifiable, instead of a secondary target of much lesser importance.

While attacking battleships was understandable, only a small number of crews adhered to their pre-attack target priority and attacked cruisers. In hindsight, if Fuchida had the chance to parcel out targets to his dive-bombers, he should have pulverized the Navy Yard area with its two heavy cruisers and three Brooklyn-class light cruisers (including *Helena* at the 1010 Pier). These were the most valuable ships in the harbor when the second wave arrived.

Attacking destroyers and auxiliaries made no sense. It probably occurred as dive-bombers were forced to abort their attack runs on other, more valuable targets because of a bad target lineup or American fire. Nevertheless, it appears that 18 dive-bombers elected to expend their bombs against ships of little value.

While using Japanese sources provides a relatively coherent picture of what targets were selected, it paints a fanciful picture of the number of hits scored. According to Fuchida's chart he developed after the attack using the debriefs of the squadrons involved (the same chart he used

THE SECOND ATTACK WAVE

Hits Claimed by Second-Wave Dive-bombers, December 7, 1941

Target	Number of hits
Battleships	
Nevada	8
California	5
Pennsylvania	1
Maryland	12
West Virginia	1
Cruisers	
Raleigh	1
Helena	6
Heavy cruiser inside Navy Yard	3
Light cruiser inside Navy Yard	1
Light cruiser inside Navy Yard	1
Light cruiser outside Navy Yard	2
Light cruiser outside Navy Yard	2
Destroyers	
Cassin	1
Downes	1
Shaw	1
Auxiliary	
Oiler *Neosho*	3
Total	49

to personally brief the Emperor on December 27, 1941), dive-bomber hits totaled 49.[42]

The claim of 49 hits and their distribution was a near-complete fabrication. Since the dawn of military aviation, it has been common for aviators of all countries to make exaggerated combat claims. On the morning of the attack, the propensity to over-claim was reinforced by poor visibility conditions. Fuchida almost certainly realized that the claims were exaggerated but chose to use them anyway. Probably not coincidentally, the final number of hits claimed reflected the pre-attack estimation of the number of hits expected, thus vindicating the planning of Fuchida and Genda. It is also a number that reflects success by the dive-bomber pilots (especially those killed during the attack), averting any loss of honor. Fuchida's analysis of the damage inflicted by the dive-bombers reflects his knowingly sanitized version of events for external consumption and in no way comports with reality.

Nevertheless, the claims of the dive-bomber pilots are interesting for several reasons. Almost all pilots reported hitting a high-value target – a battleship or cruiser. Only a few admitted to attacking a destroyer or an auxiliary. The claims against the two light cruisers outside the Navy Yard remain mysterious. One was in the location of light cruiser *Phoenix*. She was a worthy target but did not report having been attacked. The second was against a target in the channel and probably reflects the attack on *Helm*. Surprisingly, the Japanese did not claim any of the ships attacked by dive-bombers as being sunk, with the exception of *Neosho*.[43]

Using American records of the actual number of hits inflicted on the ships inside Pearl Harbor gives a much different and more accurate picture. In addition to the direct hits, damaging near misses included one on both *Honolulu* and *Helm*.[44] By this calculation, the overall dive-bomber accuracy rate was 20 percent, compared with the pre-attack practice rates of 55 percent. Amazingly only one hit was scored on the pre-attack top-priority target (after the carriers which were not present) and this was against an antiquated light cruiser with little combat capability.

Actual Hits by Japanese Second-Wave Dive-bombers, December 7, 1941[45]

Target	Number of hits
Battleships	
Nevada	5
California	1
Pennsylvania	1
Cruisers	
Raleigh	1
Destroyers	
Cassin	3
Downes	1
Shaw	3
Auxiliary	
Seaplane tender *Curtiss*	1
Total	16

THE SECOND ATTACK WAVE

REASONS FOR THE DISASTER

There were many reasons for the failure of the dive-bombers in the second wave to inflict significant losses on the Pacific Fleet. Some have already been discussed – the assumption that weather conditions would be favorable and the failure to come up with a plan if they were not. Fuchida's orders were a big part of the problem. They were unclear, contradictory, and beyond the capabilities of any but the most experienced crew to follow in the heat of battle. Fuchida wanted the dive-bombers to concentrate their attacks to sink ships, not just inflict damage. At the same time, they were told not to overconcentrate on a single target, unless it happened to be an aircraft carrier, in which case they were to be bombed into oblivion. In the absence of carriers, the crews were expected to adhere to a complex target prioritization plan. Further, the four different squadrons were to strike nearly simultaneously, but this proved impossible under the prevailing weather conditions.[46]

During the attack, there was virtually no command and control. Each *chutai* leader, or section leader of three aircraft, had to find their own target through the clouds. The only thing resembling command and control was when Makino from *Kaga* led almost his entire squadron against *Nevada*. Otherwise, the attacks were typically conducted by single sections or even by one or two aircraft.

After arriving over the harbor, the dive-bombers were faced with a cloud layer between 3,500 and 5,000 feet. Flying above the clouds, the dive-bomber crews were understandably reluctant to begin their dives without seeing what was below. Some pilots reported flying around looking for a hole in the clouds so they could use their normal dive-bomber attack profile. In the process *chutai* fragmented, accounting for a number of attacks conducted by one or two aircraft. Once the dive-bombers broke through the clouds, they faced intense antiaircraft fire. If only one or two dive-bombers attacked at a time, the Americans could concentrate their fire. Unable to use the dive-bombing profile they had been intensely training for, the Japanese were forced to use less accurate glide-bombing approaches. Using this profile, the pilots were unable to use their bomb sights, forcing them to make their drops by eye.[47]

Under these conditions, it is not surprising that bombing accuracy suffered. The Japanese claimed 49 hits, but the actual number was 16.

Later in the war, the same crews achieved amazingly high accuracy rates against maneuvering targets. In addition to poor accuracy, the dive-bomber pilots at Pearl Harbor were guilty of poor target selection and even worse damage assessment reporting.

In exchange for their weak haul, the Japanese lost 14 second-wave dive-bombers. As will be detailed later, the numbers of aircraft ditched, jettisoned overboard after landing, or damaged to varying degrees far exceeded the number of aircraft shot down. The scale of these losses had real implications in regard to any Japanese discussion of a potential follow-on attack.

SECOND-WAVE ATTACKS AGAINST AIRFIELDS

As the dive-bombers were busy over Pearl Harbor, the rest of the second-wave attackers were trying to finish off American air power at facilities all over Oahu. These efforts were led by the level bombers from *Shokaku* and *Zuikaku*, augmented by the fighters from all six carriers.

NAS Pearl Harbor
The nine Kates from *Shokaku* ordered to attack Ford Island were under the command of Lieutenant Irikiin Yoshiaki. This was the third *chutai* of *Shokaku*'s carrier attack squadron. One of the Kates carried two No. 25 Type 98 bombs; the other eight carried one Type 98 bomb and six No. 6 Type 99 132-pound ordinary bombs. At around 0900, these aircraft appeared southwest of Pearl Harbor at about 8,000 feet, flying in a compact V formation.

Irikiin began his bomb run at 0916. For reasons hard to understand, the initial attack was a fiasco. Acting on the orders of the lead bombardier, the group released its bombs early – most landed harmlessly on Waipio Peninsula to the west of Ford Island. Only a single bomb hit the northwest shore of Ford Island.[48]

By the end of the raid, NAS Pearl Harbor suffered only minor damage to its facilities. However, of the 30 PBYs assigned to VP-22, 23, and 24, only nine were flyable. Bellinger's force of 78 PBYs, located at NAS Pearl Harbor and NAS Kaneohe (and deployed to Midway) suffered heavy losses – 56 PBYs were out of action, with 40 destroyed or damaged beyond repair.[49]

THE SECOND ATTACK WAVE

Hickam Field

Twenty-seven Kates from *Zuikaku*, under the command of Shimazaki, were allocated against Hickam Field. Each aircraft in Shimazaki's lead *chutai* was armed with two No. 25 Type 99 ordinary bombs. The second *chutai*, led by Lieutenant Iwami Jozo, carried a single Type 99 551-pound bomb and six No. 6 Type 99 132-pound bombs. Lieutenant Tsubota Yoshiaki's third *chutai* was armed identically to the aircraft of the second *chutai*.

Following a fly-by near Hickam Field, Shimazaki issued his attack orders at 0855. Each *chutai* assumed a nine-plane arrowhead formation with just over 1 mile between *chutai*. At 0900, the Japanese began their attack run some 2.5 miles from Hickam at just under 10,000 feet. Flying to the target from the east-northeast, Shimazaki noticed no American fighters and no antiaircraft fire. However, heavy clouds obscured the target area. When the Japanese bombers approached the target, the lead bombardier in each *chutai* determined that an arrowhead formation was unsuited for bombing a narrow target area since many of the bombs would land in vacant areas. Accordingly, all three *chutai* aborted their first attack run and reversed course to set up a new attack.[50]

On the second run to the target, the first and second *chutai* used a column formation better suited for narrow targets. The third *chutai* remained in an arrowhead formation. Approaching from the west-southwest, the first *chutai* found holes in the clouds to bomb its primary target – the Hawaiian Air Depot hangars. Bombing accurately, a series of approximately 25 hits smashed into the hangars and adjacent aprons. This barrage of bombs was described by the Americans as "small bombs." It is likely that the delayed fusing on the Type 98 bombs led to a high percentage of duds and low-order detonations, thus accounting for the American description.[51]

Only the first *chutai* was able to drop its weapons on the second attack run. The other two *chutai* aborted again and headed southwest to set up another run. On the third run, the *chutai* commanders reduced their altitudes to get a better look at the target. To get under the clouds, Iwami's second *chutai* made its third run at just under 5,000 feet. Apparently, the lead bombardier misjudged his release since almost all of the bombs landed in the largely vacant area between the hangars and the barracks. Only aircraft from the lead section were accurate – two hangars were hit and a third was missed. On its third run, the third *chutai* flew at almost 9,000 feet, but by the time it arrived over the target the clouds had cleared. A total of 63 bombs were released on the Air Corps Barracks. A series of direct hits resulted in heavy casualties. Adding to the carnage, a number of unexploded USN 3- and 5-inch antiaircraft shells fell to earth in the same area, adding to the personnel losses.[52]

Following the departure of the level bombers, 18 Zeros arrived over Hickam to conduct strafing attacks. However, heavy smoke from the bombing attacks limited the areas the Zeros could strafe. Nine Zeros from *Kaga* were the first to arrive under Lieutenant Nakaido Yasushi. Their main target was NAS Pearl Harbor, but a short flight took them over Hickam to look for new targets. They reported strafing ten aircraft and setting fire to six.[53]

Shindo's nine *Akagi* Zeros were next. Shindo claimed he set a bomber afire, but his group was only able to strafe one more bomber. In his words:

> The base had already been bombed by the first wave and was covered with black smoke. We couldn't see any parked airplanes very well... However, regardless of the dangers we strafed the base twice and then departed for our mother ship.[54]

Some Zeros, finding no bombers to strafe, hit other parts of the base. After making two strafing runs, Shindo took his *chutai* to the west and headed for Ewa. By 1100, it was clear that the attack was over and the personnel on Hickam began efforts to clean up and to prepare for a next attack that many feared could occur at any time. The base was a shambles, with the barracks area suffering heavy damage. Six of the ten hangars were heavily damaged but the other four incurred only minor damage.

Surprisingly, the aircraft based there did not suffer catastrophic losses. At 1100, three B-17Ds, three B-18s, and five A-20As were ready to fly. By evening, the frantic efforts of the ground crews raised the total to five B-17s, 11 B-18s, and eight A-20s. Another 16 bombers were judged to be repairable. Only 13 were declared to be total losses.[55]

NAS Kaneohe Bay

The rest of *Shokaku*'s horizontal bombers under the command of Lieutenant Ichihara Tatsuo were given the task of finishing off what the

THE SECOND ATTACK WAVE

first wave had begun at Kaneohe Bay. Ichihara personally led the first of two *chutai*. His formation circled to the east after leaving the main formation. When Kaneohe came into sight, Ichihara made an immediate assessment of the target. There was no sign of antiaircraft fire, but patchy clouds extended over the bay and the facility, enough that making an accurate drop was jeopardized. Ichihara's orders were to attack the target from the usual altitude of just under 10,000 feet, but dropping through the clouds would obviously affect the accuracy of the attack. Not wanting to make an attack with poor results, Ichihara changed the plan. He decided to descend to 1,640 feet to get under the clouds and to approach the target from the southwest. Ichihara's *chutai* was in the lead, with Lieutenant Hagiwara Tsutomu's *chutai* about a half mile behind.[56]

This new course of action presented new problems. At the low altitude of 1,640 feet, the bombsight on the Kate could not be used. The skill of the lead bombardier would be heavily taxed since the drop had to be based on his intuition. Dropping from this altitude made the formation vulnerable to machine-gun fire, whereas from the usual 10,000 feet, there was no such danger.

Observers on the ground spotted the approaching Japanese over the ocean 15 miles out, giving personnel on the station time to seek any available cover. Ichihara's *chutai* released their weapons at 0907. With each Kate carrying two Type 98s, 18 551-pound bombs were sent hurtling toward the target, which was probably Hangar 2. On this occasion, Japanese accuracy was poor. The bombs were dropped too early and half of them landed in the water short of the apron in front of the hangars. A few bombs hit the apron but missed the aircraft parked there. However, bomb fragments or chunks of concrete from the explosion set at least one VP-12 PBY on fire. Though the Americans fired back at the attackers with any weapon they had access to, including .30- and .50-caliber machine guns, none of Ichihara's bombers were hit.[57]

When Hagiwara's *chutai* made its appearance at 0910, the Americans were more than ready. Still flying at 1,640 feet and making only 130 knots, Hagiwara's aircraft suffered from a storm of fire from the ground. His personal aircraft was hit 18 times and one of his wingmen's aircraft was also seriously damaged. Facing heavy fire and the smoke from Ichihara's strike, the lead bombardier elected to abort the attack run. The *chutai* circled around for another run. This time, Hagiwara ordered his formation to bomb from 8,200 feet, bringing it out of the effective range of the American machine guns. On the ground, the Americans were heartened by the apparent failure of the second raid and indications that several of the attackers had been damaged.[58]

Before Hagiwara could make his second run, 17 Zeros from *Soryu* and *Hiryu* made an appearance at 0915. The fighters approached from the northwest and roared in to make low-level strafing attacks. Nine Zeros from *Soryu* were the first to attack under Lieutenant Iida Fusata. The low-flying Japanese faced a hail of machine-gun fire, which hit several of Iida's fighters. Five of the Zeros claimed kills against six PBYs. Despite the heavy ground fire, Iida's Zeros made two more firing passes. Two VP-14 PBYs were launched into the bay between attack waves, only to be set alight by Iida's Zeros. *Hiryu*'s eight Zeros, under Lieutenant Nono Sumio, made their attack in the middle of the assault by Iida's fighters; after claiming two PBYs destroyed on the ground, they turned south to Bellows Field.[59]

The efforts of the Americans to defend the base were brave, and seemingly suicidal as men set up machine guns on the unprotected aprons to take on the strafing Japanese. Chief Petty Officer John W. Finn epitomized this bravery by manning a .50-caliber machine gun from an exposed position. Hit by two bullets and multiple pieces of shrapnel, he survived and was awarded the Medal of Honor, the first of World War II.

After circling around the base, Hagiwara's *chutai* approached again from the southwest, this time at 8,200 feet. According to the definitive account of the Kaneohe raid, Hagiwara's *chutai* had difficulty identifying the target through the clouds and had to make two runs. In the first run, Hagiwara made an adjustment by ordering his aircraft to spread out to cover more of the target and to only drop one of their two bombs in case the run turned out to be inaccurate. This was prescient since the lead bombardier had only a brief view of the target and ordered a drop too early. The bombs fell in the bay, well short of the apron.[60]

For the final attack run, Hagiwara made another adjustment. This time he ordered an approach from the northwest, parallel to the line of hangars. At 0920, the final nine bombs were sent on their way with Hangar 1 as the target. This time the bombing was accurate; three bombs scored direct hits, and two more struck inside the hangar but failed to explode or experienced only a low-order detonation. Two other

THE SECOND ATTACK WAVE

bombs hit outside the hangar amidst the aircraft wreckage from earlier attacks. The final two bombs missed.[61]

After the last bombs exploded, Iida's fighters resumed their work. In the final stages of the attack, smoke in the hangar and apron areas drove the Zeros to strafe buildings and vehicles. Iida's men finally ran out of targets and, under his direction, made the short flight south to hit Bellows Field. There his Zeros made two quick and ineffective firing passes. With this, at about 0930, Iida ordered his men to head north to rendezvous and return to the Striking Force. While flying north, the full cost of conducting multiple strafing attacks against withering fire was revealed. Several aircraft in the first and third sections were damaged. In particular, Iida's Zero was leaking fuel. Aware that it was now impossible for him to make it back to *Soryu*, Iida decided to return to Kaneohe to crash-land on a suitable target.[62] Before launching from *Soryu*, Iida had made this promise: "In case of trouble I will fly straight to my objective and make a crash dive into an enemy target rather than make an emergency landing."[63] Leaking fuel and flying erratically, Iida's Zero ended up crashing 1 mile north of the hangar line where it caused no damage. Iida was given a respectful military funeral by the Americans on the afternoon of December 8.

Following Iida's self-immolation, the full tally of damage at Kaneohe could be calculated. Eight of VP-11's 12 aircraft were destroyed or damaged beyond repair. The other four were not flyable but could be repaired.[64] VP-12 suffered almost the same fate, with eight aircraft destroyed and four others suffering heavy to moderate damage. VP-14 also had six aircraft destroyed and four damaged. All three aircraft away on training missions during the attack were from VP-14 and were undamaged. Heavy infrastructure damage included the destruction of one of the two main hangars. Personnel casualties totaled 19 dead and 69 wounded. The base was virtually knocked out, and PATWING 1 was left with only three flyable aircraft. Eventually, ten of the damaged PBYs were brought back into service.[65]

Ewa Mooring Mast Field
The Marines at Ewa Mooring Mast Field were heavily strafed in the first attack. Even though most of the aircraft of Marine Aviation Training Support Group 21 (MAG-21) had been destroyed, Genda's plan called for additional attacks by aircraft from the second wave.

Given time to bring additional weapons into action, the Marines prepared for a more robust defense against the second-wave attackers. By 0820, six .30-caliber and seven .50-caliber machine guns were in action and the Marines were in the process of emplacing seven 3-inch guns on the field's parade ground.[66]

The final attack directed at Ewa occurred at about 0930, when approximately 15 Vals from *Kaga* and *Hiryu* appeared over the treetops to resume strafing runs. No bombs were available since these had been expended against naval targets in Pearl Harbor, but the dive-bombers still carried plenty of 7.7mm rounds. Compared to the earlier dive-bomber attack, the last Val raid was "light and ineffectual" according to Lieutenant Colonel Claude Larkin, commander of MAG-21. He attributed this to the heavy volume of fire that the Marines were able to produce.[67]

MAG-21 was virtually annihilated by the end of the attack. Thirty-three of Ewa's aircraft were destroyed: eight SB2U Vindicator and ten SBD Dauntless dive-bombers (out of 32 bombers), nine Wildcat fighters (out of 11), and six utility aircraft. Fifteen more aircraft were damaged. Only a single aircraft of the 49 present at the base was undamaged.[68]

Bellows Field

Despite getting information that attacks were occurring all over Oahu, it took until 0827 to put Bellows Field on alert. Shortly thereafter, one of the first-wave Zeros, piloted by Lieutenant Kaneko and fresh from shooting up Kaneohe, headed to its secondary target. At 0840, he made a single firing pass from the seaward side of the field and estimated that 35 aircraft were present. The was about the twice the number actually there; lined up in two rows were 11 P-40s from the 44th Pursuit Squadron and five O-47B and two O-49 observation aircraft from the 86th Observation Squadron.[69]

The only effect of this first attack was to warn the Americans on Bellows that a larger attack could be imminent and allow them time to disperse the aircraft at the field. The P-40s had their armament removed the previous day for maintenance and cleaning. Ground crews furiously began to reinstall the weapons, but this was a lengthy process. By 0900, only three P-40 aircraft were ready. Another indication that combat was taking place elsewhere was provided between 0845 and 0900 when, on its second attempt, a B-17C approached with two engines smoking. It crash-landed onto an adjacent pineapple field.

THE SECOND ATTACK WAVE

Usually forgotten in the histories of the attack are the efforts by the Americans to get fighters into the air to mount a defense. During the morning, this included a total of 21 sorties. Most of these came from Bellows and Haleiwa which were not heavily attacked by the Japanese.

By 0930, the first three 44th Pursuit Squadron P-40s were preparing to launch. These fighters were manned by Second Lieutenants Samuel Bishop, George A. Whiteman, and Hans C. Christiansen. Just as the Americans were preparing to take off, Lieutenant Nono Sumio from *Hiryu* showed up with eight Zeros from the north-northwest. The Zeros were organized into three sections, with two apparently assigned to strafe targets on the ground. The third section with two Zeros was positioned to intercept any aircraft attempting to take off. By this time the Americans had dispersed the aircraft, making strafing much more of a challenge. However, Christiansen was killed in the cockpit of his P-40 by the strafers. Whiteman was attacked by Zeros seconds after taking off – his aircraft crashed on the nearby beach, killing him. Bishop got into the air and headed over water. Pursued by two Zeros, his P-40 crashed into Kailua Bay, but he survived.[70]

After dealing with the fighters attempting to take off, the Japanese turned their attention to systematically strafing the aircraft left on the ground. This continued for 15 minutes against little opposition. One O-47 was used as a machine-gun position and fired back throughout the attack. These efforts were not entirely fruitless since one Zero was seen streaming fuel. This was the aircraft of Flight Petty Officer First Class Nishikaichi Shigenori. Judging that he was unable to make it back to *Hiryu*, Nishikaichi headed to Ni'ihau Island, the westernmost of the main Hawaiian Islands, where submarine *I-174* was stationed south of the island as a plane guard.[71]

Haleiwa Field

The most effective American fighter response was mounted from Haleiwa Field. This was a dispersal field used for target practice and was unknown to the Japanese. On December 7, the 47th Pursuit Squadron was located there. At 0840, two pilots of the squadron returned to the dispersal field by car and lifted off on their own initiative with the first two ready P-40s. The only instructions given to Second Lieutenants George Welch and Kenneth Taylor were to proceed to Barbers Point at 8,000 feet and look for Japanese. After the departure of Taylor and

Welch, a single Val conducted several strafing runs of the field. When the Japanese plane was finished, Second Lieutenant John Dains took off in the third ready P-40. After 0900, Haleiwa continued to feed aircraft into the fight as they were ready. The next group to take off included a P-40B and two P-36As. These fighters failed to contact the Japanese.

Taylor and Welch encountered plenty of Japanese in the vicinity of Barbers Point. After the second-wave dive-bombers finished their attack, one of their preliminary rendezvous areas was 10 miles west of Barbers Point. When Taylor and Welch reached Barbers Point, they saw no Japanese but at about 0845 noticed 20–30 aircraft over nearby Ewa Field. Getting closer, they recognized them as Japanese. With Welch in the lead, they attacked the trailing bombers. Welch hit a Val from *Hiryu* and punctured its fuel tank. Though he claimed a victory, the damage was not severe enough to prevent the dive-bomber from returning to its carrier. Taylor attacked a second *Hiryu* bomber and watched as it crashed just inland from Ewa Beach. Welch engaged another Val, this one from *Akagi*, but the Japanese rear-gunner hit the pursuing P-40's engine. With his engine smoking, Welch was forced to escape into the clouds. Taylor intervened and finished off the offending Val with a single burst. The Val crashed into the ocean southwest of Ewa. Its pilot survived and wandered around Barbers Point until being killed on December 9 after encountering American soldiers. Three other Vals reported being damaged at this time, two from *Akagi* and one from *Kaga*. Both Taylor and Welch headed to Wheeler to rearm.[72]

Meanwhile, the third P-40 from Haleiwa piloted by Dains was chasing down the sole dive-bomber that had strafed the field. Dains caught up with the Val and downed it over the west side of Oahu. Because he was killed less than two hours later, Dains was unable to make a formal claim for his victory, but other evidence confirms that he had indeed scored the first American fighter kill of the war. On his third sortie of the morning, Dains was killed by friendly fire from Schofield Barracks in his P-36A, crashing at 1143.[73]

Taylor and Welch were far from done. While reloading ammunition at Wheeler, the base came under attack from an unknown number of *Kaga* dive-bombers approaching from the south at 0930. Welch was the first to take off while under fire from the Vals. Taylor followed, taking off in the same way as Welch – directly into the attacking Vals. Taylor reversed course and latched on to what he thought was the last dive-bomber in the formation. This was not the case – Lieutenant Makino (leader of the *Kaga* dive-bomber squadron) came to the aid of his squadron mate and attacked Taylor from behind. Caught by surprise, Taylor was slightly wounded in the arm and thigh but was able to keep flying. At this point, Welch came to Taylor's aid by diving to attack Makino's Val. The dive-bomber's rear gunner put several rounds into Welch's engine, but he was able to pour fire into the Val. Makino's aircraft burst into flames and crashed into a private home just outside the gate to Wheeler Field.[74] Despite his wounds, and the fact he only had a single operational machine gun, Taylor chased down another *Kaga* Val and shot it down north of Schofield Barracks. Welch flew south toward Barbers Point and encountered an unknown Japanese aircraft 5 miles off the coast. Welch was certain he was stalking another dive-bomber, but it was probably a Zero from *Kaga*. After several bursts, the aircraft plunged into the ocean.[75]

Taylor proceeded to Wheeler a second time for more ammunition. Taking off for a third time, he headed northwest and encountered a dive-bomber from *Kaga*. Taylor succeeded in severely damaging the Val, which later crashed.

Wheeler Field
At the Hawaiian Air Force's main fighter base, ground crews were struggling to fight fires and move undamaged aircraft to safety. On the east end of the apron, the 18th Pursuit Group lay in ruins. The 15th Pursuit Group on the western end of the apron was in better shape since many of its aircraft were hidden under smoke. Ground crews from the 46th Pursuit Squadron readied four P-36As for flight. The aircraft had to have their machine guns reinstalled and ammunition loaded. After the departure of the first attack wave, they were ready for combat. Pilots from the 46th Pursuit Squadron competed to man the available aircraft. At about 0930, the fighters took to the air piloted by First Lieutenant Lewis M. Sanders and Second Lieutenants Philip M. Rasmussen, John M. Thacker, and Gordon H. Sterling, Jr.

Led by Sanders, this flight took part in the largest fighter engagement of the entire attack. Coming up from the south was *Soryu*'s fighter unit after it had strafed NAS Kaneohe Bay. From there the Zeros flew to Bellows and were now headed north. When Sanders radioed for orders, he was instructed by the Information Center at Fort Shafter that there were Japanese aircraft near Bellows. Sanders took his flight in that direction and gained altitude. As they approached Kaneohe Bay, they spotted Japanese aircraft at a lower altitude. Five *Soryu* Zeros were in formation, but one broke off and did not take part in the action. Sanders set up a textbook attack on the unsuspecting Zeros, diving out of the sun from behind with an altitude advantage.[76]

The Americans were unable to convert their initial advantage into success, though both Sanders and Sterling probably scored hits on their initial pass. Lieutenant Junior Grade Fujita Iyozo, now in command of the *Soryu* fighter unit after the death of Iida, survived this initial assault. Seeing his wingman under attack by a P-36A on his tail, he turned to rescue him and got on the tail of the inexperienced Sterling. Before Sanders could intervene, Fujita sent Sterling down in flames. Meanwhile, Thacker and Rasmussen were involved in a dogfight against the more maneuverable Zeros. In a turning dogfight the Americans were at a clear disadvantage and soon a Zero got a beam deflection shot against Thacker's P-36A. Thacker was forced to take his damaged aircraft into the clouds. In return, Rasmussen was set up with a perfect shot. An extended burst resulted in nine hits, but the Zero was able to return to *Soryu*. In the final stage of the dogfight, Fujita and Rasmussen engaged in head-to-head combat with Fujita attempting to ram the American. Rasmussen's fighter was badly damaged (544 holes were counted in his fuselage and wings after he landed), but he was able to use the clouds to escape. Fujita nursed his badly damaged Zero back to *Soryu*.[77]

Other fighters followed Dains, Taylor, and Welch from Haleiwa. Second Lieutenant Harry Brown joined with First Lieutenant Bob Rogers. After an inconclusive dogfight, Rogers got entangled in a second dogfight in the vicinity of Haleiwa Field against two or three Vals. Rogers was forced to take his damaged P-36A out of the fight, but Brown got a good shot at a dive-bomber and drilled it full of holes. The aircraft, probably from *Soryu*, was seen to crash. Brown ran into another large formation of Japanese aircraft but was able to escape. He then joined with First Lieutenant Malcom Moore who attacked a single Japanese aircraft flying at 3,000 feet. After six long bursts, the aircraft was left smoking and losing altitude. This was possibly one of Lieutenant Iida's Zeros damaged over Kaneohe Bay.[78]

The last 47th Pursuit Squadron aircraft to engage the Japanese was flown by First Lieutenant John J. Webster. He charged into a group of

THE SECOND ATTACK WAVE

Japanese aircraft; two turned on him and hit him. Webster was forced to break off the engagement and return to Haleiwa.[79]

Sanders' flight of four P-36As was not the only activity out of Wheeler during the morning. Second Lieutenant Henry W. Lawrence, Jr, found another P-36A ready to go and took off a few minutes later. He joined with a P-40 flown by First Lieutenant Woodrow B. Wilmot and a P-36A piloted by Second Lieutenant William F. Haning, Jr. The group flew to Hickam to look for bombers to escort. Seeing none, and encountering antiaircraft fire over Pearl Harbor, the flight made a circle around the island before returning to Wheeler. A lone P-40 piloted by Second Lieutenant Fred B. Schifflet also flew to Hickam. Upon returning to Wheeler, it faced "friendly" ground fire and was lucky to make a landing with only two flat tires. Later, two additional P-36As departed from Wheeler and headed for the western part of Oahu. These also encountered no Japanese.

The activities of a small number of American fighters over Oahu on December 7 give a glimpse into what might have happened if the American air defense had been alert and functioning. As it was, at least 12 fighter pilots engaged the Japanese during the morning; another nine took off during the raid but reported no contact. A total of 49 other fighters took to the air on December 7 without an opportunity to engage the Japanese.[80] The 12 that reported making contact, most of whom were inexperienced second lieutenants, gave a good account of themselves. The best available information indicates they shot down eight aircraft with another probable kill, and damaged at least four more. Only three American fighters were lost in aerial combat, and two of these were shot down immediately after taking off.

The failure of the Americans to use even passive defenses, like placing their fighter aircraft in the numerous available revetments at Wheeler Field, made a huge impact in elevating both the level of damage and casualties inflicted on American forces. Short's insistence on placing the aircraft in the open made it possible for limited numbers of Japanese attackers to destroy a large number of fighters. The effectiveness of dispersal, even without revetments, was clearly shown at Bellows and Haleiwa where aircraft losses to strafing were nonexistent (but to be fair, the level of strafing was also much less than at Wheeler).

Japanese fighter deployments made it easy for the American fighters to score on the limited occasions they were able to take off. Japanese fighters were not tasked with escort duties. Rather, they were employed offensively. After accompanying the bombers to their target areas, they were free to conduct strafing attacks on airfields. Once the Zeros shifted to strafing missions, the bombers were left undefended. Even inexperienced pilots flying P-36As and P-40s easily outclassed a Val or a Kate. Had the numbers of American fighters left undamaged after the first wave been higher, instead of just the handful that were available, the slaughter of unescorted Vals would have been commensurately higher.

THE JAPANESE RETURN TO THE STRIKING FORCE

The first aircraft of the first wave arrived in the vicinity of the Striking Force at about 0950 hours and immediately began their recovery. As this was occurring, at about 1000 hours, the last Japanese aircraft made their attacks, and all aircraft, including that of strike leader Fuchida, had headed north. By 1115 hours, the second-wave aircraft began their recovery. Heavy seas made the recovery difficult.

Invariably, there were some difficulties with the recovery of such a large strike. One of the first-wave dive-bombers from *Shokaku* lost its way on the return flight. At 1307, long after the rest of the first-wave aircraft had landed, the commander of the bomber sent a radio message that it was about to ditch. Unwilling to ask *Shokaku* for a course to the Striking Force because the crew did not want to compromise the fleet's position, the commander instead apologized for the loss of a valuable aircraft due to his navigational error. Both the aircraft and the two crewmen were never seen again.[81]

A group of nine dive-bombers from the second wave, including two from *Akagi* and seven from *Hiryu*, faced challenges on their return trip. Led by Lieutenant Nakagawa from *Hiryu*, the Vals first encountered a PBY-5 from VP-14 north of Oahu. Launching an attack, they claimed a kill against the flying boat, but it suffered only light damage and survived. Further north, the dive-bombers ran into a B-17E from the 88th Reconnaissance Squadron on its way to Oahu flying at wave-top level. Despite multiple passes over the span of 11 minutes, the Vals were unable to bring the rugged bomber down. However, they did succeed in damaging its two port-side engines, forcing the B-17E to crash on the Kahuku Golf Course near the northern tip of the island. After ceasing efforts to dispatch the B-17, Nakagawa's group encountered a Zero

THE SECOND ATTACK WAVE

visibly leaking fuel, headed back to Oahu with the obvious intention of launching a final attack. Eight additional Zeros looking for navigational assistance joined the Vals returning to the Striking Force. In heavy mist, Nakagawa had problems finding the fleet. After arriving at what he believed to be the rendezvous point, the fleet was nowhere to be seen. After a couple of turns, Nakagawa saw the faint trace of a ship's wake and succeeded in bringing all the aircraft under his charge back to their ships. The two Vals from *Akagi* were the last to land on the flagship. After doing so, Nagumo came down from the bridge, embraced the senior aircrewmen, and remarked "It's good to see you've made it back!"[82]

The last dive-bomber to recover from the second wave landed on *Kaga* at 1246. Having suffered battle damage, the single Val flew over one of the Striking Force's three submarines. The crew decided not to ditch next to the submarine, but to continue the search for their carrier. Upon landing, the pilot forgot to deploy his tailhook, and the engine gave out from lack of fuel as the aircraft passed over the carrier's stern. Both aircraft and crew were safe when the pilot jammed on his brakes just short of the arresting barrier.[83]

After the strike had recovered, the combat air patrol also returned, and the fleet took a heading of 330 degrees at 26 knots to meet the tankers of the First Supply Group. The Pearl Harbor attack was over.

After the return of the last aircraft, the Japanese could begin to tally the status of their six air groups. In terms of overall losses, the cost of the raid was seemingly light. While only 29 aircraft were lost, there was more to the story.

First-Wave Japanese Aircraft Losses[84]
Number of aircraft involved/lost/damaged

	Kates employed as level bombers	Kates employed as torpedo bombers	Vals	Zeros	Totals
Akagi	15/0/3	12/0/4	None in first wave	9/1/3	36/1/10
Kaga	14/0/2	12/5/5	None in first wave	9/2/2	35/7/9
Soryu	10/0/2	8/0/1	None in first wave	8/0/2	26/0/3

(continued)

	Kates employed as level bombers	Kates employed as torpedo bombers	Vals	Zeros	Totals
*Hiryu**	10/0/at least 1	8/0/Unk	None in first wave	6/0/Unk	24/0/1+
Shokaku	None in first wave	None in first wave	25/1/4	6/0/Unk Total damaged for both *Shokaku* and *Zuikaku*: 4)	31/1/4+
Zuikaku	None in first wave	None in first wave	26/0/13	5/0/unk	31/0/13+
Totals	49/0/8+	40/5/10+	51/1/17	43/3/11	183/9/40+

* Records for *Hiryu* do not exist

From this table, several important aspects of the first wave are immediately apparent. Overall losses were low, with only nine aircraft being shot down. This emphasizes the value of surprise. However, surprise did not provide blanket immunity, as another 46 aircraft (and this total would be higher if records from *Hiryu* were available) were damaged. The degree of damage to these aircraft is unknown, but the total number of aircraft destroyed and damaged reached 55, or 30 percent of first-wave aircraft. The bombers suffered surprisingly few losses – no horizontal bombers were lost, only a single dive-bomber was shot down, and all five of the torpedo bombers lost were in the last group to attack as the benefits of surprise were wearing off.[85]

There are several important points to make about the second-wave losses. Compared with the first wave, losses were much greater, amounting to 51 percent of all aircraft destroyed or damaged. Most of the bombers in this wave were dive-bombers, and they suffered extremely high attrition. Seventy-one percent of the Vals taking part in the second-wave attack were destroyed or damaged, and this fails to consider *Hiryu*'s damaged aircraft. With one exception, all six Japanese air groups suffered heavy attrition rates.

The scale of the losses suffered by the second-wave attackers provides insight into the projected scale of losses should a third attack been

THE SECOND ATTACK WAVE

Second-Wave Japanese Aircraft Losses[86]

	Kates employed as level bombers	Vals	Zeros	Totals
Akagi	None in second wave	18/4/12	9/0/1	27/4/13
Kaga	None in second wave	26/6/16	9/2/3	35/8/19
Soryu	None in second wave	17/2/13	9/3/4	26/5/17
*Hiryu**	None in second wave	17/2/Unk	8/1/Unk	25/3/Unk
Shokaku	27/0/14	None in second wave	None in second wave	27/0/14
Zuikaku	27/0/2	None in second wave	None in second wave	27/0/2
Totals	54/0/16	78/14/41+	35/6/8+	167/20/65+
Grand total from both waves	143/5/34+ (all Kate sorties)	129/15/58+	80/9/19+	352/29/111+

Number of aircraft involved/lost/damaged
* Records for *Hiryu* do not exist

Loss Rates for Japanese Second-Wave Air Groups

Ship	Percentage of aircraft destroyed and damaged
Akagi	63
Kaga	77
Soryu	85
Hiryu	Unknown, but probably equal to *Soryu*'s losses
Shokaku	52
Zuikaku	7

attempted. In total, 40 percent of the attacking aircraft on the raid were destroyed or damaged. This is real testimony to the quick recovery of the Americans.

Unfortunately, it is not possible to provide additional insight into the severity of damage to the many aircraft targeted in the two raids. One aircraft was known to have ditched near a destroyer, a Kate level bomber from the first wave.[87] A second aircraft also ditched.[88] More importantly, the number of aircraft that were tossed over the side of the carriers after landing due to battle damage is unclear. It is certain that there were "several" badly damaged aircraft treated in this manner, but the best source indicates that about 15 aircraft were so severely damaged that they were jettisoned over the side.[89] Another source using Japanese records paints a similar picture, stating that about a dozen seriously damaged aircraft, half of them dive-bombers, were pushed over the side.[90]

What would the Japanese have had available for any potential third wave? Giving a precise number is impossible since records are incomplete. In terms of Kates, the total would have been just over 100. These would have only been used for level bombing since with surprise lost there was no possibility of repeating a torpedo attack. In terms of dive-bombers, the number of available aircraft was much lower. Most of the losses inflicted against the attacking Japanese were incurred by their dive-bombers. Losses in the second wave were particularly heavy.

Dive-bombers would have been the spearhead of any third attack. Under normal circumstances, they were more survivable than the Kates and were able to deliver more precise strikes than level bombers. This was not a particularly impressive total; importantly, it should be noted that the great majority of available dive-bombers were from the inexperienced air groups of Carrier Division 5.

Just considering the fighters used in the first two strikes, as many as 60 fighters might have been available. This total could have been increased had the Japanese augmented a potential attack force with any of the 39 Zeros held back from the attack to perform CAP duties over the task force. This makes the grand total approximately 220 aircraft: 100 Kates, about 60 Vals, and 60 fighters. However, the many factors

Dive-bomber losses and availability, December 7, 1941[91]

Ship	Losses	Available after strike recovery
Akagi	4	2
Kaga	6	6
Soryu	2	7
Hiryu	2	Unknown
Shokaku	1	22
Zuikaku	0	14
Total	15	51+

THE SECOND ATTACK WAVE

shaping whether the Japanese could have conducted a third strike make it all but certain that the actual number available for such an endeavor would have been far less than 220. The following chapter examines this question in more detail.

In addition to mounting two large strikes on the morning of December 7, Nagumo and Genda maintained a strong defense over the Striking Force in the event of an American aerial counterattack. A total of 39 Zeros were retained for CAP duties.[92] According to the Japanese official history, the CAP was executed in four different phases. In the first, flown from 0600 to 0900, 15 Zeros were active (three from Carrier Division 2 and 12 from Carrier Division 5). In the second phase, from 1000 to 1115, 23 Zeros were allocated to CAP (five from Carrier Division 1, six from Carrier Division 2, and 12 from Carrier Division 5). The next phase, from 1115 to 1300, included three fighters from Carrier Division 2 and 12 from Carrier Division 5. Finally, between 1300 and 1730, there were 18 and then nine Zeros airborne drawn equally from the three carrier divisions.[93] It is clear that Genda was heavily emphasizing offensive operations at the expense of CAP. The number of fighters airborne at any one time was barely adequate to mount patrols around the Striking Force and clearly inadequate to counter a concerted attack. Furthermore, most of the sorties were mounted by the inexperienced pilots from Carrier Division 5. It is true that the remaining portion of the 39 Zeros not airborne could have been scrambled with sufficient warning, but it is probably fortunate for the Japanese that the Americans were unable to mount any kind of aerial counterattack.

9

The American Reaction and the Myth of the Second Attack

Though totally surprised at the onset of the attack, the Americans responded quickly. Even the Japanese admitted that the reaction was quicker than they expected. However, aside from antiaircraft crews getting their guns into action and the efforts of a handful of fighter pilots, the overall American response was ineffective.

Within minutes of coming under attack at Ford Island, Commander Logan Ramsey (operations officer for Patrol Wing Two) began efforts to initiate search operations to find the Japanese fleet. Before an effective response could be mounted against the Striking Force, the Japanese had to be located. Ramsey planned a 360-degree search around Oahu since at this early point there was no indication from which direction the Japanese attack had been mounted. He planned to use 18 PBYs, including the seven already airborne, and Army Air Force aircraft in the search. Orders to this effect went out at 0800. Ramsey's efforts were almost immediately superseded by events (Kaneohe and Hickam had been struck and the aircraft intended to mount searches destroyed) and by communication problems with the airborne aircraft.

Since the four airborne VP-24 PBYs had not responded to the 0800 orders from Ramsey, Bellinger (commander of the patrol aircraft force) sent out a new set of orders just before 0900. The aircraft were directed to search west of Oahu to cover the sectors from 240 to 280 degrees. They were to fly out 300nm before heading south for 15nm and then returning to base. One of these aircraft encountered seven Vals from *Hiryu*. The nimble dive-bombers attacked and hit the PBY 11 times,

THE AMERICAN REACTION AND THE MYTH OF THE SECOND ATTACK

but the slow patrol plane suffered no serious damage and dove to hug the surface of the ocean to survive.[1]

Bellinger had some resources to work with, even after the last Japanese aircraft left Oahu. Eleven PBYs were ready, though seven of these were already airborne. Squadron VJ-1, with a collection of shorter range aircraft, reported it was ready for orders. Anxious to get a location on the Japanese carrier force, Bellinger launched a PBY-5 from VP-23 at 1000. The three airborne VP-14 PBYs were ordered to move to the northwest. One was tasked to conduct a search out to 375nm. By orders of Commander Knefler McGinnis, Commander Patrol Wing One, the other two aircraft were moved from the northern sectors to the west of Oahu. This command confusion greatly reduced any chance that the Striking Force would be spotted on December 7.[2] To fill the gap between the VP-14 and VP-24 searches, Bellinger resorted to using aircraft from VJ-1. Five Sikorsky JRS-1s were ordered to fly out to 250nm north and northwest of Oahu, and three Grumman J2F Ducks were sent to search at shorter ranges to cover the west and southwest sectors. Use of these utility aircraft was a desperate measure since neither type was really suitable for search operations or survivable if they encountered the enemy. One JRS-1 pilot accepted the offer from two Marines to come along with their Springfield '03 bolt-action rifles. Otherwise, the aircraft would have been unarmed.[3]

The various search aircraft failed to find the Striking Force, but at 1058 a PBY from VP-23 did locate Task Force 8 southwest of Kauai. This was one of several times *Enterprise* encountered friendly search aircraft during the day. Other encounters were not as friendly. At 1310, a JRS-1 encountered one or more Zeros from *Zuikaku* south of the Striking Force. The pilot was able to disappear into a cloud before coming under attack.[4] This was the closest an American aircraft came to Nagumo's force during the day. Another JRS-1 flying to the west encountered a Zero near Ni'ihau Island. The Zero attempted a firing pass from astern but the flying boat was able to gain the shelter offered by nearby clouds. The identity of the Zeros remains unknown, with wayward aircraft from either *Hiryu* or *Kaga* being the best candidates.[5]

Bellinger was nothing if not tenacious, but he was acting with a minimal amount of information on the possible location of the Japanese carriers. Two more VP-23 PBYs were launched at 1330 and 1400 to patrol to the southwest of Oahu. By 1400, two SOCs and four OS2U-3s (two from *Arizona* and two from *Maryland*) were dispatched to search south and southwest of Oahu. Two of the battleship floatplanes were lost to unknown causes, and none of the aircraft reported contact.[6]

THE PLIGHT OF *ENTERPRISE*'S AIR GROUP

Enterprise launched 18 of her Dauntless dive-bombers – the air group commander's aircraft, 13 aircraft from Scouting Squadron 6 (VS-6) and four aircraft from Bombing Squadron 6 (VB-6) – at dawn on December 7. Operating in pairs, the aircraft were ordered to scout an arc extending from northeast to southeast of the ship. Once the mission was complete, they were under orders to land at Ford Island. Unfortunately for the American aviators, after finding nothing they arrived over Pearl Harbor only to be caught between the attacking Japanese aircraft and the defensive antiaircraft fire from the ships and shore installations in and around the harbor. One Dauntless was attacked by Vals from *Shokaku* and *Zuikaku* – the aircraft and its two-man crew were never seen again. Another was seen to collide with a Zero, and again the crew was lost. Two more were shot down by Zeros; in each instance only the pilot survived. A fifth Dauntless disappeared and was presumed to have been shot down by Zeros. Again, both of the crewmen were lost. The last aircraft lost was claimed by American antiaircraft fire. The Dauntless was forced to ditch south of Oahu with both crewmen being wounded. In total, six aircraft were lost, eight aviators and airmen were killed, and three more were wounded.[7]

A group of seven aircraft under Lieutenant Wilmer E. Gallaher, VS-6's executive officer, was advised that Ford Island was under attack, so he circled south of Oahu for more than an hour to let the situation calm down. At about 0945, Gallaher decided to land at nearby Ewa. This was done, but after coming to a stop Marines told Gallaher and his six other aircraft to get back into the air to avoid being strafed. All seven aircraft got off safely, but when they flew to Ford Island they encountered heavy antiaircraft fire from jittery American gunners expecting another attack. Gallaher and his two wingmen were able to land at about 0955, but the other four aircraft turned back and landed at Ewa at about 1015.[8]

At 1100, the Americans were trying to put together a counterattack. All available aircraft were directed to rendezvous with a group of B-17s

THE AMERICAN REACTION AND THE MYTH OF THE SECOND ATTACK

over Hickam. Three of the *Enterprise* Dauntlesses at Ewa took off at 1115 (the fourth had suffered damage and was under repair) to meet up with the makeshift attacking force. Finding nothing, they recovered at Ford Island.[9]

The bulk of VS-6 at Ford Island was the most potent American striking force on Oahu. However, nothing could be done until the Japanese were located. Anxious to strike back at the Japanese, Gallaher conducted a search mission off Barbers Point from 1030 to 1145 and found nothing. Later, nine Dauntlesses took off from Ford Island at 1210 and headed north for about 200nm. Since the Striking Force had already moved away from Oahu, the mission found nothing and recovered at 1545.[10]

At 1630, reports of a Soryu-class carrier south of Oahu were received. Vice Admiral William Halsey on *Enterprise* responded quickly, launching a strike at 1642 with 19 Douglas TBD-1 Devastators with six Dauntless dive-bombers to lay protective smoke, and an escort of six Wildcats. Since the report was spurious, nothing was found. The bombers were directed to return to *Enterprise*, with the short-range Wildcats ordered to land at Ford Island. Despite approach directions to the Wildcats to reduce their vulnerability to trigger-happy American gunners and arrangements with antiaircraft batteries not to fire, surface ships in the harbor opened up when the Wildcats attempted to land. In what became an orgy of gunfire, three were shot down with the loss of their pilots. A fourth Wildcat ran out of fuel, but the pilot bailed out and survived.[11]

HAWAIIAN AIR FORCE OPERATIONS

Throughout December 7, the American air response was handicapped by a lack of communication between the Army and Navy. Under the duress of sudden combat, both services reverted to their usual practice of noncooperation. There was no sharing of intelligence, no informing the other of what assets each service had available, and therefore no chance of a coordinated response.

To his credit, Major General Martin did act on the intelligence he had available. After receiving information that Japanese aircraft over Oahu had been engaged while heading to the southwest, Martin and his staff assessed that a Japanese carrier was located 25–40nm south of

Barbers Point. Bellinger had already conducted searches in this area but had failed to share any intelligence with Martin. With the skimpiest intelligence on the location of the Japanese carriers, Martin decided to act. He ordered the commander of the 5th Bombardment Group, Lieutenant Colonel Edwin B. Bobzien, to conduct a search for the enemy. In response, five A-20A light bombers were each loaded with two 600-pound bombs and took off from Hickam at 1127. Flying about 100nm to the south, they found nothing and at about 1215 reversed course and headed back to Hickam. Thirteen minutes later, three B-17s departed after their escort of four P-40s arrived over Hickam. The search and strike mission got off to a rocky start after one B-17 crashed shortly after takeoff, and the escorting fighters left the remaining two bombers after they got in the air.

Heading south, the B-17s sighted *Enterprise*, which they identified as a friendly carrier. After that, the two aircraft broke up to conduct individual searches. One bomber flew out about 250nm before being forced to turn back due to engine trouble. It returned to Hickam at 1630. The second B-17 flew out 400nm to the northwest, found nothing, and returned to base by 1900.[12]

More intelligence reached Martin in the form of a flight chart from the Zero that had crashed at Fort Kamehameha. Courses plotted on the chart suggested that the Zero's flight had begun to the north of Oahu. Armed with this knowledge, Martin ordered Bobzien to conduct searches out to the north.[13]

To respond to this new order, Bobzien had very few assets left. He tapped the 58th Bombardment Squadron to arm two A-20As with two 600-pound bombs. Three B-18s from the 5th and 11th Bombardment Groups were the only other aircraft available. These were loaded with four 600-pound bombs. Using staggered take-off times, the five aircraft were tasked to search a 15-degree sector north of Oahu. The two A-20As took off at 1255. Only two B-18s could be prepared in time for the scheduled takeoff at 1330.[14]

After inexplicably searching only 30nm north of Oahu, the A-20s returned just before 1600. The two B-18s, one with a composite crew from different units, were much more aggressive. Under the command of Lieutenant Colonel Russell Waldron, they flew some 400nm to the north of Oahu. The flight crew reported that there were clouds in the area up to around 2,000 feet, making detection of the Japanese more difficult.

THE AMERICAN REACTION AND THE MYTH OF THE SECOND ATTACK

They got to 50nm west of the Striking Force. Had they found the Japanese, one crew planned to initiate a bomb run from 1,800 feet at 130 miles per hour. Such a profile would have been suicidal in the face of defending Zeros. Luckily for the B-18 crews, they failed to contact the Striking Force. The two bombers returned at 1655.[15]

The last American attempt to locate and attack the Japanese was mounted late in the afternoon. Three of the newly arrived B-17s from the 88th Reconnaissance Squadron were made ready by the tireless efforts of the ground crews. In response to a request by the Navy, Bobzien ordered the B-17s to search southeast of Oahu. Taking off at 1710, the bombers flew only 70nm to the southeast before returning shortly after dark. This was in spite of their orders to fly out to maximum range.

Command and control issues prevented an effective American offensive response on December 7. The best information on the location of the Striking Force was the radar tracking data from the morning as the Japanese attack formations approached Oahu from the north. This information never reached the commanders struggling to ascertain the location of the Japanese carriers and trying to assemble a counterattack. Thus, the Japanese prediction that they would lose two carriers to air attack was never in danger of coming true. It is fortunate for the few bombers that departed Oahu looking to attack the Japanese that they never found their target since the Japanese fighter patrols were entirely capable of defeating piecemeal attacks. With the exception of the dive-bombers from VS-6, which lacked the range to attack the Striking Force on December 7, if the few Army Air Force bombers had located the Japanese, there was an extremely thin chance their ill-trained crews using only bombs dropped from high altitude would have inflicted any damage on the Japanese.

THE SECOND ATTACK CONTROVERSY

One of the attack's salient myths was that the Japanese seriously considered a follow-up attack against Pearl Harbor on the afternoon of December 7. Only after a fierce debate on the bridge of his flagship did Nagumo decide not to pursue this option but to retreat instead. The second part of this myth follows the first: if a second attack had been approved, it would have focused on naval infrastructure on Oahu and could have easily destroyed these facilities. The third and final piece of this myth was that by not destroying the infrastructure the Japanese committed a strategic blunder. All portions of this multi-headed fable are based on little or no evidence, and all are demonstrably false.

The Debate That Never Was

As previously detailed, there was no possibility of Nagumo approving a second attack. He had made this clear to Genda on multiple occasions prior to the attack. Nevertheless, many accounts mention a debate between Nagumo and Fuchida as the latter pressed his boss to finish off the Americans. What really happened on the bridge of *Akagi* in the early afternoon hours of December 7?

In the words of Fuchida, he was having a quick meal on the flight deck when he saw the order "Preparations for attack canceled." Then he saw the signal flags on *Akagi* that the Striking Force was moving to the northwest – away from Oahu. He rushed to the bridge to protest. After saluting Nagumo he asked: "Why are we not attacking again?" Before Nagumo could reply, Kusaka injected: "The objective of the Pearl Harbor operation has been achieved. Now we must prepare for other operations ahead." In this version, provided to historian Gordon Prange in 1963, Fuchida indicated disappointment and outrage over the decision. Unable to speak, he abruptly departed, "a bitter and angry man." For the remainder of the operation, Fuchida only spoke to Nagumo when necessary.[16]

The same story with minor modifications is repeated in Prange's 1990 book *God's Samurai*, which traces Fuchida's life. It is based on interviews with Fuchida given in 1948, 1949, and 1963.[17] In another account provided by Fuchida, published in the US Naval Institute's *Proceedings* in 1952, Fuchida speaks of a fierce debate: "I was called to the bridge as soon as the plane stopped, and could tell on arriving there that Admiral Nagumo's staff had been engaged in heated discussions about the advisability of launching the next attack."[18] The best known depiction of this event was in the 1970 movie *Tora, Tora, Tora* in which Fuchida is depicted arguing strongly for a second attack.

These postwar interviews regarding a second attack were dramatically different than the one Fuchida gave in October 1945 when he was initially interrogated by the Americans as part of the postwar strategic bombing survey. On this occasion, when asked pointedly why the Japanese did not launch a repeat attack, Fuchida related that it was

THE AMERICAN REACTION AND THE MYTH OF THE SECOND ATTACK

because the American carriers were not located, the extent to which the Hawaiian Air Force had been attrited was unknown, and the knowledge that four battleships had been sunk, thus fulfilling the objective of the operation. He made no mention of a desire to launch a second attack and did not lament that it had not been done.[19]

Kusaka was also on the bridge when Fuchida was called up to make his report. He makes no mention of any angry or forceful attempt by Fuchida to advocate for a second attack.[20] Genda was less emotional than Fuchida but just as aggressive. He was in favor of mounting multiple attacks but had gotten nowhere in the weeks before the actual event in convincing Nagumo of the wisdom of doing so. Genda would have certainly remembered any discussion of a potential second attack as he would have advocated for it. However, in his 1967 memoirs, he is also clear that such a discussion never took place:

> According to Dr Prange's book *Tora, Tora, Tora* and others, a fierce argument took place on the bridge of *Akagi* as regards the proposal for a second strike. That's not true. The author had been on the bridge for some eight hours before the start of operations and remained there over the following four days… Such a proposal was never made.[21]

Thus it is clear that no debate ever took place regarding a second strike. This was an invention of Fuchida from 1963 that became embedded in the mythology of the attack when it became a powerful scene in *Tora, Tora, Tora*. No Japanese figure in this drama was convinced enough at the time to advocate publicly and forcefully for a second attack. The supposed wisdom of a second attack only became apparent after the event.

Fuchida's Story

Prange had the opportunity to interview Fuchida several times over many years. In the 1963 interview, Fuchida created the story of a dramatic confrontation on *Akagi*'s bridge. This is one of the pillars of the second attack myth – it was only the ignorance of Nagumo that stood in the way of a great strategic success by the Japanese.

According to Fuchida, on the flight back to *Akagi* he was making mental notes of targets for a second attack. On this list he included the fuel tank farms, the facilities at the Navy Yard, and a couple of ships left untouched from the first attack.[22]

Among the pilots, enthusiasm was great for a second attack. In the words of Lieutenant Goto Jinichi, one of the torpedo bomber aircrewmen on *Akagi*: "Most of the young flying officers were eager to attack Pearl Harbor again because they wished to inflict as much damage as possible. It was the chance of a lifetime, and many of the pilots felt the chance should not be passed up."[23] When the flying officers from *Akagi's* first wave were trying to do their initial bomb damage assessment on a blackboard on the flight deck near the bridge, they urged a second attack to Genda who had come down from the bridge. After listening, Genda offered no opinion on the matter, at least not to the gathered aircrew.[24]

Things got more interesting once Fuchida landed back aboard *Akagi* at about noon. Nagumo summoned him at once up to the bridge, but Fuchida wanted to compare his observations with the results tabulated on the blackboard. After another messenger told Fuchida he was wanted on the bridge, he finally went to see Nagumo and his key staff officers.

In the following discussion, Fuchida provided his best assessments to the pointed questions he was posed. He started out by stating that four battleships had sunk and four more were damaged. He went on to list the other ships struck during the attack. Nagumo asked, "Do you think the US Fleet could not come out from Pearl Harbor within six months?" In reply, Fuchida stated, "The main force of the US Pacific Fleet will not be able to come out within six months." When Kusaka followed with a question on what the targets should be for the next attack, Fuchida gave him the target list fresh in his mind: fuel tanks, naval facilities, and the occasional ship. Kusaka and another officer then zeroed in on whether the enemy could launch a counterattack against the Striking Force. In response to this pointed question Fuchida responded, "I believe we have destroyed many enemy planes, but I do not know whether we have destroyed them all. The enemy most probably could still attack the Fleet."[25]

Obviously, the prospects of an American counterattack concerned Nagumo. Genda was not at all concerned, stating, "Let the enemy come! If he does, we will shoot his planes down." Adding to Nagumo's concerns was Fuchida's response to Nagumo's question on the location

THE AMERICAN REACTION AND THE MYTH OF THE SECOND ATTACK

of the American carriers. Again, he made no attempt to sugarcoat the situation, simply responding that he did not know but that they were obviously looking for the Striking Force.[26]

Noteworthy in this discussion was the lack of any drama. Fuchida simply gave honest answers to pointed and legitimate questions and made no plea for a second attack. After Fuchida was dismissed, Genda weighed in with a plan not for a second attack, but to linger in the area for several days to find the American carriers. This was similar to the plans already pitched to Nagumo that he had always dismissed.

After this brief interaction, Nagumo received Kusaka's recommendation that there be no second attack. Nagumo concurred. He ordered a withdrawal – there would be no second attack.

It is clear that there was no chance that Nagumo would approve such a course of action. Only a direct order from Yamamoto would have changed anything. And Yamamoto made it his declared policy not to interfere with the commander on the scene. Other observers saw the situation differently. By not attacking, Nagumo was missing a huge opportunity. With the Americans on their knees, a second attack was guaranteed to succeed. The naval base could have been destroyed. Its destruction would have had strategic implications. This is the bedrock of the second and third parts of the Second Attack Myth.

Support behind the Second Attack Myth is strong. The first to lend credence to the notion that the Japanese had committed a strategic blunder was historian Samuel Eliot Morison in his semi-official account of the attack written in 1948. In it, he stated:

> There is some question, however, whether the aviators were directed to the right targets, even from the Japanese point of view. They knocked out the Battle Force and decimated the striking air power present; but they neglected permanent installations at Pearl Harbor, including the repair shops which were able to do an amazingly quick job on the less severely damaged ships. And they did not even attempt to hit the power plant or the large fuel oil "tank farm," filled to capacity, whose loss (in the opinion of Admiral Hart) would have set back our advance across the Pacific much longer than did the damage to the fleet.[27]

Prange's co-authors make the same point:

> One stroke of luck for the Americans on 7 December was the fact that the Pearl Harbor attack plan contained no provision for destroying the Navy Yard. Had the Japanese done so, they would have put the U.S. Pacific Fleet out of action far more effectively than by wrecking individual ships. The fleet would have had no choice but to return to the Pacific Coast. This withdrawal could have significantly altered the course of the war.[28]

Even Nimitz weighed in on the Japanese mistake:

> In concentrating on ships, the Japanese neglected the machine shops, leaving repair facilities virtually intact. They had overlooked the 4,500,000 barrels of oil exposed in tank farms near the harbor. This slowly accumulated fuel reserve was almost irreplaceable in view of America's European commitments. Without it, fleets could not have operated from Pearl Harbor for months.[29]

Prange, the leading Pearl Harbor historian, also falls into the camp that the Japanese had missed a golden opportunity:

> By failing to exploit the shock, bewilderment, and confusion on Oahu, by failing to take full advantage of its savage attack against Kimmel's ships, by failing to pulverize the Pearl Harbor base, by failing to destroy Oahu's vast fuel stores, and by failing to seek out and sink America's carriers, Japan committed its first and probably its greatest strategic error of the entire Pacific conflict.[30]

Had the Japanese possessed the capability to do the things listed by Prange and others, his words would have been fateful. In reality, all of these things were beyond the means of the Japanese.

Just because Fuchida stated he had been making mental notes about a target list for a second attack and that fuel tanks and naval yard facilities topped his list, that is a far stretch from assuming that a second attack would have focused on infrastructure. As the Japanese struggled to create a targeting plan under great time constraints, it would have been much more likely that they would have reverted to their ingrained

THE AMERICAN REACTION AND THE MYTH OF THE SECOND ATTACK

instincts regarding naval strategy. The Japanese were strict adherents to Mahanian concepts of sea power. This mindset was reflected in the pre-attack priority list in which naval installations were last. It was epitomized by Genda himself. When asked by an American interrogator after the war why the fuel tanks were not bombed, he replied that nobody had thought of this target.[31] Genda's aggressive plan to launch attacks over the span of several days was aimed at attacking ships, not installations. If attacking infrastructure was so important and offered the potential to cripple Pacific Fleet operations, then it would have been a part of target planning.

The leaders of the Imperial Navy were steeped and trained in the classic tenets of Mahan. This required them to engage the enemy fleet in a decisive battle, destroy that fleet, and then accrue the benefits of sea control enjoyed by the victor. This is what Yamamoto aimed to accomplish at Pearl Harbor. In this context, it would have been inconceivable that the Japanese would have placed attacks on a naval facility on the same plane, or given it greater importance as advocated by some, to attacking units of the Pacific Fleet. None of the Japanese principals wanted to inject striking installations into the planning. Only Fuchida, addressing the matter 22 years after the event when the notion of attacking infrastructure was gaining favor, contended that the lack of focus on infrastructure was a mistake. As he did for other events in the war, Fuchida loved to inflate his role and give himself credit for insight not possessed by others.[32]

OPERATIONAL FACTORS PRECLUDING A SECOND ATTACK

The Striking Force was conceived and built as a raiding force. It was not designed as a power projection force. To perform the latter mission, it had to be capable of sustained operations in enemy waters. This required several capabilities: a large supply train capable of delivering fuel, ordnance, replacement aircraft, and pilots; and the capability of defending itself against enemy attack for sustained periods. At no point during the war did the Japanese carrier force develop these capabilities.

The Striking Force was fully capable of striking the ships and aircraft on Oahu, exhibiting the classic function of a raiding force. To destroy the infrastructure of the naval base at Pearl Harbor was another thing altogether. Such a huge facility could not be destroyed by a single raid or even by a handful of raids. Destruction of a facility this large required power projection over a sustained period, something for which the Striking Force was neither suitable nor prepared.

In addition to the Striking Force not being the proper instrument to neutralize Pearl Harbor's extensive naval and aviation infrastructure, there were several operational factors that would have precluded a second attack.

Timing

For several reasons, any second attack had to be conducted on December 7. Waiting until December 8 to launch a second strike was not realistic. Nagumo and his staff were extremely concerned about the prospects of American land-based heavy bombers finding and attacking the Striking Force. The ineffectiveness of these aircraft in a maritime attack role had yet to be revealed. If they came under air attack, the Japanese fully expected to lose carriers. In addition to the threat of land-based aircraft, there was the specter of American carriers and submarines finding the task force. The longer the Striking Force lingered, the greater the threat of American retaliation became, at least in Nagumo's mind.

Another factor limiting the attack to December 7 was the task force's fuel situation. Nagumo's destroyers were running low on fuel. His resupply force was positioned well to the northeast, out of range from American action. To conduct the refueling necessary for a second attack, the Japanese would have to move the Striking Force to a safe point away from the Hawaiian Islands and then make a high-speed run to return to a position off Oahu. The earliest this could have been done was December 11. During this period the Striking Force would have been exposed to detection and possible attack. The additional time also gave the Americans time to prepare their defenses. Nagumo would never have countenanced such a delay and that degree of additional risk.

Assuming that a second attack would have had to be conducted on the afternoon of December 7 presented a very challenging timeline for the Japanese. The bulk of the second wave recovered aboard their carriers by 1215 with the last aircraft returning at 1246. From this point the timeline to determine the feasibility of mounting a second attack begins.

THE AMERICAN REACTION AND THE MYTH OF THE SECOND ATTACK

Since there were no reserve aircraft, a second attack had to be assembled from the aircraft of the first two waves. This would have been a lengthy process. Since there was no contingency plan on the shelf, Genda would have had to come up with one on the fly. Aircrew would have had to be debriefed. A targeting plan would have had to be built, based on the morning's damage assessment, and then this plan would have had to be briefed to all the pilots. It would have had to be sent from *Akagi* to the other five carriers without using radio, so by signal light alone. It would have been a hurried operation. If the target prioritization and target selection shown by the first two waves had been less than tidy, the second strike's target selection would almost certainly have been more chaotic. It also would have been much less accurate since the Japanese had no precise intelligence on structures within the Navy Yard and therefore would have been unaware of the location of critical machine shops.

As the plan was being created and disseminated, the aircraft would have had to be readied. Those aircraft that were damaged would have to be inspected and repaired if required. Aircraft would have to be refueled, and ordnance loaded. Ordnance would have been an issue. It is not known how many 1,760-pound land bombs were carried on board the six carriers; for attacking a large area target like the Navy Yard or fuel farms, this weapon was preferred. Failing their availability, the Vals and Kates would have been loaded with the Number 80 Type 25 551-pound bombs. These were unsuited for attacking area targets, and as demonstrated during the morning strike, had little destructive power against land targets. None of the refueling and rearming could have begun until the plan was firm enough to determine which aircraft would be taking part.

Given all the components of preparing a large-scale strike, it is hard to see it being ready until 1500 at the earliest. That assumes that all aspects of the planning and preparation process did not encounter difficulties. There would have been many opportunities for the friction of war to surface. For example, at the Battle of Midway when the Striking Force faced another dynamic target preparation cycle, rearming began at approximately 0745 and was not complete by 1030 when the Japanese carriers were struck. Simply spotting aircraft on the flight deck and warming them up for launch would take some 40 minutes. Therefore, a launch time of 1500 is probably optimistic, but with the proper command emphasis and the demonstrated proficiency of the flight deck and hangar crews, possibly achievable.

Next comes the launch, requiring another 15 minutes. Flying to and from Oahu required at least three hours. The additional time needed to execute the attack extends the total time required to at least four hours. This brings the strike aircraft back to the Striking Force after dark, at about 1900, introducing an entirely new set of problems.

In 1941, recovering aircraft in darkness was quite dangerous. Sunset on December 7 was at 1712. Nautical twilight, the last light in the western sky, was at 1805. The difficulty of the recovery would have been heightened by the fact that many aircraft would have been damaged, and because of the heavy seas and high winds. In these conditions, launching and then recovering a large strike would have been possible only with many casualties.[33] There is no possibility that Nagumo and Kusaka would have approved such a risky undertaking with the potential of losing a high number of irreplaceable aircraft and aircrew on the first day of the war.

Because any second attack would have been a hurried operation, it was not an ideal situation for the staff of the Striking Force which, as was shown at multiple points in the months to follow, did not deal well with dynamic situations. They had months to plan the opening attack on Pearl Harbor, and it was still riddled with problems. Any plan to attack Pearl Harbor on the afternoon of December 7 would almost certainly have been a poorly planned, highly improvised, rapidly executed, and in the final analysis, a perilous undertaking.

Forces Available for a Second Attack

Japanese

In raw numbers alone, the power of a second attack would have been significantly reduced compared with the first. Of the 350 aircraft taking part in the two waves of the first attack, 29 were shot down and 111 damaged. (It is unclear if the two ditched and 15 jettisoned aircraft are included in this total.) Calculating the numbers of undamaged aircraft results in approximately 100 Kates, 50–60 Vals, and 50–60 Zeros available for a second attack. This would have comprised a formidable strike force, but raw numbers do not tell the whole story.

Key to any second attack were the 50–60 dive-bombers. These were capable of more precise bombing, vital if the attack was going to strike remaining ships, oil tanks, or specific facilities within the Navy Yard. With each aircraft carrying only a single bomb, that did not leave Genda much flexibility in selecting targets. Plus, the majority of these were from *Shokaku* and *Zuikaku* – their inexperienced aircrews lacked the ability to service targets with precision.

Because of their vulnerability, Genda had decided not to employ the Kates as torpedo bombers. Of course, the Kates would still have been useful in the level bombing role, but this was much less accurate when flying at the usual 10,000 feet. For both the dive-bombers and level bombers, weather on Oahu would have been a huge factor. If the cloud cover was anything like the morning, it would have severely impacted accuracy. In fact, the clouds present over the harbor in the morning did not clear during the remainder of the day.

Several additional factors would have limited the number of Kates available for a second strike. First, many would have been required for search operations around the Striking Force to locate the missing American carriers or to ensure they posed no threat. Second was the need to retain a strike force that could react if the carriers were located. Nagumo was very concerned with the lack of information on American carriers. Since they were not in Pearl Harbor, they were possibly lurking somewhere nearby. If they could be located, attacked, and sunk, it would have gone a long way to making the entire operation a complete success.

Since the Striking Force was moving quickly through enemy waters and the Japanese began with no idea regarding the possible location of the American carriers, finding them would have been a resource-intensive undertaking. Usually, a heavy burden of search missions was assumed by the escorting battleships and heavy cruisers employing their floatplanes. However, on December 7 the seas were rough (by some accounts getting worse as the day wore on), so launching and recovering floatplanes in the afternoon was problematic. Accordingly, the entire burden of searches would have fallen on the Kates. If a nominal 10-degree search sector was covered by each search aircraft, the number required could be quickly calculated. Genda would have been wise to execute a full 360-degree search, but at this point in the war the Japanese habitually skimped on using strike aircraft for search missions. Nevertheless, a considerable number of Kates, perhaps as many as 35, would have had to been allocated for search operations.

Another potential drain on the strike aircraft was the creation of a reserve force to immediately react to the discovery of an emergent American naval threat. This would probably have been primarily composed of Kates, which were more potent against naval targets than dive-bombers. The small number of dive-bombers available would have likely precluded any from being held in reserve. The reserve force would also have required escort fighters either pulled from those allocated to CAP or those earmarked for strike escort. This would have been the first time in the war that Genda was faced with concurrent operations against both land and naval targets, so it is unknown whether he would have felt the necessity to create a reserve force.

Defense of the Striking Force was a paramount concern. A robust CAP had to be maintained with at least as many fighters as used for the morning patrols when 39 were held back. This left the 50–60 undamaged fighters from the morning strikes as the potential fighter component of a second attack.

In the final analysis, a second attack force would have been smaller and capable of less destructive power than the morning attack. There was no real prospect of the Japanese being able to launch a full attack in the limited hours of daylight remaining on December 7. Waiting until the following day would have increased the potential size of the strike force but would have exposed the Striking Force as well as the aircraft of the strike to greater danger.

American
An afternoon strike would have had to contend with an aroused and determined American defense. Lack of surprise would have made a huge difference for the prospects of Japanese success. As the officers from *Akagi*'s aircrews were gathered around a blackboard on the flight deck near the bridge trying to tabulate the results of the attack, they agreed that the American response was surprisingly quick. The consensus was that their great success would have been impossible without the element of surprise.[34] Examining the results from the second wave of the first attack gives a good indication of what might have occurred in a second attack. The scale of losses from the second wave could be used as a starting point to determine losses for a possible third wave in the afternoon.

THE AMERICAN REACTION AND THE MYTH OF THE SECOND ATTACK

American defense of the key facilities around Oahu would have been robust in the afternoon of December 7. The six radar sites would have been operational, virtually guaranteeing that a large formation of Japanese aircraft approaching from the north would have been detected. Likewise, the Information Center would have been fully manned. Provided with radar tracking and the certainty that any large formation approaching Oahu would have been hostile, there was a high probability that American fighters would have been successfully vectored against the Japanese. Once the American fighters encountered the Japanese, the Japanese doctrine of not using fighters for close escort would have probably resulted in at least some of the American fighters getting a shot at the strike aircraft before the Zeros came to their rescue.

According to Hawaiian Air Force records, there was a significant number of fighters still operational after the initial attack. While the few P-26s had no utility unless they encountered unescorted Vals or Kates, the P-40s and P-36s had already demonstrated earlier on December 7 that they could exact a toll from the Japanese. With 45 of these fighters available, they would have been almost numerically equal to the Japanese fighters allocated to a second attack.

Whether or not the remaining American fighters successfully intercepted the Japanese, the hundreds of antiaircraft guns from the fleet and the Army would have been on the highest alert. As they demonstrated in a number of "friendly" fire incidents during the day, they were fully capable of shooting down aircraft approaching at low level. Against the Kates, employing a typical 10,000-foot bombing run and forced to fly a constant course, the hundreds of Navy 3- and 5-inch guns would have been effective, as would the Army's 3-inch antiaircraft batteries.

American Fighters Operational after the Initial Japanese Attack[35]

Fighter Type	Number Operational
P-40C	2
P-40B	25
P-36A	16
P-26A/B	4
Total	47

Significant units of the Pacific Fleet would have been out and searching for the Striking Force. *Enterprise* was in the area west of Oahu with her escorts. *Lexington*, at the heart of Task Force 12 with three heavy cruisers and five destroyers, departed Pearl Harbor on December 5, 1941, to ferry 18 Marine Corps dive-bombers to Midway. She also embarked 65 of her own aircraft. When word of the attack reached Task Force 12, it was some 500nm southeast of Midway. After news of the attack was received, the ferry mission was canceled and *Lexington* was ordered to rendezvous with ships from Pearl Harbor 100nm west of Ni'ihau Island. Had the Striking Force lingered beyond December 7 near Oahu, *Lexington* and *Enterprise* would have been in a position to search for it and possibly launch strikes against it.

Aside from the offensive power from their two carriers, the Americans retained a small strike force on Oahu. This force included four B-17Ds, 11 B-18s, and nine A-20As that remained operational after the attack.[36] In addition, most of *Enterprise*'s VS-6 was on Oahu, and the ten surviving B-17s from the December 7 ferry flight were available as soon as ground crews could prepare them. Overall, this was an unimpressive strike force, but Nagumo was unaware of this and had a healthy respect for land-based air power.

THE ATTACK THAT NEVER WAS

With all the factors discussed above, it is reasonable to assume that the Japanese could have assembled a force of 60 Vals and 60 Kates employed as horizontal bombers for a second attack. This meant that Genda and his strike planners would potentially have approximately 180 551-bombs (each Val carrying one, and each Kate with two) to service the array of targets left. What could the Japanese have done with 180 bombs?

It would have been unlikely that all Japanese weapons would have reached their designated targets through the immense antiaircraft barrage the Americans were capable of creating and through the intercepting fighters. It is also unlikely that all the bombs dropped on a specific target would have hit it. Even those that did hit had limited lethality against a land target. The Type 25 551-pound bomb had a 0.2-second delay. As evinced in many photographs of the first attack, this meant the bomb went deep into the ground before exploding.

THE AMERICAN REACTION AND THE MYTH OF THE SECOND ATTACK

The result was often a deep crater with little damage to surrounding structures. Also as evinced during the first attack, many Japanese bombs failed to explode or experienced low-order detonations.[37]

If the Japanese had decided to target the Navy Yard, the effect of whatever proportion of the 180 bombs hitting the target would have in no way guaranteed that the Navy Yard would have been destroyed or even severely damaged. The Navy Yard was a large target, some 498 acres. An American 500-pound bomb had the potential to destroy approximately 4,400 square feet of an industrial facility, and Japanese bombs were demonstrably less powerful. The math of the problem was not kind to the Japanese – only a minute proportion of the Navy Yard would have been destroyed. Furthermore, hitting a structure does not mean that the equipment or machines inside would have been destroyed, as the extensive bombing of Germany and Japan later proved.[38]

Thus, knocking out the Navy Yard with a small number of bombs was impossible. Neutralizing such a large target would have required repeated attacks, again as demonstrated by the resilience of German and Japanese industries later in the war. In addition, there was an excess capacity to make up the difference from any damage incurred by the facilities in the Navy Yard. The Pacific Fleet possessed a large number of tenders, and many were already at Pearl Harbor. These included three repair ships, two destroyer tenders, two seaplane tenders, and a submarine tender. Each had highly capable repair facilities. In addition, there were civilian facilities on Oahu that proved very capable during the salvage efforts following the attack. Additional manpower for any repair operation was available from the crews of the sunken battleships. All of this capacity was available to support fleet operations after the attack, or to repair any critical components of the Navy Yard that had been damaged or destroyed. American ingenuity, determination, and technical know-how – so often displayed throughout the war as the United States built a comprehensive logistical network around the world – would have addressed any requirements to support the fleet at Pearl Harbor. The idea that a relatively small number of bombs could have brought Pacific Fleet operations to a halt by damaging a small portion of the Navy Yard is simply unsupported by the facts.

A similar situation pertained when analyzing whether the Japanese could have destroyed the Pacific Fleet's fuel supplies. There were two major fuel farms on Oahu: the larger one between the Navy Yard and Hickam Field, and the smaller one near the submarine base. In these facilities there were 54 fuel tanks. These are easily identifiable in many of the photographs taken during the attack. In full view of Japanese aircraft, they would seem to be unmissable targets that would have been easy to knock out. The sides of each tank were built with steel .75 to 1.5 inches thick and a flat top that floated to eliminate fuel vapors.

However, destroying such a target was not as easy as it seemed. The 7.7mm machine guns on Japanese aircraft lacked the ability to ignite the fuel. The 20mm cannons on the Zeros either lacked the capability to penetrate the sides of the tanks (because the shells were fused to explode on contact) or lacked the ability to start a fire.[39] Bombs were required to destroy the tanks. Depending on the number of bombs employed, many of the fuel tanks would have been destroyed.[40] Any fuel tanks hit by bombs and ignited would have produced huge smoke columns, making subsequent targeting of the fuel farm much more difficult. Since the hypothetical level of effort exerted by the Japanese against the fuel tanks is unknown (and of course any bombs aimed at the fuel farm would not have been available to hit the Navy Yard and vice versa), and because of the inherent difficulty of hitting even a stationary target, it is impossible to calculate how many of the 54 fuel tanks would have been destroyed. But considering their available air assets, it would have been impossible for the Japanese to fully destroy the fuel farms or even a significant number of the tanks in either one.

In all probability, the majority of the fuel tanks and the stored fuel would have remained untouched. Any discussion of the effectiveness of a strike against the fuel tanks at Pearl Harbor needs to consider the regenerative power of the Americans. Later in the war, the Americans proved their mastery in quickly building new bases or bringing shattered ports back to life. Rebuilding a number of fuel tanks would have taken only weeks and could have been restocked with oil brought by a handful of tankers. As an interim solution fuel could have been brought to Pearl Harbor and stored in several of the 200 tankers under American control at this period of the war. This was an extremely inefficient use of valuable tankers but would have no longer been necessary once the tanks had been rebuilt or the secret Red Hill Underground Fuel Storage Facility begun in September 1940 was completed.

THE AMERICAN REACTION AND THE MYTH OF THE SECOND ATTACK

With only minor damage to the fuel farms, and given the American capability to rebuild any destroyed fuel tanks and assign the required number of tankers to refill them, the notion that the Pacific Fleet could have been forced by the effects of a single strike to fall back to the West Coast for an extended period of time is a myth. Any destruction of fuel tanks would have had an effect, but not to the extent of crippling operations. The new Pacific Fleet commander would have faced some fuel issues, and would have had to adjust to the shortfall. There were viable solutions, like sending the surviving battleships to operate from the West Coast as he did historically.

When considering what a second attack on Pearl Harbor would have accomplished, the Japanese attack on Midway is a good example of what the results might have been against a well-defended and fairly small facility. Against Midway Atoll, the Striking Force employed 36 Vals and 35 Kates carrying 1,800-pound bombs. The 36 escorting Zeros prevented the intercepting American fighters from destroying any more than four of the bombers. Flying through heavy antiaircraft fire, the 67 remaining bombers caused significant but by no means crippling damage to the facilities on Midway. Overall, American operations suffered minimal degradation. In addition, Japanese losses were very severe, totaling 11 aircraft lost and another 43 damaged, 14 heavily enough to make them nonoperational.

NAGUMO DECIDES

At about 1352 on December 7, Nagumo made his decision to retire. He explained his rationale as such:

1. The first attack had inflicted all the damage we had hoped for, and another attack could not be expected to greatly increase the extent of that damage.
2. Enemy return fire had been surprisingly prompt even though we took them by surprise; another attack would meet stronger opposition and our losses would certainly be disproportionate to the additional destruction that might be inflicted.
3. Intercepted enemy messages indicated at least fifty large planes still operational, and we did not know the whereabouts of the enemy's carriers, cruisers, and submarines.

4   To remain within range of enemy land-based planes was distinctly to our disadvantage, especially since the effectiveness of our air reconnaissance was extremely limited.[41]

Kusaka was Nagumo's most trusted advisor. His recommendation to withdraw after the first attack weighed heavily with Nagumo and reflected his own views. He and Nagumo agreed that the operation was 80 percent successful and that the other 20 percent was not worth the risk. In Kusaka's words:

> The objective of this operation was to protect the flank and rear of the Southern Force. Inasmuch as its objective was almost accomplished, I concluded that we should not remain ... on the scene and also should not be distracted into lengthening the game indefinitely...
>
> We had to strike a reasonable balance between fighting spirit and resources. With Japan's limited means and America's potential, Japan just could not afford to gamble her ships recklessly nor run risks where the potential dividends were unclear.[42]

When asked by his aviators about Nagumo's decision, Genda provided a similar explanation. In the moment, he gave three reasons defending the withdrawal: the operation had already achieved its desired results, lingering for a second attack would expose the Striking Force to considerable damage, and the location of the American carriers was unknown. These were logical reasons and were largely in accordance with Nagumo's thinking. At the same time, he called Nagumo "a miscast misfit," suggesting that he agreed with his impetuous aviators and would have preferred to launch a second attack.[43]

If the Japanese were convinced that a second attack was the correct thing to do, the Combined Fleet commander could have ordered Nagumo to do it. Yamamoto's chief of staff, Ugaki, never a fan of Nagumo, was in favor of a second attack. In his diary on December 9 he recorded: "Since our loss is not more than thirty planes, it is most important for us to expand our results."[44] There was an attempt by senior staff officer Kuroshima and other more junior members of the Combined Fleet staff to intervene and convince Yamamoto to order a second strike. Kuroshima was in favor of additional attacks and presented his thoughts

THE AMERICAN REACTION AND THE MYTH OF THE SECOND ATTACK

to Yamamoto on the morning after the attack. Yamamoto had a firm policy of not interfering with the commander on the scene who had the best feel for the actual conditions (this policy failed to survive more than a few months into the war). Obviously, Yamamoto was fully invested in the success of the Pearl Harbor operation, but he was also wise enough to look at things as part of a bigger perspective. Against all the odds, the operation achieved its goals without the loss of a single ship of the Striking Force. The war had just begun. Not wanting to order Nagumo to change his original decision (which would have been a stinging rebuke), Yamamoto decided not to intervene.

The planning for Pearl Harbor and its execution initiated an uneasy relationship between Yamamoto and Nagumo. According to one of his staff members, Yamamoto "was still not satisfied with Nagumo" and he never forgot his subordinate's opposition to his bold concept for a Pearl Harbor attack. At Pearl Harbor, Rear Admiral Tomioka (chief of the Operations Section of the Naval General Staff) observed that Nagumo had carried out his orders but did not go beyond them to exploit any opportunities. In late 1942, according to Vice Admiral Ozawa (who assumed command of the carrier force in late 1942, after Nagumo was reassigned), Yamamoto confessed to him that: "Events have shown that it was a great mistake not to have launched a second attack against Pearl Harbor."[45] If anything, that demonstrates the shortcomings of Yamamoto as a commander and a strategist. If he wanted his bold plan to achieve its fullest potential, he needed to have a more aggressive admiral in command of the Striking Force. If the risk-averse Nagumo was in command, Yamamoto's orders needed to be more explicit regarding post-strike options.

For its part, the Naval General Staff took the same stance. The Pearl Harbor attack was only a single component in a much larger plan. The important thing was to conclude operations in the south. Any attempt to expand the results achieved at Pearl Harbor would have to wait until the Southern Operation was complete.[46]

From the author's perspective, there is no doubt that Nagumo made the correct decision. His instincts for caution saved him from gutting the air groups of the Striking Force on the first day of the war for what almost certainly would have been marginal returns. He was clearly thinking beyond Pearl Harbor and understood that the Striking Force was utterly essential to future Japanese successes. The ships, aircraft, and aircrew of the Striking Force were irreplaceable. Expecting Nagumo to exceed the scope of his orders and expose his irreplaceable fleet to greater risk after the original objectives of the plan had been achieved is totally unrealistic. There was never any possibility of Nagumo doing so without a direct order from Yamamoto.

The decision not to attack revealed another problem with Japanese planning. In the event that the attack enjoyed a degree of success, but not complete success (like was the case late on the morning of December 7), there was no contingency plan of how to exploit such a situation. Further, what if the American carriers weren't present – was there a backup plan of how to find and engage them? Was there a plan on the shelf to attack the infrastructure on Oahu if the opportunity presented itself? There was nothing, just the hope that the original plan would succeed.

Adding to the inertia was the lack of imagination shown by Nagumo and his staff. There was no search plan to find the American carriers that were now known not to be in harbor. In fact, no search aircraft were launched at all after the early morning of December 7. No attempt was made to conduct coordinated operations with the submarines arrayed around Oahu. This lack of flexibility was demonstrated again by the commander and staff of the Striking Force in the Indian Ocean in April 1942 and most dramatically off Midway Atoll in June 1942.

In conclusion, it is absurd to assert that the course of the Pacific War for the next two years was dependent on the oil tanks or repair facilities at Pearl Harbor. The nation that was capable of fighting a two-ocean war and supplying the Allied powers with weapons was able to address a relatively minor level of damage at a single naval base. The entire notion of the importance of the Pearl Harbor installations was born well after the attack on Pearl Harbor. The Japanese never saw their importance, and the Americans were so unconcerned that they were content to leave them undefended and undispersed.

10

The Forgotten Offensive: Japanese Submarines off Hawaii

Japanese planning for the Hawaii Operation focused on the Striking Force. The apparent success of this aspect of the attack has overshadowed another almost forgotten part of the operation – the large-scale commitment of the best units of the Imperial Navy's submarine force. Despite the security risks involved in moving a large number of submarines to the Hawaiian Islands, Yamamoto decided to include them in the operation. An even riskier decision was made to include midget submarines in the attack. This better-known part of the submarine operation was a complete failure that was later mirrored by the operations of the fleet submarines assigned to operate in Hawaiian waters.

It is important to recognize that at the beginning of World War II, all submarines were effectively surface vessels that could submerge for relatively brief periods, unlike modern submarines that are designed to operate submerged, surfacing only for brief periods. During the war, torpedoes were often fired while surfaced, and deck-mounted naval guns were used for both engagements against merchant shipping and bombardment of coastal targets. Submarines of the period were also equipped with machine guns for antiaircraft defense.

Submarines were a key component in the Imperial Navy's prewar strategy against the USN. As part of the anticipated decisive fleet engagement, Japanese submarines were expected to inflict significant pre-battle attrition on the American battle fleet. To do this in the expanse of the Pacific, the Japanese designed and built a series of large submarines suitable for conducting reconnaissance and attack missions at extended ranges. The concept of extended reconnaissance included monitoring the USN's battle fleet at sea and even in port. In turn, this required that Japanese submarines carry aircraft, making it the only navy to fully embrace the concept of aircraft-equipped submarines.

Once enemy forces were located, Japanese submarines were tasked to conduct long-range intercept and attack operations against American fleet units. Coordination of this effort required each Japanese submarine squadron to possess a flagship with the space to accommodate extensive communications equipment and room for a command staff. Originally, light cruisers were intended to play the role of flagships. In enemy-controlled waters and at extended ranges, this was impractical. At the start of the Pacific War, the Imperial Navy had two Type A1 command submarines in service, which were more survivable than light cruisers in enemy waters. In addition to additional space for a larger communications suite and an embarked command staff, each Type A1 boat carried a single floatplane.

All Imperial Navy fleet submarines were larger than their foreign counterparts in order to carry enough fuel for long-range operations. High speed was also a critical requirement to conduct attacks against USN fleet units. While all Japanese fleet boats were designed with the requisite long range and high speed, it became evident that as the attritional strategy developed, Japanese submarines had several tasks to perform and that a single submarine design could not fulfill all of them. Accordingly, several submarine classes were developed to handle specialized missions.[1]

Cruiser submarines (or *junsen*) were designed with extra-long range for independent operations. The series of *junsen* submarines included the J3-type boats, the largest built by the Imperial Navy before the war. These featured a hangar and other aircraft facilities and were large enough to act as flagships. Because of their size, they were not considered to be suited to attack enemy fleet units. Their immense range made them more suited for long-range attacks on enemy bases and SLOCs.

Large fleet-type (or *kaidai*, abbreviated from *kaigun-dai*) boats possessed long range and higher speeds, making them better suited for attacks on USN fleet units. The KD6A and KD6B boats maximized speed and possessed a top surface speed of 23 knots – the highest of any submarine when they entered service in 1934. Type B1 boats combined the functions and capabilities of the kaidai and junsen designs.

THE FORGOTTEN OFFENSIVE: JAPANESE SUBMARINES OFF HAWAII

Carrying powerful diesel engines, they could generate speeds of 23.5 knots on the surface, retained a range of 14,000nm at cruising speed, and carried 17 torpedoes. They could also perform scouting duties with a single embarked floatplane. Against USN fleet units, this class proved the most successful of the Pacific War. Finally, the Type C boat was designed as an attack submarine and thus maximized firepower – they could carry 20 torpedoes. The five Type C1 boats were selected for modification to carry midget submarines for the Hawaii Operation.

While the Imperial Navy devoted considerable thought and resources to its submarine designs, it failed to devote the same energy to developing effective tactics for them. A series of exercises in 1938 revealed serious problems with the plan to attack enemy fleet units. During these exercises, submarines could not get close to "enemy" fleet units without being judged to have been sunk. Communications directing their movements were not received, making coordination against fast-moving enemy fleet units impossible. Tactical issues were even more pronounced as it proved impossible to position the submarines into their optimal firing positions in front of the target ship's course.[2]

As a result of the exercises in which the vulnerability of submarines was demonstrated, the Imperial Navy altered its tactics to stress the importance of concealment. As a result, submarine skippers were instructed to remain submerged whenever possible and even to conduct torpedo attacks while submerged. Using these modified tactics, exercises in 1939–40 demonstrated that Japanese submarines were unable to locate, track, or attack surface forces.[3] In 1941, additional exercises were conducted which again highlighted these difficulties. The Japanese assessed that their submarines were unable to conduct adequate surveillance operations, lacked adequate speed, and remained at risk of being detected and destroyed by enemy antisubmarine forces. Exercises also exhibited the ability of enemy forces to leave their bases undetected and that Japanese submarines were unable to track them and failed to gain proper firing positions.[4]

By the start of the war, the standard Imperial Navy tactic for countering enemy fleet units was to form a scouting line across the projected line of advance of an enemy task force. If contact was made, the submarine would be in a potentially favorable firing position. However, even if a contact was made, submarine skippers invariably opted for concealment over an aggressive attack. This translated into a submerged attack in which the submarine simply waited for an enemy ship to steam by and make itself a target. In this case, the submarine remained submerged until making a final periscope check with its periscope for a target range and bearing. The actual torpedo firing would be conducted by sound bearings without use of the periscope.[5]

As described above, Japanese submarines were ordered to a predesignated patrol area to form a scouting line across the enemy's projected line of advance. As intelligence became available, the submarines were directed to shift to new positions by the submarine's higher command or from the deployed flagship. The result was usually a chaotic to and fro resulting from inaccurate or outdated intelligence. To arrive at their new position, submarines would have to use their superior surface speed, greatly increasing their vulnerability. The combination of all these factors made it very challenging for Japanese submarines to play an effective role against enemy fleet units. The Hawaii Operation was the first test of these tactics in wartime.

At the start of the war, the Imperial Navy had 63 submarines in commission.[6] Of those boats in service, 48 were I-class (fleet boats) and the other 15 were short-ranged RO-class boats. The Imperial Navy's primary submarine force was the Sixth Fleet, under the command of Vice Admiral Shimizu Mitsumi. At the start of the war, Shimizu was on his flagship, a training cruiser, at Kwajalein Atoll in the Marshall Islands in the Central Pacific.

Shimizu was a curious choice as commander of the Sixth Fleet. Other than a stint as the executive officer of a submarine tender, he had no background in submarines. He assumed the rank of vice admiral in November 1939 and was appointed commander of the Sixth Fleet in July. As such, he became one of the key command figures in planning the Hawaii Operation. His command of the submarine fleet lasted only until March 1942.[7]

Japanese submarines were organized into divisions, usually composed of three boats. Between two and four divisions made up a squadron, commanded by a rear admiral. By December 1941, the Imperial Navy had organized seven submarine squadrons. Three squadrons, the 1st, 2nd, and 3rd, with the most modern and capable boats, were assigned to the Sixth Fleet. A total of 26 fleet boats, and another four larger boats used as flagships, were available to Shimizu.[8]

THE FORGOTTEN OFFENSIVE: JAPANESE SUBMARINES OFF HAWAII

SUBMARINES IN THE HAWAII OPERATION

Planning for the Hawaii Operation was already well under way when Yamamoto informed the Sixth Fleet on July 29 that it would play a role in the operation. To the Combined Fleet, adding the submarines was not a mere afterthought – it was an essential part of the operation. In part, this was due to the uncertainty of success by the carrier force, but it also reflected the misplaced confidence the Japanese had in their submarines. Since the entire Hawaii Operation was seen as a giant risk, there seemed little harm in adding the submarines to the equation. It is important to emphasize that the large-scale commitment of the Imperial Navy's best submarines were seen as an insurance policy against the failure of the air attack launched from the striking Force. In the words of Combined Fleet Chief of Staff (from November 1939 to April 1941) Vice Admiral Shigeru Fukudome:[9]

> It was my belief that, even if the Task Force's aerial attack ended in failure, the Submarine Force's operation would not fail. My belief was based on the expectation that no hitch would arise in the submarines' operations. They had a cruising radius of 10,000 miles, with no need of refueling at sea. Besides, submarines were best suited for stealthy movements, and a blockading operation of Hawaii would be very easy for the highly trained Japanese submarines. Furthermore, I expected that more damage would be inflicted by submarine attacks, which would be continued over a longer period, than by air attacks, which would be of comparatively short duration.[10]

Shimizu approved the Sixth Fleet's operations plan on November 10. His submarines were assigned several important tasks: pre-attack reconnaissance, sinking American ships fleeing from the air attack, and intercepting an American counterattack directed at the Striking Force. To accomplish these, all 30 of the Sixth Fleet's submarines were assigned to take part in the operation.

The 30 submarines committed to the Hawaii Operation were divided into five groups. Three boats from Submarine Squadron 1 – *I-19*, *I-21*, and *I-23* – were assigned directly to the Striking Force. During the transit across the North Pacific, they were to act as reconnaissance units in advance of the main force. Once the attack was launched, these boats were available to rescue downed aircrew and help defend the carrier force from an American surface counterattack.

A Special Attack Unit, also known as the Sasaki Group (after Captain Sasaki Hanku, commander of Submarine Division 3) was given the dangerous mission of approaching within a few miles of Oahu to launch five midget submarines. Each of the five boats in this group – *I-16*, *I-18*, *I-20*, *I-22*, and *I-24* – carried a single midget submarine clamped to the deck aft of their sail. All were ordered to reach a position some 300nm south of Oahu by December 3 and then, in order to not be discovered, spend the next several days slowly closing in on the island. Sasaki Group submarines had to be in place to launch their charges early on the morning of December 7 and then remain off Oahu to recover the crews that evening.

Most of the submarines assigned to the Hawaii Operation were assigned patrol areas near or around Oahu. Submarine Group 1 was positioned in a scouting line 150nm north of Oahu. Rear Admiral Tsutomu Sato commanded the four submarines of this group: *I-9*, *I-15*, *I-17*, and *I-25*. From this position well to the north of Oahu, they were expected to attack any American ships escaping to the north and to intercept any American counterattack approaching the Striking Force.[11]

Another seven boats (*I-1*, *I-2*, *I-3*, *I-4*, *I-5*, *I-6*, and *I-7*, all *junsen*-type units) comprised Submarine Group 2. Of these, *I-1*, *I-2*, and *I-3* were stationed west of Oahu in a picket line from Oahu to Kauai. Three other boats – *I-4*, *I-5*, and *I-6* – were positioned east of Oahu to form another picket line from Oahu to Molokai. The final boat of this group, *I-7* (the headquarters boat with Rear Admiral Yamazaki Shigeki embarked), was positioned some 50nm north of Oahu between the two picket lines.[12]

Seven submarines comprised Submarine Group 3 under Rear Admiral Miwa Shigeyoshi. *I-68*, *I-69*, *I-70*, *I-71*, *I-72*, *I-73*, and *I-75* were deployed south of Oahu to attack American units departing Pearl Harbor and to intercept any counterattack force headed north toward the Striking Force. Three of these – *I-71*, *I-72*, and *I-73* – were ordered to scout the Lahaina anchorage off Maui where the Japanese suspected the Pacific Fleet could be located if it was not in Pearl Harbor.

THE FORGOTTEN OFFENSIVE: JAPANESE SUBMARINES OFF HAWAII

This information had to be transmitted to the Striking Force by December 6, allowing Nagumo time to adjust the attack plan to strike any ships anchored there.[13] If the Pacific Fleet was located in the anchorage, submarines would guard the three channels leading into the anchorage and other submarines would be moved off their stations near Pearl Harbor to attack ships in the anchorage. *I-74* was assigned aircrew rescue duty by lying off Ni'ihau Island, which had been designated as an emergency landing area for those aircraft too damaged to return to their carriers. Miwa's flagship, *I-8*, was positioned between Oahu and Ni'ihau.[14]

So as to avoid detection, the submarines were ordered to transit to the Hawaiian Islands moving only at night on the surface and at their much slower submerged speeds during the day. Strict radio silence was also ordered. Except for the three submarines in direct support of the Striking Force, overall command of submarine operations in support of the Hawaii Operation was exercised by the Sixth Fleet.

The Sixth Fleet's final two submarines were assigned operations loosely in support of the Hawaii Operation. Each was to conduct reconnaissance of distant American bases; if nothing was located, they were under orders to move to a position between Hawaii and the mainland United States by December 7.

The first of these, *I-10*, departed Yokosuka on November 16 and headed for the Fiji Islands. After refueling at Kwajalein on November 23, she arrived off Fiji on November 30. Using her E9W1 (later given the Allied reporting name of "Slim") floatplane, a reconnaissance of the waters off Suva was conducted. The pilot reported nothing in the bay but subsequently failed to return to *I-10*. After an unsuccessful three-day search for the missing aircraft, *I-10* relocated to Pago-Pago Harbor, site of a USN base on Tutuila, the main island of American Samoa. During a submerged reconnaissance of the harbor on December 3, the skipper noted the presence of an Astoria-class heavy cruiser. By December 7, *I-10* was located some 1,300nm south of Oahu.[15]

I-26 departed Yokosuka three days after *I-10*, headed for the Aleutian Islands. Under the command of Commander Yokota Minoru, the boat had orders to reconnoiter any American naval units in the Aleutians and then proceed to a point halfway between Hawaii and San Francisco to report on the possible movement of American naval reinforcements en route to Hawaii. This long-range operation would test the endurance of the boat and her crew. To have enough rations for the extended deployment, the aircraft hangar was filled with food.[16]

Yokota remained on the surface until he was within 600nm of the Aleutians when he submerged during the day to avoid detection. Between November 26 and 28, *I-26* made periscope observations of Attu, Kiska, and Adak Islands in the Aleutians. Nothing of significance was observed at any of these locations and Yokota assessed that American preparations were "very inadequate."[17] On November 29, the same mission was performed at the American naval base at Dutch Harbor, on Amaknak Island, Alaska, but again nothing was found. With this, Yokota headed for his planned position between Hawaii and San Francisco.[18]

On December 6, *I-26* sighted a small cargo ship some 300nm off San Francisco. This was the 2,140-ton *Cynthia Olson*, chartered by the US Army to carry lumber and other supplies from Tacoma, Washington, to Honolulu. Yokota decided to track it until the following morning when he could attack as soon as hostilities began.[19]

In one of the first actions of the Pacific War, *I-26* closed on *Cynthia Olson* on the morning of December 7. Yokota surfaced his boat and ordered a warning shot from her deck gun. The small freighter sent a distress call and lowered her two lifeboats with 35 men aboard. Although *I-26* fired 18 shells from her 5.5-inch gun, *Cynthia Olson* refused to sink. During this attack, the Japanese intercepted Fuchida's radio message that the air attack had gained surprise. Yokota then submerged for a torpedo attack; one torpedo was fired from 450 yards but missed astern. Yokota opted to come to the surface and fired another 29 rounds at the defenseless ship. When *Cynthia Olson* appeared to be settling, Yokota decided she was finished. He left the area, fearing an American air attack. This encounter represented the first American merchant ship lost to the Japanese during the war.[20]

THE SAGA OF THE MIDGET SUBMARINES

In October it was decided to add another dimension to the Pearl Harbor attack: five fleet submarines were to be fitted to carry midget submarines. After some deliberation, these small submarines were ordered to penetrate into the harbor before the air attack began. How this happened is evidence of the inchoate planning process for the Hawaii Operation.

THE FORGOTTEN OFFENSIVE: JAPANESE SUBMARINES OFF HAWAII

The five Type A midget submarines committed to the Hawaii Operation were among the 12 available for combat operations at the time (a 13th boat was used for training). These were designated *HA-3* through *HA-15*, HA being the third character of *katakana*.[21]

Originally, these boats were designed to participate in the decisive battle between the USN and the Imperial Navy. Their existence was top secret. Given their mission of operating in the open ocean after being launched within close proximity of the American battle fleet, they were designed with a high top speed but possessed limited endurance. Type A midget submarines had a two-man crew, were 78.5 feet long, and had a submerged displacement of 46 tons. Each was armed with two 17.7-inch torpedoes placed in two tubes at the front of the submarine. Their major weakness was short range. Using batteries, the 600-horsepower electric motor could make 23 knots surfaced or 19 knots submerged, but endurance was limited to 80nm at 6 knots or 100nm at 2 knots.

The idea of repurposing the Type A midget submarines to attack enemy ships in port came from Lieutenant Iwasa Naoji, the chief test pilot of the secretive midget program. He proposed the concept to the father of the midget submarine program, Captain Harada Kaju. Harada was impressed enough to allow Iwasa to present the idea to Lieutenant Commander Ariizumi Ryunosuke, a submariner assigned to the Naval General Staff, when Ariizumi visited the tender ship of the midget subs. Iwasa's premise was that it was more likely for the midget subs to find and torpedo the enemy in harbor rather than search for him in the open ocean. Ariizumi became a convert and made sure the concept was presented to the Combined Fleet staff and Yamamoto.[22] According to Fukudome, Yamamoto only agreed to the scheme after his staff made a full study to ensure that it was possible for the crews to survive the attack.[23]

During the October 4–5 planning conference to discuss the details of the Pearl Harbor operation, Captain Harada proposed using midget submarines to attack the Pacific Fleet in harbor. After making his pitch on the first day, Harada was asked by Yamamoto to reconsider his plan and return the following day. When Harada returned, he did so with Iwasa and another midget submarine pilot, both of whom made a direct plea to be allowed to participate in the attack. By the October 11–13 planning conference, Yamamoto gave his approval and named the midget submarine attack *Shinki* (Divine Turtle) Operation

Number 1. Genda and the other aviators on Yamamoto's staff were strongly against using the midget submarines in the attack. As surprise was paramount, they feared that the early detection of the midget submarines entering the harbor would jeopardize the security of the entire operation. When Fuchida learned of it in November, he was upset. In his view, expressed to Prange after the war, Yamamoto was jeopardizing the entire operation just to give the submarine force a share of the glory. He never reconciled himself to the role of the midget submarines and made no attempt to hide his view.[24] Despite the concerns of the aviators, Yamamoto overruled them and ordered that work begin immediately on modifying five midget submarines with increased harbor penetration capabilities and on adapting five I-class boats to carry them to Oahu.

There was little time to integrate the midget submarines into the overall plan. Twenty-four men had already been hand-picked (not voluntarily) for training on the midget submarines.[25] Iwasa demanded that he be allowed to lead the attack since the scheme was his. After much reflection, Harada relented to Iwasa's demands. Arduous training of the crews progressed on schedule, and in the middle of October they learned their probable target was either Pearl Harbor or Singapore. At the end of October, their training was completed. Before taking a ten-day leave, they were called to a meeting with Yamamoto on his flagship *Nagato*. The commander in chief urged the young officers to exert their best efforts since their work was highly important and was expected to render significant results.[26]

As the midget submarine crews were completing training, Sasaki was observing modifications to his submarines. In November, when he asked Commander Matsumura Midori, senior staff officer of the Sixth Fleet, what the purpose of the work was, he learned for the first time that it was to carry midget submarines to Pearl Harbor. Sasaki was appalled that he was learning of this at such a late stage. After the war, he remarked that the submarine part of the Hawaiian Operation was done in a rush: "There was too much hurry, hurry, hurry."[27]

On November 14, Sasaki was visited by Captain Arima Takayasu from the Combined Fleet staff. He carried an urgent message from Yamamoto that it was imperative that the midget submarines not try to force their way into the harbor. If conditions were not ideal, they were to abandon their penetration attempt and head toward the meeting point off Lanai Island where they would be recovered by their mother submarine. Arima also stressed that every effort was to be made to rescue the crews after the attack.[28]

Even after Yamamoto approved the midget submarine operation, there was continuing turmoil as to whether it should actually be conducted. On November 15, Yamamoto met privately with Shimizu. Yamamoto was concerned that the operation was no more than a suicide mission and with the difficulties of rescuing the crews if they survived their journey into Pearl Harbor. He instructed Shimizu to cancel the mission if he considered it to be suicidal. Shimizu responded that he wanted to talk with the crews before making any decision.[29]

Shimizu had already met with the crews the day before when he went to see the midget submarines for the first time and to explain the plan to them. Originally, it was planned that the midgets would launch the night before the attack, enter the harbor, and then settle on the bottom. Absolutely no attacks were permitted until the night of the air attack, i.e., after the air attack. Upon hearing this, Iwasa pointed out that remaining submerged for an extended period would be dangerous and that the time to strike was immediately after the air attack when the enemy was still confused. Shimizu thought that a daylight attack was suicidal, but the midget submariners all supported the notion of causing maximum damage while the Americans were still reeling. Shimizu relented and changed the plan.[30]

In retrospect, it is clear that the entire planning process for including the midget submarines in the overall attack was ruled by emotion, not by a hard calculation of their chances for success. Yamamoto authorized the inclusion of the midget submarines, against the advice of Genda and other Combined Fleet staff officers. The fervent pleas of the midget submarine crews won them permission to proceed inside Pearl Harbor before the execution of the air raid. It is hard to understand why Yamamoto placed the honor of ten submarine crewmen over the potential that their heroic penetration into the harbor could jeopardize the entire operation. Yamamoto's angst over the fate of the midget submariners rings false – everybody involved in the operation, including the crews themselves, knew that their chances of survival were negligible. Not for the last time in the war, the Japanese were entrapped by their fixation on allowing brave men the opportunity to sacrifice themselves. Writing in his diary after watching the fleet submarines laden with midgets depart Japan on November 18, Ugaki captured this sentiment:

> No one can predict what results they will bring about. Young lieutenants are seen on their deck smiling. They expect never to return alive; they are ready to die at the scene of battle. Their preparedness is admirable. Our old "death-defying spirit" never changes. We can fully rely on them.[31]

THE ATTACK OF THE MIDGET SUBMARINES

After an uneventful transit, Sasaki's mother submarines reached the waters south of Oahu on December 5. All five edged closer to their launch positions during the next day. According to schedule, *I-16* launched her midget at 0042 hours on December 7. Iwasa was next to launch at 0116 from *I-22*, followed by *I-18*'s midget at 0215 hours. *I-20* launched her charge at 0257. Last to launch was Ensign Sakamaki Kazuo from *I-24*.

It did not take long for the midget submarines to run into trouble. At 0342 hours, minesweeper *Condor* spotted what appeared to be a submarine in the restricted area a little over a mile south of the entrance buoys to the Pearl Harbor channel. *Condor* summoned the duty destroyer *Ward*, under Lieutenant William Outerbridge who had assumed command just the day before, to the scene. *Ward* arrived in the area by 0408 but after an hour's search found nothing. This may have been the midget launched from *I-16*.

At 0630, stores ship *Antares* spotted a suspicious-looking object 1,500 yards off her starboard quarter. It was described as a possible small submarine with its conning tower awash and periscope partially raised.[32] A PBY flying boat quickly arrived to mark the contact with smoke for *Ward*, which was racing to the scene. When she arrived, her bridge crew identified the object as a conning tower with a periscope, unlike anything they had ever seen in the USN. Outerbridge was called to the bridge. He sounded General Quarters at 0640 and at full speed headed toward the contact. After coming close abeam to the contact, *Ward* opened fire at 0645 hours. The first shot of the Pacific War missed its target, but the second hit the submarine at the base of its sail. The submarine was observed to sink, but *Ward* dropped depth charges to ensure the sub's destruction.[33] Having fired the first shots of the war, *Ward* sent a signal at 0651 hours. Wanting to be more definite, Outerbridge's second message stated: "We have attacked fired upon and dropped depth charges upon submarine operating in defense sea area." The fleet radio station logged receipt of the message at 0653 hours.

The submarine sunk by *Ward* was discovered in August 2002 in 1,330 feet of water 2.6nm offshore. Just as the crew had claimed, the wreck was complete with a 4-inch shell hole readily discernable in the base of its sail.[34] In 1942, *Ward*'s Number 3 4-inch/50-caliber gun was removed upon her being converted to a high-speed transport. In 1958, it was installed as a memorial at the Minnesota State Capitol in St Paul.

The report of this action, occurring just over one hour before the start of the air attack, gave the Americans a potential window to prepare their defenses to counter any further attack. The message was received at fleet headquarters at 0712 and by 0720 was in the hands of the 14th Naval District watch officer. He tried to reach Admiral Bloch's aide but failed. He then called Captain John B. Earle, Bloch's chief of staff. He also notified the Pacific Fleet's duty officer and gave the report to his assistant. This assistant got in touch with the duty officer, Commander Vincent Murphy. After finally getting in touch with the watch officer who took the report, and after learning more about *Ward*'s action, Murphy called Kimmel. Neither Earle nor Kimmel was convinced that this was a real attack, primarily because of the many previous false reports of submarine activity.

When Bloch became aware of the incident, he decided not to take any action, as he was waiting for orders from Kimmel. As the various naval officers pondered what to do, the Japanese first attack wave was drawing closer to Oahu. Critically, nobody thought to contact the Army. The Pacific Fleet's command and control system was awake but lacked the speed to react to emergent events in a timely manner, even one as dramatic as attacking an unknown submarine at the entrance to Pearl Harbor.

After the air attack had begun, additional reports of submarine activity were recorded. At 0817, destroyer *Helm* was exiting the channel when it spotted the conning tower of a submarine located on her starboard side, off the western shore of the channel. *Helm* opened fire with her 5-inch guns, but the contact submerged and disappeared.[35]

This could have been Sakamaki's submarine since his account claimed he was fired on by a destroyer.

At least one of the midget submarines did succeed in penetrating into the harbor. Not surprisingly, a number of ships reported seeing the submarine and several took it under fire. The first ship to record spotting a "strange submarine" was destroyer-minesweeper *Zane* at about 0830 hours. It was some 200 yards astern of repair ship *Medusa*. *Zane* was unable to bear her guns on the target, but destroyer-minesweeper *Perry* was already engaging it.[36] Personnel aboard seaplane tender *Curtiss* spotted the submarine 700 yards off her starboard quarter at 0836 hours. Two 5-inch guns on *Curtiss* engaged the target, claiming two hits.[37] The midget fired one of its torpedoes at *Curtiss* but missed. After firing, the submarine broached and then was hit by a 5-inch shell from *Curtiss*.

Monaghan was the other ready duty destroyer. At 0753, she received orders to support *Ward* at the entrance to the channel. Getting under way at 0827, her bridge crew sighted the submarine just minutes later (0835), 200–300 yards off the starboard quarter of *Curtiss*. The destroyer's skipper, Lieutenant Commander William Burford, ordered full speed to ram the object. The midget submarine responded by turning to face the destroyer and fired its second torpedo. It missed the oncoming destroyer some 20–30 yards off its portside. The submarine was struck by *Monaghan* at 0844 and forced under the destroyer. *Monaghan* proceeded to drop two depth charges. After ramming the submarine, *Monaghan*'s momentum carried her into a dredge. Burford's ship suffered minor damage and it cleared the entrance of the channel at 0908.[38] Almost certainly, the midget submarine causing so much commotion inside the harbor was the one launched from *I-22* piloted by Iwasa. As the most experienced midget submarine pilot, only he was able to find the entrance of the channel at night and navigate successfully up it. Two weeks later, his midget submarine was raised off the harbor floor. Among the artifacts found inside was a lieutenant's rank insignia, marking it as Iwasa's, the only full lieutenant among the five pilots. The hulk was later used as landfill.

The submarine launched from *I-24* was piloted by Ensign Sakamaki. Even before launching, Sakamaki discovered that his gyroscope was not functioning. Unsurprisingly, he informed the commander of the *I-24* that he would continue the mission.[39] By the time he found the entrance to the channel, it was about 0700 hours and already daylight. Destroyer *Helm* may have spotted one of Sakamaki's attempts to enter the channel at 0817 when she observed a submarine caught on the coral reef. The effects of the collisions with the reef, combined with the increasingly foul air, incapacitated Sakamaki and his other crewman, Chief Warrant Officer Inagaki Kiyoshi. Sakamaki's boat drifted to the east past Diamond Head. In the early morning hours of December 8, the boat's battery failed. After grounding on a reef near Bellows Field, Sakamaki decided to scuttle the midget with a charge provided for that purpose. He set the fuse and jumped overboard. Sakamaki endured more bitter disappointment when he watched Inagaki drown and the scuttling charges fail to work. After making it to shore, he collapsed and passed out. When he came to on a beach, he was looking up at an American soldier. Sakamaki had the dubious distinction of becoming the first Japanese sailor taken prisoner during the war. His submarine was salvaged and used for fundraising tours during the war. It still exists and since 1990 has been on display at the National Museum of the Pacific War in Fredericksburg, Texas.[40]

Part of the enduring mystery regarding the fate of the other two midget submarines was clarified in 1960 when a midget was discovered in the Keehi Lagoon off the entrance to Pearl Harbor. Found in 76 feet of water, the boat showed evidence of depth-charge damage and retained both its torpedoes. This was probably the midget from *I-18*. After the front section with the two torpedoes was removed, the rest of the boat was returned to Japan. It is on display at Etajima, the former Imperial Navy Naval Academy and current Japanese Maritime Self Defense Force Officer Candidate School.

Much debate has ensued over the fate of the last midget submarine. The author believes this is linked to a torpedo attack against light cruiser *St Louis* as she was clearing the harbor just after 1000 hours on December 7. *St Louis* got under way at 0931 and headed for the open sea. While still just inside the channel, two torpedoes were fired at the cruiser's starboard beam from a distance of 2,000 yards. Even though the torpedoes were set for shallow running, they exploded on a shoal. *St Louis* engaged the object from which the torpedoes originated with 5-inch fire between 1004 and 1007 hours without success. The object was not identified as a submarine at the time. Only later, when the ship's commanding officer, Captain George Rood, had the opportunity to see a midget submarine, did he realize that the object he saw on the morning of December 7 was a midget submarine.[41]

In addition to the information in *St Louis*'s action report, other information supports the notion that the cruiser was the target of a torpedo attack. Multiple witnesses clearly saw the two torpedoes headed for the cruiser, one following the other. Rood was convinced that his ship was about to be hit and alerted others. He ordered emergency full power and began to zig-zag the best he could inside the narrow channel. Luckily for the Americans, the torpedo hit a spit only 200 yards from the ship. The resulting geyser drenched the ship with water. The second torpedo, about 10 degrees off the first, was apparently destroyed by the explosion of the first.[42] There can be little doubt that *St Louis* came under torpedo attack as she exited the channel. Given this, the actions of the fifth midget submarine are accounted for since there were no I-boats near the channel.

This description from multiple witnesses indicates that the fifth midget submarine was in fact waiting off the channel to ambush American warships exiting the harbor. Of note, this meant that the crew was following orders to only attempt a passage of the channel if conditions were perfect. *St Louis* was certainly a worthy target, but the submarine fired too close to shore. In the words of Captain Rood, "That Jap got over-anxious."[43] After firing its torpedoes, the crew scuttled their boat, as ordered. Subsequently, the boat was discovered in 1950 and raised. In 1951, without fanfare, it was cut into three pieces and dumped in deeper water.[44] Between 1992 and 2001, three pieces of a Type A midget submarine with the unique Pearl Harbor modifications were located 3 miles off the channel. When the bow section was located in 2001, it was confirmed that both torpedoes were missing. All three sections were in the same areas, having been dumped together.[45]

Claims that the fifth midget submarine got into the harbor and successfully launched its torpedoes at Battleship Row are unsupported by fact. These originated with author Burl Burlingame and were elaborated upon in a sensationalist television show titled *Killer Sub in Pearl Harbor*.[46] The only evidence offered to support this theory is a single image purporting to show a midget sub inside the harbor in the opening minutes of the air attack. Retired naval officer Alan Zimm devotes an entire chapter in his book *Attack on Pearl Harbor* to demolish the myth of the midget submarine firing on Battleship Row. In the simplest

THE FORGOTTEN OFFENSIVE: JAPANESE SUBMARINES OFF HAWAII

of terms, the author contends that it would have been impossible for a midget sub to appear undetected in perfect position to attack Battleship Row, fire its torpedoes, and then disappear, all without eyewitnesses of a submarine which had to use its periscope for navigation. Proof that this would have been impossible was provided by the fate of the only midget submarine to have penetrated the harbor. Before being rammed by *Monaghan*, it was sighted and visually identified by many observers on multiple ships.

The heroic, though unsuccessful, efforts of the midget submarines were quickly wrapped up in mythology by the Japanese. Nine of the men were heralded as heroes and given a state funeral on April 8, 1942. Sakamaki was obviously whitewashed from Japanese history since he had committed the ultimate shame of allowing himself to be captured. To give their sacrifice meaning, the destruction of *Arizona* was credited to the midget subs, much to the dismay of the aviators who knew that proper credit belonged to a Kate crew. A radio transmission from one of the midgets at 2241 hours on December 7, probably from the midget submarine launched from *I-16*, claimed a successful attack. About the same time, the skipper of *I-69* reported "a very large flame heaving heavenward – a flame like a ship exploding in Pearl Harbor."[47] This report, combined with the message from one of the midget submarines, gave birth to the narrative that a midget submarine had scored a major success, maybe even accounting for *Arizona*'s demise. This story confirmed the prowess of the warrior gods on the midget submarines and was widely repeated in the Japanese press in early 1942.[48] In 1946, disgraced prisoner-of-war Sakamaki Kazuo was repatriated to Japan, married, and raised a family and worked for the Toyota Motor Corporation until his retirement in 1987. In 1991, 50 years after the events detailed above, he visited the National Museum of the Pacific War in Texas where he was reunited with his midget submarine.

The reality of the midget submarine attack was quite different than the fable fabricated by the Japanese. Though conducted with incredible bravery and tenacity, it ended in total failure. All five midget subs were lost without exacting any toll from the Americans. Of the ten torpedoes on the five submarines, only four were launched. Only one of the submarines succeeded in penetrating the harbor. This was no small feat of navigation and was only performed by the most experienced pilot. Iwasa missed with his two torpedoes even though he was literally surrounded by targets. Using the Type A midget submarines for a mission they were not designed for was folly. Attacking a well-defended naval base is extremely challenging for a weapon system with short range and low speed. In their desire to employ this novel weapon, the Japanese set aside the reasonable concern that the midget submarines might be detected on their way to their targets. Moving into and then through the narrow channel into Pearl Harbor required several hours, during which the periscope would have to be used often. Even at night, the chances for detection, especially in the narrow channel, were high. In what could have been a worse-case scenario for the Japanese, one midget sub was detected over four hours before the planned start of the air attack. Given this amount of time, the early discovery of the midget submarine could have been catastrophic to the Japanese hopes of gaining surprise. It was not a chance worth taking.

THE FAILURE OF THE FLEET SUBMARINES

Despite the fact that there were 25 Japanese submarines deployed around Oahu and other Hawaiian islands, only one reported contact with any American naval units on December 7. *I-69* was ordered to move its patrol position from southwest of Pearl Harbor to the east. At 2000, she reported sighting four destroyers. After they dodged a torpedo fired by *I-69*, the destroyers conducted a depth-charge attack with no success. On December 9, *I-69* reported being depth-charged again following an unsuccessful attack on a cargo ship. That night, the submarine became entangled with an antisubmarine net. It took Lieutenant Commander Watanabe Katsuji 38 hours to break his boat free.[49]

The only successful submarine attack on the opening day of hostilities was *I-26*'s sinking of *Cynthia Olson* well to the east of the Hawaiian Islands. Aside from the exploits of *I-69*, no other boat reported any contact. This difficult-to-explain lack of contacts continued until early on December 10 when *I-6* spotted what was reported as a Lexington-class carrier in the Molokai Channel that separates the islands of Oahu and Molokai. The carrier was reported to be with two heavy cruisers and was headed northeast at 20 knots. The skipper of *I-6* tried unsuccessfully to launch an attack, but in accordance with doctrine elected for concealment over aggression, and submerged. He reported the contact several hours later.

THE FORGOTTEN OFFENSIVE: JAPANESE SUBMARINES OFF HAWAII

This was exactly the kind of target the submarines had been sent to Hawaii to attack. From his flagship at Kwajalein Atoll, Vice Admiral Shimizu ordered Submarine Group 1, located north of Oahu, to chase down this lucrative target. In this first test of the Imperial Navy's ability to orchestrate submarine operations against a high-value target, all of the prewar difficulties observed during training exercises were on full display.

Shimizu's target was actually the carrier *Enterprise*. The submarines assigned to the chase took off after the carrier using their surface speed. An examination of the records of all 25 submarines in the Hawaiian Islands indicates that none spotted or attacked the carrier. After two days, the pursuit was called off. The Imperial Navy's first attempt to attack a major USN fleet unit with submarines ended in failure. Adding to Japanese frustrations, *Enterprise* accounted for the first Japanese submarine loss of the war. On the morning of December 10, Douglas SBD-2 Dauntless dive-bombers from *Enterprise*'s VS-6 spotted *I-70* on the surface some 200nm northeast of Oahu. A near miss was scored by a 1,000-pound bomb, resulting in damage that prevented the submarine from submerging. That afternoon, another Dauntless from VS-6 spotted the damaged *I-70*. Despite the efforts *I-70* made to defend herself with her solitary 25mm antiaircraft mount, the dive-bomber was able to place another bomb directly alongside the submarine. *I-70* disappeared in less than a minute, and all 93 men aboard were lost.[50]

While the Japanese submarine offensive against the USN was completely ineffective, Japanese submarines did enjoy very limited success against merchant targets. The exploits of *I-26* in the opening minutes of the war have already been detailed. In the days following the Pearl Harbor attack, *I-9* and *I-10* each sank a merchant ship in the vicinity of the Hawaiian Islands.

Following her unsuccessful pursuit of *Enterprise*, *I-9* came across the steamer *Lahaina* on December 11 some 700nm northeast of Oahu. The small cargo ship was carrying 745 tons of molasses and 300 tons of scrap iron on her way to Hawaii. Not wanting to waste a torpedo on such a target, the submarine surfaced to engage *Lahaina* with gunfire. After firing a warning shot which allowed the crew to abandon ship, 25 5.5-inch shells set the ship afire. The next morning, the crew attempted to reboard the ship but found the fires and flooding beyond control. Just after noon, *Lahaina* sank. Thirty of the 34 crewmen survived.[51]

Another success by the I-boats was recorded by *I-10*. While some 700nm southeast of Hawaii, *I-10* spotted and attacked the 4,473-ton Panamanian-flagged cargo ship *Donerail* after nightfall on December 9. The ship was carrying a cargo of sugar and pineapples from Suva, Fuji, to Vancouver, Canada. The boat's commanding officer, Commander Kayabara Yasuchika, fired a single torpedo and missed. Kayabara then ordered the submarine to surface and to engage the target with his 5.5-inch deck gun. Twenty rounds were fired and at least one was observed to have hit. The unfortunate ship sank two hours after the start of the attack; only eight of the 43 crew members survived.[52]

After these paltry successes, the three submarines of the Patrol Unit, and the four submarines of Submarine Group 1, were ordered to join *I-10* and *I-26* and head to the US West Coast to attack merchant shipping. Though beyond the scope of this book, the operations of these submarines caused no damage to the USN and accounted for only a handful of merchant ships. None of the submarines were lost and they returned to Kwajalein between January 11 and 15, 1942.

Submarine Group 2 remained in Hawaiian waters until January 11. Before departing, *I-4* sank the Norwegian freighter *Huegh Merchant* off Oahu on December 14. The flagship boat of this same group, *I-7*, used her floatplane to conduct a daring dawn scouting mission over Pearl Harbor on December 17 to confirm the results of the air raid. The crew of the E9W1 Slim floatplane reported four battleships, one aircraft carrier, five cruisers, and 30 smaller ships, including three destroyers. One of the battleships was reported as heavily damaged.[53] This was not a valuable report since it failed to convey the extent of damage inflicted by the air attack. The floatplane was able to return its submarine. Not wanting to remain on the surface long enough to crane the aircraft aboard, disassemble it, and move it inside the hangar, the skipper of *I-7* ordered the aircraft to be scuttled.

Submarine Group 3 left the Hawaiian Islands on December 17. Before departing, *I-75* spotted the 3,545-ton American merchant *Manini* on December 17 180nm south of Hawaii. *I-75* hit the merchant with one torpedo, resulting in fatal damage and the death of a single crewman.[54] Also from Submarine Group 3, *I-72* spotted the 5,113-ton freighter *Prusa* on the morning of December 19 some 150nm south of Oahu. Hit by a single torpedo, the steamer sank within nine minutes. All 24 crewmen were eventually rescued.[55]

THE FORGOTTEN OFFENSIVE: JAPANESE SUBMARINES OFF HAWAII

The results of the Hawaiian Operation during which the IJN deployed a total of 30 fleet submarines and five midget submarines were extremely disappointing from the Japanese perspective. This enormous investment of resources paid scant results. Not a single USN warship was damaged or sunk. Against totally undefended merchant traffic in the Hawaiian Islands area, five I-boats were able to attack a single merchant each. The price for even this minor success was high – one fleet and five midget submarines were lost.

The reasons for this failure are understandable once Japanese submarine doctrine and tactics are understood. In spite of the known shortcomings of their submarines, primarily their inability to track and attack enemy fleet units, the Combined Fleet assigned their submarines missions they were unable to perform. The performance of the 25 submarines operating in the Hawaiian Islands from December 7 until December 19, when all but the seven *junsen* boats of Submarine Group 2 departed, was dismal. Sixteen of these boats reported making no contact at all, even as dozens of American ship movements, both naval and merchant, were made through the area. Only five boats made any kind of attack – the four boats that sank a merchant, and *I-69*, which made an unsuccessful attack on a cargo ship on December 9. An additional four boats reported sightings that they were unable to convert into an attack. This is a complete condemnation of the prevailing Japanese submarine tactics used by the overcautious skippers. This explains how it was possible for Japanese submarine skippers to operate off busy harbors or in busy shipping lanes and report few or no contacts.[56]

The abysmal failure of the submarine operation, which was an important part of the overall Pearl Harbor attack, undermines the often-expressed view that the Imperial Navy's Hawaii Operation was flawless. The fleet submarines failed in spectacular fashion, as did the midget submarines. Only the fact that that the Americans were unprepared for battle prevented the midget submarine operation from eliminating the prospect of surprise for the entire operation.

There is a postscript to Japanese submarine operations in the immediate aftermath of the Pearl Harbor attack. Three of the submarines which had delivered midget submarines on December 7 (*I-18*, *I-22*, and *I-24*) were ordered to return to the Hawaiian Islands after refueling at Kwajalein. Departing the atoll on January 3, they joined the seven submarines of Submarine Group 2 still operating in the area.

On the morning of January 9, 1942, *I-18* sighted a Lexington-class carrier and a heavy cruiser near Johnston Atoll headed west. Admiral Yamazaki on *I-7* ordered the nearby boats of Submarine Group 2 to establish a north-south scouting line and work to the west.[57] On this occasion, the scouting line tactic paid dividends when, at 1740 hours on January 11, *I-6*, operating in the northern part of the picket line, sighted a Lexington-class carrier, one cruiser, and two destroyers some 420nm southwest of Oahu. After getting into a favorable firing position, *I-6* launched a spread of three Type 89 torpedoes from 4,700 yards.[58]

The target was carrier *Saratoga*. As the largest and longest ship in the entire fleet, she was notoriously difficult to maneuver and was unable to avoid all of the torpedoes aimed at her. One of the torpedoes hit the carrier amidships on the port side. It killed six crewmen and flooded three boiler rooms through damaged piping. *Saratoga* took on 1,100 tons of water but was never in danger of sinking. She was even able to increase speed from 15 to 18 knots to escape the danger area.[59] Lieutenant Commander Inaba Michimune, the boat's skipper, reported the carrier as probably sunk, based on two loud explosions heard on the submarine's hydrophones followed by what was assessed to be sounds of the ship breaking up.[60]

In fact, *Saratoga* was able to steam to Pearl Harbor for temporary repairs, and in early February proceeded to the Navy Yard at Bremerton, Washington, for repairs and modernization. Nevertheless, Inaba had scored an important success since *Saratoga* was out of action for both the battles of Coral Sea and Midway. The IJN doctrine of coordinating submarine attacks on USN fleet units had shown promise. Simply placing several submarines in the same water space as a high-value target created the potential for a successful attack. On this occasion, *I-6* benefitted from a large degree of luck when *Saratoga* changed course to literally present herself as a target to an undetected submarine.

11

The Reckoning

JAPANESE LOSSES

The Hawaii Operation was far less costly for the Japanese than anticipated. Far from losing a third of the carriers in the Striking Force and half of their aircraft, no ships were lost or even damaged. Aircraft losses were low, with only 29 aircraft (nine fighters, 15 dive-bombers, and 5 Kates) shot down. This figure does not tell the whole story since another two Kates were forced to ditch, and another 15 aircraft of various types were jettisoned overboard after landing due to heavy damage. The total of 46 aircraft lost still represents a mere 13 percent of the total attacking force sent to Oahu. Though far from insignificant, this level of loss in no way inhibited near-term operations. However, as a steady rate of attrition occurred during the first six months of the war, and new production of Vals and Kates failed to keep pace with losses, the four carriers of the Striking Force present at Midway carried fewer total aircraft than they did at Pearl Harbor. In addition, 45 aviators were lost during the attack.

Often forgotten is the toll suffered by the Japanese submarine force in the Hawaii Operation. Though not strictly framed as a suicide mission, none of the five midget submarines were recovered. All ten crewmen were lost (bringing the total of Japanese killed on December 7 to 55); one midget crewman was captured and became the first Japanese prisoner-of-war in the hands of the Americans. The destruction of fleet submarine *I-70*, occurring only three days after the air attack, should also be included in Japanese loss totals. The submarine was sunk with the loss of all 93 hands, becoming the first Japanese fleet submarine lost in the war.

AMERICAN LOSSES

As the last of the Japanese aircraft headed north to return to the Striking Force, the Americans were left to count their losses and prepare for a long war. December 7 had been a calamitous day, but what did it mean for the USN and its ability to conduct the war over the next few months as the Japanese wave crested over the Pacific?

Most of the Pacific Fleet had been caught in port and subjected to a surprise attack. Usually, this would have been a recipe for disaster. Most accounts of the attack state that it succeeded in crippling the Pacific Fleet. In fact, in military terms, the raid resulted in little long-term impact to American naval capabilities. Of the 100 ships (half of which were combatants) caught in port, 18 were sunk or damaged. On the surface, sinking or damaging just 18 percent of the ships in Pearl Harbor does not constitute a crippling loss, and it must be remembered that much of the Pacific Fleet was elsewhere on the morning of December 7. It is important to look at the types of ships lost, their utility in the Pacific War in the months and years that followed, and whether or not they ever re-entered service.

As will be made clear, the loss of ships on December 7 was insignificant to American naval capabilities. However, in human terms it was a catastrophic day for the United States. This table shows the scale of personnel losses from the Japanese attack.

This was a shocking toll for the first day, or any day, of the conflict. Almost half of the total number of dead resulted from the magazine

American Casualties on December 7,[1] 1941[2]

	Killed, missing, or died of wounds	*Wounded*
US Navy	2,008	710
US Army	218	364
US Marine Corps	109	69
Civilians	68	35
Totals	2,403	1,178

explosion on board *Arizona*. The total of men killed aboard just two ships, *Arizona* and *Oklahoma*, accounted for almost 80 percent of the total number of dead sailors. For the United States, it was the greatest death toll in any single day of the Pacific War, and probably all of World War II.[3]

Most of the personnel losses and the most consequential ship losses were suffered by the eight battleships present. Of the eight battleships, four were sunk, one was moderately damaged and run aground, and the other three suffered only light damage. If the Pacific War was going to be a battleship war, then this would have constituted a crippling loss, at least in the short term. This demonstrated another Japanese cognitive disconnect regarding the Pearl Harbor operation and the reason for mounting it. If on the first day of the war, aircraft carriers were able to launch a devastating strike resulting in the destruction of multiple battleships, then the war was destined to become a carrier war, not one dominated by battleships. In essence, the Japanese had demonstrated the obsolescence of battleships, thus undermining their reasoning for the entire Pearl Harbor operation.

DAMAGE TO THE PACIFIC FLEET AND ITS IMPACT

The Japanese struck 18 ships of the Pacific Fleet as outlined below.

Pacific Fleet Ships Sunk or Damaged, December 7, 1941

Ship	Type	Condition	Returned to service
Arizona	Battleship	Sunk	No
Oklahoma	Battleship	Sunk	No
California	Battleship	Sunk	Yes (January 1944)
West Virginia	Battleship	Sunk	Yes (July 1944)
Tennessee	Battleship	Light damage	Yes (February 1942)
Maryland	Battleship	Light damage	Yes (December 1941)
Nevada	Battleship	Moderate damage	Yes (June 1943)
Pennsylvania	Battleship	Light damage	Yes (December 1941)
Helena	Light cruiser	Heavy damage	Yes (September 1942)
Raleigh	Light cruiser	Heavy damage	Yes (February 1942)
Honolulu	Light cruiser	Light damage	Yes (December 1941)
Shaw	Destroyer	Moderate damage	Yes (June 1942)

(continued)

Ship	Type	Condition	Returned to service
Cassin	Destroyer	Constructive loss	Yes (Rebuilt 1944)
Downes	Destroyer	Constructive loss	Yes (Rebuilt 1944)
Vestal	Repair Ship	Light damage	Yes (February 1942)
Curtiss	Tender	Light damage	Yes (December 1941)
Oglala	Minelayer	Sunk	Yes (February 1944)
Utah	Training Ship	Sunk	No

Most of the damage inflicted against the battleships, seven of which were moored along Ford Island, occurred in the opening minutes of the attack. *Oklahoma* and *West Virginia* were the most exposed to torpedo damage and suffered the brunt of this torpedo damage. Hit by five torpedoes, *Oklahoma* capsized to port within ten minutes of being stuck by the first torpedo. Such sudden movement and lack of effective counterflooding to prevent her from capsizing resulted in greatly increased personnel casualties. Losses totaled 415 men, though rescue efforts resulted in the rescue of 32 men who were able to escape through holes cut into *Oklahoma*'s overturned hull. Two men on *Oklahoma*, Ensign Francis Flaherty and Seaman First Class James R. Wood, were awarded Congressional Medals of Honor for sacrificing their lives to allow others to escape from a gun turret.

A similar situation unfolded on *West Virginia*. Before her ordeal began with the explosion of the first of what was eventually seven torpedo hits, an alarm was sounded that brought many men from below decks, much reducing the eventual casualty list. Under the direction of Lieutenant Claude V. Ricketts, who instituted an unorthodox but effective counterflooding effort, and the ship's commanding officer, Captain Mervyn S. Bennion, losses were reduced to 105 men killed or missing and 52 wounded.[4] Considering the damage inflicted on *West Virginia*, this was a remarkedly low count. Bennion, hit in the abdomen by shrapnel from a Japanese bomb, refused to leave his post. He was awarded a posthumous Medal of Honor.

Another battleship hit by torpedoes was *California*, Pye's flagship in his capacity as commander of the Pacific Fleet's battleships. She was hit by two torpedoes and then again by a bomb from a second-wave divebomber. Total losses from her crew of 120 officers and 1,546 men were six officers and 92 enlisted men killed or declared missing. Another 48 men were wounded.⁵ For their bravery in fighting the ship, four crewmen were awarded the Medal of Honor, three posthumously.

Arizona was not sunk by torpedoes, but by an instantaneous explosion when a 1,760-pound armor-piercing bomb struck her magazine. The resulting explosion was cataclysmic and resulted in a huge loss of life. *Arizona*'s entire forward section was destroyed, taking 1,177 men out of her complement of 1,514. Among the lost were the ship's captain, Franklin Van Valkenburgh and Rear Admiral Isaac C. Kidd, commander of Battleship Division 1. Both were awarded Medals of Honor. Another officer, Lieutenant Commander Samuel G. Fuqua, survived the explosion and directed firefighting efforts and the rescue of wounded men, He too was awarded the Medal of Honor.

Nevada was subjected to a single torpedo hit and then a barrage of 551-pound bombs from the second-wave dive-bombers. Most of the bombs hit well forward, and the ship was beached, saving lives aboard. Of the ship's crew on December 1 of 94 officers and 1,390 enlisted men, three officers and 47 men were killed in the attack with another 109 wounded.⁶ Chief Boatswain's Mate Edwin J. Hill led the effort to cast off the lines so the ship could get under way and then swam back to the ship. While attempting to let go the anchors, he was killed by bomb explosions from the dive-bombers. His bravery was recognized by a Medal of Honor. Another *Nevada* crewman, Chief Machinist's Mate Donald K. Ross, was also a recipient of the Congressional Medal of Honor.

The two battleships moored inboard suffered little damage. *Maryland* was hit by two 1,760-pound bombs that killed four men and wounded 14. *Tennessee* was hit by two large armor-piercing bombs, but neither exploded with full force. Only four men were killed and 23 wounded. *Pennsylvania* was struck by a single bomb, resulting in the death of 18 men and injury to another 30.⁷

As events later in the war proved, subtracting the battleships from the Pacific Fleet's order of battle did not greatly detract from its fighting power. Only two of the sunken battleships (*Arizona* and *Oklahoma*) failed to return to service. The three most lightly damaged battleships – *Maryland, Pennsylvania,* and *Tennessee* – were back in service within three months. Joining with *Colorado*, which was in Bremerton, Washington, on December 7, undergoing overhaul at the time of the attack, and later by the three New Mexico-class battleships that returned from the Atlantic, the new Pacific Fleet commander had a formidable force of seven battleships by June 1942. Demonstrating what Nimitz and his staff thought about the fighting value of the old battleships, they were given no role in the planning for the Battle of Midway. They lacked the speed to operate with the carriers and were deficient in antiaircraft protection. In addition, Nimitz lacked the fuel and tankers to support them operating from Pearl Harbor and the destroyers to properly screen them. Accordingly, they were sent to San Francisco, out of harm's way, where they would not be a burden to fleet operations.

Three of the battleships damaged in the attack received a massive rebuilding before returning to service. *Nevada* had her antiaircraft battery extensively modernized and returned to service in June 1943. The last two ships, *West Virginia* and *Tennessee*, were rebuilt from the main deck up, giving them the same offensive capabilities as the modern battleships. Both returned to service in 1944. However, all of the Pearl Harbor-era battleships remained very slow ships. With a speed of approximately 20 knots, they were unsuited for operations with the main fleet. In contrast, being heavily armed and carrying huge 14- and 16-inch main battery guns, they were excellent platforms for supporting amphibious operations.

The first time the old battleships could prove their worth in supporting amphibious operations occurred during the Aleutians campaign from May to August 1943, when three Pearl Harbor survivors were among the five battleships taking part in the reconquest of Attu and Kiska. This was in a secondary theater, but in November 1943 the Pacific Fleet opened its Central Pacific drive by invading the Gilbert Islands. Among the seven old battleships taking part were three Pearl Harbor survivors. From this point, old battleships became a staple of amphibious operations for the remainder of the war.

The loss of the battleships at Pearl Harbor, most of them only temporarily, did not degrade American operations in 1942 at Midway or during the subsequent Guadalcanal campaign fought between August 1942 and February 1943. Though available, none of the old battleships were employed in these actions. Only after the Pacific Fleet's offensive was in full swing did the old battleships find a useful role. The delay in *West Virginia* and *Tennessee* not returning to service until 1944 would have occurred anyway since the USN would have taken some of the more capable older battleships out of action for a rebuild to greatly enhance their capabilities. So in the final analysis, the loss of the battleships at Pearl Harbor meant almost nothing to the Pacific Fleet.

Only three cruisers were hit in the attack, although had the Japanese followed their own target prioritization this number should have been much higher. *Honolulu* returned to service in December 1941, but *Helena*, another Brooklyn-class cruiser, did not return until September the following year in time to take part in the Guadalcanal campaign. After a brief but outstanding career, she was sunk in July 1943 at the Battle of Kula Gulf after being struck by three torpedoes. The third cruiser, *Raleigh*, was struck by a torpedo that would have been fatal if the damage had occurred in the open sea. The cruiser was repaired locally and returned to service by mid-February 1942. The Omaha class were all second-line units, and after returning to service, *Raleigh* spent the rest of the war in the Northern Pacific.

Of the 29 destroyers present in Pearl Harbor, only three were placed out of service. *Shaw* had her bow blown off but returned to service in mid-1942. *Cassin* and *Downes* were constructive losses and were not worth the effort to repair. However, the USN retrieved their machinery and used them as the basis for two new destroyers that were given the same name as the original ships. These returned to service in 1944. The loss of three destroyers, one only for a short period, was insignificant.

Only four auxiliaries were damaged or sunk in the attack. None was worth attacking in the first place. Target ship *Utah* performed a valuable service by absorbing two torpedoes that could have been targeted against more valuable ships. She never returned to service. The most valuable auxiliary to suffer damage was seaplane tender *Curtiss*, but she was quickly repaired and returned to full service before the end of December 1941. Repair ship *Vestal*, despite taking two bomb hits, got under way and was beached to prevent her from sinking. By February 1942, she had returned to service. Even the aged minelayer *Oglala*, sunk along the 1010 Dock, was repaired and returned to service. Though she offered very little in capabilities, this was accomplished by early 1944.

The absence of the 18 ships damaged or sunk, all but three for only for a temporary period, had almost no effect on the Pacific Fleet's capabilities in the short or long run. In fact, in the short run the reduction of the Pacific Fleet's battle line simply hastened the recognition that the carrier was now the centerpiece of the fleet. Forced to embrace this new reality, the new Pacific Fleet was structured around its aircraft carriers. These were the forces that conducted a series of raids in 1942 against Japanese installations and forces in the Central and Southern Pacific before stopping the Japanese advance into the South Pacific in May 1942 at the Battle of Coral Sea and into the Central Pacific at Midway the following month. Conversely, the battleships from Pearl Harbor did not see their first action in a primary combat zone until November 1943. Despite Admiral Ernest J. King, commander of the Atlantic Fleet, urging him to do so, Nimitz did not employ the older battleships during the six-month-long Guadalcanal campaign in which the surface forces of the Pacific Fleet were almost stretched to the breaking point.

In the long run, the losses suffered by the Pacific Fleet were irrelevant in view of the industrial capacity of the United States and its ability to build a whole new navy. Yamamoto's bold gamble meant little to the naval balance in the Pacific after the Pearl Harbor attack. The Combined Fleet outnumbered the Pacific Fleet in all categories (except submarines) before the attack; as a result of the attack, the Japanese increased their margin of superiority in battleships, but this meant little in a war dominated by air power, either from carriers or land bases.

AMERICAN AIR POWER LOSSES AND THEIR IMPACT

More than half of the Japanese sorties over Oahu were devoted to attacking American air power distributed on the many aviation facilities on the island. This level of effort achieved its objective of neutralizing American air capabilities so that an effective counterstroke against the Striking Force would be impossible. A high number of American aircraft were destroyed or damaged in the process, but this did not translate to a significant reduction of American air power for more than the immediate period of the attack and the next few following weeks. The loss of 175 aircraft had an obvious short-term impact on the ability of the Army and Navy to defend Hawaii from potential additional attacks. Since these attacks were not forthcoming, the losses meant nothing.

Exact American aircraft losses are difficult to determine since the official accounts differ and it is unclear how many of the damaged aircraft were eventually scrapped. Total aircraft losses are detailed below.

American Aircraft Destroyed on December 7, 1941

Service	Total
Army Air Force	76
Army Air Force B-17s arriving at Oahu	2
US Navy at NAS Pearl Harbor and NAS Kaneohe Bay	54
Enterprise aircraft	10
US Marine Corps	33
Total	175 (plus approximately 24 scrapped aircraft)

The Hawaiian Air Force started the day with 234 aircraft of all types available of which 146 were operational. Of these, 76 were destroyed and only 83 were left operational after the attack. Exact losses by type of aircraft are displayed in the table below. In addition, 81 fighters, six patrol aircraft, and 34 bombers were damaged; of these, 20 percent were eventually written off.[8]

Hawaiian Air Force Strengths, December 7, 1941[9]

Aircraft Type	Total Available	Operational	Destroyed	Operational after attack
B-17D	12	6	5	4
B-24A	1	1	1	0
B-18	33	21	12	11
B-12A	3	1	0	1
A-20A	12	5	2	9
A-12A	2	2	0	1
P-40C	12	9	5	2
P-40B	87	55	37	25
P-36A	39	20	4	16
P-26A/B	14	10	6	4
AT-6	4	3	1	2
OA-9	3	3	2	1
OA-8	1	1	0	1
O-47B	7	5	0	5
O-49	2	2	1	1
C-33	2	2	0	0
Totals	234	146	76	83

Despite their arriving in the middle of the attack, losses to the 12 B-17C/E that stumbled into the airspace above Oahu on December 7 were light. Of the six B-17Es from the 88th Reconnaissance Squadron (Heavy), five were in commission at the end of the day. The bomber ending up on the Kahuku Golf Course was repairable. The 38th Reconnaissance Squadron (Heavy) fared a bit worse. Both its B-17C bombers were operational after arriving at Hickam Field, as were two of its B-17Es. One B-17E was destroyed at Hickam. The single B-17E that landed at Bellows Field was deemed repairable, but it was used for spare parts and was never returned to service.[10]

Army Air Force losses looked severe but were incurred by obsolete or obsolescent aircraft types. The heavy losses of P-40s proved almost inconsequential since total P-40 production was 13,738, making the loss of 42 aircraft only a few days' worth of production. Fighter losses were replaced by more modern P-40 variants – the P-40D and E models – and bomber losses were replaced by much more capable variants of the B-17, and by B-25 and B-26 medium bombers.

Navy losses were also high, some 54 in total.[11] Most important was the loss of 40 PBYs. Of the 67 PBYs present subordinate to six patrol squadrons, 40 were destroyed and 56 knocked out of commission.[12] Navy PBY losses were very high and crippled search operations in the near term. However, PBY-5 production was in full gear. With 684 built between September 1940 and July 1943 (approximately 20 per month), Pearl Harbor losses could be made up in just over two months. By the Battle of Midway in June, PBY squadrons were back at full strength. Added to the toll of Navy aircraft lost were the six dive-bombers and four fighters from *Enterprise*.

MAG-21 lost 33 of 49 aircraft present at Ewa Field.[13] The primary units caught at Ewa and subjected to heavy losses were fighter squadron VMF-211 and scout bomber squadron VMSB-232. Both squadrons were quickly reequipped and made ready for combat. VMF-211 was reorganized by April 1942 and deployed to Palmyra Atoll. VMSB-232 was provided with the latest variant of the Dauntless dive-bomber and was one of the first two squadrons sent to Guadalcanal in August 1942 where it achieved an outstanding combat record.

THE RECKONING

THE OVERALL IMPACT OF AMERICAN LOSSES

From a strictly military perspective, the Pearl Harbor attack was merely a tactical victory for the Japanese. The Pacific Fleet had suffered damage to 18 ships, but few of these represented a real loss in its fighting capabilities. The core of the Pacific Fleet was untouched. Yamamoto failed in his objective of crippling the Pacific Fleet.

At the operational level, the Pearl Harbor attack did force the Americans to reevaluate their planned amphibious operations in the Central Pacific as outlined in war plan Rainbow-5. A complete rethink of future operations was in order as the scope and pace of Japanese offensive operations expanded throughout the Pacific. However, the delay in launching offensive operations into the Central Pacific was not a direct result of the Pearl Harbor attack.

The Pacific Fleet did not possess the offensive power and logistic support to begin its Central Pacific drive until November 1943. That was only after a critical prerequisite had been achieved at Midway when Japanese offensive power was blunted and the initiative shifted to the Americans. American strategy focused on the protection of the sea lines of communications between the United States and Australia, so the initial American offensive of the Pacific War was directed at the unknown island of Guadalcanal in the southern Solomon Islands where a Japanese airfield was about to be completed. As long as the Japanese were pursuing offensive operations in the South Pacific, the initial American offensive had to counter it. All this points to late 1943 as the earliest point at which the Pacific Fleet could have begun its long-planned offensive in the Central Pacific, highlighting the false notion held by the Japanese that the Pearl Harbor operation was necessary to forestall an American advance into the Central Pacific that could have threatened the all-important Southern Operation.

Whatever results the Japanese gained in terms of ships sunk or damaged, they could always point to the fact that the Pacific Fleet was unable to directly interfere with the Southern Operation. Unknown to the Japanese was the weakness of the Pacific Fleet's logistic train, which would have made immediate large-scale offensive operations in the Central Pacific impossible anyway.

12

Why Pearl Harbor Matters

> ...the surprise attack on Pearl Harbor, far from being a "strategic necessity," as the Japanese claimed even after the war, was a strategic imbecility. One can search military history in vain for an operation more fatal to the aggressor... On the strategic level it was idiotic. On the high political level it was disastrous.
>
> Samuel E. Morison[1]

THE WAR CREATED BY PEARL HARBOR

Japan's attack on Pearl Harbor was the single most important event of the Pacific War and one of the two most important events of World War II. First and foremost, it brought the world's most powerful nation into the war. The entry of the United States into the conflagration transformed the ongoing conflicts in Europe and Asia into a world war. Germany followed Japan's ill-considered attack on the United States by making its own grand strategic self-inflicted wound with a declaration of war on the United States on December 11, 1941. With its immense war-making potential and favorable geographic position beyond the reach of its enemies, the addition of the United States to the Allies made the defeat of the Axis powers all but inevitable.

For Japan, it was bad enough that the United States was thrust into the war – even worse was the way it happened. The manner of the Pearl Harbor attack increased the degree of outrage shared by all Americans. After months of negotiations with the goal of reducing tensions in the Pacific, the Japanese attacked in the middle of those negotiations.

To the American populace, it seemed as if the entire process had been nothing more than a farce simply to hide Japan's real intentions. The surprise attack on Pearl Harbor created a different United States. America entered the war not as a divided nation with lingering isolationist sentiment, but as an angry nation with a singular purpose.

THE JAPANESE NOT BREAKING OFF NEGOTIATIONS

On top of the Japanese strike having been a surprise attack, it had been conducted without the international legal façade of a preceding declaration of war. The Japanese thought of this and made plans for issuing such a declaration just before they opened the Pearl Harbor attack. Admiral Nomura, the Japanese ambassador to the United States, and Special Envoy Kurusu arrived at the Department of State building at 1405 (local time in Washington) and were received by Secretary of State Cordell Hull at 1420. Upon entering, Nomura apologized for being late, as his government instructed him to deliver the message he was carrying at 1300 (0730 in Oahu). With the attack scheduled to begin at 1330 Washington time (0800 in Oahu), there was little room for error. By intent, there would also be little time for the Americans to react to the delivery of the note. The delay, he conceded, was caused by problems decoding the message. This was only partially true, as the primary reason was the availability of a qualified typist to produce a readable copy of the message for the Americans.

Using Purple machines to decrypt the 14-part Japanese message, the Americans were decoding it faster than the Japanese could produce a typed copy of it. By the time the Japanese arrived at the State Department, Hull had already seen a copy of the complete message. The final part of the message stated:

> Thus the earnest hope of the Japanese Government to adjust Japanese-American relations and to preserve and promote the peace of the Pacific through cooperation with the American Government has finally been lost. The Japanese Government regrets to have to notify hereby the American Government that in view of the attitude of the American Government it cannot but consider that it is impossible to reach an agreement through further negotiations.

There was ambiguity in the meaning of the final sentence. It was not a declaration of war, and nor did it even break diplomatic relations. Even at this point, the Japanese chose not to be clear on their intentions.

Roosevelt, who had learned of the attack at 1340, ordered Hull not to reveal to the Japanese that he was already aware of what had transpired on Oahu. Hull read the message as if he had never seen it before. According to his aide, Hull delivered this stinging rebuke to the Japanese:

> In all my 50 years of public service I have never seen a document that was more crowded with infamous falsehoods and distortions – infamous falsehoods and distortions on a scale so huge that I never imagined until today that any Government on this planet was capable of uttering them.[2]

This formal response has gone down in history as the extent of Hull's reply, but it included much more salty language. A State Department official overheard Hull refer to the Japanese as "scoundrels and pissants" and this was probably not the full extent of this abuse.[3] Hull dismissed them without giving them a chance to respond.

Thus, it was a formal Japanese declaration of its intent to break off negotiations that was delivered to the Americans well after the opening of the attack. This was of little consequence to the government in Tokyo – military results mattered much more than diplomatic niceties. There was no concern whatsoever about the timing of the delivery of the note. Had this mattered, there would have been a greater margin of error built into the process. Conversely, to Yamamoto, the timing of the delivery of the note mattered greatly. He saw his operation as "a strategic surprise attack" and not as "a political sneak attack." When reports on American radio described the operation as a "sneak attack," Yamamoto ordered his staff to look into what happened. Because the Japanese Foreign Ministry did not cooperate, it was only possible to determine that the 14-part note had been delivered but that the timing remained unclear. According to Kusaka and Kuroshima, Yamamoto was troubled by this and he seemed "to have an unpleasant feeling about it." Apparently, he never realized that there was an hour delay between the opening of the attack and the presentation of the note.[4] The perception that the Japanese had played the American leadership for suckers by negotiating for a peaceful solution while preparing for war and then proceeded to open hostilities without a formal declaration of war was a major factor in the intense rage shared by all Americans.

Word to the nation that the Japanese had begun hostilities was issued by the White House at 1422. Shortly after 1500, Roosevelt met with Hull, Stimson, Secretary of the Navy Frank Knox, and Marshall as reports of the disaster continued to arrive from Oahu. At 2030, Roosevelt met with his cabinet, during which the President read them his draft message for Congress to be delivered the next day. Following this meeting, congressional leaders arrived for a follow-up meeting that did not break up until 2300.

In his address to Congress on December 8, Roosevelt was calm and resolute. He reflected the mood of the nation to overcome a heavy initial blow and to gain vengeance. The President admitted that severe damage had been incurred by American naval and air forces and many lives had been lost. He promised "absolute victory." In the last sentence of the address, he demanded: "I ask that the Congress declare that since the unprovoked and dastardly attack by Japan on Sunday, December 7, 1941, a state of war has existed between the United States and the Japanese Empire."

Congress did not need Roosevelt's impassioned speech to act promptly and decisively. A Declaration of War was then passed by the Senate (82-0, with 13 senators unable to be present due to travel problems). Just ten minutes later, the House approved its declaration with a vote of 388-1, with another 46 representatives unable to be present because of travel delays (Jennette Rankin, the first woman elected to Congress and a lifelong pacifist cast the sole "nay" vote). Within an hour, Roosevelt signed the joint resolution. The United States was now formally at war with Japan. Most importantly, the United States did not enter the war divided or uncertain of why it was fighting. As noted by Morison, this new reality made the Pearl Harbor attack a strategic calamity for the Japanese and thus was a strategic miscalculation of the first order. Any temporary gains realized during the actual attack paled by comparison.

The drastic impact of the Pearl Harbor attack on the United States is hard to comprehend today. The closest comparison would be the terrorist attack on the World Trade Center on September 11, 2001. On both occasions, the first emotions were shock and surprise, followed by grief for the fallen and humiliation that the nation had been caught flat-footed. But the overarching emotions were utter rage and a desire to retaliate. After 9/11, this desire for retaliation was sufficient to lead to an ill-defined and seemingly interminable "War on Terror" which exacted a high toll in American treasure and lives. After the Pearl Harbor attack, the same emotions led to a rapid declaration of war and a collective hatred for its perpetrators. In turn, this affected the way the war was conducted – there was to be no mercy for the Japanese.

JAPAN'S PERSPECTIVE

When news of the attack was released to the Japanese population, euphoria swept the nation. There was no moral uncertainty for the Japanese or a sense of guilt – the heavy blow struck at the United States promised a chance to end the war in China and make up for past humiliations at the hands of the West. The Japanese embarked wholeheartedly on a war with the United States even though it was very uncertain if such a war could end in its favor. As only a few far-sighted Japanese realized in December 1941, the conflict against a much stronger opponent would end in disaster. By August 1945, when Japan agreed to terminate the war (describing it as a "surrender" was impossible), millions of Japanese were dead, almost all its cities lay in ruin, and its empire ceased to exist. That is the ultimate legacy of Pearl Harbor for Japan.

WAS THERE AN ALTERNATIVE TO PEARL HARBOR?

From an economic perspective, the Japanese leadership assessed it had no option other than to go to war to secure the resources it needed. While Japan had enough coal to supply all its needs, this was not the case for food and other raw materials. The most critical shortfall was in oil. In mid-1941, Japan's domestic production accounted for only 10 percent of its total requirements. The balance came from imports, with 10 percent of total requirements from the DEI and the remainder from the United States. When the United States and its allies imposed an oil blockade, Japan was thrown into economic peril as 90 percent of its oil needs were no longer available.[5]

Of course, the Japanese were aware of this vulnerability and had assembled a reserve of 58,000,000 barrels of oil by mid-1941. During the period between the imposition of the Allied blockade and the initiation of hostilities, some 7,000,000 barrels of the oil reserve were consumed. This proved that doing nothing was unsustainable, as domestic production (including production of crude oil and synthetic production) was far short of the 7,000,000 barrels used over a few months. Solving this problem required that the oil-producing and refining facilities in the DEI be captured and brought into service as soon as possible. If the facilities on Borneo, Java, and Sumatra could be seized, their total production in 1940 of 65,000,000 barrels would cover Japan's estimated requirement for 37,800,000 barrels from September 1941 until September the following year.[6]

However, there were other factors that pointed to problems with the Japanese solving their oil problem, even after facilities in the DEI had been captured. The Japanese tanker fleet was too small to carry the necessary fuel from the DEI to facilities in Japan. Another unknown factor was the time required to return the captured facilities to full operation. One key assumption was that during the first three years of the war, only a single major fleet engagement (for which an astounding 3,150,000 barrels of oil was needed) would be conducted. However, none of the assumptions used in the prewar estimates were correct. In the first year of the war, the Imperial Navy used 60 percent more oil than was envisioned. Even after the original estimates were refined, always in a more optimistic light, it was clear that by 1944 Japan would be facing an oil crisis.[7]

More than oil was at stake. Japan needed iron, primarily from Malaya and the Philippines. Other materials were unavailable domestically and could only be acquired in Malaya and the DEI. These included a number of key elements for a wartime economy – rubber, tin, bauxite, manganese, cobalt, graphite, lead, nickel, phosphate, and potash. A significant amount of foodstuffs also was imported.

Japan's gloomy economic picture dictated its strategy and operations. It was utterly essential that the resource areas in Southeast Asia be captured and that this be done as quickly as possible before the British and Dutch had the opportunity to reinforce their defenses or to destroy key facilities. This basic premise explains the Naval General Staff's vehement opposition to Yamamoto's Pearl Harbor plan.

For Japan, the most challenging part of its initial phase of operations was how to handle the United States. Accepted wisdom at the time was that the United States would not leave the fate of British and Dutch possessions in Southeast Asia up to the Japanese. It was assumed that the strategic linkage between the Americans and the Europeans would force the Americans to come to the aid of the lightly defended European colonies. Given this, it was necessary to neutralize American power in the Pacific as part of the initial wave of offensive operations. Most critical was the decision how to handle the Philippines. They were an American possession, and the Americans were making strides improving their capabilities in the archipelago. This included a growing number of modern aircraft, including long-range B-17 bombers with the range to hit targets in Japan. Whatever the state of the American forces in the Philippines, they were well positioned to strike the SLOCs between Japan and the critical resource areas that Japan intended to conquer. Leaving these forces unmolested and able to attack the SLOCs was a risk of the first order. Furthermore, if the Philippines were not neutralized, it would allow the Americans to reinforce them significantly, making it more difficult to capture them should that become necessary and increasing the risk to the SLOCs over time.

Attacking the Philippines was an obvious act of war that the United States could not ignore. By striking the Philippines, the Japanese had the opportunity to occupy smaller American possessions at Guam Island and Wake Atoll that posed a minor threat to Japanese SLOCs in the Central Pacific. If the Philippines were attacked, and the United States brought into the war, the way seemed clear to attack the Pacific Fleet in Hawaii, at least as far as Yamamoto was concerned. Leaving the Pacific Fleet undisturbed in the opening strikes of the war meant that the initiative passed to the Americans who would then be free to decide how to respond to the Japanese invasion of the Philippines. Striking the Pacific Fleet at the onset of hostilities kept the initiative in Japanese hands. More importantly, it promised to neutralize the only force in the Pacific with the potential capabilities to interfere with the Southern Operation by beginning offensive operations against Japanese holdings in the Central Pacific.

However, in the view of most Imperial Navy officers, there was a better alternative to attacking Pearl Harbor. Before Yamamoto came on the scene and changed it, the Imperial Navy's strategy for defeating the USN was built around the decisive battle strategy. At a place in the Central Pacific, changed from the Western Pacific by Yamamoto in 1940, the two fleets would meet in a climactic clash to decide the war. Following attritional attacks by submarines and bombers against the advancing Pacific Fleet, the decisive battle would be fought. The Imperial Navy had given much thought to this set-piece battle in which their superior training and tactics would carry the day. After a massive night torpedo attack, the Japanese battle line would finish off the American battle line using long-range gunnery and superior speed. Following Japan's decisive victory at sea, the United States would be forced to negotiate and concede that Japan was dominant in the Western Pacific.

The decisive battle strategy (termed the "Great All-Out Battle Strategy" by the Japanese) became dogma within the Imperial Navy and dictated training, tactics, ship design, and force structure. Incredibly though, the strategy was never fully tested in a fleet exercise.[8] Though parts of the operation were well rehearsed, like long-range gunnery and night torpedo attacks by light units, other parts, when they were attempted, could not be performed, like locating the American fleet and massing forces against it for the required attritional attacks. Furthermore, in order for the decisive battle strategy to work, the Americans had to operate according to the Japanese script. Because the Imperial Navy preferred to fight and win a short war, it needed the Americans to conduct an immediate advance into the Central Pacific rather than waiting to build a fleet much more powerful than the Combined Fleet. In the actual battle, it was assumed the Pacific Fleet would steam willingly into the trap set by the Japanese, regardless of the losses suffered during the attritional phase, while ignoring Japanese preparations to surround the Pacific Fleet before the great climactic battle.

Though the Great All-Out Battle Strategy had problems, most Japanese Navy officers thought that the Imperial Navy and the nation would have been better served by sticking to the original defensive plan that the Japanese had trained so hard to master during the interwar period. Even if some aspects of the Great All-Out Battle Strategy were impracticable, it did offer the benefits of being on the defensive. These included removing the possibility of overextension and reducing logistical demands. Air power advocates, such as Yamamoto's close ally Admiral Inoue Shigeyoshi, wanted to enhance the viability of the defensive strategy by increasing the strength of the Imperial Navy's land-based, long-range air strength to turn Japanese possessions in the

Central Pacific into a chain of impregnable fortresses.[9] Most importantly, it avoided the requirement to attack the Americans directly on their sovereign territory of Hawaii, thus eliminating the political risk of inflaming American public opinion.

One action never seriously considered by the Japanese was to forego attacking any American possessions at all. It is impossible to know if and when the Americans would have responded to a Japanese attack solely against Dutch and British colonies, but it is clear that Roosevelt did not have the required level of support to take America to war in 1941 over such Japanese aggression.

THE JAPANESE PLAN FOR VICTORY

Japan went to war against the most powerful nation in the world with only an ill-defined notion of how it would defeat such a formidable enemy. There was no concept of a classic victory against the United States in which Japan could dictate peace terms. Rather, it was envisioned that a negotiated settlement would be possible once the Americans realized the futility of trying to pry Japan's new-found gains in the Pacific away from it. Essentially, Japanese spirit would substitute for the lack of resources compared with the Americans and eventually would force the United States to acquiesce to a new order in the Western Pacific.

As flawed as this war termination planning was, what little hope of success existed in this scenario rested on American war-weariness. The Pearl Harbor attack put to rest any prospect of a negotiated settlement by the Americans. Perhaps the American public would not be willing to risk never-ending casualties for Chinese sovereignty or to recover lost European colonies, but there was no price too high to pay to avenge Pearl Harbor. With the slogan "Remember Pearl Harbor" drilled into every American, there was little prospect the United States would compromise on the outcome of the war.

In military terms, the Japanese plans for a favorable peace were ambitious and based on faulty assumptions. In the initial phases of war, Japan planned to strengthen its defensive posture and cut off Australia from the United States. Isolating Australia was considered critical since it could no longer be used as a staging area for an American counteroffensive. With their defensive position solidified, and with the Combined Fleet operating from interior lines, the Japanese planned to defeat any American attempt to penetrate its defensive perimeter. After a period of 18–24 months of fruitless attacks, the Japanese believed that the Americans would grow tired of the heavy losses suffered against such a determined enemy as the Japanese and be ready to make peace. Another factor working in their favor, the Japanese believed, was that the war in Europe would require most of America's resources. In the negotiated peace to follow, Japan would retain most of its conquests. After making peace with the Americans and their allies, the war against an isolated China would resume.

Yamamoto's vision of victory, symbolized by the Pearl Harbor attack, and later by the ill-fated Midway operation, did not comport with Japan's best hope for victory. It was impossible to beat the Americans by pursuing a strategy of expansion. It was impossible to seize or neutralize areas supporting the American wartime economy, and expansion only overextended the Japanese, making them more vulnerable to the inevitable American counterattack. Likewise, seeking a decisive battle against the USN was foolhardy since it could never be defeated in a single battle or even a series of battles given the enormous industrial capacity of the United States to build a new wartime navy much larger than the prewar American or Japanese navies. The best, and only, hope for Japanese victory was a strategy of prolonged attrition after which a compromised peace might be possible. If the political scenario could be created that the Americans were only fighting to recover European colonies or to reoccupy the Philippines, which had already been promised independence by the Americans, then prospects for a negotiated peace were enhanced. If, on the other hand, the Americans were fighting for vengeance against a treacherous enemy, then prospects for any negotiations were greatly reduced.

The Japanese vision of victory was a collection of assumptions and hopes and not a concrete plan that would place the United States in a position where it had no choice but to stop the war. Japanese assumptions regarding the overall war-making potential and social cohesiveness of the Unites States were seriously mistaken. Incredibly, these assumptions were based on no academic research and scholarly analysis of the economic or psychological characteristics of the United States. Imperial Army intelligence efforts were focused on China and the Soviet Union, ignoring the United States and other Western powers. Because of the secrecy of the Pearl Harbor attack plan, neither Imperial Navy intelligence, nor any civilian agencies or universities, were tasked to look into American war-making potential before the decision for war was made.[10]

While the Japanese were generally aware of the superior production capabilities of the United States, these were considered secondary to the societal weakness of the Americans. Just as the Americans assumed that the inferior Japanese lacked the strength and capabilities to take on the might of the United States, the Japanese made a series of assumptions about the United States that supported the concept that the Americans were incapable of mobilizing for and sustaining a long war against the determined Japanese. Americans were known to be soft, selfish, and egotistical. This was reflected in a number of characteristics – isolationism, labor agitation, racial strife, political factionalism, among others – that the Japanese believed made it impossible for the United States to fight a successful war.[11]

The views of Yamamoto, as the driving force behind the Pearl Harbor attack, were critical. In spite of his supposed expertise on America and Americans, his assessments were spectacularly wrong. Yamamoto subscribed to the notion that Americans were weak and that a major defeat (like sinking a number of battleships) could break American morale. Therefore, the Pearl Harbor attack was designed to deliver a psychological shock to the Americans.

The psychological aspect of Yamamoto's Pearl Harbor attack has been underplayed. Yamamoto targeted battleships for a reason. Onishi told Genda that: "Yamamoto not only intends to cripple the US Pacific Fleet severely at the beginning of hostilities; he counts heavily on smashing the morale of the American people by sinking as many battleships as possible."[12] Since most observers in Japan and the United States still assessed that battleships were the final arbiters of naval power, Yamamoto assessed that destroying a number of them at the onset of the war would smash the American spirit. After the fall of Singapore, the occupation of the Philippines, and the seizure of resources in the DEI, Japan needed to continue the war, the United States would be forced to negotiate. Yamamoto did not believe in the Great All-Out Battle Strategy, but his notion that sinking battleships at Pearl Harbor would deliver a huge psychological blow to the Americans had no basis in reality.

Yamamoto's naiveté regarding Americans was demonstrated conclusively by his insistence that the 14-part message be delivered half an hour before the attack, since by observing the diplomatic particulars of "declaring" war the level of American anger could somehow be curbed. For the man who claimed to understand Americans so well, it defies belief that Yamamoto would have thought that, by delivering a quasi-declaration of war a few minutes before a surprise attack, the American people would have considered the Japanese any less dastardly.[13]

Because of the secrecy of the planning, Japanese naval intelligence was not asked to make an assessment of the psychological impacts of the Pearl Harbor attack.[14] Had there been an intelligence assessment in this regard and it contradicted the assumption that a successful attack would be a huge psychological shock to the Americans, it would have been summarily ignored, as the Imperial Navy typically ignored intelligence assessments that did not support operational planning. So, the unsupported and incorrect beliefs of Yamamoto were left unchallenged.

STRATEGIC BENEFITS OF THE PEARL HARBOR ATTACK

At the operational and tactical levels, the attack on Pearl Harbor was partially successful. However, these benefits were fleeting. On the strategic level, it was unsuccessful as it failed to cripple the Pacific Fleet or negatively impact the morale of the American populace. In spite of all obstacles, the Imperial Navy had approached within striking range of the most important American naval base in the Pacific and delivered a heavy blow, while suffering only minor losses. This was achieved in spite of a plan that embraced excessive risk.

The stated objective of the Hawaii Operation was to cripple the Pacific Fleet for at least six months, thus preventing it from interfering with the conquest of Southeast Asia. Nominally, this was a success, since the occupation of Malaya and the DEI succeeded as planned. With only light losses, the Imperial Navy completed the conquest of these critical areas by early March 1942. In fact, because the Pacific Fleet did not possess the necessary forces or logistics train to conduct a major offensive in late 1941 or early 1942, the Hawaii Operation was unnecessary on a strategic level. That the Japanese military did not recognize that was both a command and an intelligence failure.

The inability of the Pacific Fleet to intervene against Japanese operations in Southeast Asia was clearly understood by the Americans. In the words of Captain Vincent R. Murphy, Kimmel's assistant war plans officer, when asked about a Japanese air attack on Pearl Harbor:

I did not think that such an attack would be made. I thought it would be utterly stupid for the Japanese to attack the United States at Pearl Harbor... I thought that the Japanese could probably have gone into Thailand and Malaya, and even the Dutch East Indies... I did not think they would attack at Pearl Harbor because I did not think it was necessary for them to do so, from my point of view. We could not have materially affected their control of the waters that they wanted to control, whether or not the battleships were sunk at Pearl Harbor. In other words, I did not believe that we could move the United States Fleet to the Western Pacific until such time as auxiliaries were available, as the material condition of the ships were improved, especially with regard to anti-aircraft, and until such time as the Pacific Fleet was materially re-enforced. I thought it would be suicide for us to attempt, with an inferior fleet, to move into the Western Pacific.[15]

The Japanese had a clear understanding of the prewar order of battle of the Pacific Fleet and were aware that a sizeable part of the fleet had been sent to the Atlantic. They must have understood the logistics requirements of mounting an offensive into the Central Pacific. A brief look at a chart of the Pacific confirms the significant distances involved. Yet they convinced themselves that it was a strategic necessity to attack the Pacific Fleet in Pearl Harbor.

Yamamoto was content to emphasize the supposed benefit that his Pearl Harbor attack would cripple the Pacific Fleet for at least six months as a reason to have the attack approved by the Naval General Staff. However, Yamamoto had much bigger things in mind than just a temporary respite from a potential intervention by the Pacific Fleet. It is clear from Yamamoto's discussions before the attack that the risks of the Hawaii Operation were taken with a much larger potential payoff – nothing less than the permanent crippling of the Pacific Fleet and more grandly the crippling of American morale at the onset of the war, which would reduce the United States' willingness to continue the war. Yamamoto's bold gambles to cripple the Pacific Fleet and damage American morale were both unsuccessful. Neither were they really achievable by a single raid on Pearl Harbor. If either had been, the risky Hawaiian Operation was worth undertaking. Yamamoto overestimated the impact of his operation.

WHY PEARL HARBOR MATTERS

Yamamoto's strategic failure at Pearl Harbor to permanently cripple the Pacific Fleet was demonstrated only a few months later. He still had to put together a plan to complete the destruction of the Pacific Fleet. This led to the Yamamoto-backed concept to attack Midway and draw the American fleet into battle. As he had at Pearl Harbor, Yamamoto threatened to resign if he didn't get his way. Again, the Naval General Staff relented, and again the result was disastrous. At Midway, four of the Pearl Harbor carriers were destroyed by American carriers. The Japanese planning process at Midway by Yamamoto's Combined Fleet staff had some of the earmarks of the planning before Pearl Harbor, with its wildly inaccurate strategic assumptions and lack of planning precision for operational and tactical details. Defeat at Midway marked the end of the prewar Striking Force and ended Japan's offensive phase of the war. Midway was a direct result of the failure of the Pearl Harbor attack to achieve Yamamoto's strategic objectives.

Competing Japanese strategies and the obvious flaws possessed by each call into question Japan's ability to formulate viable plans in a modern war. The decisive battle concept was based on their experiences from the Russo-Japanese War of 1904–05. The Great All-Out Battle Strategy was not a strategy at all – it was grand tactics masquerading as strategy. Even if the "decisive" battle had been fought, it would have been a battle within the opening campaign of the war, not a strategy to deliver war-winning results to Japan. Yamamoto's faulty understanding of the United States, leading to his assumption that a psychological shock could make the Americans accept a negotiated peace on Japanese terms, was even more flawed.

The final conclusion must be that Pearl Harbor provided no strategic military gain for the Japanese. If he could have curbed his impatience, Yamamoto would have been in a much better situation had the Americans actually attempted to mount a drive across the Central Pacific that the Japanese had been planning to counter for the last two decades. In this scenario, the old battleships of the Pacific Fleet, provided with inadequate air cover, would not have sunk in harbor, allowing the majority of their crews to be rescued and the ships themselves to be salvaged, but would have sunk at sea, where personnel losses would probably have been higher and ship losses permanent. In any event, the Pacific Fleet, even if untouched on December 7 and ordered to move immediately against the Japanese, could not have interfered with the Japanese invasion of the DEI and Malaya. This was demonstrated later during the war when the Americans attempted just that. In November 1943 an infinitely more powerful and prepared Pacific Fleet began its drive into the Central Pacific and took until October 1944 to reach the Philippines. Yamamoto's desire to gain time by a preemptive strike against the USN at Pearl Harbor was as unnecessary as it was ill-considered.

Another indication of the futility of the Pearl Harbor attack and the failure of the Japanese to understand the productive capability of the United States is provided by the expansion of the USN during the war. The groundwork for this growth was the Two Ocean Naval Expansion Act of June 1940 in the aftermath of the Fall of France. It included funding for 11 battleships, six large cruisers (the Alaska class, often referred to, incorrectly, as battlecruisers), 18 fleet carriers, 27 cruisers, 115 destroyers, and 43 submarines. This was an act of immense importance. It signaled that the Americans had decided to build the largest and most powerful fleet in the world, capable of meeting security requirements in the Atlantic and Pacific. Once this program was complete (scheduled for 1946–48), or after the bulk of the ships had joined the fleet, the Imperial Navy would be grossly overmatched. It also meant that no matter what losses the Americans suffered early in the war against a temporarily superior Imperial Navy, the flood of American naval construction was guaranteed to overwhelm the IJN at some point.

In the end, it did not matter what the result of the Japanese attack on Pearl Harbor was. The losses suffered by the Pacific Fleet were insignificant when placed in the overall context of American wartime naval production.

American Ships Commissioned from 1941 to 1945[16]

Battleships	8
Fleet carriers	18
Light carriers	9
Escort carriers	77
Large cruisers	2
Heavy cruisers	11
Light cruisers	33
Destroyers	349
Destroyer escorts	420
Submarines	203

WHY PEARL HARBOR MATTERS

Even with the loss of every ship present in Pearl Harbor on December 7, 1941, the IJN would still have faced unsurmountable odds by 1944.

THE AMERICAN PERSPECTIVE

In the United States, "Remember Pearl Harbor" became the rallying cry for the remainder of the war. It would be incorrect to state that the Japanese attack on Pearl Harbor was solely responsible for a war that was fought with ferocity and brutality on both sides. Clearly, there was a racial component to why the Americans disdained the Japanese, but after Pearl Harbor there was little reason to show restraint. Tales of unjustified Japanese brutality throughout the war served to solidify the "no quarter – no surrender" mentality. Pearl Harbor set a tone for the American conduct of the war that followed.

Pearl Harbor is imbedded deep within the American psyche. The attack achieved total surprise, and the results were not only disastrous but embarrassing. Never again would the United States be "Pearl Harbored." The day of the attack is still memorialized each year, but with the passing of the last few survivors who were on Oahu on December 7, 1941, the nature of these commemorations has and will further change. What will not change are the enduring lessons of Pearl Harbor. Though held up as perhaps the ultimate example of an intelligence failure in American history, that has not prevented a series of intelligence failures since 1945. Another lesson was that, with its immense capabilities, the United States was able to absorb an initial blow and then marshal its resources to achieve final victory. This was an incredibly quick process since, in less than four years, Japan was defeated and occupied. Even more remarkably, this was accomplished concurrently with the defeat of Nazi Germany.

In the grand strategic context, the Japanese attack at Pearl Harbor, coming as it did early in the war, was fortuitous for the United States. Instead of having to bide its time to enter the war after the full scope of Axis expansion had played out, the United States was brought into the conflict before the Axis powers had a chance to digest their gains and while the British Empire and the Soviet Union were powerful allies. In this sense, the entry of the United States into the war in late 1941 brought the war to an end in the shortest time possible.

PEARL HARBOR

OPERATIONS OF THE "CRIPPLED" PACIFIC FLEET

The notion that the Pearl Harbor attack succeeded in crippling the Pacific Fleet remains largely unchallenged. Was this really the case? It is true that the Imperial Navy possessed a numerical advantage over the Pacific Fleet in December 1941, but this advantage was less imposing than is usually believed. The numerical balance was affected by two major factors in early 1942. Most of the Imperial Navy was tied down in the Western Pacific seizing First Operational Phase objectives through March–April 1942. Additionally, the Americans were able to constantly reinforce Nimitz's fleet. Only a few hours after news of the attack reached Washington, Stark ordered Admiral Ernest J. King King, commander of the Atlantic Fleet, to reinforce the Pacific Fleet. Among the units to be transferred were the carrier *Yorktown*, battleships *New Mexico*, *Mississippi*, and *Idaho*, a squadron of destroyers, and three squadrons of patrol aircraft.[17]

Even before these important reinforcements could reach Hawaii, Kimmel and his staff were taking stock of what they had left to work with. The situation was not as bleak as might be imagined. Because the Japanese had concentrated on the battle line, there was little damage to the other combat elements of the fleet. *Helena*, a valuable light cruiser, was out of action, as was the antiquated *Raleigh*. Only three destroyers were removed from the American order of battle. Damage to the battle line was extensive, but even here there were reasons for optimism. The three New Mexico-class ships, considered the most capable of the "old" battleships, would soon return to the Pacific. *Colorado* was untouched; *Maryland* and *Pennsylvania* suffered little damage and were made available in December. *Tennessee* was back in service by February 1942, giving the Pacific Fleet a total of seven battleships. Better still for the Americans was the arrival in the Pacific of the 16-inch fast battleship *North Carolina* in mid-June 1942, followed by two more modern battleships, *Washington* and *South Dakota*, in August. The rebuilt American battle line compared well with its Japanese counterpart of only six battleships and four much less protected Kongo-class fast battleships. Of these, only the Kongo-class units were active in fleet operations during 1942 with the exception of the Midway operation. Unknown to the Americans, superbattleship *Yamato* was commissioned on December 16, 1941, just days after the Pearl Harbor attack.

Pacific Fleet Strength after the Pearl Harbor Attack[18]

Carriers	*Enterprise, Lexington, Saratoga* (reaching Oahu on December 12), *Yorktown* en route.
Battleships	*Maryland, Pennsylvania, Tennessee* ready about December 13–17; *Colorado* ready February 1. *New Mexico, Idaho, Mississippi* en route from the Atlantic.
Heavy cruisers	Eight operating near Oahu; *Pensacola* en route Suva to Brisbane; *Louisville* en route Samoa to Honolulu; *New Orleans* and *San Francisco* about to proceed to West Coast for completion of repairs.
Light cruisers	*St Louis, Phoenix; Boise* operating with the Asiatic Fleet; *Honolulu* in Oahu soon to finish repairs. One old unit – *Detroit*.
Destroyers	50 modern and 17 old.
Submarines	17 modern and 4 old.

Too important to be risked, she sat at anchor at Truk Atoll for most of 1942. In the end, even the Japanese edge in battleships, created by the losses of the Pearl Harbor attack, proved illusory.

The Pacific Fleet compared most unfavorably with the Combined Fleet in the category of aircraft carriers. At the start of the war, the USN possessed only seven fleet carriers in service, and only three of these were in the Pacific. No additional fleet carriers entered service until late 1942. Of the seven pre-Pearl Harbor carriers, *Ranger* was assessed to be unfit for service in the Pacific, leaving only six for potential use against the Japanese. By April, five of these were assigned to the Pacific, with the sixth, *Wasp*, arriving in June. In comparison, the IJN possessed a total of six fleet carriers. In addition, it had four smaller carriers in service in December 1941, giving it the imposing total of ten carriers. Three more, converted from auxiliaries as part of a plan to circumvent treaty limitations on carrier construction, also entered service early in 1942. This numerical advantage was less imposing than it seemed since one prewar light carrier was unsuitable for fleet operations, the first escort carrier was used only for ferry operations at this point in the war, and the conversions from auxiliaries lacked the protection and speed to be considered the equal of fleet carriers. Though heavily outnumbered by the IJN in carriers, the total aircraft capacity of the Pacific Fleet's fleet carriers was broadly similar to the Japanese capacity of the period.

All of the Pacific Fleet's 12 heavy cruisers remained operational after the Pearl Harbor attack. Even more valuable than these treaty heavy cruisers were the nine Brooklyn-class light cruisers. Of these, three were operational with the Pacific Fleet, and *Boise* was temporarily under the operational command of the Asiatic Fleet. Four more units were assigned to the Atlantic Fleet, but *Nashville* was quickly transferred from the Atlantic to the Pacific. By the time *Helena* rejoined the fleet in September 1942 and *Boise* was repaired after suffering damage in the DEI, six Brooklyn-class cruisers were active in the Pacific. This total of 18 front-line cruisers compared well with the IJN's 18 heavy cruisers, though on a ship-for-ship basis, the Japanese ships were superior. Japanese light cruisers were numerous (17 in total, with three more training cruisers) but were antiquated and were designed primarily to act as flagships for destroyer squadrons.

The Pacific Fleet was always short of destroyers at this point of the war, but the total of American destroyers in service was greater than the total of Japanese destroyers. Throughout 1942, the Pacific Fleet received a constant flow of new destroyers as transfers from the Atlantic or from new production. In comparison, the IJN was unable to cover losses in 1942 with new construction. The same situation existed in the submarine force of both navies.

In the immediate aftermath of the Pearl Harbor attack, the Pacific Fleet was reorganized into a number of task forces each built around a carrier. Task Force 12 (later 11) was centered on *Lexington*. *Enterprise* remained at the center of Task Force 8. *Saratoga* hurriedly departed San Diego and when she arrived at Pearl Harbor on December 13 became the hub of Task Force 16.[19] Each carrier task force was assigned two or three heavy cruisers and six to nine destroyers. When *Yorktown* arrived in the Pacific she headed up Task Force 17. There was no place in the new post-Pearl Harbor Pacific Fleet for the old battleships. It was impossible for them to participate in operations with the carriers since they were over 10 knots slower. They also burned fuel at prodigious rates, which was challenging to support from Pearl Harbor with the fuel stocks and oilers available. At this point, the only purpose found for them was to perform convoy escort duty between the West Coast and Hawaii while being based on the West Coast. Without much fanfare, the battleship passed from its central position in American naval thinking and operations, and the carrier assumed the central role in the fleet.

THE NEXT SIX MONTHS OF PACIFIC FLEET OPERATIONS

Once hostilities had begun, Kimmel planned to use his fleet offensively and intended to make Wake Atoll a pivotal part of his operations. Ironically, this opportunity was open to him even after the disaster of December 7. Part of the initial Japanese war plan was to seize Guam and Wake. Guam fell without much of a fight on December 10. The initial Japanese attempt to take Wake Atoll was mounted during the early morning hours of December 11. Marine shore batteries sank a destroyer and a second was sunk by Marine aircraft. The invasion attempt was abandoned.

The failure of the Japanese landing attempt provided an opportunity that Kimmel had long desired – engaging part of the Japanese fleet using Wake as a lure. Kimmel earmarked all three of his carrier task forces for a proposed relief operation. Had he decided to mount the operation quickly and to mass his carriers, there was the possibility that it would have been successful. *Saratoga*, at the center of an improvised task force that included seaplane tender *Tangier*, which was loaded with supplies, ammunition, and equipment for the Marines on Wake, led the relief force. She also carried a squadron of Marine fighters for the atoll. *Lexington* was ordered to conduct a raid against Jaluit in the Marshalls to pin down Japanese forces there. *Enterprise* was placed in a passive position to protect Oahu while standing by to support the other two carrier task forces.

As Kimmel tried to get his force into position, the Japanese acted quickly to prepare a second invasion. Not until December 14 did the *Saratoga* task force depart Pearl Harbor. Meanwhile, on December 15, *Soryu*, *Hiryu*, heavy cruisers *Tone* and *Chikuma*, and two destroyers were detached from the Striking Force to cover the second invasion of Wake Island scheduled for December 23. On December 17, Kimmel was relieved and replaced temporarily by Admiral Pye. On December 20, Pye ordered the *Lexington* task force to abandon its planned strike and head north to support the *Saratoga* task force then approaching Wake. Rear Admiral Frank Fletcher, in command of the *Saratoga* task force, was aware that the position of the Marines on Wake was increasingly perilous.

By late evening on December 21, his force was about 600nm from Wake. Instead of making a high-speed run to deliver aid to the beleaguered garrison, he elected to spend most of December 22 refueling his destroyers, a process which was still incomplete on December 23.

As the Americans demonstrated no alacrity, the Japanese were quicker off the mark. A larger invasion force was gathered, and *Soryu* and *Hiryu* began air strikes against Wake on December 21. Per Japanese doctrine, the landing occurred during the early hours of December 23. The Marines put up a brief, sharp fight, but surrendered beginning at 0730 on December 23. Even before he learned of the Marines' surrender, Pye ordered the operation canceled.

The Wake relief operation had the potential to retrieve Kimmel's reputation and provide a huge boast to American morale. If Kimmel had not been removed from command on December 17, he likely would have ordered Fletcher to continue, prompting a carrier battle. If pressed with alacrity and with all three carriers, Kimmel's relief operation had the possibility of fighting a battle with the two weakest carriers of the Striking Force. The results of such a battle cannot be reliably predicted, but it was unlikely that the Pacific Fleet was going to be placed in a better position to defeat part of the Striking Force in detail. As it was, after the Americans were slow to mount a relief attack and had dispersed their available forces, Pye made the correct decision to recall the *Saratoga* task force – losing a carrier immediately after the Pearl Harbor attack could not be risked. Pitting *Saratoga* against two Japanese carriers would have most likely resulted in an American defeat.

Following the Wake debacle, morale in the Pacific Fleet plummeted. Rejuvenation began with the appointment of Admiral Chester W. Nimitz on December 17. On December 31, he assumed command of the fleet. One of his first actions was to meet with Kimmel's former staff and assure them that the new Pacific Fleet commander still had confidence in them. Nimitz was exactly the right choice for the job and led the Pacific Fleet through to final victory.

In the aftermath of the Pearl Harbor disaster, the aggressive offensive plans for the Pacific Fleet to attack the Marshalls had no basis in reality. King, who had replaced Stark as Chief of Naval Operations, changed the fleet's mission to the defensive, keyed on two areas of near equal importance. One was protecting the Midway–Johnston–Hawaii triangle, and the second was the much more ambitious task of securing the sea lines of communication between the United States, Australia, and New Zealand. Neither King nor Nimitz was content to remain entirely on the defensive for long. Responding to King's demands for action, Nimitz planned a series of carrier raids on Japanese-held areas in the Central and South Pacific.

Nimitz needed no prodding to attack the Japanese. On February 1, *Enterprise* aircraft, supported by cruiser bombardments, hit three islands in the northern Marshalls. Concurrently, *Yorktown* hit Makin Island in the Gilberts and two more islands in the northern Marshalls. Both carriers approached their targets without being detected and faced only weak opposition. Little damage was inflicted on the Japanese, and *Enterprise* was undamaged by two air attacks.

The next raid did not go as planned. *Lexington* was ordered to attack the newly captured Japanese base at Rabaul in the South Pacific. However, on February 20, Japanese flying boats detected the task force some 460nm east of Rabaul, forcing Vice Admiral Wilson Brown to cancel the raid. In the resulting Japanese reaction, 17 medium bombers were sent to attack *Lexington*. Only two bombers survived fighter interception and antiaircraft fire, and no damage was suffered by the Americans. Meanwhile, in the Central Pacific, *Enterprise* hit Wake Atoll on February 24 and then Marcus Island on March 4.

Japanese Second Operational Phase objectives focused on the South Pacific, with the ultimate goal of blocking the SLOCs to Australia. Nimitz sent *Yorktown* to join *Lexington* in the region. On March 8, the Japanese landed troops at Lae and Salamaua on New Guinea. Fletcher, in charge of the carrier force, raced north to attack Japanese shipping off the two invasion points on March 10. Flying against no air opposition, American aviators mounted several attacks on the invasion force. Japanese losses, though minor, were the greatest so far in the war for a single day. Losses aside, this raid had strategic implications. With American carriers operating in the South Pacific, the Japanese assessed that further advances would require support from the carriers of the Striking Force.

Carrier *Hornet* joined the Pacific Fleet in March 1942. Now Nimitz had four operational carriers – *Saratoga* had been torpedoed by a Japanese submarine on January 9 and did not return to service until June.[20] With his latest reinforcement, Nimitz planned the most audacious raid yet. Protected by *Enterprise*, *Hornet* embarked 16 Army Air

Force B-25 medium bombers to strike Tokyo and two other Japanese cities on Honshu, Japan's largest island. Though launched from a longer range than planned, the Doolittle Raid achieved surprise and struck its targets. In fact, it was no more than a stunt conducted at the behest of Roosevelt to improve American morale. The operational penalty paid was the inability to get *Enterprise* and *Hornet* into the South Pacific in time to face the next major Japanese offensive.

In the first week of April, the Japanese decided on their sequencing of operations for the next few months. *Shokaku* and *Zuikaku* would detach from the Striking Force to lead a major thrust into the Coral Sea to occupy Port Moresby in early May. Once that operation was complete, the Combined Fleet would mass to occupy Midway during the first week of June. The Americans discerned enough from breaking IJN operational codes to understand that the first offensive was slated for the South Pacific. Nimitz left *Yorktown* and *Lexington* in the region to oppose it. He was even successful in convincing King to allow him to move *Enterprise* and *Hornet* into the region, leaving Oahu unprotected by carriers.

The first carrier-versus-carrier battle of the war, fought between May 7 and 8 in the Coral Sea, was both a strategic and tactical defeat for the Japanese. Both sides missed opportunities in the chaotic clash of carriers, and both sides suffered heavily. Japanese losses included light carrier *Shoho* sunk, *Shokaku* heavily damaged by bombs, and *Zuikaku* rendered out of action because of heavy losses to her air group. In exchange, *Lexington* was sunk and *Yorktown* moderately damaged. In addition, the invasion of Port Moresby was canceled, marking the first strategic Japanese defeat of the war.

To Yamamoto, the South Pacific adventure was just a sideshow. His primary operation was planned in June against Midway Atoll during which it was assumed Nimitz would commit his remaining forces. However, the Imperial Navy was reaching its culminating point. The three carriers lost at the Coral Sea meant that the Striking Force's fleet carrier edge over the Pacific Fleet was down to only one. Yamamoto designed his Midway operation as a decisive battle to finish off the Pacific Fleet, but Nimitz was not going to blindly stumble into a Japanese trap. Instead, armed with exquisite intelligence about Yamamoto's plans, he planned an ambush of the Striking Force. Yamamoto's planning was so poor that he failed to allow for an unforeseen American reaction,

WHY PEARL HARBOR MATTERS

and his forces were so spread out that even though this was the largest operation mounted by the Combined Fleet during the war, the Striking Force fought alone and was actually outnumbered in ships and aircraft.

Midway was the ultimate result of Yamamoto's failure at Pearl Harbor. Having poorly sequenced his operations and assembled the worst imaginable operational plan, his ill-considered bid for a decisive battle went awry. The Striking Force was totally defeated, losing *Akagi*, *Kaga*, *Soryu*, and *Hiryu*. *Yorktown* was also lost, but Japanese offensive power was blunted.

In less than six months after the attack on Pearl Harbor, the Combined Fleet reached its zenith and then began a slow decline. The Pacific Fleet, for which the future seemed so hopeless after the Pearl Harbor disaster, had kept the Japanese off balance with a series of pinprick raids, and then stopped a major Japanese offensive in the South Pacific. Faced with the massed strength of the Combined Fleet off Midway, Nimitz led his fleet to victory through the synchronized use of land- and carrier-based air power. Battleships were not even included in Nimitz's operational scheme. In contrast, Yamamoto, the bold gambler and supposed air power zealot, fought a battle based in part on the Great All-Out Battle Strategy, which included a major role for his battleships. It was as if Yamamoto learned little from his Pearl Harbor attack. As Nimitz was leading the Pacific Fleet into the carrier war that the Pacific War had become, Yamamoto still clung to the notion that the carrier was not the principal striking force of the fleet. By June 1942, it was absolutely clear that the Japanese had gained nothing from their temporary success at Pearl Harbor.

13

Kimmel and Short: Responsibility Misplaced?

All right, Morgan – I'll give you your answer. I never thought those little yellow sons-of-bitches could pull off such an attack, so far from Japan.[1]

                       Admiral Kimmel to Congressional Pearl Harbor
                  investigation Assistant Counsel Edward P. Morgan

This frank admission by Kimmel after the war may have been pithy, but investigations into the Pearl Harbor disaster began almost immediately after the attack. The first of no fewer than ten from 1941 until 1995 was conducted by Secretary of the Navy Frank Knox. From December 9 to 14, 1941, he went on an inspection trip to Oahu to survey the damage and talk to the principals. Both Kimmel and Short were honest with Knox and admitted that they had not expected an air attack. Knox expressed this mindset in a letter written on December 18: "They evidently had convinced themselves that an air attack by carrier born [sic] planes was beyond the realm of possibility, because they made no preparation whatever for such an attack."[2] Kimmel also related his opinion that he considered a submarine attack as the principal danger.[3] In short, both Kimmel and Short came across as unprepared for what had transpired. It was clear that neither commander considered an air attack as anything more than an extremely unlikely Japanese course of action. The underlying reason for this command failure was the expectation that any Japanese action would be conducted against targets in the Far East and that the Japanese had no means with which to strike a serious blow on Pearl Harbor.[4]

KIMMEL AND SHORT: RESPONSIBILITY MISPLACED?

Upon returning to Washington late on December 14, Knox proceeded to the White House to debrief Roosevelt. The following day, Knox returned to the White House and was joined by Hull, Stimson, and several others. Roosevelt provided guidance on what could be released to the public regarding losses. Later that day, Knox held a press conference during which he depicted the attack in a generally accurate manner. The loss of *Arizona, Utah, Cassin, Downes, Shaw,* and *Oglala* were announced. Several other ships were described as damaged, including *Oklahoma*. The full extent of personnel casualties was also released. Because it could not be avoided, the fact that the defenses were not on alert against an air attack was admitted. Knox promised an immediate investigation to gain the facts leading to the tragedy. Of note, the Army made no attempt at this point to ascertain the facts behind the attack. Knox's early efforts created the impression that the Navy alone was at the center of the tragedy.[5]

This first indication of American commanders on Oahu bearing responsibility for the failure to mount a respectable defense was sufficient cause for President Roosevelt to relieve both Kimmel and Short effective on December 17. In the months and years that followed, they became the focal points of ongoing efforts to attribute blame for the tragedy. General Martin was also relieved of his command, though he was given another post of lesser importance. Admiral Bellinger was left in place. Admiral Bloch also remained at his post, at least for the time being.

After Secretary Knox returned to Washington, Roosevelt directed a full-blown investigation to be started by a panel led by Supreme Court Associate Justice Owen J. Roberts along with two Army and two Navy flag officers. Stimson and Marshall agreed that the Army officers on the commission be Major General Frank R. McCoy, an infantry officer, and Brigadier General Joseph T. McNarney, the latter chosen because he was an Army Air Force pilot. The Navy members were Admiral William H. Standley, a retired former Chief of Naval Operations, and Rear Admiral Joseph M. Reeves, a proponent of naval aviation. It was difficult to find senior military officers who could act in a completely unbiased manner. On the surface, all four officers seemed very qualified. But there were signs that Stimson and Knox picked their respective members carefully with the thought that they would minimize the role Washington played in the disaster.

Standley was respected for being fair, as Roberts later admitted. Reeves had been hand-picked by Roosevelt to oversee Lend-Lease aid to Russia. At least one observer thought he was "very antagonistic to Kimmel and Short." After the commission issued its findings, Kimmel described him as such: "He was a Roosevelt man body and soul if indeed he had a soul."[6] McCoy came with a very high reputation and appeared set on getting to the bottom of the Pearl Harbor debacle. After the commission released its findings, Kimmel stated that McCoy was out to clear Washington by condemning Short and himself. McNarney was on his way to a new job to reorganize the War Department and was tied up on the Roberts Commission. Both Kimmel and Short expressed strong negative opinions on him, with Kimmel stating: "McNarney was a lying s.o.b. who had no more morals than a crawling snake."[7]

From the start, Justice Roberts focused on whether Washington, specifically the War Department, issued war warnings to commanders on Oahu. The newly appointed commission members got off to an uncertain start on December 17 when its members met with Secretary of War Henry Stimson and Secretary Knox. Stimson requested the meeting, even though he was obviously peripherally complicit in Pearl Harbor's lack of preparedness. Knox was also a primary player in the weeks before the attack, yet he was also allowed to discuss the results of his recent trip with the commission. Such a meeting was highly prejudicial. Another misstep followed on December 18 and 19 when the commission heard unsworn testimony from General George Marshall and Admiral Stark and key members of their staffs. Taking the unsworn testimony of key witnesses who asserted they had given Kimmel and Short adequate warning was also highly prejudicial.

On December 22, the commission began its hearings in Hawaii. Short testified the following day; Kimmel first appeared on December 27. Both men gave truthful and honest testimony while admitting that they had made errors. The last day of testimony was January 9, after which the commission departed Hawaii, arriving in Washington on January 15. Work was finished on January 23, and a copy of the report was delivered to the White House the next day. After surveying the report, Roosevelt directed that it be released to the public the next day.

The final version was presented in three parts. First was an introduction, followed by the findings of facts, and then the conclusions. Among the important conclusions were that Hull, Stimson, and Knox

KIMMEL AND SHORT: RESPONSIBILITY MISPLACED?

had fulfilled their obligations by monitoring the course of negotiations with Japan and passed pertinent information to Marshall and Stark. For their part, Marshall and Stark were found to have fulfilled their obligations by issuing warnings to Oahu. However, some fault was assigned to Washington since its warnings emphasized potential Japanese aggression in the Far East and possible sabotage on Oahu while failing to highlight the possibility of a major attack on Oahu. The War Department was also criticized for its failure to reply to Short's response to the "War Warning" message.

In the view of the commission, the blame for the failure to respond more forcefully to the Japanese attack fell squarely upon Kimmel and Short. The most important conclusions were:

16. The failure of the commanding general, Hawaiian Department, and the commander in chief, Pacific Fleet, to confer and cooperate with respect to the meaning of the warnings received and the measures necessary to comply with the orders given them under date of November 27, 1941, resulted largely from a sense of security due to the opinion prevalent in diplomatic, military, and naval circles, and in the public press, that any immediate attack by Japan would be in the Far East. The existence of such a view, however prevalent, did not relieve the commanders of the responsibility for the security of the Pacific Fleet and our most important outpost.

17. In the light of the warnings and directions to take appropriate action, transmitted to both commanders between November 27 and December 7, and the obligation under the system of coordination then in effect for joint cooperative action on their part, it was a dereliction of duty on the part of each of them not to consult and confer with the other respecting the meaning and intent of the warnings, and the appropriate measures of defense required by the imminence of hostilities. The attitude of each, that he was not required to inform himself of, and his lack of interest in, the measures undertaken by the other to carry out the responsibility assigned to such other under the provisions of the plans then in effect, demonstrated on the part of each a lack of appreciation of the responsibilities vested in them and inherent in their positions as commander in chief, Pacific Fleet, and commanding general, Hawaiian Department.

18. The Japanese attack was a complete surprise to the commanders and they failed to make suitable dispositions to meet such an attack. Each failed properly to evaluate the seriousness of the situation. These errors of judgment were the effective causes for the success of the attack.[8]

Significantly, Kimmel and Short were accused of dereliction of duty, not just the sin of misjudgment. Martin, Bloch, and Bellinger, along with the other subordinate commanders on Oahu, were spared. The entirety of the blame was cast at the two principal commanders. Much of the resulting concern with the commission's conclusion was the verdict of "dereliction of duty," though no such crime existed in the regulations governing the actions of American military personnel. The reason behind the use of this term remains cloudy, but when it was established, the commission was directed to ascertain whether "derelictions of duty" or "errors in judgment" were in evidence. Using the much harsher "dereliction of duty" may have simply been the result of the commission taking its instructions literally and using the terms provided to it.

Of all the Pearl Harbor investigations, the Roberts Commission was the most impactful, coming so soon after the event and initially being seen as an honest attempt to get at the truth. Its finding that "dereliction of duty" was in play also makes it the most controversial. It is also clear that the commission conducted its work with little regard for existing legal standards, with its Supreme Court justice exercising little oversight. The testimony gathered provided an invaluable source for understanding the events of December 7, 1941. In the immediate aftermath of the attack, it was clear that something had gone terribly wrong. The only question was whether this was due to errors in Washington or Oahu, or both. The Roberts Commission assessed that the commanders on Oahu had been given adequate warning. Ultimately, the readiness of the forces on Oahu was the responsibility of the senior commanders on the island, making them primarily responsible for what ensued.

Though published without the full supporting testimony (not released until February 17, 1946), the commission's report was generally supported by the nation. That it was released so quickly was also generally praised. However, no investigation conducted so soon after the causal event could have been perfect, and the Roberts Commission's work was not without flaws. The primary area of contention was the conclusion that the failures of Kimmel and Short were the result of "derelictions of duty."

Following the release of the report, Kimmel and Short came under increasing pressure to resign their commissions. When neither received any indication that they would be retained on active duty in some capacity, both requested they be allowed to retire. On February 28, the Navy and War Departments announced that their requests had been accepted, with Short's retirement effective that day and Kimmel's on the next. The announcement also indicated that both would be tried by courts-martial at a suitable time on the charges of "dereliction of duty."

Interest in a court-martial continued even as the war raged. One complicating factor was the two-year statute of limitations for a court-martial, which in this case would have been December 7, 1943. Both Kimmel and Short realized that their courts-martial could not be held during the war, and both agreed to a waiver of the statute of limitations.

To prepare for the upcoming but still not scheduled courts-martial of Kimmel and Short, Knox announced on February 25, 1944 that he had assigned Admiral Thomas C. Hart the job of collecting testimony from those with knowledge about the attack. Knox's intent was to get the testimony from key observers before they were possibly killed in the war. He gave little direction to Hart before dying on April 28, 1944. A well-connected and highly regarded officer, Hart was perhaps the perfect person for the job. Highly intelligent and experienced, he commanded the Asiatic Fleet at the start of the war.

Beginning on February 22, 1944, Hart interviewed a series of 40 witnesses, of which 19 had not been interviewed previously. Wanting to be fair, he urged Kimmel to take part in the process by also interviewing the witnesses, introducing information he thought pertinent. By this point, Kimmel was convinced that everyone was against him and he declined the opportunity to participate. By doing so, Kimmel probably lost the best chance to present his case. The Hart investigation concluded on June 15, 1944.

Despite Hart's work, Congress was not satisfied. At the behest of Kimmel and his lawyers, Congress introduced legislation for both an Army Board and a Navy Court of Inquiry. The twin investigations ran concurrently, the Army Board from July 20 until October 20 and the Navy Court of Inquiry from July 24 to October 19, 1944. Both panels were loaded with clearly biased officers. For the Army Board, Marshall selected members with whom he was not friendly and asserted that: "The only reason for their assignment was their availability."[9] Those who were chosen had a variety of grudges against Marshall.

For the Navy board, the biases were much more apparent. Kimmel still engendered sympathy and support in much of the Navy. The Navy Judge Advocate General, Rear Admiral T. L. Gatch, made no secret of his pro-Kimmel bias and predicted that the proceedings would develop into a contest between the Army and Navy to see which service would bear the primary fault for the disastrous lack of preparedness.[10]

First to appear before the Navy Court of Inquiry was Admiral Stark, who was ordered to return from Europe to render his testimony. His testimony was not as pro-Kimmel as certain members of the board desired. Short's testimony did not serve him well and seemed to strengthen the hand of those ready to blame the Army for everything. Kimmel took his turn on August 15. He blamed the Army for failing in its duty to protect the fleet. Most of all, he took issue with the finding of the Roberts Commission that his shortcomings represented a "dereliction of duty." On August 28, Kimmel won a hard-earned victory by obtaining the Magic reports. These were placed into the record despite justifiable security concerns.

The Army Pearl Harbor Board was held under different rules. There were no rules of evidence and hearsay, and speculation on the part of the witnesses was allowed. General Short and his lawyer could not attend the sessions of other witnesses or cross-examine them. Short testified on August 11 and 12 and again came across poorly.

The Army Board report was riddled with inaccuracies and unwarranted grievances over United States prewar policy. A bias against the War Department was evident. In its conclusion, the board stated that the Pearl Harbor disaster was due primarily to two causes. The first was Short's failure "adequately to alert his command for war" and the second was the War Department's failure to direct Short to order an adequate level of alert and to keep him fully informed about the state of relations between the United States and Japan, which, had it been done, might have made Short change his inadequate alert posture. Short was held responsible for not being ready to deal with an enemy attack and for not having implemented joint action with the Navy. The board reserved its full condemnation for Marshall and for his former Chief of War Plans, Brigadier General Leonard T. Gerow, who had drafted the November 27 "War Warning" message. Marshall was faulted for not keeping Short fully informed of developments and for not knowing the Hawaiian Department's true condition of readiness. Gerow was accused of a multitude of omissions, including producing a confusing message, not following up on Short's inadequate reply, and not directing Short to go to a higher level of alert.[11]

The report of the Navy Court took a different approach. Kimmel and his commanders were spared criticism because of extenuating circumstances – the general lack of resources for a full defense. It even supported Kimmel's decision not to use his PBYs for long-range patrols. Stark came in for some muted criticism for his failure to share some information with Kimmel. But no naval officer had committed any offenses, because "The attack of 7 December 1941, on Pearl Harbor, delivered under the circumstances then existing, was unpreventable. When it would take place was unpredictable."[12]

Rear Admiral Gatch endorsed the report with little comment. However, Chief of Naval Operations King rendered a much more sober assessment of the board's findings. He agreed that a court-martial did not seem consistent with the evidence, but that administrative action might be proper. To his credit, he also stated the obvious:

> Despite the evidence that no naval officer was at fault to a degree likely to result in conviction if brought to trial, nevertheless the Navy cannot evade a share of responsibility for the Pearl Harbor incident. That disaster cannot be regarded as an "act of God," beyond human power to prevent or mitigate.

In his view, the measures taken by Kimmel and Stark were faults of omission rather than ones of commission.[13]

With Roosevelt's blessing, neither report was made available to the public. In a public statement about the report, the new Secretary of the Navy James Forrestal only went as far to state that the available evidence did not warrant a court-martial of any naval officer but admitted that errors of judgment were made both in Washington and Hawaii. Stimson followed with his statement on December 1, 1944, asserting that Short's relief after the attack was appropriate because of errors in judgment, but that was sufficient action in itself. At this point, the finding of "dereliction of duty" in the Roberts Commission was off the table.

Not all questions had been answered by the Navy Court, so Forrestal decided to conduct a supplemental inquiry. He selected Vice Admiral H. Kent Hewitt, who was a capable officer with a fine war record but who was frank in his admiration of Kimmel.[14] From May 15 until July 11, 1945, Hewitt interviewed 37 witnesses, 21 of whom had not been previously interviewed. Many of those interviewed were involved with intelligence. At the end of this process, Hewitt's report included 29 conclusions. His report differed from the Navy Court's as Hewitt did not try to exonerate Kimmel, as he believed that Kimmel had received adequate indications that war was imminent. The report listed a number of measures Hewitt thought that Kimmel should have taken. For his part, Stark was admonished for not fully sharing pertinent information with Kimmel.[15]

Gatch endorsed the report and believed that neither Kimmel nor Stark was guilty of anything beyond errors of judgment. However, he also believed that the Navy was "morally obligated to order Admiral Kimmel tried by court-martial," if Kimmel insisted on requesting one.[16] King also concurred in general with Hewitt's report and with Gatch's recommendations.

Stimson had problems with the Army Board's efforts, particularly with regard to Magic not being adequately addressed. To gather the requisite information, he appointed Major Henry C. Claussen, the assistant recorder of the Army Board. Armed with a broad enabling memorandum, he interviewed 92 people from November 23, 1944 to September 12, 1945. Since the subjects were directed to provide testimony without reference to classification, Claussen was able to add much new information to the record.

Concurrently, Marshall ordered another investigation, this one by Colonel Carter W. Clarke, from September 14 to 16 and from July 13 to August 4, 1945. His efforts focused on gathering additional information on the handling of Magic. Twelve witnesses were interviewed. In particular, Clarke's inquiry provided valuable testimony on the November 28 "Winds Message" controversy, which resulted from the contention that the US had intercepted a clear warning of an impending Japanese attack on Pearl Harbor. The primary source fueling the controversy was Captain Laurance R. Safford, a well-respected senior Navy cryptologist who had testified at the Hart Inquiry, the Army

Board, and the Navy Court of Inquiry. From the testimony of others interviewed, it eventually became clear that no "winds execute" message had been received and that there was no record that any such message had been destroyed by Army intelligence personnel.

The death of President Roosevelt on April 12, 1945 complicated matters. The new President, Harry S. Truman, wanted the public to see the results of the Navy Court of Inquiry and the Army Board. Released on August 29, they were almost universally seen as not having gotten to the truth. As such, a full investigation by a joint committee of Congress was seen as necessary.

The Joint Congressional Committee on the Investigation of the Pearl Harbor Attack began its work on November 15, 1945 and ran until May 31, 1946. Ten members were appointed to the committee – three Democrats and two Republicans from both the House and Senate. As would be expected for such a controversial subject, invariably politics was injected into the process. As a result, the promise of revealing the truth was trampled as partisan politics came to dominate the proceedings. The Republicans wanted to show that the Roosevelt Democratic administration was fully aware of Japanese plans and wanted to drag the United States into war. In this scenario, Kimmel and Short were innocent victims.

Kimmel made his appearance on January 15 and proceeded to read a prepared statement of 108 pages. During the statement and in the days of testimony that followed until he was dismissed on January 21, he never admitted any fault. He placed all the blame for the surprise attack on Washington. He never admitted to any mistakes in the weeks leading to the attack, not even one of judgment. Short followed on December 22 with another long, prepared statement of his own. He also laid blame on Washington for not keeping him fully informed.

After five extensions to its original deadline, the committee released its report on July 20, 1946. In reality, it was divided into two parts, one focused on the surprise attack and the other on United States prewar foreign policy. As expected, the report was not unanimous. In the majority report, there were 12 conclusions. Five pertained to the prewar posturing and found that the Japanese bore "ultimate responsibility" for opening hostilities – in other words, the Japanese had not been tricked or provoked into attacking the United States. In regard to the responsibility for the Pearl Harbor disaster, the report came down hard on the commanders on Oahu. Failures in the following areas were noted:

(a) To discharge their responsibilities in the light of the warning received from Washington, other information possessed by them, and the principle of command by mutual cooperation.
(b) To integrate and coordinate their facilities for defense and to alert properly the Army and Navy establishments in Hawaii, particularly in the light of warnings and intelligence available to them during the period November 27 to December 7, 1941.
(c) To effect liaison on the basis designed to acquaint each of them with the operations of the other ... and to exchange fully all significant intelligence.
(d) To maintain a more effective reconnaissance within the limits of their equipment.
(e) To effect a statement of readiness throughout the Army and Navy establishments designed to meet all possible attacks.
(f) To employ the facilities, material, and personnel at their command ... in repelling the Japanese raiders.
(g) To appreciate the significance of intelligence and other information available to them.[17]

These conclusions were well reasoned. In the view of the committee, they were the result of errors of judgment and not derelictions of duty. Overall, the congressional investigation was the most valuable of the many inquiries into the Pearl Harbor attack.

Even after the series of investigations, there remained many officers and members of the public who believed that Kimmel and Short did all they could under the circumstances and were unfairly singled out for blame. In 1995, at the request of the Kimmel family, 95-year-old South Carolina Senator Strom Thurmond and chairman of the Senate Armed Services committee demanded that the Department of Defense reopen the case. The inquiry, the tenth since 1941, was led by Edward L. Dorn, Undersecretary of Defense for Personnel and Readiness.

Coming as it did 50 years after the end of the Pacific War, the Dorn Report represented an examination of the Pearl Harbor debacle by a new generation of officials. As such, it contained the promise of a detached and unbiased analysis of events. As had been the trend in the investigations following the Roberts Commission report, the Dorn report issued in December 1995 gave a balanced view and started: "Responsibility for the Pearl Harbor should not fall solely on the shoulders of Admiral

KIMMEL AND SHORT: RESPONSIBILITY MISPLACED?

Kimmel and General Short; it should be broadly shared."[18] The report detailed the shortcomings of the November 27 "War Warning" messages to both commanders and mentioned that Kimmel and Short did not receive some critical Magic-derived information.

After stating that responsibility for the disaster should be shared more broadly, the report did not absolve Kimmel and Short of accountability. The report recognized the unique position of a commander and his responsibility for the welfare of the personnel under his command and the extra requirements for judgements for high-level commanders. Perhaps the most important section of the Dorn Report states:

> The intelligence available to Admiral Kimmel and General Short was sufficient to justify a higher level of vigilance than they chose to maintain. They knew that war was imminent, they knew that Japanese tactics featured surprise attacks, and Admiral Kimmel (though not General Short) knew that the U.S. had lost track of Japan's carriers. Further, they had the resources to maintain a higher level of vigilance. Admiral Kimmel believed that the optimum aerial reconnaissance would require covering 360 degrees around Hawaii for a sustained period. The Navy clearly did not have enough planes for that. This does not mean, however, that Admiral Kimmel had to choose between ideal aerial reconnaissance and no aerial reconnaissance. The fleet also had cruisers and destroyers that could have been used as pickets to supplement air patrols, but were not.[19]

The report highlights what information was available to Kimmel and Short. This body of knowledge included:

- That their primary mission was to prepare for war with Japan, and that war with Japan was highly likely.
- That the Japanese would strike the first blow and that a surprise attack would precede a declaration of war.
- Such a surprise attack could include Japanese aircraft, submarines, or both.
- Pearl Harbor could be the target in the initial Japanese attacks; if so, these could be launched from aircraft carriers.
- The outline of a potential Japanese air attack had already been provided by Kimmel's and Martin's staffs. Both Kimmel and

Short made statements before the attack that they were aware of this possibility.
- Kimmel was aware that the Japanese carrier force was unlocated.
- Both knew that a Japanese attack could occur within days or weeks.[20]

The Dorn Report concluded that Kimmel and Short had not been victims of unfair official actions. In fact, their treatment was described as "substantively temperate," as it included only their relief from duty (described as warranted in the report) and reversion to two-star rank upon retirement, in accordance with the laws in force at the time. Thus, in response to the original request from Senator Thurmond, the Dorn Report did not recommend their promotion on the retired list.

The Pearl Harbor case continued to live on. In May 1999, Senators William V. Roth Jr and Joseph Biden, both from Delaware, responding to pressure from Kimmel supporters in their state, sponsored a nonbinding resolution to exonerate Kimmel and Short and restore them to their final ranks. It passed the Senate, 52-47. On October 30, 1999, Congress passed the 2001 National Defense Authorization Act, which included a section asking President Bill Clinton to restore Kimmel's and Short's ranks. Neither President Clinton nor his successor George W. Bush took any action on the matter.[21]

WHO WAS RESPONSIBLE?

There was plenty of blame to go around for the greatest disaster in American military history. Obviously, to place all the blame on one or two individuals would be unfounded. Early investigations made every attempt to place all of the blame on the two principal commanders on Oahu. This was unjust as the investigations subsequent to the Roberts Commission made clear.

Washington's Faults
There is no doubt that much of the responsibility for the Pearl Harbor disaster can be laid at Washington's door. It is important to remember that the Pearl Harbor attack was set up in 1940 by Roosevelt ordering the Pacific Fleet to Pearl Harbor as a deterrent to the Japanese.

KIMMEL AND SHORT: RESPONSIBILITY MISPLACED?

This deployment failed to achieve its objective. If Japanese leaders were faced with a situation they considered essential to the nation's survival, the presence of the fleet in Pearl Harbor (or back on the West Coast) would not matter. The transfer of the fleet to Pearl Harbor placed it in a potentially vulnerable position since it was no longer immune to a potential Japanese carrier air attack.

The case against Washington is built around the notion that it failed to provide warning to Kimmel and Short of the impending attack. This premise is flawed, as Washington did not possess information that Pearl Harbor was the planned target of a Japanese attack. What Washington did have was a growing body of evidence that a Japanese attack was likely, but no firm indication that Pearl Harbor was the intended target. There were disparate data points that provided hints that Pearl Harbor was under threat. But Washington was unable to connect the dots in time, and to suggest that analysts on Oahu would have done better is pure speculation. Despite conspiracy theorists' claims, there is no indication whatsoever that Washington possessed a clear idea of the targets and timing of the opening Japanese blow and deliberately withheld that information from commanders on Oahu.

On November 27, Washington issued "War Warning" messages to both Kimmel and Short. The clear intent of these was to increase the readiness of American forces throughout the Pacific and to prepare commanders for the probability of imminent hostilities with the Japanese. However, the actual effect of these messages was to divert attention away from Hawaii by highlighting the prospects for Japanese action in Southeast Asia. This brings two key points to the fore. The first was that there was no intelligence that any Japanese action was planned against Hawaii, while almost all available intelligence pointed to imminent Japanese action in Southeast Asia. This leads to the second point that elements of groupthink existed between Hawaii and Washington. The Japanese were on the march, but their aim was to seize critical areas in Southeast Asia, not to attack the Pacific Fleet. With this firm conviction, there was no likelihood that analysts in either location would correctly read the few signs pointing to Pearl Harbor as a target and contextualize them with Japan's opening blow. An example of this was provided when on December 3 Kimmel received word from Washington that the Japanese had ordered certain consulates and embassies to destroy their codes. Kimmel failed to appreciate the importance of this development.

A salient example of Washington failing to provide pertinent information to Oahu was the October 9 "bomb plot" message. The "bomb plot" involved a decoded Japanese message to their consulate in Hawaii that tasked a spy posing as the Foreign Office chancellor to divide the harbor into five sub-sections in grid format and note where particular ships were moored. Analysts in Washington did not appreciate the message's importance and failed to forward it to Oahu. Nevertheless, it was reasonable for Kimmel and Short to expect that any traffic between Tokyo and its diplomatic facilities that dealt with ships and facilities on Oahu would be provided to them.

If Washington's intent on November 27 was to force commanders on Oahu to recognize that war was coming, and that it was not beyond imagination to think that Oahu could be struck, the warning should have been more focused. For example, Rear Admiral Kelly Turner, author of the message from Stark to Kimmel, testified before the congressional hearings that he put the odds at 50-50 that the Japanese would conduct an air raid on Pearl Harbor. This was a postwar statement, so was likely influenced by his knowledge of actual events. But if this was Turner's thinking at the time, it failed to come across in the "War Warning" message.[22]

It is also clear that Washington failed to exert proper oversight of the commanders on Oahu. In particular, Short was directed to report what actions he was taking. When he did so by indicating that he was taking additional measures to guard against possible sabotage, Army officers in Washington, including Marshall, failed to point out to Short that his response was not adequate or in compliance with the spirit of the "War Warning" message. The same was true for Stark and the senior officers on the Navy Staff in Washington. Kimmel was neither given detailed instructions nor told to report on what measures he had taken. Assumedly, as war grew ever closer, Washington had every need to understand the posture of its most important military outpost in the Pacific. Had the principal commanders on Oahu been directed to provide regular situation reports on their actions, it would have become apparent very quickly that there was a huge gap between expectations in Washington and actions being implemented on Oahu.

Kimmel's and Short's Faults
The author believes that the bulk of the blame for the Pearl Harbor disaster falls on Kimmel and Short, and that Short was particularly culpable.

KIMMEL AND SHORT: RESPONSIBILITY MISPLACED?

Their collective intellectual unpreparedness and simple lack of imagination remains as breathtaking today as it was at the time and is simply indefensible. Blaming their inaction on Washington was an abdication of their responsibilities as commanders. Given their convictions that an attack on Oahu was impossible, even if Washington had provided everything it had on Japanese intentions, the notion that Kimmel and Short, aided by their staffs, could have correctly interpreted this information and fit it into the bigger picture of Japanese intentions is ludicrous. Having ascertained a potential threat to Oahu, it cannot be assumed that Kimmel and Short would have directed their forces to take prompt and effective action. Another massive handicap in this scenario was Kimmel's and Short's abysmal use of intelligence that focused on ascertaining Japanese intentions while totally disregarding Japanese capabilities.

There were sufficient forces on Oahu to put up a resolute defense had they been properly used. Just from the first descriptions of the attack coming into Washington, it was immediately apparent that something had gone terribly wrong. Roosevelt lamented to journalist Edward R. Murrow on the night of the attack: "Our planes were destroyed on the ground, by God, on the ground."[23] Another informed observer, Senator Tom Connally, chairman of the Foreign Relations Committee, was similarly astounded by the first reports: "I am amazed at the attack by Japan, but I am still more astounded at what happened to our Navy. They were all asleep. Where were our patrols?"[24]

While the shortcomings of senior commanders in Washington were serious, that does not absolve the commanders on Oahu from blame. At no point in the months leading up to the attack, as tensions mounted between Japan and the United States, did Kimmel or Short put into motion an agreement for joint operations and unity of command to defend Oahu. Though Kimmel and Short got along well personally and both had done an effective job tamping down the habitual friction that existed between the Army and the Navy, this goodwill never resulted in joint operations. This was utterly essential since neither service had the capability to defend Oahu by itself. Though monitoring the waters around Oahu was technically an Army responsibility, only the Navy had the trained assets available to perform that mission and had accepted responsibility for it. Air defense of the island and the fleet while in port was an Army responsibility but one dependent upon adequate early warning best provided by search planes from the Navy.

Though wholesale cross-service rivalry was not evident on Oahu, the two services were not able to work together efficiently. This was especially true with regards to sharing information. For example, tracking the principal Japanese threat to Hawaii – the Japanese carrier force – was a Navy responsibility. Kimmel never shared the information with Short that the Japanese carriers were not being tracked and that it was only assessed that they remained in Japanese home waters. For his part, Short failed to inform Kimmel that his reaction to the "War Warning" message was to emphasize defense against sabotage, not against an external threat.

The failure of Kimmel and Short to exchange information had far-reaching implications. In the case of Short, he was left to assume that the Navy was conducting robust long-range reconnaissance and was keeping much of the fleet at sea. Confident that he would receive warning to place his command on a higher alert status if necessary, he assumed Alert Number 1.[25] Asked by the Robert Commission's General McNarney why he didn't seek more detailed information on the status of Navy reconnaissance around Oahu, Short replied: "I did not feel that it was my business to try to tell Admiral Kimmel how he would conduct his reconnaissance. I think he would have resented it very much."[26] Kimmel had his own unfounded assumptions regarding Short's defensive preparedness and thus felt comfortable not bringing the fleet to a higher alert level.

When he received the "War Warning" message, Kimmel did not bother to consult with all his key officers regarding potential actions. Rear Admiral Bloch, as Commander of the 14th Naval District and thus responsible for local defense, did not see it until the following day. It failed to stir him to action. This is not surprising since he had consistently placed administrative factors over security of the fleet. His lack of flexibility was demonstrated when he advocated with Admirals Richardson and Kimmel for a fixed schedule of fleet operations so as to save tug costs and to not interfere with dredging operations in the channel.[27] He was also content to let the PBY force remain on normal alert because he considered conditions to be normal, even after receipt of the "War Warning" message.[28] Bellinger's command fell under Bloch's authority, yet the latter made no attempt to initiate or coordinate joint

KIMMEL AND SHORT: RESPONSIBILITY MISPLACED?

Army–Navy air operations to surveil the waters around Oahu. Kimmel did not show the "War Warning" message to his commander, Arthur C. Davis, his fleet aviation officer, or Rear Admiral Bellinger, Commander Patrol Wing Two, who would have been the principal drivers in instigating an enhanced search program. Kimmel also decided not to share the message with his lower level subordinate commanders. Had this been done, it is very likely that many of the ships in harbor on December 7 would have been at a higher alert level.

By its very nature, a Japanese attack against the formidable defenses on Oahu was going to be a surprise attack. As the Martin-Bellinger Report from March 1941 pointed out, such an attack could come without any warning. Even if Washington provided no warnings, there were signs available to Kimmel and his staff that the Japanese were planning something. The Japanese carriers had disappeared, and on December 1 the Imperial Navy took the unprecedented step of changing its call signs for the second time in a month. None of this made Kimmel reconsider his focus on training and move to a defensive posture. Kimmel may not have been well served by his staff, in particular by Bloch or his intelligence officer Layton, but it was the commander who set the tone on Oahu that he was not concerned as to a direct attack on the fleet.

The first duty of a commander is to safeguard his forces from enemy action – what is called "force protection" in current jargon. Both Kimmel and Short utterly failed in this regard. Neither took any measure to prepare against a Japanese air attack, clearly the most dangerous enemy course of action. Kimmel was focused on his own offensive plans, which were impossible without ensuring the safety of his own forces from attack. Though it was clear from the available intelligence and from the "War Warning" message that hostilities with Japan were imminent and perhaps only days away, Kimmel took no measures to safeguard the fleet. Movement of forces to Wake Island and Midway Atoll were prudent measures, but these were linked to Kimmel's planned offensive actions and not defense of the fleet in Pearl Harbor.

On December 7, none of Kimmel's 67 PBY long-range patrol aircraft were on patrol missions around Oahu. This action alone meant that the Japanese were virtually guaranteed of achieving surprise. This lack of reconnaissance activity was not coordinated with the Army, nor was the Army even informed of it. In his 1955 book explaining his actions,

Kimmel stated: "A search of all sectors of approach to an island base is the only type of search that deserves the name."[29] Such a claim indicates clearly that Kimmel did not understand what was required. Kimmel explained his reasoning for not having ordered any search operations with this assertion:

> If I had instituted a distant search of any one hundred twenty-eight-degree sector around Oahu on or after November 27, within the foreseeable future, I would have deprived the Pacific Fleet of any efficient patrol plane force for its prescribed war missions.[30]

Thus Kimmel reaffirmed his ill-considered prioritization of training over operational security.

As the prospect of hostilities increased, Kimmel handled his fleet poorly. On December 7, the majority of the fleet was present at Pearl Harbor, including all eight of the fleet's operational battleships. Both of the fleet's operational carriers were absent, but it should be highlighted that *Enterprise* was slated to return by the morning of December 7 but had fallen behind schedule due to heavy seas. Had she been in harbor that morning, the Japanese would have been presented with almost all of Kimmel's capital ships as targets. This overconcentration was entirely preventable and Kimmel should have been aware of the potential danger. The primary objective of an air raid on Pearl Harbor was the ships of the Pacific Fleet. Having so much of the fleet's fighting strength in port at the same time was unwise. The reason given by Kimmel why he did not order some of the battleships out of harbor after receiving the "War Warning" message was to avoid alarming the population. Such a consideration was clearly secondary to the safety of a significant portion of the fleet; furthermore, had dispersal of the fleet been practiced in the weeks or months before the attack, it would not even have been noticed. In addition, none of the ships massed in port were at a higher level of readiness aside from the duty destroyers. Ship's boilers were cold and at least two battleships had hatch covers open or loosened over anti-torpedo bulges.

Another step that Kimmel could have taken was to augment the number of antiaircraft guns that were manned and ready for action. Per the existing state of readiness laid down in an October 14, 1941 letter to the fleet, only one ship with at least four antiaircraft guns was required to always be ready in any sector.[31] Vice Admiral Pye had also ordered that his battleships maintain two 5-inch and two .50-caliber machine guns in a ready status.[32] This proved inadequate in the opening minutes of the attack. In the days following the "War Warning" message, a higher state of readiness would have been warranted. Had more guns been manned and ready for immediate action, the success of the initial wave of torpedo bombers would have been reduced.

In his 1955 book, Kimmel also defended his handling of the fleet in the days before the attack. He puts forth the self-serving argument that: "At no time during 1941 were all ships of the fleet in Pearl Harbor."[33] While this was undoubtedly true, it tells only half the story. On December 7, 1941, nine of the fleet's ten operational capital ships were scheduled to be in port. The Japanese had been recording the fleet's predictable operating pattern and picked Sunday, December 7 as the attack day based on the fleet's demonstrated routine. Kimmel offered two reasons for the concentration of fleet assets. One was a fueling issue represented by declining fuel stocks and only a handful of oilers. Like his approach to the use of long-range patrol aircraft, Kimmel viewed matters in an all-or-nothing context. The other reason was that, since the two carriers were assigned other missions in the days immediately before the attack, "the battleship force was kept in Pearl Harbor. To send them to sea without air cover for any prolonged period would have been a dangerous course."[34] Of course, leaving them in port and vulnerable to air attack was even more dangerous.

Of the two principal commanders, General Short deserves a greater share of blame. That stems from the fact that he appeared not to understand his primary operational mission of protecting the fleet. This was shown early after he assumed command when he ordered that Army Air Force personnel on Oahu needed to undergo six to eight weeks of training as infantrymen at the expense of their air-related duties and training.[35] This failure to understand the nature of the threat resulted in aircraft lined up in neat rows. Short's lack of air defense preparations was egregious. This began with the failure to create a functioning and effective Information Center as part of the island's air warning system. Without this capability, effective air defense was impossible. Of course, the Navy had to fully participate in the operation of an effective

Information Center, so the failure to create this critical command and control capability rests with both Kimmel and Short. However, Short controlled the operations of the six radar stations. On the day of the attack, they performed well when active but since the information they gained had nowhere to go to receive the importance it deserved, this capability was irrelevant.

Of the 138 modern fighters on Oahu on the morning of the attack, only 84 were operational.[36] On December 77, not a single American fighter was fully armed, fueled, and ready to respond to a potential warning. This fact alone underlines the culpability of Short and his failure to give any credence to the possibility that an external threat existed to the forces and facilities on Oahu. That these fighters were not dispersed but lined up in neat rows for the Japanese to target is inconceivable. Short was content to expose his entire fighter force to destruction in the worst-case scenario of a large-scale Japanese air attack while overcompensating for the sabotage risk that might have resulted at worst in the destruction or damage of a few dispersed fighters at the hands of a small number of saboteurs. Short's overall response to the "War Warning" was to degrade his readiness to deal with an external threat – a black mark that no amount of revisionist history can undo. For his part, the safety of Kimmel's fleet while in port was totally dependent on the steps taken by the Army. To his discredit, Kimmel never made any effort to verify with Short whether these defenses were adequate or not.

Neither of the principal commanders created any urgency for their commands to stress combat readiness. A peacetime garrison mentality with a focus on training was allowed to become the norm as Oahu was far away from any expected Japanese attack. The result was an inability to take advantage of any of the many warnings received from the Japanese on December 7 that an attack was imminent. Kimmel's command and control system proved resistant to warnings about enemy submarine activity hours before the air attack. Even though Kimmel expected potential submarine activity, this was treated in isolation as there was no way the personnel on watch could conceive it was part of a coordinated attack. When reports were received of enemy submarine activity, the peacetime command system was not able to respond quickly enough. The same peacetime mentality prevailed for the Army garrison. The air warning system designed to protect the fleet failed utterly despite the excellent performance of multiple radar stations on Oahu. When reports of potentially hostile air activity were generated, there was no ability to examine them with any degree of rigor. Instead, they were easily explained away, allowing the peacetime mentality to remain undisturbed.

Appendix 1

United States Order of Battle, December 7, 1941

United States Navy

United States Pacific Fleet
Commander: Admiral Husband E. Kimmel
Chief of Staff: Captain William W. Smith
Operations Officer & Assistant Chief of Staff: Captain Walter S. DeLany
War Plans Officer: Captain Charles H. McMorris

Forces in or near Pearl Harbor
(does not include non-commissioned craft)

Battle Force
Commander: Vice Admiral William S. Pye
Chief of Staff: Captain Harold C. Train

Battleships, Battle Force
Commander: Rear Admiral Walter S. Anderson

    Battleship Division 1
    Commander: Rear Admiral Isaac Campbell Kidd

        Battleships
        Arizona (BB 39) (Captain Franklin Van Valkenburgh)
        Nevada (BB 36) (Captain Francis W. Scanland)
        Pennsylvania (BB 38) (Captain Charles M. Cooke, Jr)

APPENDIX I

Battleship Division 2
Commander: Rear Admiral David W. Bagley

   Battleships
   California (BB 44) (Captain Joel W. Bunkley)
   Oklahoma (BB 37) (Captain Howard D. Bode)
   Tennessee (BB 43) (Captain Charles E. Reordan)

Battleship Division 4
Commander: Rear Admiral Walter S. Anderson

   Battleships
   Maryland (BB 46) (Captain D. C. Godwin)
   West Virginia (BB 48) (Captain Mervyn Bennion)

Cruisers, Battle Force
Commander: Rear Admiral Herbert F. Leary

   Cruiser Division 6
     Heavy cruisers
     New Orleans (CA 32)
     San Francisco (CA 38)

   Cruiser Division 9
     Light cruisers
     Phoenix (CL 46)
     Honolulu (CL 48)
     St Louis (CL 49)
     Helena (CL 50)

Destroyers, Battle Force
Commander: Rear Admiral Milo F. Draemel

Destroyer Flotilla 1
Commander: Rear Admiral Robert A. Theobald

     Light cruiser: *Raleigh* (CL 7)
     Destroyer tenders: *Dobbin* (AD 3), *Whitney* (AD 3)

Destroyer Squadron 1
Destroyer: *Phelps* (DD 360)

Destroyer Division 1
Destroyers: *Dewey* (DD 349), *Hull* (DD 350), *MacDonough* (DD 351), *Worden* (DD 352)

Destroyer Division 2
Destroyers: *Farragut* (DD 348), *Dale* (DD 353), *Monaghan* (DD 351), *Aylwin* (DD 355)

Destroyer Squadron 3
Destroyer: *Selfridge* (DD 357)

Destroyer Division 5
Destroyers: *Reid* (DD 369), *Conyngham* (DD 371), *Cassin* (DD 372), *Downes* (DD 375)

Destroyer Division 6
Destroyers: *Cummings* (DD 365), *Case* (DD 370), *Shaw* (DD 373), *Tucker* (DD 374)

Destroyer Flotilla 2
Commander: Rear Admiral Milo F. Draemel

Light cruiser: *Detroit* (CL 8)

Destroyer Division 7
Destroyers: *Bagley* (DD 386), *Blue* (DD 387), *Helm* (DD 388), *Henley* (DD 391)

Destroyer Division 8
Destroyers: *Jarvis* (DD 393), *Mugford* (DD 389), *Ralph Talbot* (DD 390), *Patterson* (DD 392)

Minecraft, Battle Force
Commander: Rear Admiral William R. Furlong

APPENDIX I

Minelayer: *Ogala* (CM 4)

Mine Squadron 1

Mine Division 1
Light minelayers: *Preble* (DM 20), *Pruitt* (DM 22), *Sicard* (DM 21), *Tracy* (DM 19)

Mine Division 2
Light minelayers: *Breese* (DM 18), *Gamble* (DM 15), *Montgomery* (DM 17), *Ramsay* (DM 16)

Mine Squadron 2

Mine Division 4
High-speed minesweepers: *Perry* (DMS 17), *Trever* (DMS 16), *Wasmuth* (DMS 15), *Zane* (DMS 14)

Aircraft, Scouting Force
Commander: Rear Admiral Patrick N. L. Bellinger
Operations Officer: Captain Logan C. Ramsey

VJ-1	NAS Pearl Harbor	9 J2F Duck, 9 JRS
VJ-2	NAS Pearl Harbor	10 J2F Duck, 2 PBY-1 Catalina
Patrol Wing 1	NAS Kaneohe Bay	1 OS2U Kingfisher
VP-11	NAS Kaneohe Bay	12 PBY-5 Catalina
VP-12	NAS Kaneohe Bay	12 PBY-5 Catalina
VP-14	NAS Kaneohe Bay	12 PBY-5 Catalina

Seaplane tender (Small): *Avocet* (AVP 4)
Seaplane tender (Destroyer): *Hulbert* (AVP 6)

Patrol Wing 2	NAS Pearl Harbor	
VP-22	NAS Pearl Harbor	14 PBY-4 Catalina
VP-23	NAS Pearl Harbor	12 PBY-5 Catalina
VP-24	NAS Pearl Harbor	6 PBY-4 Catalina

Seaplane tenders: *Curtiss* (AV 4), *Tangier* (AV 8)
Seaplane tender (small): *Swan* (AVP 7)
Seaplane tender (destroyer): *Thornton* (AVD 11)

In addition to the Catalinas on Ford Island, there were many other aircraft present which were normally based on the Pacific Fleet's large warships. These included at least 15 Vought OS2U Kingfishers from the battleships and at least four Curtiss SOC Seagulls from the cruisers.

Ford Island was also the home of a small number of reserve aircraft for the Pacific Fleet's three carrier air groups. These included one F4F Wildcat from *Saratoga*'s VF-3; three F2A Buffalo fighters from *Lexington*'s VF-2, and one reserve SBD Dauntless for *Lexington*; *Enterprise* had four reserve Wildcats for VF-6 and two Dauntlesses at Ford Island.

Submarines, Scouting Force
Commander: Rear Admiral Thomas Withers, Jr

Submarines: *Narwhal* (SS 167), *Dolphin* (SS 169), *Cachalot* (SS 170), *Tautog* (SS 199)

Submarine rescue ship: *Widgeon* (ASR 1)

Submarine tender: *Pelias* (AS 14)

Base Force
Commander: Rear Admiral William L. Calhoun

Miscellaneous auxiliaries: *Argonne* (AG 31), *Sumner* (AG 32), *Utah* (AG 16)

Cargo ship: *Vega* (AK 17) (located at Honolulu)

Service Squadron 2
Repair ships: *Medusa* (AR 1), *Vestal* (AR 4)
Base repair ship: *Rigel* (ARb 1)
Hospital ship: *Solace* (AH 5)

APPENDIX I

Ocean-going tug: *Keosanqua* (AT 38), *Navajo* (AT 64) (12nm outside Pearl Harbor entrance)

Service Squadron 6
Minesweepers: *Bobolink* (AM 20), *Grebe* (AM 43), *Rail* (AM 26), *Tern* (AM 31), *Turkey* (AM 13), *Vireo* (AM 52)

Service Squadron 8
General stores issue ships: *Castor* (AKS 1), *Antares* (AKS 3) (at Pearl Harbor entrance)
Oilers: *Neosho* (AO 23), *Ramapo* (AO 12)
Ammunition ship: *Pyro* (AE 1)

14th Naval District
Commandant, Rear Admiral Claude C. Bloch

Gunboat: *Sacramento* (PG 19)

Destroyer Division 80
 Destroyers: *Allen* (DD 66), *Chew* (DD 106), *Schley* (DD 103), *Ward* (DD 139)

Coastal minesweepers: *Cockatoo* (AMc 8), *Condor* (AMc 14), *Crossbill* (AMc 9), *Reedbird* (AMc 30)

Ocean-going tugs: *Ontario* (AT 13), *Sunnadin* (AT 28)

Coast Guard cutter: *Taney* (berthed in Honolulu)

Pacific Fleet Forces not in Pearl Harbor

Returning from Wake Island: Task Force 8
Commander: Vice Admiral William F. Halsey

Carrier: *Enterprise* (CV 6)
 Air Group: VF-6 (19 Grumman F4F Wildcats)
   VB-6/VS-6 (38 Douglas SBD Dauntlesses)
   VT-6 (22 Douglas TBD Devastators)

PEARL HARBOR

Heavy cruisers: *Chester* (CA 27), *Northampton* (CA 26), *Salt Lake City* (CA 25)
Destroyers: *Balch* (DD 363), *Benham* (DD 397), *Craven* (DD 382), *Dunlap* (DD 384), *Ellet* (DD 398), *Fanning* (DD 385), *Gridley* (DD 380), *Maury* (DD 401), *McCall* (DD 400)

Returning from Midway Atoll: Task Force 12
Commander: Rear Admiral John H. Newton
Carrier: *Lexington* (CV 2)
   Air Group: VF-2 (16 Grumman F2A Buffalos)
                    VB-2/VS-2 (32 Douglas SBD Dauntlesses)
                    VT-2 (14 Douglas TBD Devastators)

Heavy cruisers: *Astoria* (CA 34), *Chicago* (CA 29), *Portland* (CA 33)
Destroyers: *Drayton* (DD 366), *Flusser* (DD 368), *Lamson* (DD 367), *Porter* (DD 356), *Mahan* (DD 364)

En route Midway Atoll: Seaplane Tender: *Wright* (AV 1)

On Midway Atoll: VP-21 (12 PBY-4 Catalinas)

In the vicinity of Johnston Atoll:
Heavy cruiser: *Indianapolis* (CA 35)
High-speed minesweepers: *Dorsey* (DMS 1), *Elliot* (DMS 4), *Hopkins* (DMS 13), *Long* (DMS 12)

South of Oahu:
Heavy cruiser: *Minneapolis* (CA 35)
High-speed minesweepers: *Boggs* (DMS 3), *Chandler* (DMS 9), *Hovey* (DMS 11), *Lamberton* (DMS 2)

Located southeast of Oahu: Minesweeper *Robin* (AM 3)

In the area of Phoenix Islands:
Heavy cruiser: *Pensacola* (CA 24) escorting motor torpedo boat tender *Niagara* (AGP 1), Navy transports *Chaumont* (AP 5), *Republic* (AP 33), and six Army transports and freighters

APPENDIX I

Returning from Manila:
Heavy cruiser: *Louisville* (CA 24) escorting two Army transports

Located at Lahaina:
Seaplane tender (destroyer): *McFarland* (AVD 14)
VJ-3 (4 JRB, 2 BT-1, 1 JRF, 1 J2F)

Submarines:
Gudgeon (SS 211) (off Lahaina)
Thresher (SS 200) and destroyer *Litchfield* (DD 363) (50nm northwest of Oahu returning from Wake Atoll patrol)
Plunger (SS 179), *Pollack* (SS-180), *Pompano* (SS 181) (200nm east of Oahu)
Tambor (SS 200), *Triton* (SS 201) off Wake Island
Argonaut (SS 166), *Trout* (SS 202) off Midway Atoll

En route to Wake Island: Ocean-going tug: *Sonoma* (AT 12)

On the West Coast or off Alaska (either in port or in transit):
Carrier: *Saratoga* (CV 3)
Battleship: *Colorado* (BB 45)
Light cruiser: *Concord* (CL 10)
9 destroyers
10 submarines
25 auxiliaries of various types

In Panama: Light cruiser: *Trenton* (CL 11)

United States Marine Corps

Marine Air Group 21   Marine Corps Air Station Ewa
Commander: Colonel Claude A. Larkin

VMF-211	Ewa	11 F4F Wildcats, 1 SNJ-3 (12 Wildcats on Wake Island)
VMSB-231	Ewa	7 SB2U-3 Vindicators (18 SB2U-3 Vindicators on Midway Atoll)

VMSB-232   Ewa   22 SBD Dauntlesses
VMJ-252   Ewa   2 R3D-2, 2 J2F-4, 1 JO-2, 1 JRS-1, 1
                 SB2U-3, 1 SBD Dauntless

United States Army

Hawaiian Department
Commander: Lieutenant General Walter C. Short

Hawaiian Air Force
Commander: Major General Frederick L. Martin

Hickam Field, 17th Air Base Group
Commander: Colonel William E. Farthing

Aircraft present on December 7, 1941:
12 B-17D, 32 B-18, 12 A-20A, 2 P-26A, 2 A-12A, 2 C-33, 1 B-24A

18th Bombardment Wing
Commander: Brigadier General Jacob H. Rudolph

5th Bombardment Group
   23rd Bombardment Squadron
   31st Bombardment Squadron
   58th Bombardment Squadron
   72d Bombardment Squadron
   4th Reconnaissance Squadron

11th Bombardment Group
   26th Bombardment Squadron
   42d Bombardment Squadron
   50th Reconnaissance Squadron

Wheeler Field, 18th Air Base Group
Commander: Colonel William J. Flood

APPENDIX I

Aircraft present on December 7, 1941:
12 P-40C, 87 P-40B, 39 P-36A, 6 P-26A, 6 P-26B, 3 B-12A, 4 AT-6, 3 OA-9, 1 OA-8

14th Pursuit Wing
Commander: Brigadier General Howard C. Davidson

15th Pursuit Group
    45th Pursuit Squadron
    46th Pursuit Squadron
    47th Pursuit Squadron (deployed to Haleiwa Field prior to December 7)
    72d Pursuit Squadron

18th Pursuit Group
    6th Pursuit Squadron
    19th Pursuit Squadron
    44th Pursuit Squadron (deployed to Bellows Field prior to December 7)
    73rd Pursuit Squadron
    78th Pursuit Squadron

Bellows Field
Commander: Lieutenant Colonel Leonard D. Weddington
86th Observation Squadron

Aircraft present on December 7, 1941:
2 O-49, 7 O-48B, 1 B-18

Appendix 2

Imperial Japanese Navy Forces Involved in the Attack on Pearl Harbor

Combined Fleet (Admiral Yamamoto Isoroku)

1st Air Fleet (Vice Admiral Nagumo Chuichi)
Chief of Staff: Rear Admiral Kusaka Ryunosuke
Senior Staff Officer: Commander Oishi Tamotsu
Air Officer: Commander Genda Minoru

Air Attack Unit
  Carrier Division 1 (Nagumo)

  Carrier *Akagi* (flag) (Captain Hasegawa Kiichi)
    Air Officer: Commander Shogo Masuda
    Horizontal Bomber Unit: Commander Fuchida Mitsuo
    Torpedo Bomber Unit: Lieutenant Commander Murata Shigeharu
    Carrier Bomber Unit: Lieutenant Chihaya Takehiko
    Fighter Unit: Lieutenant Commander Itaya Shigeru

  Carrier *Kaga* (Captain Okada Jisaku)
    Air Officer: Commander Sata Naohito
    Horizontal Bomber Unit: Lieutenant Commander Hashiguchi Kakuichi
    Torpedo Bomber Unit: Lieutenant Kitajima Kazuyoshi
    Carrier Bomber Unit: Lieutenant Makino Saburo
    Fighter Unit: Lieutenant Shiga Yoshio

APPENDIX 2

Carrier Division 2 (Rear Admiral Yamaguchi Tamon)

Carrier *Soryu* (flag) (Captain Yanagimoto Ryusaku)
    Air Officer: Commander Kusumoto Ikuto
    Horizontal Bomber Unit: Lieutenant Abe Heijiro
    Torpedo Bomber Unit: Lieutenant Nagai Tsuyoshi
    Carrier Bomber Unit: Lieutenant Commander Egusa Takeshige
    Fighter Unit: Lieutenant Suganami Masaji

Carrier *Hiryu* (Captain Kaku Tomeo)
    Air Officer: Commander Amagai Takahisa
    Horizontal Bomber Unit: Lieutenant Commander Kosumi Tadashi
    Torpedo Bomber Unit: Lieutenant Matsumura Hirata
    Carrier Bomber Unit: Lieutenant Kobayashi Michio
    Fighter Unit: Lieutenant Okajima Kiyoguma

Carrier Division 5 (Rear Admiral Hara Chuichi)

Carrier *Shokaku* (Captain Jojima Takatsugu)
    Air Officer: Commander Wada Tetsujiro
    Carrier Attack Plane Unit: Lieutenant Ichihara Tatsuo
    Carrier Bomber Unit: Lieutenant Commander Takahashi Kakuichi
    Fighter Unit: Lieutenant Kaneko Tadashi

Carrier *Zuikaku* (Captain Yokokawa Ichibei)
    Air Officer: Commander Shimoda Hisao
    Carrier Attack Plane Unit: Shimazaki Shigekazu
    Carrier Bomber Unit: Lieutenant Commander Akira Sakamoto
    Fighter Unit: Lieutenant Sato Masao

Directly attached to Carrier Division 5: Destroyer *Akigumo*

Support Unit (Vice Admiral Mikawa Gunichi)

Battleship Division 3 (Mikawa)

    Battleships *Hiei* and *Kirishima*

Cruiser Division 8 (Rear Admiral Abe Hiroaki)

    Heavy Cruisers *Tone* and *Chikuma*

Escort Unit (Rear Admiral Omori Sentaro)

    Destroyer Squadron 1 (Omori)

    Light Cruiser *Abukuma* (flag)
    Destroyer Division 17
        Destroyers *Hamakaze, Isokaze, Tanikaze, Urakaze*
    Destroyer Division 18 (Detached from Destroyer Squadron 2)
        Destroyers *Arare, Kagero, Kasumi, Shiranuhi*

Midway Neutralization Unit (Captain Ohishi Kaname)

    Destroyer Division 7
        Destroyers *Sazanami, Ushio*
        Oiler *Shiriya*

Patrol Unit (Captain Imaizumi Kijiro)

    Submarine Division 2
        Submarines *I-19, I-21, I-23*

Supply Unit (Captain Daido Masanao)

    First Supply Train
        Oilers *Kyokuto Maru, Kenyo Maru, Kokuyo Maru, Shinkoku Maru* (*Akebono Maru* was also available but did not take part in the operation)

    Second Supply Train
        Oilers *Toho Maru, Toei Maru, Nippon Maru*

Sixth Fleet (Vice Admiral Shimizu Mitsumi)

    Submarine Squadron 1 (Rear Admiral Tsutomu Sato)

APPENDIX 2

Submarines *I-9*, *I-15*, *I-17*, *I-25*

Submarine Squadron 2 (Rear Admiral Yamazaki Shigeki)
Submarines *I-1*, *I-2*, *I-3*, *I-4*, *I-5*, *I-6*, *I-7*

Submarine Squadron 3 (Rear Admiral Miwa Shigeyoshi)
Submarines *I-8*, *I-68*, *I-69*, *I-70*, *I-71*, *I-72*, *I-73*, *I-74*, *I-75*

Special Attack Unit (Captain Sasaki Hanku, embarked on *I-22*; Lieutenant Iwasa Naoji, commander of the midget submarines)
Submarines *I-16* (with Type A midget submarine *I-16A*); *I-18* (with Type A midget submarine *I-18A*); *I-20* (with Type A midget submarine *I-20A*); *I-22* (with Type A midget submarine *I-22A*); *I-24* (with Type A midget submarine *I-24A*)

Submarine Reconnaissance Unit
Submarines *I-10*, *I-26*

Appendix 3

Fates of Imperial Japanese Navy Ships Involved in the Attack on Pearl Harbor

The fate of the ships taking part in the Hawaiian Operation is representative of Japan's fate. Not only was the nation destroyed by the ensuing war, but almost every ship taking part in the attack was sunk during the course of the war. The only exception was destroyer *Ushio*, which did not take part in the main attack but in the subsidiary operation to shell the airfield on Midway Atoll.

CARRIERS

Akagi – struck by aircraft from carrier *Enterprise* at the Battle of Midway on June 4, 1942; scuttled on June 5

Kaga – struck by aircraft from carrier *Enterprise* at the Battle of Midway on June 4, 1942; scuttled on June 4

Soryu – struck by aircraft from carrier *Yorktown* at the Battle of Midway June 4, 1942; scuttled on June 4

Hiryu – struck by aircraft from carriers *Enterprise* and *Yorktown* at the Battle of Midway on June 4, 1942; sank June 5

Shokaku – sunk by American submarine *Cavalla* on June 19, 1944 during the Battle of the Philippine Sea

Zuikaku – sunk by American carrier aircraft on October 25, 1944 off Cape Engano during the Battle of Leyte Gulf. *Zuikaku* was the last Pearl Harbor carrier to be sunk, a fact gleefully noted by the Americans at the time.

APPENDIX 3

BATTLESHIPS

Hiei – crippled by USN surface units on November 13, 1942 during the First Naval Battle of Guadalcanal; sank after a series of American air attacks later in the day

Kirishima – Sunk by battleship *Washington* on November 15, 1942 during the Second Naval Battle of Guadalcanal

HEAVY CRUISERS

Chikuma – sunk by aircraft from three escort carriers on October 25, 1944 in the Battle off Samar during the Battle of Leyte Gulf

Tone – struck by carrier aircraft from Task Force 38 near Kure on July 24 and 28, 1945; scuttled on July 29

LIGHT CRUISER

Abukuma – torpedoed by an American PT Boat on October 25, 1944 in the Battle of Surigao Strait during the Battle of Leyte Gulf; sunk by Army Air Force B-24 bombers on October 26

DESTROYERS

Akigumo – sunk by submarine *Redfin* on April 11, 1944 southeast of Zamboanga Island in the Philippines

Arare – sunk by submarine *Growler* on July 5, 1942 off Kiska Island in the Aleutians

Hamakaze – sunk by carrier aircraft from Task Force 58 on April 7, 1945 during battleship *Yamato*'s sortie to Okinawa

Isokaze – struck by carrier aircraft from Task Force 58 on April 7, 1945 during battleship *Yamato*'s sortie to Okinawa; scuttled the same day

Kagero – struck a mine on May 8, 1943 southwest of Rendova Island in the Solomons; sunk by American aircraft later in the day

Kasumi – struck by carrier aircraft from Task Force 58 on April 7, 1945 during battleship *Yamato*'s sortie to Okinawa; scuttled the same day

Shiranuhi – sunk by carrier aircraft from Task Force 77 on October 27, 1944 off Panay Island in the Philippines

Sazanami – sunk by submarine *Albacore* on January 14, 1944 southeast of Yap Island

Tanikaze – sunk by submarine *Harder* on June 9, 1944 near Tawi Tawi in the Philippines

Urakaze – sunk by submarine *Sealion* on November 21, 1944 off Formosa

Ushio – surrendered in a damaged condition at Yokosuka at the end of the war, making her the only combatant involved in the Pearl Harbor attack to survive the war

SUBMARINES

I-1 – sunk by New Zealand corvettes *Kiwi* and *Moa* on January 29, 1943 off Guadalcanal

I-2 – sunk by destroyer *Saufley* on April 7, 1944 in the Bismarck Sea

I-3 – sunk by *PT-59* on December 10, 1942 off Guadalcanal

I-4 – sunk by submarine *Seadragon* on December 21, 1942 off New Ireland Island

I-5 – sunk by destroyer escort *Wyman* on July 19, 1944 east of Guam

I-6 – lost in June 1944 near Saipan but cause remains unknown

I-7 – destroyed by destroyer *Monaghan* on June 22, 1943 near Kiska Island

I-8 – sunk by destroyers *Morrison* and *Stockton* on March 31, 1945 southeast of Okinawa

I-9 – sunk by destroyer *Frazier* on June 13, 1943 off Kiska Island

I-10 – sunk by destroyer *David W. Taylor* and destroyer escort *Riddle* on July 4, 1944 off Saipan

I-15 – sunk by destroyer *Southard* on November 10, 1942 north of San Cristobal Island in the Solomons

I-16 – sunk by destroyer escort *England* on May 19, 1944 north of the Solomons

I-17 – sunk by a New Zealand corvette *Tui* and American aircraft on August 19, 1943 southeast of New Caledonia Island

I-18 – sunk by destroyer *Fletcher* on February 11, 1943 south of San Cristobal Island

I-19 – sunk by destroyer *Radford* on November 25, 1943 west of Makin Island in the Gilberts

I-20 – sunk by destroyer *Ellett* on September 3, 1943 northeast of Espiritu Santo

APPENDIX 3

I-21 – probably sunk by aircraft from escort carrier *Chenango* on November 29 near Tarawa in the Gilberts

I-22 – possibly sunk by American aircraft on October 6, 1942 in the Solomons

I-23 – missing in mid-February 1942 south of Oahu; cause unknown

I-24 – sunk by an American subchaser on June 11, 1943 northeast of Attu Island in the Aleutians

I-25 – probably sunk by destroyer *Patterson* on August 25, 1943 in the lower Solomons

I-26 – lost in the area east of Leyte in November 1944; cause unknown

I-68 – sunk by submarine *Scamp* on July 27, 1943 north of New Hanover Island

I-69 – sunk by American land-based aircraft on April 4, 1944 at Truk

I-70 – sunk by aircraft from carrier *Enterprise* on December 10, 1941 in the Hawaiian Islands

I-71 – sunk by destroyers *Guest* and *Hudson* on February 1, 1944 off Buka Island in the Solomons

I-72 – sunk by destroyer *McCalla* on November 3, 1942 southwest of San Cristobal Island

I-73 – sunk by submarine *Gudgeon* on January 27, 1942 west of Midway

I-74 – sunk by American land-based aircraft on April 12, 1944 off Truk

I-75 – sunk by destroyer *Charrette* on February 4, 1944 east of Wotje Atoll in the Carolines

OILERS

Kenyo Maru – sunk by submarine *Guardfish* on January 14, 1944 south of Sorol Island in the Central Pacific

Kokuyo Maru – sunk by submarine *Bonefish* on July 30, 1944 northeast of Borneo

Kyokuto Maru – sunk by carrier aircraft from Task Force 38 on September 21, 1944 in Manila Bay

Nippon Maru – sunk by submarine *Scamp* on January 14, 1944 south of Sorol Island in the Central Pacific

Shiriya – sunk by submarine *Trigger* on September 21, 1943 in the East China Sea

Shinkoku Maru – sunk by carrier aircraft from Task Force 58 on February 18, 1944 at Truk

Toei Maru – sunk by submarine *Silversides* on January 18, 1943 southwest of Truk

Toho Maru – sunk by submarine *Gudgeon* on March 29, 1943 in Makassar Strait

Appendix 4

The Alternative Pearl Harbor Attack

In the actual attack, every factor imaginable aligned to make Japanese surprise as complete as possible. By changing only a few variables, the all-important element of surprise could have been lost to the Japanese. Had this happened, the outcome of the attack would have been much different.

A SHORT HISTORY OF THE BATTLE OF PEARL HARBOR

Kimmel's response to the November 27 "War Warning" message failed to impress the Plans Division at the Navy Department in Washington. It provided additional guidance, approved by Admiral Stark, directing Kimmel to increase reconnaissance efforts around Oahu. Though still reluctant to do so, Kimmel conferred with Bloch and Bellinger to heighten the patrol activity of the fleet's PBY force. Kimmel instructed Bellinger to use no more than 10 percent of his Catalina force on reconnaissance. This translated to five or six sorties per day, not anywhere near enough for a complete search. Using the March Martin-Bellinger Report as a guide, Bellinger decided to concentrate this effort on the area north of Oahu with a secondary focus west of the island. The three to four sorties per day allocated to search north of the island departed Oahu in the pre-dawn hours and were ordered to fly 600nm before making a return to base. While the Pacific Fleet made this effort to search the waters around Oahu, no attempt was made to contact the Army to advise them of this development or to seek assistance in expanding the search.

As the Americans debated their search options, Nagumo's Striking Force continued its trek to Pearl Harbor. No incidents were encountered during the transit. When Japanese spies on Oahu provided information on the additional patrols by American long-range aircraft, Nagumo made no change to the Striking Force's planned route. With the Pearl Harbor attack just a single part of the coordinated Japanese offensive across the Pacific, there was no room to change the transit route to any great degree.

On the morning of December 7, the Striking Force was on schedule to launch its first strike and remained confident that surprise had been achieved. However, all was not as it seemed. On this Sunday, five PBYs were assigned to search operations; of these, three were allocated routes north of Oahu. By 0645, these aircraft were some 100nm north of Oahu. A Catalina from VP-14 was in the sector due north from Oahu. At 0646, it spotted a large group of aircraft through intermittent clouds. Knowing at once that such a huge formation was not from an American carrier, the aircraft commander ordered an immediate message be sent to Oahu: "MANY AIRCRAFT HEADED PEARL HARBOR." After spotting the formation, the PBY broke for the deck to avoid detection. Another message was sent ten minutes later: "A LARGE FORMATION OF OVER 100 AIRCRAFT WAS SPOTTED AT 0646 120 MILES DUE NORTH OF OAHU HEADED SOUTH. THESE AIRCRAFT ARE PRESUMED TO BE JAPANESE."

Received by PATWING 2 headquarters at 0702 and 0704, these two messages had an electrifying effect. The duty officer called Bellinger at once and passed the information to Kimmel's headquarters. The seven other PBYs on training duties in addition to the five aircraft on search missions were ordered to head north to locate the source of the large formation of aircraft.

At Kimmel's headquarters, tensions were already on the rise after the receipt of a report from destroyer *Ward* that she had attacked a submarine in the security zone. The report from the VP-14 PBY on the large group of aircraft approaching from the north convinced those present that a coordinated Japanese attack was under way. At 0741, Kimmel issued this order: "ALL UNITS ASSUME HIGHEST READINESS CONDITION. A JAPANESE ATTACK IS IMMINENT."

This left little time for action. Ships in the harbor went to General Quarters and set to watertight condition, sealing all doors and hatches.

APPENDIX 4

Immediate steps were taken to break out ammunition and get gun crews to their weapons. These were still in motion as the first Japanese aircraft arrived over the harbor.

Kimmel called Short at 0743 to brief him on what had transpired. Unbeknownst to both, Army radar stations had also tracked a large formation coming south. With no idea what the Navy had already detected, the Information Center had dismissed the radar contact as a formation of B-17s. After talking to Kimmel, Short immediately contacted Martin's headquarters. With only minutes before the arrival of the Japanese, there was very little that could be done. An alert was passed to all fields. At Wheeler, Bellows, and Haleiwa, the process of arming aircraft began, and the fighters were moved out of the neat rows they were parked in. The same hectic dance was also taking place at Hickam.

To Commander Fuchida, leading the Japanese formation approaching Oahu, surprise appeared intact. Not having sighted the PBY north of Oahu, and with no American aircraft evident, Fuchida sent the signal for a surprise attack. When his first flare failed to bring the results he wanted, Fuchida fired another, giving his dive-bomber leader the impression that the signal for an opposed attack had been given. In this case, the miscommunication worked in the favor of the Japanese since, unbeknownst to them, surprise had been lost.

When the first Japanese aircraft appeared over Wheeler and Hickam Fields, they saw indications that the Americans were scrambling to launch aircraft. Nevertheless, with no antiaircraft guns deployed and with only a few machine guns set up to defend the bases, opposition was initially weak. The Japanese proceeded to strafe and bomb largely unimpeded. At Wheeler, the efforts to disperse the fighters were partially successful, and losses were mainly restricted to those aircraft remaining on the flight apron. At Hickam, the arrival of 12 B-17s from the West Coast occurred right in the middle of the attack; most of the aircraft were forced to divert to other fields.

The real impact of just a few minutes' warning was felt most at Pearl Harbor. *Shokaku*'s dive-bombers assigned to strike Naval Air Station Pearl Harbor attacked Ford Island, as the Americans frantically tried to move aircraft to more dispersed locations. The Japanese hope that the dive-bomber attack would provide cover to the subsequent torpedo bomber attack proved unfounded. When the first torpedo bombers commenced their attack on the ships moored on the northwestern part of Ford Island, they were surprised at the amount of antiaircraft fire already in evidence. Under heavy fire, the aircrews were unable to distinguish that the targets present were not worthy of their torpedoes. Of the 16 torpedo bombers, all but three attacked the ships moored in this location. Of the 13 that attacked, seven were shot down before they could launch their weapons. One of the remaining six succeeded in hitting light cruiser *Raleigh* with a single torpedo. She remained afloat due to the tireless efforts of her crew to save their ship. Target ship *Utah* drew three Kates; one hit the former battleship with a torpedo, but with full watertight integrity set, *Utah* settled slowly to the bottom of the harbor. The last three torpedo bombers bypassed these secondary targets and headed for the 1010 Dock where light cruiser *Helena* was moored. Gun crews on the fully alert cruiser shot down two Kates and the third was seen to drop its torpedo early; the torpedo struck the pier well aft of the cruiser.

On the other side of Ford Island, 24 torpedo bombers from *Akagi* and *Kaga* also encountered a storm of fire. The defenders exploited the flawed Japanese attack plan in which every torpedo plane used the same approach route. Of the 24 Kates, only half were able to launch their weapons. Heavy antiaircraft fire accounted for the other 12. From those 12 Kates that were able to launch their Type 91 torpedoes, seven struck a target. Three hit *Oklahoma*, three more slammed into *West Virginia*, and one struck *Nevada*. Both *Oklahoma* and *West Virginia* assumed an immediate list, but flooding was reduced by the setting of full watertight integrity, and the list was corrected by prompt counterflooding. Eventually, both *Oklahoma* and *West Virginia* settled onto the harbor floor with a minimal loss of life.

Fuchida's horizontal bombers also faced a barrage of antiaircraft fire. Flying at 10,000 feet in formation and maintaining a steady course, the 3- and 5-inch guns from the ships around the harbor had a field day. Of the 49 level bombers, 11 were shot down and several more were seen smoking as they departed the area. More importantly, their accuracy was greatly diminished. Japanese records indicate that 30 aircraft dropped their bombs; American records confirm only six hits. A salvo of five bombs dropped against *Arizona* was very accurate, with three hits being recorded. Two were duds, but the third hit the bridge and penetrated deep into the ship, causing a serious fire. Damage control crews took over three hours to extinguish the flames – over 100 men were killed and as many wounded. *Tennessee* and *West Virginia* were also hit, but none of the bombs achieved full detonation. On both ships, damage and casualties were minor.

Japanese attacks on air facilities experienced some success since there was inadequate time to get any fighters airborne or to fully disperse aircraft. Wheeler Field was hit hard, but with some dispersal already complete and more aircraft being moved even as the attack progressed, losses were merely heavy instead of being catastrophic. About half of the fighters lined up on the apron were saved. At Kaneohe Bay, it proved impossible to move the big PBYs before the attack began, and the Japanese bombers and strafers inflicted severe damage. Of the 30 PBYs present, almost half were destroyed or rendered unflyable. A similar scale of losses was visited upon NAS Pearl Harbor. Nearby Hickam Field benefitted from the intense antiaircraft fire from ships in the harbor, so the impact of the 17 horizontal bombers assigned to bomb the facility was reduced. Nevertheless, about half the aircraft present at Hickam were destroyed or damaged. Communication problems prevented Ewa Field from receiving a timely warning, leading to heavy losses from Japanese fighters conducting strafing attacks.

By the end of the first attack wave, the Hawaiian Air Force was making an impact on the battle. The first fighters got airborne from Bellows, Haleiwa, and Wheeler Fields at 0845. By 0900, 45 were in the air. Japanese fighters were busy strafing their assigned targets, leaving the retreating first-wave bombers largely unprotected. In a series of dogfights between small groups of American fighters and the retreating Japanese bombers, 18 Japanese aircraft were lost. When the Zeros intervened, they exacted a high toll on the Americans, shooting down 11 P-36 or P-40s.

Noting the growing opposition, Commander Shimazaki sent his second-wave Zeros ahead of the bombers. Many of the American fighters had returned to Wheeler for more ammunition, but the Zeros encountered almost 20 American fighters in the air and claimed them all in a series of dogfights. Actual American losses were much less than those of the Japanese, and by the time the Japanese second-wave bombers reached Oahu there were 38 American fighters active over the island. The Zeros were unable to counter the onslaught of American fighters that, according to Japanese pilots, seemed to come from all directions. Several groups of P-40s succeeded in attacking the second-wave dive-bombers before the Zeros could intervene.

Of the 78 second-wave dive-bombers, only 62 reached the target area. Many ships were attempting to depart the harbor, led by battleships *California* and *Nevada*. Most of the dive-bombers focused on these two large targets. Against intense antiaircraft fire and unable to use a full dive-bomber profile because of the presence of low clouds, the results were disappointing for the Japanese. *California*, the lead ship, was attacked by over 20 dive-bombers but was only struck by three bombs. She proceeded to steam down the channel and reached the open sea. Frustrated by the lack of apparent success against the first battleship, up to 30 dive-bombers attacked *Nevada*. Five hits were placed forward, causing large fires to break out. The ship was ordered to beach. The other 12 dive-bombers attacked targets all over the harbor, but Battleship Row appeared to be their main focus. *Maryland* and *Tennessee* were both hit by a single bomb. Damage to both was light. A group of two dive-bombers selected *Pennsylvania* as their target. The bombers missed the battleship and struck the two destroyers in the same drydock. A fuel-fed conflagration broke out and both ships were eventually declared constructive losses. Of the 78 dive-bombers, only 40 survived. Twenty-three were shot down by antiaircraft fire and another 15 by fighters either approaching or departing the target area. In exchange for these heavy losses, results were meager. The dive-bombers scored only 11 hits, resulting in damage to four battleships and the destruction of two destroyers. In addition, one crippled dive-bomber intentionally crashed onto seaplane tender *Curtiss*. The resulting fire was quickly put out, but 22 men were killed.

As the Japanese air attack was playing out, the Americans were contemplating how to strike back. With 12 PBYs headed to the area north of Oahu, it was inevitable that one would locate Nagumo's force. The first Catalina to do so spotted the Japanese fleet just before 0900. The lumbering PBY was detected and attacked by Zeros on CAP before the American aircraft could send a contact report. Just over 30 minutes later, a PBY from VP-23 approached the Striking Force from the west. Using clouds skillfully, the crew was able to get close enough to identify five carriers in formation, prompting the urgent message "JAP CARRIER FORCE LOCATED." Subsequent reports gave the

APPENDIX 4

location of the Japanese and their course and speed. Now the Americans could plan their counterattack.

Martin ordered his heavy and medium bombers into action. The availability of aircraft and their different cruising speeds meant the attacks were conducted in a piecemeal fashion. The first to arrive over the Striking Force was a group of three B-17s at 1405. Bombing from 22,000 feet, they hit nothing but suffered no damage to the Zeros that conducted a few timid firing passes before departing. The next group consisted of five B-18s. Arriving at 1430, they approached the Striking Force at 10,000 feet. Spotted by the CAP, the ponderous bombers were all dispatched within minutes. None had a chance to drop their weapons.

A more promising attack was launched by four A-20As just before 1500. Flying at 3,000 feet, the small formation was not spotted until it reached within 6nm of the Striking Force. Late-arriving Zeros were able to shoot down two of the light bombers, but the other two continued toward their targets. Both aircraft dropped bombs against a carrier at the rear of the Japanese formation which turned out to be *Shokaku*. The closest bomb landed 200 yards from the carrier; both aircraft were shot down as they exited the Japanese formation.

At about 1630, the Hawaiian Air Force made its biggest attack of the day. Turning around the B-17s that had just arrived from the mainland, seven heavy bombers from three squadrons were made available. This time, the Japanese fighters spotted the approaching American bombers some 12nm away. A series of attacks by the Zeros damaged two B-17s. The Americans selected *Akagi* as their target and dropped their bombs from 23,000 feet. Japanese observers held their breath as the carrier was enveloped in a forest of bomb splashes, but Nagumo's flagship emerged unscathed. Martin contemplated sending out more B-18s, but in view of the morning massacre made the brave decision not to send more men to a needless death.

Not just the Hawaiian Air Force noted the location of Nagumo's force and made plans to attack it. Aboard carrier *Enterprise*, Admiral Halsey was determined to get his task force into action. However, the morning report indicating that five Japanese carriers were present was sobering. Halsey did not believe that the Japanese could operate five carriers together, but it was clear that *Enterprise* was outnumbered. Reports from Pearl Harbor that the Japanese had taken heavy losses but had been able to sink or damage several ships drove Halsey to take vengeance. He and his staff determined that a dusk air attack would even the odds by allowing him to close the Japanese force and mount a surprise attack. This course of action also gave him the opportunity to recover the remaining dive-bombers from VB-6 and VS-6 which had flown to Ford Island in the morning and then encountered friendly fire. Unfortunately, the last Catalina contact report was from before 1300, but when Martin passed the location of the second B-17 attack, Halsey had enough targeting information to work with.

Moving toward the Japanese force, Halsey delayed the launch until 1600 when he was within 175nm of the projected location of the Japanese. A total of 25 Dauntlesses, 18 Devastators, and ten Wildcats were launched. When the launch took longer than planned, Halsey ordered the dive-bombers to proceed on their own, with the torpedo bombers and fighters to follow. In fact, the position passed by Martin was incorrect, and as the Japanese force continued to steam to the northwest, the distance to the target was longer than planned. As a result, *Enterprise*'s torpedo bombers never came close to the Japanese fleet. The dive-bombers arrived at the supposed location of Nagumo's force and found nothing. Making an educated guess, the leader of the formation took his aircraft to the northwest and quickly found the Japanese.

Warning from one of the outlying Japanese escort ships that a formation of American aircraft was approaching was too late. By the time the Zeros began to attack, the Dauntlesses were already in their dives. The formation leader divided his dive-bombers to attack two targets, which turned out to be *Shokaku* and *Soryu*. Against weak antiaircraft fire, the Dauntlesses struck *Shokaku* with a single bomb hit forward. Though large fires resulted, the ship was in no danger of sinking. *Soryu* suffered under the blows from two bomb hits. One penetrated to the hangar deck and started a major conflagration. When the fires reached the forward engine room, speed dropped to only 6 knots. This placed Nagumo in the middle of a major dilemma. He was determined to withdraw and save the Striking Force from further attacks. After much debate, it was decided to take *Soryu*'s crew off and scuttle the ship.

The next day, December 8, was also filled with action. Nagumo continued his hasty withdrawal and looked certain to make his escape. Unlike on the previous day during which the Striking Force flew no afternoon searches, Nagumo and his staff made a maximum search effort to locate any threats near the Striking Force. The Japanese missed

APPENDIX 4

finding *Enterprise*, but just before 0900, search aircraft from heavy cruiser *Tone* reported a Lexington-class carrier 240nm northwest of the Striking Force. This was *Lexington* hurrying down from Midway to support Halsey. Within an hour of receiving the contact report, the Japanese had a strike of 26 torpedo bombers and 28 dive-bombers in the air. This was the maximum number of strike aircraft available after heavy losses on the previous day. Attacking at 1130, the Japanese made short work of *Lexington*, hitting her with seven torpedoes and seven bombs. She sank with heavy loss of life.

The Pearl Harbor attack was a climactic event that brought the United States into the war. The Americans claimed victory, but one bought at a great price. Personnel casualties from the December 7 attack totaled 437 missing or dead and 755 wounded. Two battleships, *Oklahoma* and *West Virginia*, were sunk, but both were back in service by late 1943. *Nevada* was damaged by one torpedo and several bombs and forced to beach, but she also returned to service in late 1943. *Arizona* suffered moderate damage and was back in service by May 1943. Bomb damage to *California*, *Maryland*, and *Tennessee* was comparatively minor; all were back in service by March 1942. The torpedoed *Raleigh* was placed back in service by July 1942. No effort was made to salvage target ship *Utah*. The two destroyers destroyed in drydock were rebuilt and returned to the fleet in 1944. In total, ten ships were damaged or sunk, not including *Curtiss*, which was fully operational within days.

Aircraft losses were heavy, with 57 Navy and Marine Corps aircraft destroyed and almost 40 damaged. The Hawaiian Air Force reported the loss of 67 aircraft and damage to another 99.

By far the most consequential American loss was *Lexington*. Another 342 men were lost when she sank. Overall, the scale of the losses on December 7–8 and the attempted sneak attack launched by the Japanese enraged the American public. Avenging Pearl Harbor became the slogan of the day and helped shape American actions for the rest of the Pacific War.

Yamamoto's daring raid was viewed within the Imperial Navy as only a partial success. Reports from surviving aircrews confirmed that the Pacific Fleet's battle line had been ravaged, but that only two battleships were sunk. What saved the Hawaii Operation from being a tremendous disappointment was the sinking of *Lexington* the following day.

Heavy losses were expected by the Japanese, and with the loss of surprise this prediction became a reality. Of the 350 aircraft taking part in the two attack waves, losses were extremely heavy. One hundred and two aircraft were shot down or forced to ditch on their way back to the Striking Force; another 145 were damaged to some degree – a whopping 70 percent of the aircraft committed. Air crew losses were correspondingly heavy. The air groups of all six carriers were severely attrited. One of the six carriers was lost, and another damaged; *Shokaku* was able to return to service within three months.

After the events of December 7–8 were analyzed, it became apparent to the Japanese that the cost of the raid had been too high. Obviously, the Pacific Fleet had not been crippled and the power of the Striking Force had been much reduced. As a result, Yamamoto's reputation was badly dented and his credibility as a strategist shattered. From this point on, the Naval General Staff dictated Japanese naval strategy. This led to a major Japanese thrust into the South Pacific and a major defeat at the Second Battle of the Coral Sea in June 1942. Before that point, Nagumo had been relieved of his command for what was regarded as a timid performance at Pearl Harbor. Yamamoto supported Nagumo, saying that he had been charged to execute a risky plan, but pressure for his resignation grew until Yamamoto relented in early February.

Kimmel's reputation also took a beating, and he too was forced to resign in February. Halsey came out of the battle as a national hero. He was feted as "the man who chased off six Japanese carriers with one of his own." Short was sacked immediately after the attack, while Martin's reputation survived largely intact.

Forced by the Japanese to defend the sea lanes from the United States to Australia, the new commander of the Pacific Fleet, Admiral Chester Nimitz, sought to bring the Combined Fleet to battle as quickly as possible. After an inconclusive battle in the Coral Sea in May, Halsey led the Pacific Fleet's carrier force to a major victory in the same waters in June. Tied down in the South Pacific and the Solomons through the end of 1943, the Pacific Fleet's Central Pacific drive did not begin until November 1943. From there the advance toward Japan continued relentlessly until the Japanese capitulation in August 1945.

Bibliography

ARCHIVAL DOCUMENTS

USS *Allen* (DD 60) Action Report
USS *Antares* (AKS 3) Action Report
USS *Argonne* (AG 31) Action Report
USS *Arizona* (BB 39) Action Report
USS *Avocet* (AVP 4) Action Report
USS *Aylwin* (DD 355) Action Report
USS *Bagley* (DD 386) Action Report
USS *Blue* (DD 387) Action Report
USS *Bobolink* (AM 20) Action Report
USS *Breese* (DM 18) Action Report
USS *Cachalot* (SS 170) Action Report
USS *California* (BB 44) Action Report
USS *Case* (DD 370) Action Report
USS *Cassin* (DD 372) Action Report
USS *Castor* (AKS 1) Action Report
USS *Chew* (DD 106) Action Report
USS *Conyngham* (DD 371) Action Report
USS *Cummings* (DD 365) Action Report
USS *Curtiss* (AV 4) Action Report
USS *Dale* (DD 353) Action Report
USS *Detroit* (CL 8) Action Report
USS *Dewey* (DD 349) Action Report
USS *Dobbin* (AD 3) Action Report
USS *Dolphin* (SS 169) Action Report
USS *Downes* (DD 375) Action Report

USS *Enterprise* (CV 6) Air Group Action Report
USS *Enterprise* (CV 6) Scouting Squadron 6 Action Report
USS *Farragut* (DD 348) Action Report
USS *Gamble* (DM 15) Action Report
USS *Helena* (CL 50) Action Report
USS *Helm* (DD 388) Action Report
USS *Henley* (DD 391) Action Report
USS *Honolulu* (CL 48) Action Report
USS *Hulbert* (AVD 6) Action Report
USS *Hull* (DD 350) Action Report
USS *Jarvis* (DD 393) Action Report
USS *MacDonough* (DD 351) Action Report
USS *Maryland* (BB 46) Action Report
USS *Medusa* (AR 1) Action Report
USS *Minneapolis* (CA 36) Action Report
USS *Monaghan* (DD 354) Action Report
USS *Montgomery* (DM 17) Action Report
USS *Mugford* (DD 389) Action Report
USS *Narwhal* (SS 167) Action Report
USS *Neosho* (AO 23) Action Report
USS *Nevada* (BB 36) Action Report
USS *New Orleans* (CA 32) Action Report
USS *Oglala* (CM 4) Action Report
USS *Oklahoma* (BB 37) Action Report
USS *Ontario* (AT 13) Action Report
USS *Patterson* (DD 392) Action Report
USS *Pelias* (AS 14) Action Report
USS *Pennsylvania* (BB 38) Action Report
USS *Perry* (DMS 17) Action Report
USS *Phelps* (DD 360) Action Report
USS *Phoenix* (CL 46) Action Report
USS *Preble* (DM 20) Action Report
USS *Pruitt* (DM 22) Action Report
USS *Pyro* (AE 1) Action Report
USS *Rail* (AM 26) Action Report
USS *Raleigh* (CL 7) Action Report
USS *Ralph Talbot* (DD 390) Action Report
USS *Ramapo* (AO 12) Action Report
USS *Ramsay* (DM 16) Action Report
USS *Reid* (DD 369) Action Report

BIBLIOGRAPHY

USS *Rigel* (ARb 1) Action Report
USS *Sacramento* (PG 19) Action Report
USS *San Francisco* (CA 38) Action Report
USS *Selfridge* (DD 357) Action Report
USS *Shaw* (DD 373) Action Report
USS *Sicard* (DM 21) Action Report
USS *Solace* (AH 5) Action Report
USS *St Louis* (CL 49) Action Report
USS *Sumner* (AG 32) Action Report
USS *Swan* (AVP 7) Action Report
USS *Tangier* (AV 8) Action Report
USS *Tautog* (SS 199) Action Report
USS *Tennessee* (BB 43) Action Report
USS *Tern* (AM 31) Action Report
USS *Thornton* (AVD 11) Action Report
USS *Tracy* (DM 19) Action Report
USS *Trever* (DMS 16) Action Report
USS *Tucker* (DD 374) Action Report
USS *Turkey* (AM 13) Action Report
USS *Utah* (AG 16) Action Report
USS *Vestal* (AR 4) Action Report
USS *Vireo* (AM 52) Action Report
USS *Ward* (DD 139) Action Report
USS *Wasmuth* (DMS 15) Action Report
USS *West Virginia* (BB 48) Action Report
USS *West Virginia* (BB 48) Salvage Report
USS *Whitney* (AD 4) Action Report
USS *Worden* (DD 352) Action Report
USS *Zane* (DMS 14) Action Report
Commander Battle Force Action Report
Commander Battleships, Battle Force Action Report
Command Summary of Fleet Admiral Chester W. Nimitz, USN (Nimitz "Graybook") Volume 1 (December 7, 1941 to August 1942)
Destroyer Division 80, Battle Force Action Report
Destroyer Flotilla 1, Battle Force Action Report
Minecraft, Battle Force Action Report
Minecraft, Battle Force, Mine Division 1 Action Report
Minecraft, Battle Force, Mine Division 2 Action Report
Motor Torpedo Squadron 1 Action Report
Patrol Squadron 11 Action Report

PEARL HARBOR

Patrol Squadron 22 Action Report
Patrol Wing One Action Report
Patrol Wing Two Action Report
Pearl Harbor Mooring and Berthing Plans
Submarine Squadron 4 Action Report

PEARL HARBOR INVESTIGATIONS

Report of the Commission Appointed by the President of the United States to Investigate and Report the Facts Relating to the Attack Made by Japanese Armed Forces upon Pearl Harbor in the Territory of Hawaii on December 7, 1941 (The Roberts Commission Report)
The Hart Inquiry
Army Pearl Harbor Board
Navy Court of Inquiry
Report by Admiral H. K. Hewitt on Further Pearl Harbor Investigation
Clausen Investigation
Clarke Investigation
Congress of the United States Seventy-Ninth Congress, *Hearings Before the Joint Committee on the Investigation of the Pearl Harbor Attack*
Dorn Report on Kimmel and Short

OFFICIAL HISTORIES

Arakaki, Leatrice R. and John R. Kuborn, *7 December 1941: The Air Force Story*, Pacific Air Forces Office of History, Hickam Air Force Base, Hawaii, 1991

Conn, Stetson, Rose E. Engelman, and Byron Fairchild, *United States Army in World War II, Guarding the United States and its Outposts*, Center of Military History, Washington, 1989

Craven, Wesley, F. and James L. Cate, eds., *The Army Air Forces in World War II. Vol. 1: Plans and Early Operations, January 1939 August 1942*, Office of Air Force History, Washington, DC, 1983

Hough, Frank O., Verle E. Ludwig, and Henry I. Shaw, *History of U.S. Marine Corps Operations in World War II, Volume I Pearl Harbor to Guadalcanal*, Historical Branch, US Marine Corps, Washington, DC

Morison, Samuel Eliot, *History of United States Naval Operations in World War II, Volume III, The Rising Sun in the Pacific 1931–April 1942*, Little, Brown and Company, Boston, 1975

Preliminary Design Section, Bureau of Ships, Navy Department "Summary of War Damage to U.S. Battleships, Carriers, Cruisers and Destroyers,

17 October 1941 to 7 December 1942," NavShips A (374), September 15, 1943

Reports of General MacArthur, *Japanese Operations in the Southwest Pacific Area, Volume II, Part I*, Chief of Military History, Washington, 1994

Sherrod, Robert, *History of Marine Corps Aviation in World War II*, Combat Forces Press, Washington, DC, 1952

US Department of the Army Far East Command, Japanese Monograph No. 97, *Pearl Harbor Operations: General Outline of Orders and Plans*, General Headquarters Supreme Commander for the Allied Powers, Tokyo, 1953

US Department of the Army Far East Command, Japanese Monograph No. 113, *Task Force Operations*, General Headquarters Supreme Commander for the Allied Powers, Tokyo, n.d.

United States Strategic Bombing Survey (Pacific), *The Campaigns of the Pacific War*, United States Government Printing Office, Washington, 1946

MEMOIRS AND ACCOUNTS BY PARTICIPANTS

Evans, David C., ed., *The Japanese Navy in World War II: In the Words of Former Japanese Naval Officers* (2nd Edition), Naval Institute Press, Annapolis, Maryland, 1986

Hashimoto, Mochitsura, *Sunk*, Progressive Press, Joshua Tree, California, 2010

Holmes, W. J., *Double-Edged Secrets*, Naval Institute Press, Annapolis, 1979

Kimmel, Husband E., *Admiral Kimmel's Story*, Henry Regency Company, Chicago, 1955

Layton, Edwin T., *"And I Was There,"* William Morrow and Company, New York, 1985

Orita, Zenji with Joseph Harrington, *I-Boat Captain*, Major Books, Canoga Park, California, 1976

Sakamaki, Kazuo, *I Attacked Pearl Harbor*, Rollston Press, Honolulu, 2017

Stilwell, Paul, ed., *Air Raid: Pearl Harbor*, Naval Institute Press, Annapolis, 1981

Theobald, Robert A., *The Final Secret of Pearl Harbor*, Devin-Adair Company, New York, 1954

Ugaki, Matome, *Fading Victory*, University of Pittsburgh Press, Pittsburgh, 1991

United States Strategic Bombing Survey (Pacific), *Interrogations of Japanese Officials*, Volumes 1 and 2, United States Government Printing Office, Washington, n.d.

Werneth, Ron, *Beyond Pearl Harbor*, Schiffer Military History, Atglen, PA, 2008

BIOGRAPHIES

Agawa, Hiroyuki, *The Reluctant Admiral*, Kodahsha International, Tokyo, 1979

Bix, Herbert P., *Hirohito and the Making of Modern Japan*, HarperCollins Publishers, New York, 2000

Buell, Thomas B., *Master of Sea Power: A Biography of Fleet Admiral Ernest J. King*, Little, Brown and Company, Boston, 1980

Carlson, Elliot, *Joe Rochefort's War*, Naval Institute Press, Annapolis, Maryland, 2011

Dyer, George Carroll, *The Amphibians Came to Conquer: The Story of Admiral Richmond Kelly Turner*, Vol. 1, Washington, DC, US Government Printing Office, 1972

Mauch, Peter, "Admiral Nagano Osami and the Japanese Navy's Decision for War Against the United States" in Evan Wilson and Paul Kennedy, eds., *Planning for War at Sea*, Naval Institute Press, Annapolis, 2025

Pineau, Roger, "Yamamoto" in Field Marshal Sir Michael Carver, ed., *The War Lords: Military Commanders of the Twentieth Century*, Little, Brown, Boston, 1976

Potter, John Deane, *Yamamoto*, Paperback Library, New York, 1967

Smith, Peter C., *Fist From the Sky*, Stackpole Books, Mechanicsburg, PA, 2005

Willmott, H. P., " Isoroku Yamamoto" in Jack Sweetman, ed., *The Great Admirals*, Naval Institute Press, Annapolis, 1997

REFERENCE WORKS

Campbell, John, *Naval Weapons of World War Two*, Naval Institute Press, Annapolis, 2002

Evans, David C. and Mark R. Peattie, *Kaigun: Strategy, Tactics and Technology in the Imperial Japanese Navy 1887–1941*, Naval Institute Press, Annapolis, 1997

Francillon, Rene J., *Japanese Aircraft of the Pacific War*, Naval Institute Press, Annapolis, 1987

Friedman, Norman, *Naval Anti-Aircraft Guns & Gunnery*, Naval Institute Press, Annapolis, 2013

Fuller, Richard, *Japanese Admirals 1926–1945*, Schiffer, Atglen, PA 2011

Goldstein, Donald and Katherine Dillon, *The Pearl Harbor Papers*, Brassey's, Dulles, Virginia, 1993

Goldstein, Donald, Katherine Dillon, and Michael Wenger, *The Way it Was: Pearl Harbor*, Brassey's, Washington, 1991

BIBLIOGRAPHY

Lacroix, Eric and Linton Wells II, *Japanese Cruisers of the Pacific War*, Naval Institute Press, Annapolis, 1997

Peattie, Mark R., *Sunburst: The Rise of Japanese Naval Air Power 1909–1941*, Naval Institute Press, Annapolis, 2001

Smith, Peter C., *Aichi D3A1/2 Val*, Crowood Press, Ramsbury, 1999

Stille, Mark E., *The United States Navy in World War II*, Osprey Publishing, Oxford, 2021

Stille, Mark E., *The Imperial Japanese Navy*, Osprey Publishing, Oxford, 2014

Wildenberg, Thomas and Norman Polmar, *Ship Killer*, Naval Institute Press, Annapolis, 2010

Wildenberg, Thomas, *Gray Steel and Black Oil*, Naval Institute Press, Annapolis, 1996

SECONDARY SOURCES

Anderson, Charles R., *Day of Lightning, Years of Scorn*, Naval Institute Press, Annapolis, 2005

Asada, Sadao, *From Mahan to Pearl Harbor*, Naval Institute Press, Annapolis, 2006

Bergamini, David, *Japan's Imperial Conspiracy*, William Morrow, New York, 1971

Borch, Fred and Daniel Martinez, *Kimmel, Short and Pearl Harbor*, Naval Institute Press, Annapolis, 2005

Borg, Dorothy and Shumpei Okamoto, *Pearl Harbor as History*, Columbia University Press, New York, 1973

Boyd, Carl and Akihiko Yoshida, *The Japanese Submarine Force and World War II*, Naval Institute Press, Annapolis, 1995

Burlingame, Burl, *Advance Force Pearl Harbor*, Pacific Monograph, Kailua, Hawaii, 1992

Carpenter, Dorr, and Norman Polmar, *Submarines of the Imperial Japanese Navy*, Naval Institute Press, Annapolis, 1986

Carter, Worrall Reed, *Beans, Bullets, and Black Oil*, US Government Printing Office, Washington, 1952

Chambers, Mark with Tony Holmes, *Nakajima B5N 'Kate' and B6N 'Jill' Units*, Osprey Publishing, Oxford, 2017

Cohen, Stan, *East Wind Rain*, Pictorial Histories Publishing, Missoula, Montana, 1990

Conroy, Hilary and Harry Wray, eds., *Pearl Harbor Reexamined*, University of Hawaii Press, Honolulu, 1990

Coox, Alvin D., *Nomonhan*, Stanford University Press, Stanford, 1985

Cressman, Robert J., and J. Michael Wenger, *Infamous Day: Marines at Pearl Harbor*, Marine Corps Historical Center, Washington, DC 1992

Delgado, James P. et al., *The Lost Submarines of Pearl Harbor*, Texas A&M University Press, College Station, 2016

Dower, John W., *War Without Mercy*, Pantheon Books, New York, 1986

Dull, Paul S., *A Battle History of the Imperial Japanese Navy (1941–1945)*, Naval Institute Press, Annapolis, 1978

Frank, Richard B., *Tower of Skulls*, W. W. Norton & Company, New York, 2020

Gannon, Michael, *Pearl Harbor Betrayed*, Henry Holt and Company, New York, 2001

Hata, Tameichi, and Yasuho Izawa, *Japanese Naval Aces and Fighter Units in World War II*, Naval Institute Press, Annapolis, 1989

Hotta, Eri, *Japan 1941*, Alfred A. Knopf, New York, 2013

Hoyt, Edwin P., *Yamamoto*, McGraw-Hill Book Company, New York, 1990

Hoyt, Edwin P., *Japan's War*, McGraw-Hill Book Company, New York, 1986

Ike, Nobutaka, ed., *Japan's Decision for War*, Stanford University Press, Stanford, 1967

Ito, Masanori, *The End of the Imperial Japanese Navy*, W. W. Norton and Company, New York, 1962

Kotani, Ken, *Japanese Intelligence in World War II*, Osprey Publishing, Oxford, 2009

Lambert, John W., and Norman Polmar, *Defenseless*, MBI Publishing Company, Minneapolis, 2003

Lord, Walter, *Day of Infamy*, Henry Holt and Company, New York, 1957

Lundstrom, John B., *The First Team*, Naval Institute Press, Annapolis, 1984

Marder, Arthur J., *Old Friends, New Enemies*, Clarendon Press, Oxford, 1981

Maurer, John H. and Erik Goldstein (eds.), *The Road to Pearl Harbor*, Naval Institute Press, Annapolis, 2022

Mawdsley, Evan, *The War for the Seas*, Yale University Press, New Haven, 2019

Mawdsley, Evan, *December 1941*, Yale University Press, New Haven, 2011

Melber, Takuma, *Pearl Harbor*, Polity Press, Cambridge, 2021

Millman, Nicholas, *A6M Zero-Sen Aces 1940-42*, Osprey Publishing, Oxford, 2019

Morison, Samuel Eliot, *Strategy and Compromise*, Little, Brown and Company, Boston, 1958

O'Neil, William D., *Undefending Pearl Harbor* (Second Edition), Peter Press, Fairfax, 2016

Pike, Francis, *Hirohito's War*, Bloomsbury, London, 2015

Parshall, Jonathan and Tully, Anthony, *Shattered Sword*, Potomac Books, Washington, 2005

BIBLIOGRAPHY

Potter, E. B. and Chester W. Nimitz, eds., *The Great Sea War*, Bramhall House, New York, 1960

Prados, John, *Combined Fleet Decoded: The Secret History of American Intelligence and the Japanese Navy in World War II*, Random House, New York, 1995

Prange, Gordon, *At Dawn We Slept*, McGraw-Hill Book Company, New York, 1981

Prange, Gordon, Donald Goldstein, and Katherine Dillon, *Dec. 7 1941*, McGraw-Hill Book Company, New York, 1991

Prange, Gordon, Donald Goldstein, and Katherine Dillon, *God's Samurai*, Brassey's, Washington, 1990

Prange, Gordon, Donald Goldstein, and Katherine Dillon, *Pearl Harbor: The Verdict of History*, McGraw-Hill Book Company, New York, 1986

Salecker, Gene Eric, *Fortress Against the Sun*, Combined Books, Conshohocken, Pennsylvania, 2001

Schom, Alan, *The Eagle and the Rising Sun*, W. W. Norton & Company, New York, 2004

Slackman, Michael, *Target: Pearl Harbor*, University of Hawaii Press, Honolulu, 1990

Slackman, Michael, ed., *Pearl Harbor in Perspective*, Arizona Memorial Museum Association, Honolulu, 1986

Smith, Carl, *Pearl Harbor*, Osprey Publishing, Oxford, 2001

Smith, Myron J., *Golden State Battlewagon*, Pictorial Histories Publishing, Missoula, Montana, 1983

Stafford, Edward P., *The Big E*, Naval Institute Press, Annapolis, 1988

Stephan, John J., *Hawaii Under the Rising Sun*, University of Hawaii Press, Honolulu, 1984

Stille, Mark E., *Pacific Carrier War*, Osprey Publishing, Oxford, 2021

Stille, Mark E., *Yamamoto Isoroku*, Osprey Publishing, Oxford, 2012

Stille, Mark E., *Tora! Tora! Tora!*, Osprey Publishing, Oxford, 2011

Symonds, Craig L., *World War II at Sea: A Global History*, Oxford University Press, New York, 2018

Tagaya, Osamu, *Aichi 99 Kanbaku 'Val' Units 1937–42*, Osprey Publishing, Oxford, 2011

Takeo, Iguchi, *Demystifying Pearl Harbor*, International House of Japan, Tokyo, 2010

Tillman, Barrett, *SBD Dauntless Units of World War 2*, Osprey Publishing, Oxford, 1998

Tohmatsu, Haruo and H. P. Willmott, *A Gathering Darkness*, SR Books, Lanham, Maryland, 2004

Toland, John, *The Rising Sun*, Random House, New York, 1970

Trefousse, Hans, ed., *What Happened at Pearl Harbor*, Twayne Publishers, New York, 1958

Williford, Glen and Terrance McGovern, *Defenses of Pearl Harbor and Oahu 1907–50*, Osprey Publishing, Oxford, 2003

Willmott, H. P., *Empires in the Balance*, Naval Institute Press, Annapolis, 1982

United States Strategic Bombing Survey (Pacific), *The Campaigns of the Pacific War*, US Government Printing Office, Washington, 1946

Wenger, J. Michael, Robert J. Cressman, and John F. Di Virgilio, *"A Pitiful Unholy Mess,"* Naval Institute Press, Annapolis, 2022

Wenger, J. Michael, Robert J. Cressman, and John F. Di Virgilio, *"They're Killing My Boys,"* Naval Institute Press, Annapolis, 2019

Wenger, J. Michael, Robert J. Cressman, and John F. Di Virgilio, *"This is No Drill,"* Naval Institute Press, Annapolis, 2018

Wenger, J. Michael, Robert J. Cressman, and John F. Di Virgilio, *"No One Avoided Danger,"* Naval Institute Press, Annapolis, 2015

Willmott, H. P., *Pearl Harbor*, Cassell, London, 2001

Willmott, H. P., *The Barrier and the Javelin*, Naval Institute Press, Annapolis, 1983

Wood, James B., *Japanese Military Strategy in the Pacific War*, Rowman & Littlefield Publishers, Lanham, Maryland, 2007

Zimm, Alan D., *Attack on Pearl Harbor*, Casemate, Philadelphia, 2011

ARTICLES

Aiken, David, "Hirano's Zero," *Aviation History*, January 2009

Aiken, David, "Ghosts of Pearl Harbor," *Flight Journal*, June 2007, Volume 12, Number 3

Aiken, David, "Torpedoing Pearl Harbor," *Military History*, December 2002

Aiken, David, "Pearl Harbor's Lost P-36," *Flight Journal*, September/October 2002

Budiansky, Stephen, "Too Late for Pearl Harbor," *Proceedings*, December 1999

Di Virgilio, John F., "Seven Seconds to Infamy," *Naval History*, December 1997

Di Virgilio, John F., "Technical Report – Japanese Thunderfish," *Naval History*, December 1991, Volume 5, Number 4.

Hassan, Adeel, "Warren Upton, Who Escaped Sinking Battleship in Pearl Harbor, Dies at 105," *New York Times*, December 29, 2024

Hone, Thomas C., "The Destruction of the Battle Line at Pearl Harbor," *Proceedings*, December 1977

BIBLIOGRAPHY

Miller, Edward S., "Kimmel's Hidden Agenda," *MHQ*, Autumn 1991, Volume 4, Number 1

O'Connor, Christopher P., "A Taranto-Pearl Harbor Connection," *Naval History*, December 2022

Okumiya, Masatake, "The Japanese Perspective," *Naval History*, December 1991, Volume 5, Number 4

Parshall, Jonathan and J. Michael Wenger, "Pearl Harbor's Overlooked Answer," *Naval History*, December 2011, Volume 25, Number 6

Parshall, Jonathan, "Reflecting on Fuchida, or 'A Tale of Three Whoppers,'" *Naval War College Review*, Spring 2010, Volume 63, Number 2

Roberts, Sam, "Masamitsu Yoshioka, Last Pearl Harbor Bombardier, Dies at 106," *New York Times*, October 3, 2024

Zimm, Alan D., "The Second-Wave Attack on Battleship Row," *Proceedings*, December 2021, p. 21

Zimm, Alan D., "Commander Fuchida's Decision," *Naval History*, December 2016, Volume 30, Number 6

WEBSITES

www.combinedfleet.com
www.history.navy.mil
www.pwencycl.kgbudge.com (The Pacific War Online Encyclopedia)
www.nationalww2museum.org

Notes

INTRODUCTION

1 Sam Roberts, "Masamitsu Yoshioka, Last Pearl Harbor Bombardier, Dies at 106," *New York Times*, October 3, 2024.
2 Adeel Hassan, "Warren Upton, Who Escaped Sinking Battleship in Pearl Harbor, Dies at 105," *New York Times*, December 29, 2024.

CHAPTER 1: THE ROAD TO PEARL HARBOR

1 Richard B. Frank, *Tower of Skulls*, W. W. Norton & Co, New York, 2020, p. 11.
2 Frank, *Tower of Skulls*, p. 55.
3 Frank, *Tower of Skulls*, p. 98.
4 Ironically, the Japanese aircraft were led by Lieutenant Murata Shigeharu who was destined to lead the Japanese torpedo bombers in the Pearl Harbor attack.
5 Other accounts attribute the attack to the inability to pass *Panay*'s location, known to the Japanese, to air units operating from an advanced base. Nevertheless, the ship was well marked and it would have been inexplicable for the pilots to not know what they were attacking. John Prados, *Combined Fleet Decoded: The Secret History of American Intelligence and the Japanese Navy in World War II*, Random House, New York, 1995, pp. 48–51.
6 Frank, *Tower of Skulls*, pp. 102–04.
7 Alvin D. Coox, *Nomonhan*, Stanford University Press, Stanford, 1985, is the definitive account in English of the Japanese perspective of this little-known border war.

8 Mark R. Peattie, *Sunburst: The Rise of Japanese Naval Air Power, 1909–1941*, Naval Institute Press, Annapolis, 2001, pp. 120–21.
9 Imperial General Headquarters liaison conferences became the de facto decision-making body for major national issues. They were attended by the chiefs and deputy chiefs of the Army and Navy General Staffs and selected cabinet ministers (usually the Army, Navy, foreign, and finance). Decisions made at a liaison conference were taken to an imperial conference for formal approval. Iguchi Takeo, *Demystifying Pearl Harbor*, International House of Japan, Tokyo, 2010, p. xx.
10 Frank, *Tower of Skulls*, p. 168.
11 Nobutaka Ike, *Japan's Decision for War*, Stanford University Press, Stanford, 1967, pp. xxviii–xxix.
12 Gordon Prange, *At Dawn We Slept*, McGraw-Hill Book Company, New York, 1981, pp. 116–17; Ike, *Decision for War*, p. xxii.
13 Frank, *Tower of Skulls*, p. 172.
14 Eri Hotta, *Japan 1941*, Alfred A. Knopf, New York, 2013, p. 131.
15 Imperial conferences were convened for urgent matters of state. The Emperor attended while the prime minister chaired the meeting. Other attendees included the foreign, finance, Army, and Navy ministers, and the chiefs and deputy chiefs of the Army and Navy General Staffs. From the Emperor's household, the President of the Privy Council was also present. Takeo, *Demystifying Pearl Harbor*, p. xix.
16 Hotta, *Japan 1941*, p. 131.
17 Hotta, *Japan 1941*, p. 142.
18 Prange, *At Dawn We Slept*, p. 205.
19 Hotta, *Japan 1941*, p. 171.
20 Hotta, *Japan 1941*, p. 174.
21 Ibid.
22 Ibid.
23 Hotta, *Japan 1941*, p. 175.
24 Ike, *Japan's Decision for War*, p. 139.
25 Ike, *Japan's Decision for War*, p. 140.
26 David Bergamini, *Japan's Imperial Conspiracy*, William Morrow, New York, 1971, p. 786.
27 Prange, *At Dawn We Slept*, p. 212.
28 The author would like to thank Alan Zimm for clarifying the matter of the Japanese perspective.
29 Hotta, *Japan 1941*, pp. 197–98.
30 Takeo, *Demystifying Pearl Harbor*, p. 114.
31 Takeo, *Demystifying Pearl Harbor*, p. 115.

32 Frank, *Tower of Skulls*, p. 203.
33 Takeo, *Demystifying Pearl Harbor*, p. 109.
34 Hotta, *Japan 1941*, p. 225.
35 Hotta, *Japan 1941*, pp. 228–29.
36 Ike, *Japan's Decision for War*, pp. 203–04.
37 Ike, *Japan's Decision for War*, pp. 209–10.
38 Ike, *Japan's Decision for War*, pp. 210–11.
39 Ike, *Japan's Decision for War*, p. 205; Hotta, *Japan 1941*, pp. 237–38.
40 Takeo, *Demystifying Pearl Harbor*, p. 113.
41 Frank, *Tower of Skulls*, p. 215.
42 Frank, *Tower of Skulls*, p. 212.
43 Takeo, *Demystifying Pearl Harbor*, p. 117; Frank, *Tower of Skulls*, p. 221.
44 Takeo, *Demystifying Pearl Harbor*, p. 129.
45 Takeo, *Demystifying Pearl Harbor*, p. 137.
46 Frank, *Tower of Skulls*, p. 223.
47 Hotta, *Japan 1941*, p. 269.
48 Mount Niitake, located on Formosa, was the tallest in the Japanese Empire. It provided a cultural reference for achieving something great.

CHAPTER 2: YAMAMOTO AND THE GREAT DEBATE

1 Takuma Melber, *Pearl Harbor*, Polity Press, Cambridge, 2021, p. 81.
2 David C. Evans and Mark R. Peattie, *Kaigun: Strategy, Tactics and Technology in the Imperial Japanese Navy, 1887–1941*, Naval Institute Press, Annapolis, 1997, p. 466.
3 Sadao Asada, *From Mahan to Pearl Harbor*, Naval Institute Press, Annapolis, 2006, pp. 240–41.
4 Evans and Peattie, *Kaigun*, p. 453.
5 Evans and Peattie, *Kaigun*, p. 468.
6 H. P. Willmott, *Empires in the Balance*, Naval Institute Press, Annapolis, 1982, pp. 73–74.
7 This was light carrier *Ryujo*. Light carrier *Hosho* was unsuited for fleet work, and the new *Zuiho* was retained to operate with the battleships of the First Fleet. Escort carrier *Taiyo* was assigned to ferry duties.
8 Evans and Peattie, *Kaigun*, p. 469.
9 Evans and Peattie, *Kaigun*, p. 470.
10 At this point of the war, the Combined Fleet controlled all of the IJN's fleets and air formations. Only the China Area Fleet and naval districts with local defense forces were beyond its control. Since it controlled virtually all of the IJN's oceangoing combatants and all combat aircraft, it was by far the most important command in the IJN.

NOTES

11 This faction was led by Admiral Yonai Mitsumasa who served as Navy Minister from 1937 to 1940.
12 Evans and Peattie, *Kaigun*, p. 461.
13 Roger Pineau, "Yamamoto" in Field Marshal Sir Michael Carver, ed., *The War Lords: Military Commanders of the Twentieth Century*, Little, Brown, Boston, 1976, p. 393.
14 Yamamoto was a member of the "treaty" faction content to let the 5-5-3 ratio between Great Britain–United States–Japan from the Washington Naval Treaty of 1922 continue. The London Naval Conference extended this ratio from capital ships to other types of warships.
15 Prange, *At Dawn We Slept*, p. 13.
16 Evan Mawdsley, *The War for the Seas*, Yale University Press, New Haven, 2019, p. 179.
17 Prange, *At Dawn We Slept*, p. 11. This extract comes from a December 1940 letter to classmate Vice Admiral Shimada Shigetaro.
18 Prange, *At Dawn We Slept*, p. 12.
19 H. P. Willmott, "Isoroku Yamamoto" in Jack Sweetman, ed., *The Great Admirals*, Naval Institute Press, Annapolis, 1997, p. 450. The few biographies of Yamamoto available in English are deficient in regard to his characteristics as a commander. Willmott's short work provides a good overview. Also see the author's *Yamamoto Isoroku*, Osprey Publishing, Oxford, 2012.
20 The exception to this rule was the defeat of France in May–June 1940.
21 Evans and Peattie, *Kaigun*, pp. 473, 605.
22 Evans and Peattie, *Kaigun*, p. 473. The predictive nature of USN exercises between the wars has been overblown. Defending (and attacking) bases was a normal exercise element.
23 Evans and Peattie, *Kaigun*, pp. 473–74.
24 Evans and Peattie, *Kaigun*, p. 474.
25 Evans and Peattie, *Kaigun*, pp. 474–75, 606.
26 Paul S. Dull, *A Battle History of the Imperial Japanese Navy (1941–1945)*, Naval Institute Press, Annapolis, 1978, p. 7.
27 Evans and Peattie, *Kaigun*, p. 472.
28 Prange, *At Dawn We Slept*, pp. 28–29.
29 Prange, *At Dawn We Slept*, p. 21.
30 Evans and Peattie, *Kaigun*, p. 476.
31 Evans and Peattie, *Kaigun*, pp. 476–77.
32 Prange, *At Dawn We Slept*, p. 103.
33 Prange, *At Dawn We Slept*, p. 100.
34 Prange, *At Dawn We Slept*, pp. 103–04.

35 Prange, *At Dawn We Slept*, p. 184.
36 Prange, *At Dawn We Slept*, p. 225.
37 Prange, *At Dawn We Slept*, pp. 225–26.
38 Prange, *At Dawn We Slept*, pp. 227–28, 756. This was not a war game but was a controlled tabletop experiment to examine various courses of action.
39 Prange, *At Dawn We Slept*, p. 229.
40 Prange, *At Dawn We Slept*, pp. 229–30.
41 Prange, *At Dawn We Slept*, p. 234.
42 Prange, *At Dawn We Slept*, p. 233.
43 Ibid.
44 Prange, *At Dawn We Slept*, p. 235.
45 Prange, *At Dawn We Slept*, pp. 236–37.
46 Prange, *At Dawn We Slept*, pp. 261–62.
47 Prange, *At Dawn We Slept*, pp. 262, 759.
48 Prange, *At Dawn We Slept*, p. 263.
49 Ibid.
50 Ibid.
51 Ibid.
52 Prange, *At Dawn We Slept*, p. 281.
53 Prange, *At Dawn We Slept*, pp. 282–83.
54 Prange, *At Dawn We Slept*, p. 282.
55 Prange, *At Dawn We Slept*, p. 284.
56 Prange, *At Dawn We Slept*, p. 285.
57 Prange, *At Dawn We Slept*, p. 295.
58 Prange, *At Dawn We Slept*, p. 296.
59 Ibid.
60 Prange, *At Dawn We Slept*, p. 297.
61 Prange, *At Dawn We Slept*, p. 298.
62 Peter Mauch, "Admiral Nagano Osami and the Japanese Navy's Decision for War Against the United States," in Evan Wilson and Paul Kennedy (ed.), *Planning for War at Sea*, Naval Institute Press, Annapolis, 2025, p. 185.
63 Donald W. Goldstein and Katherine V. Dillon, *The Pearl Harbor Papers*, Brassey's, Washington, 1993, pp. 93–94.

CHAPTER 3: THE JAPANESE PLAN

1 The "Dorn Report on Kimmel and Short," December 15, 1995, p. 3.
2 Arthur J. Marder, *Old Friends, New Enemies*, Clarendon Press, Oxford, 1981, p. 314.

NOTES

3   The exception was night carrier operations, which the Royal Navy frequently employed and the Imperial Navy did not. The British attack on Taranto was a night operation.
4   Prange, *At Dawn We Slept*, p. 320.
5   Christopher P. O'Connor, "A Taranto-Pearl Harbor Connection," *Naval History Magazine*, December 2022. In an ironic parallel, the Americans also failed to learn from the lesson of Taranto. Aboard *Illustrious* was an American observer, Lieutenant Commander John N. Opie III, the assistant naval attaché to London. When *Illustrious* returned to Alexandria, Opie wrote a report which arrived in Washington in January 1941.
6   Prange, *At Dawn We Slept*, p. 367.
7   Prange, *At Dawn We Slept*, p. 315.
8   Prange, *At Dawn We Slept*, pp. 315–19.
9   Prange, *At Dawn We Slept*, p. 366.
10 Prange, *At Dawn We Slept*, pp. 366–67.
11 Prange, *At Dawn We Slept*, p. 368.
12 This arrangement was typical in Imperial Navy staffs in which flag officers did not get involved in detail. This was different in the USN; a good example would be Admiral Chester Nimitz's involvement in creating the Pacific Fleet's plan at Midway.
13 Prange, *At Dawn We Slept*, p. 19.
14 Richard Fuller, *Japanese Admirals 1926–1945*, Schiffer, Atglen, 2011, p. 187. Later in the war as the tide of battle was turning against Japan, Onishi was the driving force behind the formation of the first kamikaze units in the Philippines in October 1944. Even after the atomic bombings, he advocated that the war be continued and that all Japanese males be employed in suicide attacks. Onishi committed ritual suicide on August 16, 1945, taking 12 hours to die.
15 Prange, *At Dawn We Slept*, p. 18.
16 Prange, *At Dawn We Slept*, pp. 19–20.
17 Melber, *Pearl Harbor*, pp. 85–86.
18 Prange, *At Dawn We Slept*, p. 20.
19 Prange, *At Dawn We Slept*, pp. 21–22.
20 Prange, *At Dawn We Slept*, pp. 25–26.
21 Prange, *At Dawn We Slept*, p. 27.
22 Ibid.
23 Prange, *At Dawn We Slept*, p. 98.
24 Prange, *At Dawn We Slept*, p. 99.
25 Prange, *At Dawn We Slept*, p. 100.

26 Prange, *At Dawn We Slept*, pp. 111–12.
27 Prange, *At Dawn We Slept*, p. 755.
28 Prange, *At Dawn We Slept*, pp. 217–18.
29 Prange, *At Dawn We Slept*, p. 218.
30 Prange, *At Dawn We Slept*, p. 219.
31 Prange, *At Dawn We Slept*, p. 220.
32 Prange, *At Dawn We Slept*, p. 227.
33 Prange, *At Dawn We Slept*, p. 322.
34 Prange, *At Dawn We Slept*, p. 323.
35 H. P. Willmott, *Pearl Harbor*, Cassell, London, 2001, p. 64.
36 Goldstein and Dillon, *The Pearl Harbor Papers*, p. 101.
37 Ibid.
38 Alan D. Zimm, *Attack on Pearl Harbor*, Casemate, Philadelphia, 2011, pp. 114–15.
39 Prange, *At Dawn We Slept*, p. 322.
40 Prange, *At Dawn We Slept*, p. 378–79.
41 Prange, *At Dawn We Slept*, p. 384.
42 Zimm, *Attack on Pearl Harbor*, p. 119.
43 Prange, *At Dawn We Slept*, pp. 269–70.
44 Walter Lord, *Day of Infamy*, Henry Holt, New York, 2001, p. 22.
45 Prange, *At Dawn We Slept*, p. 321.
46 Goldstein and Dillon, *The Pearl Harbor Papers*, pp. 101–03.
47 Zimm, *Attack on Pearl Harbor*, pp. 96–97.
48 John W. Lambert and Norman Polmar, *Defenseless*, Motorbooks International, St Paul, 2003, p. 40.
49 Zimm, *Attack on Pearl Harbor*, p. 99.
50 Had either the Americans or Japanese devoted more energy to studying the histories of air attacks against surface ships in the first year of the European war, they would have drawn the proper lesson that attacking ships at sea is difficult. Neither the British, Germans, nor Italians enjoyed any real success in this regard.
51 Prange, *At Dawn We Slept*, p. 768.
52 Prange, *At Dawn We Slept*, p. 376.
53 Prange, *At Dawn We Slept*, p. 376–77.
54 Prange, *At Dawn We Slept*, p. 379.
55 Goldstein and Dillon, *The Pearl Harbor Papers*, p. 25.
56 Prange, *At Dawn We Slept*, p. 374.
57 Ibid.
58 Prange, *At Dawn We Slept*, p. 373. The information comes from a 1947 interview with Genda.

NOTES

59 Samuel Eliot Morison, *Strategy and Compromise*, Little, Brown and Company, Boston, 1958, p. 68.
60 Zimm, *Attack on Pearl Harbor*, p. 115.

CHAPTER 4: THE STRIKING FORCE

1 Mark R. Peattie, *Sunburst*, p. 148.
2 Peattie, *Sunburst*, pp. 150–51.
3 Peattie, *Sunburst*, p. 151; Prange, *At Dawn We Slept*, p. 102.
4 Peattie, *Sunburst*, pp. 152–53.
5 Prange, *At Dawn We Slept*, p. 267.
6 Prange, *At Dawn We Slept*, p. 268.
7 Fuller, *Japanese Admirals 1926–1945*, pp. 128–29.
8 Prange, *At Dawn We Slept*, p. 268.
9 Goldstein and Dillon, *The Pearl Harbor Papers*, p. 144.
10 Prange, *At Dawn We Slept*, p. 268.
11 Prange, *At Dawn We Slept*, p. 267.
12 Prange, *At Dawn We Slept*, p. 260.
13 Ibid.
14 Fuller, *Japanese Admirals 1926–1945*, p. 271.
15 Matome Ugaki, *Fading Victory*, University of Pittsburgh Press, Pittsburgh, 1991, p. 141.
16 Willmott, *Pearl Harbor*, p. 188. Willmott uses strengths from a number of Japanese sources.
17 Peattie, *Sunburst*, p. 134.
18 John B. Lundstrom, *The First Team*, Naval Institute Press, Annapolis, 1984, p. 456.
19 Peattie, *Sunburst*, p. 131.
20 Zimm, *Attack on Pearl Harbor*, pp. 139–40.
21 Prange, *At Dawn We Slept*, p. 323.
22 Prange, *At Dawn We Slept*, pp. 328–30; Zimm, *Attack on Pearl Harbor*, pp. 140–43. Prange provides an outline of the rehearsals; Zimm provides a detailed review of the critique afterwards.
23 Rene J. Francillon, *Japanese Aircraft of the Pacific War*, Naval Institute Press, Annapolis, 1987, pp. 415–16.
24 Peattie, *Sunburst*, pp. 140, 333.
25 Prange, *At Dawn We Slept*, pp. 161–62.
26 Prange, *At Dawn We Slept*, p. 268.
27 Prange, *At Dawn We Slept*, p. 268–69.
28 Peattie, *Sunburst*, p. 333.
29 Peattie, *Sunburst*, p. 140.

30 Peattie, *Sunburst*, p. 144.
31 Peattie, *Sunburst* pp. 144–45.
32 Prange, *At Dawn We Slept*, p. 160.
33 Prange, *At Dawn We Slept*, pp. 320–21.
34 John F. Di Virgilio, "Technical Report – Japanese Thunderfish," *Naval History Magazine*, December 1991, Volume 5, Number 4.
35 Francillon, *Japanese Aircraft of the Pacific War*, pp. 275–76.
36 Peattie, *Sunburst*, pp. 140–41.
37 Goldstein and Dillon, *The Pearl Harbor Papers*, p. 35.
38 Prange, *At Dawn We Slept*, pp. 271–72.
39 This bomb was fitted with a 0.2-second delay fuse designed to penetrate deeply into non-heavily armored naval targets before exploding. When used to attack ground targets, it would dig itself into even the hardest surfaces, sending the force of the explosion straight up. This produced deep holes while leaving structures only a few feet away intact.
40 Prange, *At Dawn We Slept*, pp. 272–73.
41 Peattie, *Sunburst*, p. 137.
42 Prange, *At Dawn We Slept*, p. 163.
43 David C. Evans, ed., *The Japanese Navy in World War II: In the Words of Former Japanese Naval Officers* (2nd Edition), Naval Institute Press, Annapolis, 1986, p. 136.
44 Francillon, *Japanese Aircraft of the Pacific War*, p. 281.
45 Francillon, *Japanese Aircraft of the Pacific War*, p. 410.
46 Willmott, *Pearl Harbor*, p. 189.
47 Ibid.
48 Peattie, *Sunburst*, p. 156.
49 Ibid.
50 Jonathan Parshall and Anthony Tully, *Shattered Sword*, Potomac Books, Washington, 2005, p. 136.
51 Eric Lacroix and Linton Wells II, *Japanese Cruisers of the Pacific War*, Naval Institute Press, Annapolis, 1997, pp. 241–42.
52 Lacroix and Wells, *Japanese Cruisers of the Pacific War*, p. 245.
53 Lacroix and Wells, *Japanese Cruisers of the Pacific War*, p. 244.
54 Ibid.
55 Parshall and Tully, *Shattered Sword*, p. 144.
56 The salient exception being the attack on light carrier *Shoho* on May 7, 1942, during the Battle of the Coral Sea. On this occasion, conditions were perfect for the Devastators and a variant of the Mark 13 less prone to malfunction was used. Two squadrons attacked the carrier and scored so many hits that the precise number could not be determined.

NOTES

CHAPTER 5: THE PACIFIC FLEET AND PEARL HARBOR DEFENSES

1. Prange, *At Dawn We Slept*, p. 64.
2. Prange, *At Dawn We Slept*, p. 406.
3. Congress of the United States Seventy-Ninth Congress, *Hearings Before the Joint Committee on the Investigation of the Pearl Harbor Attack* (hereafter referred to as PHA), Part 32, p. 220.
4. PHA, Part 6, pp. 2569–70, 2597, 2579, 2828; Prange, *At Dawn We Slept*, p. 470.
5. Ibid.
6. PHA, Part 6, pp. 2569–70.
7. Richardson was forced to move the fleet to Pearl Harbor in the spring of 1940 by the Roosevelt administration. When Richardson protested that the fleet would be too exposed in Hawaii, he was sacked.
8. Prange, *At Dawn We Slept*, p. 66.
9. Prange, *At Dawn We Slept*, p. 461.
10. Prange, *At Dawn We Slept*, pp. 41–42.
11. Mark Stille, *The United States Navy in World War II*, Osprey Publishing, Oxford, 2021, has been used for the details of all ships in this chapter.
12. PHA, Part 12, pp. 319–20, 323, 351–53; Part 19, pp. 3982–83.
13. Frank, *Tower of Skulls*, p. 242. The table has been modified slightly from its original form.
14. Naval History and Heritage Command website, accessed August 1, 2024.
15. Prange, *At Dawn We Slept*, p. 420.
16. Willmott, *Pearl Harbor*, p. 91.
17. Thomas Wildenberg, *Gray Steel and Black Oil*, Naval Institute Press, Annapolis, 1996, p. 169.
18. PHA, Part 36, p. 401.
19. John W. Lambert and Norman Polmar, *Defenseless*, p. 165.
20. PHA, Part 22, pp. 349–50.
21. PHA, Part 22, p. 350.
22. PHA, Part 22, pp. 350–51.
23. PHA, Part 22, p. 351.
24. PHA, Part 39, p. 304.
25. PHA, Part 39, p. 309.
26. PHA, Part 32, pp. 231–32.
27. PHA, Part 8, p. 3453.
28. Lambert and Polmar, *Defenseless*, pp. 166–67.
29. Prange, *At Dawn We Slept*, p. 136; the quotes are extracted from PHA.

30 Prange, *At Dawn We Slept*, p. 137; extracted from PHA.
31 Prange, *At Dawn We Slept*, p. 136; extracted from PHA
32 Edward S. Miller, "Kimmel's Hidden Agenda", MHQ Autumn 1991, Volume 4, Number 1. This brilliant piece of work provides an insightful overview of Kimmel's thinking.
33 Superbattleship *Yamato* was commissioned on December 16 so could have also been available.
34 PHA, Part 6, p. 2504.
35 Gordon W. Prange, Donald M. Goldstein, and Katherine V. Dillon, *Pearl Harbor: The Verdict of History*, McGraw-Hill, New York, 1986, p. 427.
36 Frank, *Tower of Skulls*, p. 238.
37 Stetson Conn, Rose E. Engelman, and Byron Fairchild, *United States Army in World War II, Guarding the United States and its Outposts*, Center of Military History, Washington, DC, 1989, pp. 168–69.
38 PHA, Part 15, p. 1635.
39 Prange, *At Dawn We Slept*, p. 58.
40 Prange, *At Dawn We Slept*, p. 91.
41 PHA, Part 12, p. 234 and Part 24, p. 1833; Leatrice R. Arakaki and John R. Kuborn, *7 December 1941 The Air Force Story*, Pacific Air Forces Office of History, Hickam Air Force Base, 1991, p. 151. There are minor differences between these sources.
42 Lambert and Polmar, *Defenseless*, p. 60.
43 Lambert and Polmar, *Defenseless*, p. 68; Prange, *At Dawn We Slept*, p. 190.
44 PHA, Part 15, p. 1626.
45 Prange, *At Dawn We Slept*, p. 62.
46 In addition to the six mobile sites, there were three fixed sites envisioned, but their towers were still located on the West Coast.
47 Prange, *At Dawn We Slept*, p. 626.
48 Ibid.
49 Conn, Engelman, and Fairchild, *United States Army in World War II, Guarding the United States and its Outposts*, pp. 168–69; PHA, Part 26, pp. 375–82; Lambert and Polmar, *Defenseless*, p. 40, provides a different number of 98 3-inch guns of which 76 were mobile. In addition there were eight 3-inch Marine guns.
50 PHA, Part 22, p. 168.
51 Terrance McGovern and Glen Willford, *Defenses of Pearl Harbor and Oahu 1907–50*, Osprey, Oxford, 2003, p. 38.
52 Prange, *At Dawn We Slept*, p. 124.

NOTES

53 Wesley F. Craven and James L. Cate, eds., *The Army Air Forces in World War II. Vol. 1: Plans and Early Operations January 1939 to August 1942*, Office of Air Force History, Washington, DC, 1983, p. 172.
54 Prange, *At Dawn We Slept*, pp. 124–25.
55 Arakaki and Kuborn, *7 December 1941 The Air Force Story*, pp. 14–15.
56 PHA, Part 27, p. 156.
57 PHA, Part 22, p. 35.
58 PHA, Part 27, pp. 138–40.
59 Craven and Cate, *The Army Air Forces In World War II, Volume One Plans and Early Operations January 1939 to August 1942*, p. 198.
60 PHA, Part 8, p. 3926; Part 9, pp. 4168, 4171.
61 PHA, Part 35, p. 82; Part 8, pp. 3399, 3896.
62 Prange, *At Dawn We Slept*, pp. 87–88; PHA, Part 4, pp. 1926–27.
63 Prange, *At Dawn We Slept*, p. 291.
64 Rochefort was the only American naval officer who met Yamamoto to come away with a less than favorable impression. He assessed him as a hothead and a menace, which he certainly became in 1941.
65 Elliot Carlson, *Joe Rochefort's War*, Naval Institute Press, Annapolis, 2011, p. 129.
66 Carlson, *Joe Rochefort's War*, p. 165.
67 PHA, Part 39, p. 304.
68 This was the same Rochefort that made dramatic penetration of JN-25(b) after Pearl Harbor and was correctly able to predict Japanese operations into the South Pacific and then against Midway. It is interesting to consider what might have happened if Rochefort and his unit had been allowed to attack JN-25(b) as early as April or May 1941 as had been briefly approved by Washington.
69 Carlson, *Joe Rochefort's War*, p. 122.
70 Carlson, *Joe Rochefort's War*, p. 131.
71 Prange, *At Dawn We Slept*, p. 362.
72 Carlson, *Joe Rochefort's War*, p. 182.

CHAPTER 6: THE STRIKING FORCE APPROACHES PEARL HARBOR

1 Prange, *At Dawn We Slept*, pp. 343–44.
2 Prange, *At Dawn We Slept*, p. 373.
3 Tabular Records of Movement for *Sazanami*, *Ushio*, and *Shiriya*, accessed on July 15, 2024; *Pearl Harbor Operations General Outline of Orders and Plans, Japanese Monograph No. 97*, Military History Section, Headquarters, Army Forces Far East, 1953.
4 Prange, *At Dawn We Slept*, p. 415.

5 Ibid.
6 Ibid.
7 Prange, *At Dawn We Slept*, p. 417.
8 Ibid.
9 Prange, *At Dawn We Slept*, p. 426.
10 Prange, *At Dawn We Slept*, pp. 427–28.
11 Prange, *At Dawn We Slept*, p. 419.
12 Prange, *At Dawn We Slept*, p. 479.
13 Prange, *At Dawn We Slept*, p. 484.

CHAPTER 7: THE FIRST ATTACK WAVE

1 George Carroll Dyer, *The Amphibians Came to Conquer: The Story of Admiral Richmond Kelly Turner*, Vol. *1*, Washington, DC, US Government Printing Office, 1972, pp. 177–79.
2 Just a few minutes' warning would have been significant. General Quarters could be set on a large ship (like a battleship) in only eight minutes. Ships that had their watertight voids open could have secured them in under 25 minutes.
3 This reveals another Japanese planning oversight. Fuchida carried only a single flare gun, meaning that there would be some period of time before a second flare could be fired. How long had the other flight leaders been instructed to wait for a possible second flare? More alarmingly, what if the single flare gun had malfunctioned?
4 Prange, *At Dawn We Slept*, p. 503.
5 Historian Alan Zimm believes that Fuchida intended to execute a no-surprise attack, probably because he incorrectly assessed that surprise had not been gained. After the war, Fuchida created the story that Takahashi, whom he considered a "blockhead," was responsible for misreading his flare signals. Given Fuchida's history of fabrication, the author agrees with this assessment. See Alan D. Zimm, "Commander Fuchida's Decision," *Naval History Magazine,* December 2016, Volume 30, Number 6, pp. 16–23.
6 David Aiken, "Torpedoing Pearl Harbor," *Military History*, December 2002, pp. 48–49.
7 USS *Utah* Report of Pearl Harbor Attack, December 15, 1941.
8 USS *Raleigh* Report of Pearl Harbor Attack, December 13, 1941.
9 Aiken, "Torpedoing Pearl Harbor," p. 50.
10 Ibid.
11 Ibid.

NOTES

12 USS *Helena* Report of Pearl Harbor Attack, December 14, 1941. *Helena* was one of two modified Brooklyn-class class light cruisers and carried 5-inch/38 guns; the first seven units of the class mounted a secondary battery of 5-inch/25 guns.
13 USS *Oglala* Report of Pearl Harbor Attack; USS *Oglala* Report of December 11, 1941; USS *Oglala* War Damage Report of December 31, 1941.
14 Aiken, "Torpedoing Pearl Harbor," p. 50.
15 Aiken, "Torpedoing Pearl Harbor," p. 51.
16 Ibid.
17 Ibid.
18 Aiken, "Torpedoing Pearl Harbor," p. 52.
19 Aiken, "Torpedoing Pearl Harbor," p. 53.
20 Ibid.
21 Ibid.
22 See Preliminary Design Section, Bureau of Ships, Navy Department, "Summary of War Damage to U.S. Battleships, Carriers, Cruisers and Destroyers, 17 October 1941 to 7 December 1942," NavShips A (374), September 15, 1943, pp. 6–10. Adding up all the ships action reports gives a figure of 25, but after the attack when a more detailed analysis could be conducted the true number was revealed.
23 Mitsuo Fuchida, "I Led the Air Attack on Pearl Harbor" in Paul Stillwell, ed., *Air Raid: Pearl Harbor!*, Naval Institute Press, Annapolis, 1981, p. 11.
24 Ibid.
25 Fuchida, "I Led the Air Attack on Pearl Harbor", p. 13.
26 Ibid.
27 Email with David Aiken, April 6, 2011; Willmott, *Pearl Harbor*, p. 190.
28 Zimm, *Attack on Pearl Harbor*, p. 196
29 John F. Di Virgilio, "Seven Seconds to Infamy," *Proceedings*, December 1997, pp. 63–64.
30 Di Virgilio, "Seven Seconds to Infamy," p. 64.
31 Di Virgilio, "Seven Seconds to Infamy," p. 65.
32 USS *Oklahoma*, Reports of Pearl Harbor Attack; Report of 18 December 1941; Report of Damage Sustained during Action at Pearl Harbor, 20 December 1941.
33 Ibid.
34 Thomas C. Hone, "The Destruction of the Battle Line at Pearl Harbor," *Proceedings*, December 1977.
35 Ibid.

36 USS *West Virginia* Report of Pearl Harbor Attack, December 11, 1941.
37 Ibid.
38 Hone, "The Destruction of the Battle Line at Pearl Harbor."
39 USS *Maryland* Report of Pearl Harbor Attack, December 15, 1941.
40 USS *Tennessee* Report of Pearl Harbor Attack, December 11, 1941.
41 Ibid.
42 Hone, "The Destruction of the Battle Line at Pearl Harbor."
43 USS *Nevada* Report of Pearl Harbor Attack, December 15, 1941.
44 USS *California* Reports of Pearl Harbor Attack, December 13, 1941 and December 22, 1941.
45 Hone, "The Destruction of the Battle Line at Pearl Harbor."
46 Ibid.
47 Ibid.
48 J. Michael Wenger, Robert Cressman, and John F. Di Virgilio, *"This is No Drill,"* Naval Institute Press, Annapolis, 2018, pp. 77–78.
49 Wenger et al., *"This is No Drill,"* pp. 80–82.
50 Wenger et al., *"This is No Drill,"* p. 87.
51 Wenger et al., *"This is No Drill,"* p. 124.
52 J. Michael Wenger, Robert Cressman, and John F. Di Virgilio, *"They're Killing My Boys,"* Naval Institute Press, Annapolis, 2019, p. 98.
53 Wenger et al., *"They're Killing My Boys,"* p. 100.
54 Wenger et al., *"They're Killing My Boys,"* p. 113.
55 Wenger et al., *"They're Killing My Boys,"* p. 116.
56 Wenger et al., *"They're Killing My Boys,"* p. 116–17.
57 Leatrice R. Arakaki and John R. Kuborn, *7 December: The Air Force Story*, Pacific Air Forces Office of History, Hickam Air Force Base, Hawaii, 1991, p. 151.
58 J. Michael Wenger, Robert Cressman, and John F. Di Virgilio, *"A Pitiful, Unholy Mess,"* Naval Institute Press, Annapolis, 2022, p. 117.
59 Wenger et al., *"A Pitiful, Unholy Mess,"* pp. 131–32.
60 Wenger et al., *"A Pitiful, Unholy Mess,"* p. 133.
61 Wenger et al., *"A Pitiful, Unholy Mess,"* pp. 141–42.
62 Wenger et al., *"A Pitiful, Unholy Mess,"* pp. 149–55.
63 Wenger et al., *"A Pitiful, Unholy Mess,"* pp. 161–64.
64 Wenger et al., *"A Pitiful, Unholy Mess,"* pp. 170–71.
65 Wenger et al., *"A Pitiful, Unholy Mess,"* p. 172.
66 Wenger et al., *"A Pitiful, Unholy Mess,"* p. 174.
67 J. Michael Wenger, Robert Cressman, and John F. Di Virgilio, *"No One Avoided Danger,"* Naval Institute Press, Annapolis, 2015, p. 8.
68 Wenger et al., *"No One Avoided Danger,"* p. 22.

NOTES

69 Wenger et al., *"No One Avoided Danger,"* pp. 70–74.
70 Robert Cressman and J. Michael Wenger, *Infamous Day: Marines at Pearl Harbor 7 December 1941*, Marine Corps Historical Center, Washington, DC, 1992, p. 16.
71 Cressman and Wenger, *Infamous Day: Marines at Pearl Harbor 7 December 1941*, pp. 16–17.
72 Cressman and Wenger, *Infamous Day: Marines at Pearl Harbor 7 December 1941*, pp. 18–19.
73 Cressman and Wenger, *Infamous Day: Marines at Pearl Harbor 7 December 1941*, p. 20.
74 Ibid.
75 Wenger et al., *"A Pitiful, Unholy Mess,"* p. 184.

CHAPTER 8: THE SECOND ATTACK WAVE

1 Peter C. Smith, *Fist From the Sky*, Stackpole Books, Mechanicsburg, PA, 2006, pp. 152–53.
2 Peter C. Smith, *Aichi D3A1/2 Val*, Crowood Press, Ramsbury, 1999, p. 63.
3 Ron Werneth, *Beyond Pearl Harbor*, Schiffer, Atglen, PA, 2008, p. 43.
4 Osamu Tagaya, *Aichi 99 Kanbaku 'Val' Units 1937–42*, Osprey Publishing, Oxford, 2011, p. 30.
5 USS *New Orleans* Report of Pearl Harbor Attack, December 13, 1942; USS *Rigel* Report of Pearl Harbor Attack, December 9, 1942.
6 Tagaya, *Aichi 99 Kanbaku 'Val' Units 1937–42*, p. 30.
7 USS *Cassin* Report of Pearl Harbor Attack, December 13, 1942; USS *Downes* Report of Pearl Harbor Attack, December 17, 1942; USS *Pennsylvania* Report of Pearl Harbor Attack, December 16, 1942; Summary of War Damage to U.S. Battleships, Carriers, Cruisers and Destroyers 17 October, 1941 to 7 December, 1942, Preliminary Design Section Bureau of Ships Navy Department, 15 September, 1943, p. 11.
8 USS *Dale* Report of Pearl Harbor Attack, December 28, 1942.
9 Tagaya, *Aichi 99 Kanbaku 'Val' Units 1937–42*, p. 31.
10 USS *Helena* Report of Pearl Harbor Attack, December 14, 1942.
11 Tagaya, *Aichi 99 Kanbaku 'Val' Units 1937–42*, p. 31.
12 USS *Dobbin* Report of Pearl Harbor Attack, December 11, 1942.
13 USS *California* Reports of Pearl Harbor Attack, December 13, 1941 and December 22, 1941; Myron J. Smith, *Golden State Battlewagon*, Pictorial Histories Publishing, Missoula, MT, 1983, p. 23.
14 Smith, *Golden State Battlewagon*, p. 23.
15 Tagaya, *Aichi 99 Kanbaku 'Val' Units 1937–42*, p. 31.

16 USS *Pennsylvania* Report of Pearl Harbor Attack, December 16, 1942.
17 Tagaya, *Aichi 99 Kanbaku 'Val' Units 1937–42*, p. 31.
18 Tagaya, *Aichi 99 Kanbaku 'Val' Units 1937–42*, pp. 31–32.
19 Commander Battle Force, Report of the Pearl Harbor Attack, January 9, 1942.
20 USS *St Louis* Reports of Pearl Harbor Attack, December 10, 1941 and December 25, 1941.
21 Tagaya, *Aichi 99 Kanbaku 'Val' Units 1937–42*, p. 32.
22 USS *Maryland* Report of Pearl Harbor Attack, December 15, 1941.
23 Tagaya, *Aichi 99 Kanbaku 'Val' Units 1937–42*, p. 32.
24 USS *Helm* Report of Pearl Harbor Attack, December 11, 1941.
25 Tagaya, *Aichi 99 Kanbaku 'Val' Units 1937–42*, p. 32; USS *Neosho* Report of Pearl Harbor Attack, December 11, 1942.
26 Werneth, *Beyond Pearl Harbor*, pp. 16–18.
27 Tagaya, *Aichi 99 Kanbaku 'Val' Units 1937–42*, pp. 32–33.
28 USS *Shaw* Report of Pearl Harbor Attack, January 29, 1942.
29 Tagaya, *Aichi 99 Kanbaku 'Val' Units 1937–42*, p. 33.
30 USS *Tangier* Report of Pearl Harbor Attack, January 2, 1942.
31 Ibid.
32 Tagaya, *Aichi 99 Kanbaku 'Val' Units 1937–42*, p. 33; Werneth, *Beyond Pearl Harbor*, pp. 43, 274.
33 USS *Raleigh* Report of Pearl Harbor Attack, December 13, 1942.
34 Tagaya, *Aichi 99 Kanbaku 'Val' Units 1937–42*, p. 33.
35 Tagaya, *Aichi 99 Kanbaku 'Val' Units 1937–42*, p. 34.
36 The myth that the Japanese could have bottled up the Pacific Fleet by sinking *Nevada* in the channel persists to this day. The maximum width of the channel averages about 400 yards (1,200 feet). Since *Nevada's* extreme length was 583 feet, it would have been impossible for her to block the channel even if she had been sunk in an exactly perpendicular position.
37 Smith, *Aichi D3A1/2 Val*, p. 65; Hone, "The Destruction of the Battle Line at Pearl Harbor."
38 Smith, *Aichi D3A1/2 Val*, pp. 65–67.
39 Smith, *Aichi D3A1/2 Val*, p. 67.
40 Ibid.
41 Tagaya, *Aichi 99 Kanbaku 'Val' Units 1937–42*, p. 34.
42 Goldstein and Dillon, *The Pearl Harbor Papers*, front and back overleaves.
43 Chart 47 contained in Japanese Monograph 113 gives another even less-valuable version of the number of hits attained by the dive-bombers. It states that 75 (and probably 78) bombs were dropped.

NOTES

Of these, at least 38 were hits. The value of the information is low since only one hit is attributed to dive-bombers from *Akagi*, only three to *Kaga*, while *Soryu* is given credit for 14 hits of 17 bombs dropped and *Hiryu* 15 hits of 16 dropped. The identity of the targets is also unclear. Japanese Monograph No. 113 (Navy) Task Force Operation, Japanese Research Division, Military History section, Headquarters, United States Army Forces, Far East, n.d., Chart 47.

44 Summary of War Damage to U.S. Battleships, Carriers, Cruisers and Destroyers 17 October, 1941 to 7 December, 1942, Preliminary Design Section Bureau of Ships Navy Department, 15 September, 1943, pp. 10–11.
45 Ibid, pp. 6–11.
46 Alan D. Zimm, "The Second-Wave Attack on Battleship Row," *Proceedings*, December 2021, p. 21.
47 Ibid, p. 22.
48 Wenger et al., *"This is No Drill,"* p. 150.
49 Wenger et al., *"This is No Drill"*, p. 191; PHA Pt. 28, pp. 854–55.
50 Wenger et al., *"They're Killing My Boys,"* p. 166.
51 Wenger et al., *"They're Killing My Boys,"* pp. 166–67.
52 Wenger et al., *"They're Killing My Boys,"* pp. 168–69.
53 Wenger et al., *"They're Killing My Boys,"* p. 182.
54 Ibid.
55 Wenger et al., *"They're Killing My Boys,"* p. 207.
56 Wenger et al., *"No One Avoided Danger,"* pp. 84–85.
57 Wenger et al., *"No One Avoided Danger,"* pp. 88–89.
58 Wenger et al., *"No One Avoided Danger,"* p. 90.
59 Wenger et al., *"No One Avoided Danger,"* p. 96.
60 Wenger et al., *"No One Avoided Danger,"* p. 100.
61 Wenger et al., *"No One Avoided Danger,"* p. 102.
62 Ibid.
63 Prange, *At Dawn We Slept*, p. 491.
64 Patrol Squadron Eleven Report for Pearl Harbor Attack.
65 Wenger et al., *"No One Avoided Danger,"* pp. 120, 123.
66 Cressman and Wenger, *Infamous Day: Marines at Pearl Harbor*, p. 20.
67 Cressman and Wenger, *Infamous Day: Marines at Pearl Harbor*, p. 22.
68 Samuel Eliot Morison, *History of United States Naval Operations in World War II, Volume III, The Rising Sun in the Pacific 1931–April 1942*, Little Brown and Company, Boston, 1975, pp. 122–23. These numbers conflict slightly with other sources on Marine aircraft present; see Frank O. Hough et al., *Volume I, Pearl Harbor to Guadalcanal, History of*

the U.S. Marine Corps Operations in World War II, Historical Branch, Headquarters, US Marine Corps, Washington DC (n.d.), p. 73; and Robert Sherrod, *History of Marine Corps Aviation in World War II,* Combat Forces Press, Washington, 1952, p. 33.
69 Wenger et al., *"A Pitiful, Unholy Mess,"* p. 184.
70 Wenger et al., *"A Pitiful, Unholy Mess,"* pp. 197–201.
71 The exploits of Nishikaichi did not end here. His crash-landing on Ni'ihau prompted the so-called Ni'ihau Incident from December 7 to 13. The inhabitants of the island, unaware of the Pearl Harbor attack, initially welcomed Nishikaichi as a guest. However, the resident who first encountered Nishikaichi prudently took his pistol and papers relating to the attack. Shintani Ishimatsu, a resident born in Japan, was brought in to interpret; he later attempted to negotiate for Nishikaichi the return of his papers. By evening, the residents learned of the attack and apprehended Nishikaichi. He was allowed to stay with the Haradas, the other two residents of Japanese descent on the island, but under guard. After Nishikaichi revealed to the Haradas about the attack they agreed to help him. Nishikaichi and Harada Yoshio escaped the guard and destroyed Nishikaichi's Zero and papers. Later they took two residents, Benehakaka "Ben" Kanahele and his wife Kealoha "Ella" Kanahele prisoner. On the morning of December 13, the Kanaheles overcame the fatigued Nishikaichi and Harada, and Ella killed Nishikaichi. Ben Kanahele was wounded in the fracas, and Harada committed suicide. Ben was decorated for his action though Ella received no official recognition. The incident became widely known in the United States with the role of the Hawaiians given prominence. The role of the three Japanese residents on the island gave cause for concern and increased distrust of Japanese American residents on Hawaii and on the mainland.
72 David Aiken, "Ghosts of Pearl Harbor," *Flight Journal,* June 2007, pp. 26–28.
73 Wenger et al., *"A Pitiful, Unholy Mess,"* p. 233.
74 Wenger et al., *"A Pitiful, Unholy Mess,"* pp. 209–10; Aiken, "Ghosts of Pearl Harbor," pp. 30–31.
75 Aiken, "Ghosts of Pearl Harbor," p. 32.
76 Wenger et al., *"A Pitiful, Unholy Mess,"* p. 216.
77 Wenger et al., *"A Pitiful, Unholy Mess,"* pp. 214–24.
78 Wenger et al., *"A Pitiful, Unholy Mess,"* p. 225.
79 Wenger et al., *"A Pitiful, Unholy Mess,"* p. 226.
80 Wenger et al., *"A Pitiful, Unholy Mess,"* p. 241.

81 Tagaya, *Aichi 99 Kanbaku 'Val' Units 1937–42*, p. 29.
82 Tagaya, *Aichi 99 Kanbaku 'Val' Units 1937–42*, p. 37.
83 Tagaya, *Aichi 99 Kanbaku 'Val' Units 1937–42*, p. 38.
84 Willmott, *Pearl Harbor*, p. 203. This information comes from the Japanese official history of the Hawaiian Operation. For the first-wave attack, these records include 185 aircraft, even though only 183 took part.
85 Another version of Japanese losses comes from a monograph prepared by former Imperial Navy officers after the war. It generally comports with more current versions and may fill in some of the gaps in damaged aircraft. In this version, losses were 29 (21 "dove into enemy" and eight unknown). One aircraft was forced to ditch and one more was so badly damaged it required depot-level repair. Damaged aircraft totaled 121 aircraft (26 Kates, 71 Vals, 24 Zeros). Monograph 113, p. 40.
86 Ibid.
87 Mark Chambers with Tony Holmes, *Nakajima B5N 'Kate' and B6N 'Jill' Units*, Osprey, Oxford, 2017, p. 24.
88 Frank, *Tower of Skulls*, pp. 289 and 614.
89 Ibid.
90 Tagaya, *Aichi 99 Kanbaku 'Val' Units 1937–42*, p. 38.
91 Ibid. Records from *Hiryu* do not exist.
92 Willmott, *Pearl Harbor*, p. 203.
93 Willmott, *Pearl Harbor*, p. 186.

CHAPTER 9: THE AMERICAN REACTION AND THE MYTH OF THE SECOND ATTACK

1 Patrol Wing Two Report for Pearl Harbor 20 December 1941; Wenger et al., "This is No Drill," pp. 160–63.
2 Patrol Wing Two Report for Pearl Harbor 20 December 1941; Wenger et al., "This is No Drill," pp. 159–60.
3 Wenger et al., "This is No Drill," p. 167.
4 Wenger et al., "This is No Drill," p. 178.
5 Wenger et al., "This is No Drill," pp. 180–81.
6 Wenger et al., "This is No Drill," pp. 185–90.
7 USS *Enterprise* (CV-6) Air Group Action Report; USS *Enterprise* (CV-6) Scouting Squadron 6 Report for Pearl Harbor Attack.
8 Cressman and Wenger, *Infamous Day: Marines at Pearl Harbor*, p. 22.
9 Cressman and Wenger, *Infamous Day: Marines at Pearl Harbor*, p. 23.
10 USS *Enterprise* (CV-6) Air Group Action Report; Wenger et al., "This is No Drill," pp. 174–76.
11 USS *Enterprise* (CV-6) Air Group Action Report.

12 Wenger et al., "They're Killing My Boys," p. 192.
13 PHA pt. 22, p. 195.
14 Wenger et al., "They're Killing My Boys," p. 196.
15 Wenger et al., "They're Killing My Boys," p. 197.
16 Prange, *At Dawn We Slept*, pp. 546–47.
17 Gordon W. Prange, Donald M. Goldstein, and Katherine V. Dillon, *God's Samurai*, Brassey's, Washington, 1990, pp. 40–41.
18 Evans, *The Japanese Navy in World War II*, "The Air Attack on Pearl Harbor," Naval Institute Press, Annapolis, 1986, p. 69.
19 United States Strategic Bombing Survey, *Interrogations of Japanese Officials Volume I*, US Government Printing Office, Washington, 1946, p. 124.
20 Goldstein and Dillon, *The Pearl Harbor Papers*, p. 162.
21 Willmott, *Pearl Harbor*, p. 156. The quote is drawn from Genda's *Recollections of the Pearl Harbor Operation* first printed in 1967 and reprinted in 1998.
22 Prange, *At Dawn We Slept*, p. 541. This is from the 1963 interview with Fuchida.
23 Prange, *At Dawn We Slept*, p. 545.
24 Prange, *At Dawn We Slept*, p. 541.
25 Prange, *At Dawn We Slept*, p. 542.
26 Prange, *At Dawn We Slept*, pp. 542–43.
27 Morison, *History of United States Naval Operations in World War II, Volume III, The Rising Sun in the Pacific 1931–April 1942*, p. 125.
28 Donald M. Goldstein and Katherine V. Dillon, *The Way it Was: Pearl Harbor*, Brassey's, Washington, 1991, p. 24.
29 E. B. Potter and Chester W. Nimitz, eds., *The Great Sea War*, Bramhall House, New York, 1960, p. 197.
30 Prange, *At Dawn We Slept*, p. 550.
31 Paul Stilwell, ed., *Air Raid: Pearl Harbor*, "A Tactical View of Pearl Harbor," Naval Institute Press, Annapolis, 1981, p. 139.
32 Jonathan Parshall, "Reflecting on Fuchida, or 'A Tale of Three Whoppers,'" *Naval War College Review*, Spring 2010, Vol. 63, No. 2, pp. 128–31.
33 Prange, *At Dawn We Slept*, p. 543.
34 Prange, *At Dawn We Slept*, p. 542.
35 Arakaki and Kuborn, *7 December 1941: The Air Force Story*, p. 151.
36 Ibid.
37 Zimm, *Attack on Pearl Harbor*, p. 310. Zimm had made a detailed assessment of the likely degree of damage Japanese bombs would have made on the Navy Yard, the highlights of which are presented here.

38 Zimm, *Attack on Pearl Harbor*, pp. 310–11.
39 Zimm, *Attack on Pearl Harbor*, pp. 317–18.
40 Zimm, *Attack on Pearl Harbor*, pp. 318–19. Zimm ran a simulation in which 280 bombs were aimed at the fuel tanks. In this favorable scenario for the Japanese, in 90 percent of the cases between 22 and 35 tanks were hit. Hitting a tank with a bomb does not automatically set it afire, and the effects of the fire-suppression systems in place at Pearl Harbor need to be considered.
41 Evans, *The Japanese Navy in World War II*, "The Air Attack on Pearl Harbor," p. 70. The source is a document provided by Fuchida.
42 Prange, *At Dawn We Slept*, p. 544. The quote is from a 1948 interview with Kusaka.
43 Prange, *At Dawn We Slept*, p. 545.
44 Ugaki, *Fading Victory*, p. 47.
45 Prange, *At Dawn We Slept*, p. 550.
46 Prange, *At Dawn We Slept*, p. 549.

CHAPTER 10: THE FORGOTTEN OFFENSIVE: JAPANESE SUBMARINES OFF HAWAII

1 Mark Stille, *Imperial Japanese Navy Submarines of World War II 1941–45*, Osprey Publishing, Oxford, 2007, pp. 4–5. The short account provides a good overview of the confusing IJN nomenclature for its submarines.
2 Evans and Peattie, *Kaigun*, pp. 428–29.
3 Evans and Peattie, *Kaigun*, p. 429.
4 Evans and Peattie, *Kaigun*, pp. 431–32.
5 Evans and Peattie, *Kaigun*, p. 432.
6 Of interest, this was the lowest number of submarines in commission by any of the primary naval powers. In contrast, the USN had 111 submarines in commission in December 1941. The IJN's relative lack of submarines was a major operational constraint during the war.
7 Fuller, *Japanese Admirals 1926–45*, p. 213.
8 Dorr Carpenter and Norman Polmar, *Submarines of the Imperial Japanese Navy*, Naval Institute Press, Annapolis, 1986, p. 12.
9 David C. Evans, ed., *The Japanese Navy in World War II* (Second Edition), Shigeru Fukudome, *The Hawaii Operation*, Naval Institute Press, Annapolis, 1986, p. 25.
10 Fukudome, *The Hawaii Operation*, p. 28.
11 Carpenter and Polmar, *Submarines of the Imperial Japanese Navy*, p. 13.
12 Carl Boyd and Akihiko Yoshida, *The Japanese Submarine Force and World War II*, Naval Institute Press, Annapolis, 1995, p. 56. This

information comes from a map in *Senshi Sosho* (War History Series), vol. 98, covering the Hawaii Operation.
13. Prange, *At Dawn We Slept*, p. 340.
14. Boyd and Akihiko, *The Japanese Submarine Force and World War II*, p. 56.
15. *I-10* TROM, accessed April 21, 2024 from www.combinedfleet.com.
16. *I-26* TROM, accessed April 21, 2024 from www.combinedfleet.com.
17. Prange, *At Dawn We Slept*, p. 431.
18. *I-26* TROM, accessed April 25, 2024 from www.combinedfleet.com.
19. Ibid.
20. Ibid.
21. James P. Delgado, Terry Kerby, Hans K. Van Tilburg, et al., *The Lost Submarines of Pearl Harbor*, Texas A&M University Press, College Station, 2016, p. 18. Use of the third character marked them as third-class submarines. The first two letters in kanji, I and RO, were used to indicate first- and second-class submarines.
22. Zenji Orita with Joseph D. Harrington, *I-Boat Captain*, Major Books, Canoga Park, 1976, p. 28.
23. Fukudome, *The Hawaii Operation*, p. 35.
24. Prange, *At Dawn We Slept*, p. 338.
25. Kazuo Sakamaki, *I Attacked Pearl Harbor*, Rollston Press, Honolulu, 2017, p. 29.
26. Prange, *At Dawn We Slept*, p. 337.
27. Prange, *At Dawn We Slept*, p. 338.
28. Orita and Harrington, *I-Boat Captain*, p. 31.
29. Prange, *At Dawn We Slept*, p. 340.
30. Prange, *At Dawn We Slept*, p. 341.
31. Ugaki, *Fading Victory*, p. 26.
32. USS *Antares* (AKS-3) Action Report. The report was written after the action when the identity of the mysterious object was known. On December 7, this would have been much less clear.
33. USS *Ward* (DD-139) Action Report.
34. Delgado et al., *Lost Submarines of Pearl Harbor*, p. 128.
35. USS *Helm* (DD-388) Action Report.
36. USS *Zane* (DMS-14) Action Report.
37. USS *Curtiss* (AV-4) Action Report.
38. USS *Monaghan* (DD 354) Action Report.
39. Sakamaki, *I Attacked Pearl Harbor*, p. 21.
40. Sakamaki, *I Attacked Pearl Harbor*, pp. 36–44.
41. USS *St Louis* (CL-49) Action Report.
42. Zimm, *Attack on Pearl Harbor*, pp. 340–41.

NOTES

43 Zimm, *Attack on Pearl Harbor*, p. 341.
44 Delgado et al., *Lost Submarines of Pearl Harbor*, p. 165.
45 Delgado et al., *Lost Submarines of Pearl Harbor*, pp. 146–47.
46 Burl Burlingame, *Advance Force Pearl Harbor*, Pacific Monograph, Kailua, 1992, p. 199.
47 Prange, *At Dawn We Slept*, p. 571.
48 Prange, *At Dawn We Slept*, p. 572.
49 *I-69* TROM, accessed April 30, 2024 from www.combinedfleet.com.
50 *I-70* TROM, accessed April 24, 2024 from www.combinedfleet.com.
51 *I-9* TROM, accessed April 24, 2024 from www.combinedfleet.com.
52 *I-10* TROM, accessed April 22, 2024 from www.combinedfleet.com.
53 *I-7* TROM, accessed April 23, 2024 from www.combinedfleet.com.
54 *I-75* TROM, accessed April 24, 2024 from www.combinedfleet.com.
55 *I-72* TROM, accessed April 25, 2024 from www.combinedfleet.com.
56 To be fair, USN submarines used much the same tactics at the start of the war which emphasized concealment over aggressive offensive action. This explains the failure of the 29 submarines in the Asiatic Fleet to exert a high toll from Japanese invasion forces attacking the Philippines and the Dutch East Indies at the start of the war. The difference is that American submarines changed their tactics and became much more effective later in the war while the Japanese never changed theirs and remained ineffective. Under special circumstances Japanese submarines did effectively attack USN fleet units, like when the Americans insisted on operating in the same area southeast of Guadalcanal for prolonged periods even though Japanese submarines were known to be present.
57 Boyd and Yoshida, *The Japanese Submarine Force and World War II*, p. 64.
58 *I-6* TROM, accessed April 25, 2024 from www.combinedfleet.com.
59 Navships, Summary of War Damage to U.S. Battleships, Carriers, Cruisers and Destroyers 17 October, 1941 to 7 December, 1942, dated 15 September 1943, p. 26; Morison, *History of United States Naval Operations in World War II, Volume III, The Rising Sun in the Pacific 1931–April 1942*, p. 260.
60 *I-6* TROM, accessed April 25, 2024 from www.combinedfleet.com.

CHAPTER 11: THE RECKONING

1 Morison, *History of United States Naval Operations in World War II, Volume III, The Rising Sun in the Pacific 1931–April 1942*, p. 126.
2 The only day in which more American casualties may have been sustained was June 6, 1944, during the invasion of Normandy. There is no definitive casualty count for D-Day, but once the fate of all the

missing personnel is resolved, the total count still would not equal that of Pearl Harbor. See Frank, *Tower of Skulls*, p. 289. On the other hand, the overall loss rate of military personnel on Oahu was low. Approximately 57,000 men were present on the island on December 7, making the loss rate of those killed only 4 percent.

3 Morison, *The Rising Sun in the Pacific 1931–April 1942*, p. 107.
4 Morison, *The Rising Sun in the Pacific 1931–April 1942*, p. 113.
5 Morison, *The Rising Sun in the Pacific 1931–April 1942*, p. 110.
6 Morison, *The Rising Sun in the Pacific 1931–April 1942*, p. 119.
7 Willmott, *Pearl Harbor*, p. 134.
8 Arakaki and Kuborn, *7 December 1941 The Air Force Story*, p. 151.
9 Arakaki and Kuborn, *7 December 1941 The Air Force Story*, pp. 157–58.
10 This figure is not firm since there is no conclusive data on the number of utility aircraft lost at NAS Pearl Harbor. Two were lost at NAS Kaneohe Bay.
11 Wenger et al., *"This is No Drill,"* p. 191.
12 Morison, *The Rising Sun in the Pacific 1931–April 1942*, p. 123.

CHAPTER 12: WHY PEARL HARBOR MATTERS

1 Morison, *History of United States Naval Operations in World War II, Volume III, The Rising Sun in the Pacific 1931–April 1942*, p. 132.
2 Frank, *Tower of Skulls*, p. 294.
3 Frank, *Tower of Skulls*, pp. 295, 615.
4 Prange, *At Dawn We Slept*, p. 580.
5 H. P. Willmott, *Empires in the Balance*, p. 68.
6 Willmott, *Empires in the Balance*, p. 68.
7 Ibid., pp. 69–70.
8 Willmott, *Pearl Harbor*, p. 39.
9 Willmott, *Pearl Harbor*, p. 179.
10 John W. Dower, *War Without Mercy*, Pantheon Books, New York, 1986, pp. 259–60.
11 Dower, *War Without Mercy*, p. 260.
12 Prange, *At Dawn We Slept*, p. 21. The quotes come from an interview with Genda.
13 Francis Pike, *Hirohito's War*, Bloomsbury, London, 2015, p. 182.
14 Dower, *War Without Mercy*, p. 260.
15 PHA, Part 26, p. 207.
16 Mark Stille, *The United States Navy in World War Two*, Osprey Publishing, Oxford, 2021. The numbers are arrived at by examining each class of ship constructed during the war. The totals include only

NOTES

ships built for the USN. More ships were launched before the end of the war but were not commissioned before the end of it.

17 Samuel Eliot Morison, *History of the United States Naval Operations in World War II, Vol. III, The Rising Sun in the Pacific 1931-April 1942* p. 214.
18 Command Summary of Fleet Admiral Chester W. Nimitz, USN (the "Nimitz Graybook"), 7 December 1941–31 August 1945, Volume 1 of 8, pp. 12, 94. The figures were updated through January 13, 1942 and do not include ships of the Asiatic Fleet.
19 Nimitz Graybook, Volume 1, p. 28.
20 This act was performed by *I-6* which was part of the original wave of fleet submarines sent to support the Pearl Harbor attack. This success could therefore be considered part of the Hawaii Operation.

CHAPTER 13: KIMMEL AND SHORT: RESPONSIBILITY MISPLACED?

1 Prange et al., *Pearl Harbor: The Verdict of History*, p. 460.
2 PHA, Part 5, p. 2338.
3 Ibid.
4 Frank, *Tower of Skulls*, p. 291; Prange, *At Dawn We Slept*, pp. 585–90.
5 Prange, *At Dawn We Slept*, p. 588.
6 Prange, *At Dawn We Slept*, pp. 593–94.
7 Prange, *At Dawn We Slept*, p. 594.
8 Report of the Commission Appointed by the President of the United States to Investigate and Report the Facts Relating to the Attack Made by Japanese Armed Forces upon Pearl Harbor in the Territory of Hawaii on December 7, 1941 (The Roberts Commission Report), pp. 20–21.
9 Prange, *At Dawn We Slept*, p. 619.
10 Prange, *At Dawn We Slept*, p. 620.
11 Report of Army Pearl Harbor Board, pp. 297–300.
12 PHA, Part 39, pp. 321 and 308. The proceedings of the Navy Court of Inquiry, and all other investigations on the attack, can be found in the Joint Committee on the Investigation of the Pearl Harbor Attack report.
13 PHA, Part 39, pp. 343–45.
14 Prange, *At Dawn We Slept*, p. 663.
15 Report by Admiral H. K. Hewitt on Further Pearl Harbor Investigation, pp. 175–80.
16 PHA, Part 39, pp. 388–89.
17 Prange, *At Dawn We Slept*, pp. 722–23.

18 Dorn Report, p. 1.
19 Dorn Report, p. 4.
20 Dorn Report, Part III, pages III-7–11.
21 Fred Borch and Daniel Martinez, *Kimmel, Short and Pearl Harbor*, Naval Institute Press, Annapolis, 2005, p. 101.
22 PHA Part 4, p. 1962.
23 Frank, *Tower of Skulls*, p. 297.
24 Frank, *Tower of Skulls*, p. 296.
25 Charles R. Anderson, *Day of Lightning, Years of Scorn*, Naval Institute Press, Annapolis, 2005, p. 97.
26 PHA, Part 22, pp. 72–75; Part 23, pp. 977, 1106, 1111.
27 PHA, Part 22, pp. 490–91.
28 PHA, Part 32, p. 504.
29 Husband E. Kimmel, *Admiral Kimmel's Story*, Henry Regency Company, Chicago, 1955, p. 66.
30 Kimmel, *Admiral Kimmel's Story*, pp. 67–68.
31 Prange et al., *Pearl Harbor: The Verdict of History*, p. 450.
32 PHA, Part 32, p. 215.
33 Kimmel, *Admiral Kimmel's Story*, p. 25.
34 Kimmel, *Admiral Kimmel's Story*, pp. 72–73.
35 Prange, *At Dawn We Slept*, pp. 189–90.
36 Arakaki and Kuborn, *7 December 1941 The Air Force Story*, p. 151.

Index

Note: Page locators in bold refer to maps, charts and illustrations.

action reports 202, 214, 219, 238–239, 240, 241, 242, 243, 244, 245, 246, 247, 310
air bases in the Philippines 58, 59, 334
air formations 115–116, 132, 137, 138, 211, 253
air speeds 131, 136, 138, 139–140, 143, 171
air warning systems 172, 372–373
   Fort Shafter Information Center 172, 174, 196, 197, 261, 287, 371–372, 395
aircraft 17, 27, 56, 59, 83, 88, 139–140, 143, 159, 162, 170, 171, 193, 223, 224, 226, 229, 230, 232, 233, 254, 258, 259, 271–272, 273, 274–275, 287, **287,** 288, 301, 314, 326, 350
   Aichi D3A1 "Val" (Japan) 25, 28, 104, 108, 136, 137, 159, 193, 194, 221, 222, 223–224, 226, 227, 228, 231, 235, 236, 239–245, 258, 260, 262, 264, 265, **265–266,** 266, **267,** 268, 270, 283, 284, 287, 288, 291, 317
   Boeing B-17 (US) 26, 58, 88, 142–143, 161, 171, 174, 175, 190, 197, 223, 224–225, 232, 233, 254, 258, 264, 272–273, 274, 275, 288, 326, 334
   Consolidated PBY Catalina (US) 27, 88, 104, 148, 159, 161, 167, 221, 222, 223, 229, 230, 252, 256, 257, 264, 270–271, 306, 326, 359, 368, 369
   Curtiss P-36 Hawk (US) 88, 170, 226, 228, 260, 261, 262, 263, 264, 287, **287**
   Curtiss P-40 Warhawk (US) 26–27, 41, 88, 170, 226, 228, 232, 233, 258, 259, 260, 263, 264, 274, 287, **287,** 326
   Douglas SBD Dauntless (US) 143, 159, 162, 223, 230, 258, 272, 273, 313, 326
   Mitsubishi A6M2 "Zero" (Japan) 24–25, 28, 74, 104, 114–115, 138, 143, 144, 170, 188, 193, 194, 195, 221, 224–225, 227, 230, 254, 256, 257, 259, 262, 264–265, **265–266, 267,** 269, 271, 272, 274, 284
   Nakajima B5N2 "Kate" (Japan) 25, 102, 107, 108, 115, 131, 134, 140, 159, 192, 193, 194, 200, 201, 203, 205, 207, 209, 210, 212, 219, 252, 253, 255, 264, **265–266, 267,** 268, 283, 284, 285, 286, 287, 288, 291, 311, 317
Aleutians campaign (May – August 1943), the 322
American Volunteer Group ("Flying Tigers"), the 41
ammunition storage and supply 170, 173, 175–176, 232
antiaircraft fire and capabilities 132, 141–142, 143, 153, 173, 209, 210, 223, 237, 238, 240, 242, 245, 251, 270, 272, 287, 288, 291
armor penetration 13, 26, 92, 101, 131, 132, 136, 137, 214, 321

Army Board inquiry, the 357–358, 360–361
Army Pearl Harbor Board, the 358

barrage balloons 191, 192
Battle of Coral Sea (May 1942), the 324, 350
Battle of Midway, the (June 1942) 20, 117, 121, 143, 283, 322, 324, 326, 341, 350–351
Bellinger, Rear Adm Patrick 23, 150, 160, 161, 162, 270, 271, 274, 353, 356, 368, 369
bomb payloads 131, 136, 143, 159, 171
and detonation failure 213, 216, 238, 289
bombing instructions 101–102
British interests and actions 41, 58

CAP (combat air patrol) missions 108–109, 140–141, 143, 194, 265, 268, 269, 286
code decryption 176–177, 179–180, 181, 184, 350
Combat Intelligence Unit (Station Hypo) 179, 183, 184
command culture in the Japanese military 122

deaths 18, 25, 26, 33, 34, 202, 205, 209, 215, 216, 217, 218, 219, 225, 240, 241, 254, 257, 259, 260, 272, 313, 316, 317, **318**, 318–319, 320, 321, 353
deck parks (flight decks) 128
DEI (Dutch East Indies), the 14, 42, 49, 58, 63, 332–333, 338
diplomatic code decryptions 176
dive-bombing 27, 92, 98, 102, 103–104, 107, 127, 129, 132, 136–137, 144, 198, 221–225, 226–227, 234, 235, 236–250, **248, 249, 250,** 258, 260, 268, **268,** 284–285
dogfights 138, 170, 262
Dorn Report, the 362–364
Draft Understanding, the 38–39

enemy COAs (courses of action) 180–181
"Essentials for Carrying Out the Empire's Policies, The" (paper) 42–43, 45
European colonial possessions 14, 36, 37, 58
European theater, the 7, 11, 14, 35, 39, 41

fighter escorts 59, 91, 108–109, 139, 141–142, 273
fire control systems 141–142, 153
Ford Island 24, 25, 104, 200
Battleship Row 25, 26, 102, 103, 115, 200, 203, 205–209, **208,** 211, 214–217, 241, 243, 310, 311
French Indochina 36–37, 40, 41, 49, 51
Fuchida, Cdr Mitsuo 16, 19, 84, 100, 101–102, 103, **105,** 109, 111, 115, 120, 122–124, 129, 130, 132, 134, 137, 188, 194, 195, 197–198, 200, 201, 211–212, 221, 236, 248–250, 251, 264, 276–279, 280, 281, 304
fuel supplies 45, 59, 74, 158, 282, 289–290, 322, 333, 346, 371
and refueling 13, 68, 72, 77, 91–92, 94, 96, 97–98, 149, 186, 187, 189, 190–191, 282, 283, 299
see also Japanese oil requirements
fuel tank farms 19, 28, 108, 215, 232, 246, 278, 279, 280, 281, 283, 289–291
Fukudome, Vice Adm Shigeru 69, 71, 73, 75, 76, 80, 93, 299, 303

Genda, Cdr Minoru 16, 17, 19, 20, 23, 64–65, 68, 73, 74, 75, 76, 78, 79, 88, 89, 90–92, 93, 94–97, 98–99, 100, 101, 103, 108, 109, 110, 111, 113–114, 115, 116, 119, 122–123, 124, 130, 132, 134, 137, 188, 189–190, 191–192, 194, 197, 198, 201, 211, 220, 221, 223, 229, 236, 237, 249, 257, 269, 276, 277, 278, 279, 280, 281, 283, 285, 286, 288, 292, 304, 305
glide-bombing profiles 239–240, 242, 251
Guadalcanal campaign (August 1942 – February 1943), the 118, 322, 323, 324, 327

Hawaiian Air Force, the 169–171, 174, 223, 226, 232, 261, 277, 287
see also USAAF (US Army Air Force), the
Hickam Field 104, 206, 223–225, 237, 238, 253–254, 290
Hirohito, Emperor 40, 43, 44–45, 47, 48, 50
horizontal bombing 123–124, 127, 129, 130–132, 134, 142, 144, 211–214, 217–218, 234
Hull, Cordell 38, 39, 50, 51, 52, 53, 54, 329, 330, 331, 353, 354–355

INDEX

IJA (Imperial Japanese Army), the 31, 34, 35, 36, 37, 39–40, 43, 46, 49, 58, 60, 62
IJN (Imperial Japanese Navy), the 8, 9, 10, 15, 21, 35, 38, 40, 41, 43, 46–47, 48, 52, 56, 57, 58, 62, 66, 84–85, 118, 119–120, 127, 165, 179, 346, 369
   battleships 121, **154,** 197, 324
   Carrier Divisions 24, 79, 91, 120, 123, 138, 184
      Div 1 120, 125, 129, 137, 138, 184, 193, 194, 220–221
      Div 2 120, 124, 125, 127, 129, 137, 138, 184, 193, 194, 220–221, 269
      Div 5 99, 121, 124, 125–126, 129–130, 229, 268, 269
   carriers 127–128, 151, **154,** 181, 345
   Combined Fleet 59, 67, 70–71, 75, 80, 81, 82, 111, 118, 121, 126, 134, 138, **154,** 164, 185, 335, 351
   Destroyer Squadron 1 126–127
   destroyers **154,** 189, 190, 193
   heavy cruisers **154,** 197
   and JN-25(b) code 179, 181, 184
   light cruisers **154,** 197, 296
   Midway Bombardment Force 187–188
   and the Naval General Staff 13, 14, 58, 59, 64, 70, 71, 72, 73, 74, 75, 76, 81, 82, 85, 86, 94, 98, 138, 190, 293, 340, 341
   Sasaki Group 300, 306
   ships 77, 89, 97, 100, 114, 120–121, 126, 127, 139, 140, 165, 186, 187, 188, 190, 191, 193, 194, 197, 235, 304, 344–346, 347, 350
      Akagi (carrier) 19, 24, 28, 61, 77, 79, 88, 94, 99, 102, 109, 111, 120, 123, 125, 132, 135, 136, 141, 186, 187, 188, 191, 192, 193, 195, 200, 205, 206, 207, 209, 221, 222, 231, 235, 237, 238, 243–245, 260, 264, 265, **265, 267, 268,** 276, 277–278, 283, 286, 351
      Hiryu (carrier) 24, 77, 99, 102, 109, 120, 125, 136, 186, 187, 193, 194, 195, 200, 201, 203, 205, 206, 207, 209, 211, 212, 213, 221, 227, 231, 234, 235, 237, 238, 241–243, 256, 258, 259, 260, 264, **266, 267, 268,** 270–271, 347, 348, 351
      Kaga (carrier) 24, 28, 77, 89, 90, 97, 99, 102, 109, 120, 125, 135, 186, 187, 193, 194, 195, 200, 209, 210, 211, 212, 213, 219, 221, 225, 231, 235, 237, 238, 245–247, 250, 254, 258, 260–261, **265, 267, 268,** 271, 351
      Shokaku (carrier) 24, 25, 77, 97, 101, 104, 109, 121, 125–126, 139, 183, 193, 194, 195, 221, 223, 229, 230, 231, 234, 252, 254, 264, **266, 267, 268,** 272, 285, 350
      Soryu (carrier) 9, 77, 99, 102, 109, 120, 125, 136, 186, 187, 193, 194, 195, 200, 201, 203, 205, 206, 207, 210, 211, 212, 221, 226, 227, 231, 235, 238–241, 256, 257, 261, 262, **265, 267, 268,** 347, 348, 351
      Zuikaku (carrier) 24, 26, 77, 97, 101, 104, 109, 121, 125–126, 139, 193, 194, 195, 221, 223, 226, 228, 229, 230, 234, **266, 267, 268,** 271, 272, 285, 350
   Sixth Fleet 77, 184, 298, 299, 301, 304
   Striking Force *(Kido Butai)* 88, 94, **95,** 96, 97, 98, 103, 109, 111, 121, 124, 125, 128–129, 139, 144, 166, 184, 186, 187, 188, 189, 193–194, 264–265, 273, 275, 281–282, 285, 288, 291, 293, 300, 317, 341, 348, 350–351
   submarines 191, 259, 295–297, 299–300, 301–302, 306, 308–309, 311, 312, 313, 314, 315, 316, 317
IJNAF (Imperial Japanese Navy Air Force), the 58, 72, 75, 76, 77, 79, 81, 89, 120, 121, 122, 123, 132, 165, 180, 181, 183
Imperial Navy Naval Academy, Etajima, the 61, 309
intelligence 8, 9–11, 22, 52, 75, 81, 84–88, 96, 176–184, 191–192, 236, 273–274, 298, 337, 339, 343, 350, 365, 367

J-code system, the 176, 177, 179, 181, 184
Japanese consulate, Honolulu 9, 85–86, 100, 103, 177, 191, 192, 366
Japanese oil requirements 42, 45, 49, 52, 81, 332
Japanese strategy 8–9, 13–15, 17–18, 35, 36, 42–43, 58–60, 63–64, 118, 140–142, 167, 220–221, 269, 292, 333–334, 339, 340, 348, 371
   and airfield attacks 220–228, 229–233, 252–264
   and the alternative decisive battle strategy 334–336, 341

and battleships and carriers 92, 98,
102–103, 112–113, 117, 119–121, 124,
185, 338, 341
and chance to avert war with the US 11,
12, 14–15
and China 11, 31–32, 49, 50, 51, 54
and the conduct of large-scale air strikes
128–129
and deception tactics 10, 183, 184–185
and development of new capabilities
143–144
and the element of surprise 16–17, 18, 20,
22, 68, 71, 72, 73, 74, 75, 86, 88, 90,
92–93, 96, 100, 107, 108, 109–110,
114, 116, 121, 144, 160, 181, 185, 187,
188, 197–198, 200, 237, 268, 286, 330,
343, 369
and fighter deployment 263–264, 287
and imperial conferences on objectives in
Southeast Asia 40–45, 46, 50
and moral cowardice in leadership 45,
48, 116
and naval planning 56–58, 64,
66–68, 70–71
and need for resources in Southeast Asia
12, 13, 14, 21, 40–41, 57, 59, 63, 68,
112, 181, 332–334, 336, 338
and negotiations with the US 12, 49–53,
328–329
and planning flaws 15, 16, 83–84, 85,
86–88, 99, 103, 116, 144, 188, 198,
236, 251, 252, 294, 341, 350–351
and lack of contingencies 71–72, 116,
236, 283, 294
and planning the Pearl Harbor attack 60,
64, 65, 66, 68–70, 71–72, 73–82, 86,
88–109, **95**, 122, 123–124, 186–187,
191–193, **199**
and affect on long-term strategy 21, 332,
341–343
and the first wave 193–219, **199, 204,
208**, 221, 264, **265–266**, 266
and logistical evaluation of 111–116
organization of attack forces **105–107**
and the second-wave 27, **106–107**,
107–108, 192, **199**, 219, 234–235,
237–250, 252–258, 266–267, **267**
and pre-war relations with the US 31, 33,
37–44, 48–53
and quasi-declaration of war 329–331, 339

and the question of a second attack 18–19,
110–111, 189–190, 275–286, 288–291,
292, 293–294
and rationale for war 42–45, 46–47, 48,
50, 53, 54–55, 336–337
and search doctrine 139–140
and Second Operational Phase objectives
349, 350
and the Southern Operation 13–14, 63,
72, 74–80, 165, 185, 293, 327, 334
and submarines 19–20, 116, 295,
297–298, 299, 300–316

kill and hit claims 203, 209, 210, 213, 217,
219, 223, 228, 229, 231, 239, 240, 241,
242, 244, 245, 248–250, **249,** 251,
256, 264, 308
Kimmel, Adm Husband E. 21–22, 23,
145–146, 147, 148–149, 154, 158,
159–160, 161, 162–163, 164, 165,
166–167, 169, 175, 177, 178, 179, 182,
183–184, 185, 195, 196, 307, 344, 347,
348, 352, 353, 354, 355–356, 357, 358,
359, 360, 361, 362–364, 365, 366–367,
368, 369–371, 372
Konoe, Prince Fumimaro 36, 38, 40, 42, 43,
44, 45, 46, 47, 54, 63, 147
Kusaka, Rear Adm Ryunosuke 16, 66, 72,
75, 76–77, 78, 79, 88, 93–94, 96, 97,
110, 114, 122, 123, 189, 191, 276, 277,
278, 279, 284, 292, 330
Kwantung Army, the 31, 32, 34

Lend Lease assistance 41, 354
logistics 112, 158
London Naval Conferences, the 61,
62, 124
Ludlow Amendment and US declarations of
war, the 33–34

Magic cryptography 52, 176, 177, 182, 358,
360, 363
Mahanian doctrine on naval power 281
maintenance and repairs 27, 226, 283, 289,
316, 322, 323
Manchukuo state 31–32
Marshall, Gen George 50–51, 167–168,
169, 173, 175, 331, 353, 354,
358–359, 366
Martin-Bellinger Report, the 160, 182

INDEX

matèriel losses 17, 20, 21, 25, 26, 27, 202, 205, 209, 210, 213, 214–215, 219, 222, 224, 225, 230, 239, 242, 252, 254, 258, 263, **265–266**, 265–268, **267, 268,** 273, 278, 291, 311, 313, 314, 317–318, **319–320,** 320–321, 324–326, **325,** 327, 350, 351, 353
  and jettisoning of aircraft 267–268, 317
merchant shipping 86, 187, 302, 312, 313–314
Midway Atoll 187–188, 291, 294
military honors 217, 218, 256, 320, 321
military production 21, 57, 133, 136, 317, 326, 332, **342,** 346
military strengths and complements 57, 88, 104, **128,** 154, **154–155,** 158–159, 162, 163, 165–166, 170, 268, 284, 298, 324, **345,** 345–346
mooring arrangements 24, 25–26, 85, 102, 103, 123, 131, 201–202, 203, 206, 212, 216, 217, 218, 219, 242
Morse code 139, 140
Murata, Lt Cdr Shigeharu 100, 101, 102, **105,** 115, 129, 134–135, 188, 198, 200, 201, 206, 207
museum exhibits and memorials 307, 309, 311

Nagano, Adm Osami 43–44, 45, 46, 47, 50, 62, 64, 70, 71, 72, 73, 80, 81, 82
Nagumo, Vice Adm Chuichi 18, 19, 23, 24, 73, 74, 75, 76, 77, 78, 79, 88, 93, 94, 96–97, 100, 108, 110, 113–114, 121–123, 124, 127, 132, 137, 140, 187, 188, 189, 190–191, 194, 234, 269, 275, 276, 278, 282, 284, 285, 288, 291–292, 293, 294, 301
NAS (Naval Air Stations) 104, 231
  NAS Kaneohe Bay 104, 114, 159, 221, 228–229, 235, 252, 254–257, 261–262, **325**
  NAS Pearl Harbor 27, 104, 159, 221, 222, 235, 237, 252–254, **325,** 397
National Defense Authorization Act (2001), the 364
nautical speeds 125, 126, 150, 151, 152, 193, 296, 297, 316, 322, 346
naval conversions 24, 125, 151, 153, 155, 202, 205, 307, 345

naval exercises and tests 66, 130, 132, 134, 135, 155, 161–162, 173–174, 181, 186, 235, 297
  see also war gaming
Naval Staff College, Tokyo 61, 63, 65, 66, 72
naval treaty restrictions 345
Navy Court of Inquiry, the 357–358, 359, 360, 361
Navy Department, the 147, 149, 160, 167, 175, 176, 178, 179, 182, 357
Navy Yard, the 24, 27, **157,** 219, 238, 242, **248, 249,** 250, 278, 280, 283, 285, 289–290
Nazi Germany 7, 11, 14, 35, 54, 59
Neutrality Act (1937), the 33
night combat 127
Nimitz, Adm Chester 20, 28, 280, 322, 324, 348, 349, 350, 351
Nomura, Adm Kichisaburo 37–38, 39, 41, 42, 47, 50, 51, 52, 54, 329

Oahu fortress, Hawaii 8, 9, 17, 22, 86–88, **87,** 148, 168, 372
ONI (Office of Naval Intelligence), the 178, 180, 181
operational readiness 159, 173, 176, 185, 258, 283, 365, 370–371, 372

Pearl Harbor attack, the 17–18, 55, 193–194, 294, 328
  and the apportioning of blame 364–365, 366–373
  and federal responsibility in Washington 364–366
  and investigations 352, 353–364
pilot and crew proficiency 128, 129, 137–138, 143, 144
Prange, Gordon 15–16, 172, 276, 277, 280, 304
public opinion 11, 33, 35, 112, 336
Purple decoding machines 176

radar systems 17, 22, 172, 174, 175, 176, 196, 197, 287, 373
radio communications 138–139
radio silence 109, 180, 184, 188–189, 301
ranges 56, 59, 67, 96, 97, 127, 131, 133, 135, 139, 140, 142, 148, 153, 159, 160–161, 165, 167, 171, 172, 200, 275, 296, 297, 299, 303, 334, 335, 368, 369, 371

445

reconnaissance 73, 100, 114, 139–140, 148, 159, 160–161, 162, 165, 171, 175, 191, 196, 292, 295–296, 301–302, 368
reporting names 131
revetments 108, 170, 226, 263
Roberts Commission, the 353–357, 358, 360, 362, 364, 368
Roosevelt, F. D. R. 11, 12, 14, 28, 33, 35–36, 37, 38, 41, 42, 46, 50, 51, 52, 54, 64, 153, 330, 331, 336, 350, 353, 354, 359, 361, 364, 367
route options to Hawaii 94–96, **95**, 97
Royal Navy, the 83, 84
Russo-Japanese War (1905), the 61, 191, 341

samurai, the 61
Satsuma Rebellion (1877), the 61
sea rescues 215, 300, 301, 305, 314, 320, 321
search missions 22, 88, 96, 114, 139–140, 161–162, 191, 194, 265, 270, 271, 273, 274–275, 285, 288, 294, 326, 370
self-sealing fuel tanks 131, 136, 138
ship designations and identification **157**, 243
Short, Lt Gen Walter C. 21–22, 23, 148, 168–169, 171–172, 173, 174–176, 177, 185, 195, 226, 263, 352, 353, 354, 355–356, 357, 358, 359, 361, 362, 363–364, 365, 366–367, 369, 371–372
Sino-Japanese War (1937–45), the 11, 32–33, 34–35, 39, 62
SLOCs (sea lines of communications) 57, 58, 59, 64, 296, 334, 349
Soviet Union, the 7, 11, 34, 37, 39, 40, 41, 54, 62, 337, 343
spare parts 159, 326
Stark, Adm Harold R. 50, 146, 147, 164, 167, 348, 355, 358, 359, 360, 366
Station Hypo (Combat Intelligence Unit) 179, 183, 184
statute of limitations and courts-martial, the 357
Stimson, Henry 52, 53, 331, 353, 354–355, 359
strafing runs 26, 104, 202, 222, 224, 225, 226, 227, 228, 229, 230, 231, 232, 254, 256, 257, 258, 259, 260, 263–264

submarines 19–20, 24, 28, 146, 148, 189, 295–297, 315
 midget submarines 20, 24, 77, 196, 295, 297, 300, 302–315, 317
 and U-boats 153
surface engagement 127

target accuracy 17–18, 25, 101–102, 123, 132, 137, 144, 211, 235, 250, 251–252, 255, 256
target allocation 108, 114, 115, 140, 236, 237, 285
torpedo-bombing attacks 17–18, 25, 27, 89, 91, 93, 99, 100, 101, 102–103, 107, 114–116, 123, 129, 130, 131–132, 146–147, 166, 188, 192, 197–211, **204, 208, 210**, 214, 215–217, 218–220, 268
 in shallow water 133–135, 143
torpedo nets 103, 131–132, 147, 148, 191, 192
traffic analysis and code decryption 180, 183
training 66, 124, 127, 129–130, 133, 134, 135, 137, 138, 139, 144, 170, 171, 175, 201, 304, 371, 372
Tripartite Pact, the 35, 36, 38, 49, 50, 52, 62
Two Ocean Naval Expansion Act (1940), the 342

underwater protection 151, 215, 220
US Army, the 167–168, 302, 367–368
 Hawaiian Division 167, 172
US Congress, the 33–34, 35–36, 57, 64, 331, 357, 364
 and Joint Congressional Committee on the Investigation of the Pearl Harbor Attack 361–362
US economic power 11–12, 57, 67, 328, 338, 342
US Marines, the 347–348
 MAG-21 (Marine Aviation Training Support Group) 230, 231, 257, 258, 326
 VMF (Marine Fighter Squadrons) 230, 326
 VMSB (Marine Scout Bomber Squadrons) 230, 326
US strategy and aims 20–21, 41, 50–53, 117–118, 146–147, 160, 161–162, 294, 307, 324, 342

INDEX

and American unpreparedness for defensive operations 16–17, 21–22, 83, 147–148, 162–163, 182, 229, 230–231, 263
and Army-Navy coordination 273, 367–369
and the Atlantic theater 153–154
and defense of the Pacific Fleet 167–168, 172–174, 185
anti-sabotage measures 174–175, 366
and the ignoring of warnings 195–197, 355–356, 365, 369, 372
and intelligence 177–178, 181, 183–184, 185
and Japanese trade embargo and restrictions 12, 14, 36, 40, 41–42, 57
and naval planning 57, 163–165, 327
Rainbow-5 163, 164, 327
Plan O-1 (Pacific Fleet Plan WP Pac-46) 163–164, 165, 166–167
and push into the Pacific 347–351
and reaction 9, 270–275, 286–288, 290, 291, 328, 329, 331–332, 343
and support for China 11, 33, 34, 37, 41, 46, 50, 53–54
and underestimation of Japanese intentions 10–11, 181, 339–340, 352
USAAF (US Army Air Force), the 142, 160, 161, 169, 171, 274, 349–350
14th Pursuit Wing 169, 226
86th Observation Squadron 232, 258
Pursuit Groups 226, 261
Pursuit Squadrons 227, 232, 259–263
Reconnaissance Squadrons 225, 264, 275, 326
USN (US Navy), the 8, 10, 56, 57, 66, 85, 113, 158, 160–161, 272, 367–368
auxiliaries 248, **248**
battleships 150–151, **154, 155,** 163, 236, 248, **248, 319,** 319–320, 322–323, 344, **345,** 346–347, 370, 371
carriers 158, 181, 236, 312, 319, 323–324, 345, **345,** 347
destroyers 152–153, **154,** 155, 157, **248,** 312, **345,** 346
heavy cruisers 151–152, **154, 155,** 158, 191, **248,** 312, **345,** 346
light cruisers 152, **154, 155,** 248, **248, 345,** 346

Pacific Fleet 20–21, 28, 35, 59, 64, 65, 67, 99–100, 111, 112, 145–146, 154, **156–157,** 163, 229, 291, 318, 327, 334, 335, 339, 344, 348, 364–365, 370
Patrol Wings 221, 222, 229, 230, 270, 369
ships 9, 24, 25–26, 27, 33, 151, 154, 155, 157, **157,** 192, 196, 201, 202–203, 205, 206, 212, 213, 218, 238, 239, 240, 241, 242, 243, 244, 245, 246, 250, **250,** 306–307, 308, 309–310, 311, 316, 321, 323, 344, 345, 346, 347, 348, 349–350, 351, 353
USS *Arizona* (battleship) 16, 18, 25, 26, 27, 151, 206, 212, 213, 214, 215–216, 217, 218, 219, 245, 246, 272, 311, 319, 321, 353
USS *California* (battleship) 151, 207, 210, 212, 213, 214, 215, 219–220, 240–241, 242, 244–245, 250, **250,** 307, 308, 309, 320–321, 347
USS *Enterprise* (carrier) 151, 155, 161, 174, 223, 271, 272, 273, 274, 288, 313, 326, 346, 347, 349, 350, 370
USS *Helena* (light cruiser) 203–205, 222, 239, 240, 241, 243, 248, 323, 344, 346
USS *Lexington* (carrier) 151, 155, 159, 161, 191, 230, 288, 346, 347, 349, 350
USS *Maryland* (battleship) 26, 151, 212, 213, 214, 215, 217, 219, 239, 242, 243, 245, 247, 272, 321, 344
USS *Nevada* (battleship) 25, 27, 151, 206, 210, 212, 214, 215, 218–219, 246–247, 250, **250,** 321, 322
USS *Oklahoma* (battleship) 25, 26, 151, 206, 207, 209, 210, 211, 214–215, 216, 319, 320, 353
USS *Pennsylvania* (battleship) 146, 151, 238–239, 241, 243, 244, **250,** 321, 344
USS *Tennessee* (battleship) 26, 151, 206, 210, 212, 213, 214, 215, 216, 217–218, 219, 321, 322, 344
USS *West Virginia* (battleship) 26, 132, 151, 206, 207, 209, 211, 212, 214, 215, 216–217, 219, 242, 247, 320, 322
submarines 28, 157
Task Forces 149–150, 155, 159, 271, 288, 346
tenders 289
VJ Utility Squadrons 222, 223, 271

VP Patrol Squadrons 222, 223, 230, 252, 255, 256, 257, 264, 271
VS-6 Scouting Squadrons 272, 273, 275, 288, 313

War Department, the 147, 148, 174–175, 176, 354, 355, 357, 358
war gaming 66, 72–75, 77–78
"War Warning" messages 365, 366, 368, 369, 370, 371, 372
Washington Naval Treaty (1922), the 56, 62, 125, 151, 152
weaponry 107, 126, 127, 131, 133, 137, 141, 142, 151, 152, 153, 173, 202, 203, 205, 209, 214, 216, 217, 219, 220, 222, 226, 235–236, 240, 241, 242, 244, 247, 252, 255, 253, 258, 283, 287, 288–289, 307, 316
   7.7mm machine gun (Japan) **106, 107,** 131, 136, 138, 224, 230, 231, 258, 290
   20mm cannon (Japan) **106, 107,** 138, 224, 230, 290
   .30-caliber machine gun (US) 225, 229, 231, 232, 255, 258
   .50-caliber machine gun (US) 153, 173, 203, 205, 209, 217, 227, 229, 241, 242, 244, 255, 256, 258, 371
   Type 91 torpedo (Japan) 133, 134, 135, 136, 187, 200, 202, 203, 207, 209
weather conditions 81, 189, 190, 193, 236
Wheeler Field 26, 108, 170, 221, 225–228, 261–264
"Winds Message" controversy, the 360–361
World Trade Center attacks (9/11), the 11, 331–332

Yamamoto, Adm Isoroku 12–14, 15, 16, 19, 20, 23, 36, 38, 46, 56, 58, 60–62, 64, 65, 66–67, 68–70, 71, 72, 73, 74, 75, 76–77, 78–81, 88–89, 90, 91, 92, 94, 98, 104, 111–113, 117–118, 119, 120, 122, 123, 124, 144, 163, 167, 178, 186–187, 188, 194, 279, 281, 292–293, 294, 295, 299, 303, 304, 305, 324, 327, 330, 334, 338, 340–341, 350, 351
   on war with the US 63, 116–117, 337

Z flag, the 191